Frances Minto (Dickinson) 1820-1898 Elliot

Old Court Life in France

Volume I.

Frances Minto (Dickinson) 1820-1898 Elliot

Old Court Life in France
Volume I.

ISBN/EAN: 9783743310193

Manufactured in Europe, USA, Canada, Australia, Japa

Cover: Foto ©Thomas Meinert / pixelio.de

Manufactured and distributed by brebook publishing software
(www.brebook.com)

Frances Minto (Dickinson) 1820-1898 Elliot

Old Court Life in France

COLLECTION

OF

BRITISH AUTHORS

TAUCHNITZ EDITION.

VOL. 1351.

OLD COURT LIFE IN FRANCE BY F. ELLIOT.

IN TWO VOLUMES.

VOL. I.

BY

FRANCES ELLIOT,

AUTHOR OF

"DIARY OF AN IDLE WOMAN IN ITALY," "PICTURES OF OLD ROME."

REVISED COPYRIGHT

EDITION.

IN TWO VOLUMES.—VOL. I.

LEIPZIG

BERNHARD TAUCHNITZ

1873.

TO MY NIECE,

THE COUNTESS OF MINTO,

THIS WORK

IS INSCRIBED.

PREFACE.

ALL my life I have been a student of French memoir-history. In this species of literature France is remarkably rich. There exist contemporary memoirs and chronicles, from a very early period down to the present time, in which are preserved not only admirable outlooks over general events, but details of language, character, dress, and manners, not to be found elsewhere. I was bold enough to fancy that somewhat, yet remained to tell;—say—of the caprices and eccentricities of Louis XIII., of the homeliness of Henri Quatre, of the feminine tenderness of Gabrielle d'Estrées, of the lofty piety and unquestioning confidence of Louise de Lafayette, of the romantic vicissitudes of Mademoiselle de Montpensier; and that some pictures might be made of these old French personages for English readers in a way that should pourtray the substance and spirit of history, without affecting to maintain its form and dress.

In all I have written I have sought carefully to work into my dialogue each word and sentence recorded of the individual, every available trait or peculiarity of character to be found in contemporary memoirs, every tradition that has come down to us.

To be true to life has been my object. Keeping close to the background of history, I have endeavoured to group the figures of my foreground as they grouped themselves in actual life. I have framed them in the frames in which they really lived.

FRANCES ELLIOT.

FARLEY HILL COURT,
Christmas, 1872.

PREFACE

TO THE THIRD EDITION OF "OLD COURT LIFE," PUBLISHED
BY BARON TAUCHNITZ*—IN REPLY TO CERTAIN CRITICS.

To relate the "Court life" of France—from Francis I. to Louis XIV.—it is necessary to relate also, the history of the royal favourites. They ruled both court and state, if they did not preside at the council. The caprice of these ladies was, actually, "the Pivot on which French history turned."

Louis XIII. was an exception. Under him Cardinal Richelieu reigned. Richelieu's "*zeal*" for France led him unfortunately to butcher all his political and personal opponents. He ruled France, axe in hand. It was an easy way to absolute power.

Cardinal Mazarin found France in a state of anarchy. The throne was threatened with far more serious dangers than under Richelieu. To feudal chiefs were joined royal princes. The great Condé led the Spanish troops against his countrymen. Yet no political murder stains the name of the gentle Italian. He triumphed by statescraft,—and married the Infanta to Louis XIV.

Cardinal de Retz possessed much of the genius of Richelieu. No cruelty however attaches to his memory. But de Retz was on the wrong side, the side of rebellion. He was false to his king and to France.

* This edition is completely revised and corrected by the author.

Great as were his gifts, he fell before the persevering
loyalty of Mazarin.

The personal morality of either of these states-
men ill bears investigation. Marion de l'Orme was the
mistress and the spy of Richelieu; Mazarin—it is to
be hoped—was privately married to the Queen Regent
Anne of Austria. Cardinal de Retz had, as a contemporary remarks, "a bevy of mistresses."

We have the authority of Charlotte de Bavière,
second wife of Philippe Duc d'Orleans, brother of
Louis XIV., in her 'Autobiographical Fragments,' "that
her predecessor, Henrietta of England, was poisoned."
No legal investigation was ever made as to the cause
of her sudden death. There is no proof "that
Louis XIV. disbelieved she was poisoned."

The number of the victims of the St. Bartholomew-
massacre is stated by Sully to have been 70,000.
(Memoirs, book I., page 37). Sully and other authorities
state "that Charles IX., at his death, manifested by
his transports and his tears the sorrow he felt for what
he had done." Further, "that when dying he sent for
Henry of Navarre, in whom *alone* he found faith and
honour." (Sully, book I., page 42).

That Sorbin, confessor to Charles IX., should have
denied this is perfectly natural. Henry of Navarre
would stink in the confessor's nostrils as a pestilent
heretic. As to the credibility of Sorbin (a bigot and
a controversialist), I would refer to the "Memoires
de l'état de France sous Charles IX." vol. 3, page 267.

According to the "Confession de Saucy" Sorbin
de St. Foy "was made a Bishop for having placed
Charles IX. among the Martyrs."

August 1873.

FRANCES (MINTO) ELLIOT.

AUTHORITIES.

Mémoires de Brantôme.

Mémoires de son Temps, Du Bellay.

Histoire de Henri Duc de Bouillon.

Mémoires de Condé.

Dictionnaire de Bayle, "*Duc de Guise.*"

Histoire des Guerres Civiles de la France, par Davila.

Mémoires pour servir à l'Histoire de France, par Champollion.

Mémoires de Coligni.

Novaes, Storia dei Pontefici.

Mémoires de Marguerite de Valois.

Journal de Henri III.

Mémoires de Sully.

Histoire de Henri IV., par Mathieu.

Histoire des Amours de Henri IV.

L'Intrigue du Cabinet sous Henri IV. et Louis XIII.

Mémoires pour l'Histoire du Cardinal de Richelieu.

Mémoires du Cardinal de Richelieu.

Histoire de la Mère et du Fils, par Mezeray.

Mémoires du Maréchal de Bassompierre.

Observations de Bassompierre.

Mémoires de feu Monsieur (Gaston) Duc d'Orléans.

Mémoires de Cinq-Mars.

Mémoires de Montrésor.

La Cour de Marie de Medici, par un Cadet de Gascogne

Lettres de Madame de Sévigné.

Mémoires de Mademoiselle de Montpensier.

Mémoires du Duc de Lauzun.

Mémoires de Madame de Motteville.

Mémoires de M. d'Artagnan.

Mémoires du Cardinal de Retz.

Mémoires de La Porte.

Mémoires de Mazarin.

Œuvres Complètes de Saint-Simon.

Mémoires de la Duchesse de la Vallière.

Mémoires de la Marquise de Montespan.

Mémoires de la Marquise de Maintenon.

Amours des Rois de France.

Dulaure, Histoire de Paris.

Histoire de la Touraine, dans la Bibliothèque Publique à Tours.

Capefigue, Ouvrages Divers.

CONTENTS

OF VOLUME I.

14 CONTENTS OF VOLUME I.

OLD COURT LIFE IN FRANCE.

CHAPTER I.

Francis I.

W<small>E</small> are in the sixteenth century. Europe is young in artistic life. The minds of men are moved by the discussions, councils, protests, and contentions of the Reformation. The printing press is spreading knowledge into every corner of the globe.

At this period, three highly educated and unscrupulous young men divide the power of Europe. They are Henry VIII. of England, Charles V. of Austria, and Francis I. of France. Each is magnificent in taste; each is desirous of power and conquest. Each acts as a spur to the others both in peace and in war. They introduce the cultivated tastes, the refined habits, the freedom of thought of modern life, and from the period in which they flourish modern history dates.

Of these three monarchs Francis is the boldest, cleverest, and most profligate. The elegance, refinement, and luxury of his court, are unrivalled; and this luxury strikes the senses from its contrast with the frugal habits of the ascetic Louis XI. and the homely Louis XII.

His reign educated Europe. If ambition led him towards Italy, it was as much to capture the arts of that classic land and to bear them back in triumph to France, as to acquire the actual territory. Francis introduced the French Renaissance, that subtle union of elaborate ornamentation with purity of design which was the renovation of art. When and how he acquired such exact appreciation of the beautiful is unexplained. That he possessed judgment and taste is proved by the monuments he left behind, and by his patronage of the greatest masters of their several arts.

The wealth of beauty and colour, the flowing lines of almost divine expression in the works of the Italian painters of the Cinque-cento, delighted the sensuous soul of Francis. Wherever he lived he gathered treasures of their art around him. Such a nature as his had no sympathy with the meritorious but precise elaboration of the contemporary Dutch school, led by the Van Eycks and Holbein. It was Leonardo da Vinci, the head of the Milanese school, who blended power and tenderness, that Francis delighted to honour. He brought Cellini, Primaticcio, and Leonardo from Italy, and never wearied of their company. He established the aged Leonardo at the Château de Clos, near his own castle of Amboise, where the painter is said to have died in the arms of his royal patron.

As an architect, Francis left his mark beyond any other sovereign of Europe. He transformed the gloomy fortress-home—embattled, turreted, and moated —into the elaborately decorated, manorial château. The bare and foot-trodden space without, enclosed with walls of defence, was changed into green lawns and over-arching bowers breaking the vista toward the royal forest, the flowing river, and the open campagne.

Francis had a mania for building. Like Louis XIV., who in the century following built among the sandhills of Versailles, Francis insisted on creating a fairy palace amid the flat and dusty plains of Sologne. Here the Renaissance was to achieve its triumph. At Chambord, near Blois, were massed every device, decoration, and eccentricity of his favourite style. So identified is this place with its creator, that even his intriguing life peeps out in the double staircase under the central tower—representing a gigantic fleur-de-lys in stone—where those who ascend are invisible to those who descend; in the doors, concealed in sliding panels behind the arras; and in many double walls and secret stairs.

Azay le Rideau, built on a beautifully wooded island on the river Indre, though less known than Chambord, was and is an exquisite specimen of the Renaissance. It owes the fascination of its graceful outlines and peculiar ornamentation to the master-hand which has graven his crowned F and Salamander on its quaint façades. The Louvre and Fontainebleau are also signed by these monograms. He, and his son Henry II., made these piles the historic monuments we now behold.

Such was Francis, the artist. As a soldier, he followed in the steps of Bayard, "Sans peur et sans reproche." He perfected that poetic code of honour which reconciles the wildest courage with generosity towards an enemy. A knight-errant in love of danger and adventure, Francis comes to us as the perfect type of the chivalrous Frenchman; ready to do battle on any provocation either as king or gentleman, either at the head of his army, in the tournament, or in the

duello. He loved all that was gay, bright, and beautiful. He delighted in the repose of peace, yet no
monarch ever plunged his country into more ruinous
and causeless wars. Though capable of the tenderest
and purest affection, no man was ever more heartless
and cruel in principle and conduct.

Francis, Duc de Valois,* was educated at home
by his mother, Madame Louise de Savoie, Duchesse
d'Angoulême, Regent of France, together with his
brilliant sister, Marguerite, "the pearl of the Valois,"
poetess, story-teller, artist, and politician. Each of
these royal ladies was tenderly attached to the clever,
handsome youth, and together formed what they chose
to call "a trinity of love.". The old Castle of Amboise,
in Touraine, the favourite abode of Louis XII., continued to be their home after his death. Here, too,
the hand of Francis is to be traced in sculptured
windows and architectural façades, in noble halls and
broad galleries, and in the stately terraced gardens
overlooking the Loire which flows beneath its walls.
Here, under the formal lime alleys and flowering
groves, or in the shadow of the still fortified bastions,
the brother and sister sat or wandered side by side,
on many a summer day; read and talked of poetry
and troubadours, of romance and chivalry, of Arthur,
Roland and Charlemagne, of spells and witcheries, and
of Merlin the enchanter, whose magic failed before a
woman's glance.

Printing at that time having become general, literature of all kinds circulated in every direction, stirring
men's minds with fresh tides of knowledge. Marguerite de Valois, who was called "the tenth Muse,"

* See Note 1.

dwelt upon poetry and fiction, and already meditated her Boccaccio-like stories, afterwards to be published under the title of the "Heptameron." Francis gloated over such adventures as were detailed in the roundelay of the "Four Sons of Aymon," a ballad of that day, devoured the history of "Amadis de Gaul," and tried his hand in twisting many a love-rhyme, after the fashion of the "Romaunt of the Rose."

In such an idyllic life of love, of solitude, and of thought, full of the humanising courtesies of family life,. was formed the paradoxical character of Francis, who above all men possessed what the French describe as "the reverse of his qualities." His fierce passions still slumbered, his imagination was filled with poetry, his heart beat high with the endearing love of a brother and a son. His reckless courage vented itself in the chase, among the royal forests of Amboise and of Chanteloup, that darkened the adjacent hills, or in a tustle with the boorish citizens, or travelling merchants, in the town below.

Thus he grew into manhood, his stately yet condescending manners, handsome person, and romantic courage, gaining him devoted adherents. Yet when we remember that Francis served as the type for Hugo's play of *Le Roi s'amuse* we pause and—shudder.

CHAPTER II.

Charles de Bourbon.

The Court is at Amboise. Francis is only twenty, and still solicits the advice of his mother, Louise de Savoie, regent during his minority. Marguerite, now married to the Duc d'Alençon, has also considerable influence over him. Both these princesses, who are with him at Amboise, insist on the claims of their kinsman, Charles de Montpensier, Duc de Bourbon,— in right of his wife, Suzanne, only daughter and heiress of Pierre, the last duke,—to be appointed Constable of France. It is an office next in power to the sovereign, and has not been revived since the treasonable conspiracy of the Comte de St. Pol, in the reign of Louis XI.

Bourbon is only twenty-six, but he is already a hero. He has braved death again and again in the battle-field with dauntless valour. In person he is tall and handsome. In manners, he is frank, bold, and prepossessing; but when offended, his proud nature easily turns to vindictive and almost savage revenge. Invested with the double dignity of General of the royal forces and Constable of France, he comes to Amboise to salute the King and the princesses, who are both strangely interested in his career, and to take the last commands from Francis, who does not now propose accompanying his army into Italy.

There is a restless, mobile expression on Bourbon's dark yet comely face, that tells of strong passions ill suppressed. A man capable of ardent and devoted love, and of bitter hate; his marriage with his cousin

Suzanne, lately dead, had been altogether a political alliance to bring him royal kindred, wealth, and power. Suzanne had failed to interest his heart. It is said that another passion has long engaged him. Francis may have some hint as to who the lady is, and may resent Bourbon's presumption. At all events, the Constable is no favourite with the King. He dislikes his *fanfaronnade* and haughty address. He loves not either to see a subject of his own age so powerful and so magnificent; it trenches too much on his own prerogatives of success. Besides, as lads, Bourbon and Francis had quarrelled at a game of maille. The King had challenged Bourbon but had never fought him, and Bourbon resented this refusal as an affront to his honour.

The Constable, mounted on a splendid charger, with housings of black velvet, and attended by a brilliant suite, gallops into the courtyard. His fine person is set off by a rich surcoat, worn over a suit of gilded armour. He wears a red and white panache in his helmet, and his sword and dagger are thickly incrusted with diamonds.

At the top of the grand staircase are posted one hundred archers; royal pages conduct the Constable through the range of state apartments.

The King receives Bourbon in the great gallery hung with tapestry. He is seated on a chair of state, ornamented with elaborate carving, on which the arms of France are in high relief. This chair is placed on a raised floor, or dais, covered with a carpet. Beside him stands the grand master of the ceremonies, who introduces the Constable to the King. Francis, who inclines his head and raises his cap for an instant, is courteous but cold. Marguerite d'Alençon is present; like Bourbon, she is unhappily mated. The Duc d'Alençon is, physically and mentally, her inferior. When the Constable salutes the King, Marguerite stands apart. Conscious that her brother's eyes read her thoughts, she blushes deeply and averts her face. Bourbon advances to the spot where she is seated in the recess of an oriel window. He bows low before her; Marguerite rises, and offers him her hand. Their eyes meet. There is no disguise in the passionate glance of the Constable; Marguerite, confused and embarrassed, turns away.

"Has your highness no. word of kindness for your kinsman?" says the Constable, in a low voice.

"You know, cousin, your interests are ever dear to me," replies she, in the same tone; then, curtseying deeply to the King, she takes the arm of her husband, M. d'Alençon, who was killing flies at the window, and leaves the gallery.

"Diable!" says Francis to his confidant, Claude de Guise, in an undertone; "My sister is scarcely civil to the Constable. Did you observe, she hardly answered him? All the better. It will teach Bourbon humility, and not to look too high for a mate."

"Yet her highness pleaded eagerly with your Majesty for his advancement."

"Yes, yes; that was to please our mother. Suzanne de Bourbon was her cousin, and the Regent promised her before her death to support her husband's claims."

Meanwhile, the Constable receives, with a somewhat reserved and haughty civility, the compliments of the Court. He is conscious of an antagonistic atmosphere. It is well known **that** the King **loves** him not; and whom the King loves not neither does the courtier.

A page then approaches, and invites the Constable, in the name of Queen Claude, to join her afternoon circle. Meanwhile, he is charged to conduct the Constable to an audience with the Regent-mother, **who** awaits him **in her** apartments.

The King had been cool and the Princess **silent** and reserved: **not** so the Regent Louise de Savoie, who **advances to** meet the Constable with unmistakable eagerness.

"I congratulate you, my cousin," **she** says, holding out both her hands to him, which he receives kneeling, **"on the** dignity **with** which my **son** has invested you. I may add, that I was not altogether idle in the matter."

"Your highness will, I hope, be justified in the favour you have shown me," replies **the** Constable coldly.

"Be seated, my cousin," continues Louise. **"I** have desired to see you alone that I might fully explain with what grief I find myself obliged, by the express orders of my **son, to** dispute with a kinsman I so much **esteem** as yourself"—she pauses a **moment,** the Constable bows gravely—"the inheritance of my poor cousin, your **wife,** Madame Suzanne de Bourbon. Suzanne was **dear to** me, and **you also,** Constable, have a high place **in my** regard."

Louise ceases. She looks significantly at the Constable, as if waiting for him to answer; but he does not reply, and again bows.

"I am placed," continues the Regent, the colour

gathering on her cheek, "in a most painful alternative. The Chancellor has insisted on the legality of my claims—claims on the inheritance of your late wife, daughter of Pierre, Duc de Bourbon, my cousin. I will not trouble you with details. My son urges the suit. My own feelings plead strongly against proceeding any farther in the matter." She hesitates and stops.

"Your highness is of course aware that the loss of this suit would be absolute ruin to me?" says Bourbon, looking hard at Louise.

"I fear it would be most disastrous to your fortunes. That they are dear to me, judge—you are by my interest made Constable of France, second only in power to my son."

"I have already expressed my gratitude, madame."

"But, Constable," continues Louise de Savoie, speaking with much animation, "why have you insisted on your claims—why not have trusted to the gratitude of the King towards a brave and zealous subject? Why not have counted on myself, who have both power and will, as I have shown, to protect you?"

"The generosity of the King and your highness's favour, which I accept with gratitude, have nothing to do with the legal rights of my late wife's inheritance. I desire not, madame, to be beholden in such matters even to your highness or to his Majesty."

"Well, Constable, well, as you will; you are, I know, of a proud and noble nature. But I have desired earnestly," and the Regent rises and places herself on another chair nearer the Constable, "to ascertain from your own lips if this suit cannot be settled *à l'amiable.* There are many means of accommodating a lawsuit, Duke. Madame Anne, wife of two kings of France, saved Brittany from cruel wars in a manner worthy of imitation."

"Truly," replies Bourbon with a sigh; "but I know not what princess of the blood would enable me to accommodate your highness's suit in so agreeable a manner."

"Have you not yourself formed some opinion on the subject?" asks Louise, looking at the Constable with undisguised tenderness.

"No, madame, I have not. Since the hand of your beautiful daughter, Madame Marguerite, is engaged, I know no one."

"But—" and she hesitates, and again turns her eyes upon him, which the Constable does not observe, as he is adjusting the hilt of his dagger—"but—you forget, Duke, that I am a widow."

As she speaks she places her hand upon that of the Constable, and gazes into his face. Bourbon starts violently and looks up. Louise de Savoie, still holding his hand, meets his gaze with an unmistakable expression. She is forty years old, but vain and intriguing. There is a pause. Then the Constable rises and drops the hand which had rested so softly upon his own. His handsome face darkens into a look of disgust. A flush of rage sends the blood tingling to the cheeks of Louise.

"Your highness mistakes me," says Bourbon. "The respect I owe to his Majesty, the disparity of our years, my own feelings, all render such an union impossible. Your highness does me great honour, but I do not at present intend to contract any other alliance. If his Majesty goes to law with me, why I will fight him, madame,—that is all."

"Enough," answers Louise in a hoarse voice, "I understand." The Constable makes a profound obeisance and retires.

This interview was the first act in that long and intricate **drama** by which the spite of a mortified woman **drove** the **Duc** de Bourbon — the greatest general of his age, under whom the arms of France never knew defeat—to become a traitor to **his** king and **to France.**

CHAPTER III.

Brother and Sister.

YEARS have passed; Francis, with his wife, Queen Claude, daughter of Louis XII. and Anne of Brittany, is at Chambord, in the Touraine. Claude, but for the Salic law, would have been Queen of France. In her childhood she was affianced to Charles, son of Philip the Fair, afterwards Charles V. of Germany, the great rival of Francis. Francis had never loved her, the **union** had been political; yet Claude is gentle and devoted, **and he says** of her, "that her soul is as a rose without a **thorn**." This queen—the **darling** of her parents—can neither bear the indifference nor the infidelity of her brilliant husband, **and** dies **of her** neglected love at the early age of twenty-five.

Marguerite d'Alençon, the Duke her husband, and **the** Court, are assembled **for** hunting in the forests of Sologne. Chambord, then but a gloomy mediæval fortress lying on low swampy lands on the banks of

the river Casson, is barely large enough to accommodate the royal party. Already Francis meditates
many changes; the course of the river Loire, some
fifteen miles distant, is to be turned in order to bathe
the walls of a sumptuous palace, not yet fully conceived in the brain of the royal architect.

It is spring; Francis is seated in the broad embrasure of an oriel window, in an oak-panelled saloon
which looks towards the surrounding forest. He
eagerly watches the gathering clouds that veil the sun
and threaten to prevent the boar-hunt projected for
that morning. Beside him, in the window, sits his
sister Marguerite. She wears a black velvet riding-
habit, faced with gold; her luxuriant hair is gathered
into a net under a plumed hat on which a diamond
aigrette glistens. At the farther end of the room
Queen Claude is seated on a high-backed chair, richly
carved, in the midst of her ladies. She is embroidering an altar-cloth; her face is pale and very plaintive.
She is young, and, though not beautiful, there is an
angelic expression in her large grey eyes, a dimpling
sweetness about her mouth, that indicate a nature
worthy to have won the love of any man, not such a
libertine as Francis. Her dress is plain and rich, of
grey satin trimmed with ermine; a jewelled coif is
upon her head. She bends over her work, now and
then raising her wistful eyes with an anxious look towards the King. The Queen's habits are sedentary,
and the issue of the hunting party is of no personal
interest to her; she always remains at home with her
children and ladies. Many attendant lords, attired
for hunting, are waiting his Majesty's pleasure in the
adjoining gallery.

"Marguerite," says the King, turning to the Duchesse d'Alençon, as the sun reappears out of a bank of cloud, "the weather mends; in a quarter of an hour we shall start. Meanwhile, dear sister, sit beside me. *Morbleu*, how well that riding-dress becomes you! You are very handsome, and worthy to be called the Rose of the Valois. There are few royal ladies in our Court to compare to you;" and Francis glances significantly at his gentle Queen, busy over her embroidery, as if to say—"Would that she resembled you!"

Marguerite, proud of her brother's praise, reddens with pleasure and reseats herself at his side. "By-and-by I shall knock down this sombre old fortress," continues Francis, looking out of the window at the gloomy façade, "and transform it into a hunting château. The situation pleases me, and the surrounding forest is full of game."

"My brother," says Marguerite, interrupting him and speaking in an earnest voice, for her eyes have not followed the direction of the King's, which are fixed on the prospect; she seems not to have heard his remarks, and her bright look has changed into an anxious expression; "my brother, tell me, have you decided upon the absolute ruin of Bourbon? Think how his haughty spirit must chafe under the repeated marks of your displeasure." They are both silent. Marguerite's eyes are riveted upon the King. Francis is embarrassed. He averts his face from the suppliant look cast upon him by his sister, and again turns to the window, as if to watch the rapidly passing clouds.

"My sister," he says at length, "Bourbon is not a loyal subject; he is unworthy of your regard."

"Sire, I cannot believe it. Bourbon is no traitor! But, my brother, if he were, have you not tried him sorely? Have you not driven him from you by an intolerable sense of injury? Oh, Francis, remember he is our kinsman, your most zealous servant;—did he not save your life at Marignano? Who among your generals is cool, daring, valiant, wise as Bourbon? Has he not borne our flag triumphantly through Italy? Have the French troops under him ever known defeat? Yet, my brother, you have now publicly disgraced him." Her voice trembles with emotion; she is very pale, and her eyes fill with tears.

"By the mass, Marguerite, no living soul, save our mother, would dare to address me thus!" exclaims the King, turning towards her. He is much moved. Then, examining her countenance, he adds, "You are strangely agitated, my sister. What concern have you with the Constable? Believe me, I have made Bourbon too powerful."

"Not now, not now, Francis, when you have, at the request of a woman—of Madame de Châteaubriand too—taken from him the government of Milan; when he is superseded in his command; when our mother is pressing on him a ruinous suit, with your sanction."

At the name of Madame de Châteaubriand Marguerite's whole countenance darkens with anger, the King's face grows crimson.

"My sister, you plead Bourbon's cause warmly—too warmly, methinks," and Francis turns his head aside to conceal his confusion.

"Not only has your Majesty taken from him the government of Milan," continues Marguerite bitterly, unheeding the King's interruption, "but he has been replaced by Lautrec, brother of Madame de Châteaubriand, an inexperienced soldier, unfitted for such an important post. Oh, my brother, you are driving Bourbon to despair. So great a general cannot hang up his victorious sword."

"By my faith, sister, you press me hard," replies the King, recovering the gentle tone with which he always addressed her; "I will communicate with my council; what you have said shall be duly considered. Meanwhile, if Bourbon inspires you with such interest, as it seems he does, tell him to humble his pride and submit himself to us, his sovereign and his master. If he do, he shall be greater than ever, I promise you." As he speaks, he glances at Marguerite, whose eyes fall to the ground. "But see, my sister, the sun is shining; and there is some one already mounting in the courtyard. Give the signal for departure, Comte de Saint-Vallier," says the King in a louder voice, turning towards two gentlemen standing at an opposite window in the gallery. The King has to repeat his command before the Comte de Saint-Vallier hears him. "Saint-Vallier, you are in deep converse with De Pompérant. Is it love or war?"

"Neither, Sire," replies the Captain of the Royal Archers, looking embarrassed.

"M. de Pompérant, are you going with us to-day to hunt the boar?" says the King, advancing towards them.

"Sire," replies De Pompérant, bowing profoundly, "your Majesty does me great honour; but, with your leave, I will not accompany the hunt. Urgent business calls me from Chambord."

"Ah, *coquin*, it is an assignation; confess it," and a wicked gleam lights up the King's eyes.

"No, Sire," says De Pompérant. "I go to join the Constable de Bourbon, who is indisposed."

"Ah! to join the Constable!" Francis pauses and looks at him. "I know he is your friend," continues he, suddenly becoming very grave. "Where is he?"

"At his fortress of Chantelle, Sire."

"At Chantelle! a fortified place, and without my permission. Truly, Monsieur de Pompérant, your friend is a daring subject. What if I will not trust you in his company, and command your attendance on our person here at Chambord?"

"Then, Sire, I should obey," replies De Pompérant; "but let your gracious Majesty remember the Duc de Bourbon is ill; he is a broken and ruined man, deprived of your favour. Chantelle is more a château than a fortress."

"Go, De Pompérant; I did but jest. Tell Bourbon, on the word of a king, that he has warm friends near my person; that if the Regent-mother gains her suit against him, I will restore tenfold to him in money, lands, and honour. Adieu, Monsieur de Pompérant. You are dismissed. Bon voyage."

Now, the truth was that De Pompérant had come to Chambord upon a secret mission from Bourbon, who wished to assure himself of those gentlemen of the Court upon whom he could rely in case of rebellion. The Comte de Saint-Vallier had just, while standing at the window, pledged his word to stand by Bourbon for life or death.

The King is **now** mounting his horse in the courtyard, a noble bay with glittering harness. He gives the signal of departure, which is echoed through **the** woodland recesses by the bugles of the huntsmen. A lovely lady attired in white has joined the royal retinue in the courtyard. She rides on in front beside the King, who, the better to converse with her, has placed his hand upon her horse's neck. This is Françoise, Comtesse de Châteaubriand, the favourite **of** the hour—at whose request Bourbon had been superseded in the government of Milan by her brother Lautrec.

Behind this pair rides Marguerite d'Alençon with **her** husband, the Comte de Guise, Montmorenci, Bonnivet, and other nobles. A large cavalcade of courtiers follows. Since her conversation with her brother, Marguerite looks thoughtful and anxious. She is so absent that she does not even hear the prattle of her husband, who is content to talk and cares not for reply. On reaching the dense thickets of the forest she suddenly reins up her horse, and, falling back a little, beckons the Comte de Saint-Vallier to her **side**.

"M. le Comte," she says in a loud voice, so as to be overheard by her husband and the other gentlemen riding in advance, "tell me when is the Court to be graced by the presence of your incomparable daughter, Madame Diane, Grande Seneschale of Normandy?"

"Madame," replies Saint-Vallier, "her husband, Monseigneur de Brézè, is much occupied in his distant government. Diane is young, much younger than her husband. The Court, madame, is dangerously full of temptations to the young."

"We lose a bright jewel **by her** absence," says Marguerite abstractedly. "M. le Comte," she continues in a low voice, speaking quickly, and motioning to him with her hand to approach nearer, "I have something private to say to you. Ride close by my side. You are a friend of the Constable de Bourbon?" she asks eagerly.

"Yes, madame, I am."

"You are, perhaps, his confidant? Speak freely to me; I feel deeply the misfortunes of the Duke. I would aid him if I could. Is there any foundation for the suspicion with which my brother regards him? You will not deceive me, Monsieur de Poitiers?"

Saint-Vallier does not answer at once. "The Constable de Bourbon will never, I trust, betray his Majesty," replies he at last, with hesitation.

"Alas! my poor cousin! Is that all the assurance you can give me, Monsieur de Saint-Vallier? Oh! he is incapable of treason," exclaims Marguerite with enthusiasm; "I would venture my life he is incapable of treason!"

A courier passes them at this moment, riding with hot speed. He nears the King, who is now far on in front, and who, hearing the sound of the horse's hoofs, stops and listens. The messenger hands the King a dispatch. Francis hastily breaks the seal. It is from Lautrec, the new governor of Milan. Bourbon is in open rebellion.

Bourbon in open rebellion! This intelligence necessitates the instant presence of the King at Paris.

CHAPTER IV.
The Quality of Mercy.

FRANCIS is at the Louvre, surrounded by his most devoted friends and councillors, Chabannes, La Tré-mouille, Bonnivet, Montmorenci, Crequi, Cossé, De Guise, and the two Du Bellays. The Louvre is still the isolated stronghold, castle, palace, and prison, surrounded by moat, walls, and bastions, built by Philippe Auguste on the grassy margin of the Seine. In the centre of the inner court is a round tower, also moated, and defended by ramparts, ill-famed in feudal annals for its oubliettes and dungeons, under which the river flows. Four gates, with posterns and towers, open from the Louvre; that one opposite the Seine is the strongest. The southern gate—which is low and narrow, with statues on either hand of Charles V. and his wife, Jeanne de Bourbon—faces the Church of Saint-Germain l'Auxerrois.* Beyond are gardens and orchards, and a house, called Fromenteau, where lions are kept for the King's amusement.

These are the days of stately manners, intellectual culture, and increasing knowledge. Personal honour as from man to man is a religion, of which Bayard is the high priest; treachery to woman, a virtue inculcated by the King. The idle, vapid life of later courts is unknown under a monarch who, however addicted to pleasure, cultivates all kinds of knowledge, whose inquiring intellect seeks to master all science, to whom indolence is impossible. His very meals are chosen moments in which he converses with authors, poets,

* See **Note 2.**

and artists, or dictates letters to Erasmus and the learned Greek Lascaris. Such industry and dignity, such grace and condescension, gather around him the great spirits of the age. He delights in their company.

It is the King's boast that he has introduced into France the study of the Greek language, Botany, and Natural History. He buys, at enormous prices, pictures, pottery, enamels, statues, and manuscripts. As in his fervid youth at Amboise, he loves poetry and poets. Clément Marot is his chosen guest, and polishes the King's rhymes, of which some delicate and touching stanzas (those on Agnes Sorel,* especially) have come down to us.

Even that witty heretic, Rabelais, found both an appreciative protector and intelligent friend in a sovereign superior to the prejudices of his age. With learning, poetry, wit, and intellect, come luxury and boundless extravagance. Brantôme speaks as with bated breath of the royal expenditure. These are the days of broad sombrero hats fringed with gold and looped up with priceless jewels and feathers; of embroidered cloaks in costly stuffs—heavy with gold or silver embroidery—hung over the shoulder; of slashed hose and richly chased rapiers; of garments of cloth of gold, embroidered with armorial bearings in jewels; of satin justaucorps covered with rivières of diamonds, emeralds, and oriental pearls; of torsades and collars wherein gold is but the foil to priceless gems. The ladies wear eastern silks and golden tissues, with trimmings of rare furs; wide sleeves and Spanish fardingales, sparkling coifs and jewelled nets, with glittering veils. They ride

* See Note 3.

in ponderous coaches covered with carving and gilding, or on horses whose pedigrees are as undoubted
as their own, covered with velvet housings and with
silken nets woven with jewels, their manes plaited with
gold and precious stones. But these illustrious ladies
consider gloves a royal luxury, and are weak in respect of stockings.

Foremost in every gorgeous mode is Francis. He
wears rich Genoa velvets, and affects bright colours—
rose and sky-blue. A Spanish hat is on his head,
turned up with a white plume, fastened to an aigrette
of rubies, with a golden salamander his device, signi-
fying, "I am nourished and I die in fire" (Je me
nourris et je meurs dans le feu).

How well we know his dissipated though distinguished features, as portrayed by Titian! His long
nose, small eyes, broad cheeks, and cynical mouth.
He moves with careless grace, as one who would say,
"*Que m'importe?* I am King of France; nought comes
amiss to me."

Now he walks up and down the council-room in
the Louvre which looks towards the river. His step
is quick and agitated, his face wears an unusual
frown. He calls Bonnivet to him and addresses him
in a low voice, while the other nobles stand back.

"Am I to believe that Bourbon has not merely re-
belled against me, but that the traitor has fled into
Spain and made terms with Charles?"

"Your Majesty's information is precise."

"What was the manner of his flight?"

"The Duke, Sire, waited at his fortress of Chantelle until the arrival of Monsieur de Pompérant from
your Majesty's Court at Chambord, feigning sickness

and remaining shut up within his apartments. After Monsieur de Pompérant's arrival, a litter was ordered to await his pleasure, and De Pompérant, dressed in the clothes of the Duke and with his face concealed by a hood, was carried into the litter, which started for Moulins, travelling slowly. Meanwhile Bourbon, accompanied by a band of gentlemen, was galloping on the road to the frontier. He was last seen at Saint-Jean de Luz, in the Pyrenees."

"By our Lady!" exclaims Francis, "such treason is a blot upon knighthood. Bourbon, a man whom we had made as great as ourselves!"

"The Duke, Sire, left a message for your Majesty."

"A message! Where? and who bore it?"

"De Pompérant, Sire, who has already been arrested at Moulins. The Duke begged your Majesty to take back the sword which you had given him, and prayed you to send for the badge which he left hanging at the head of his bed at Chantelle."

"Diable! does the villain dare to point his jests at his sovereign?" and Francis flushes to the roots of his hair with passion. "I wish I had him face to face in a fair field"—and he lays his hand on the hilt of his sword;—"but no," he adds in a calmer voice, "a traitor's blood would but soil my weapon. Let him carry his perfidy into Spain—'twill suit the Emperor; I am well rid of him. Are there many accomplices, Bonnivet?"

"About two hundred, Sire."

"Is it possible! Do we know them?"

"The Comte de Saint-Vallier, Sire, is the principal accomplice."

"What! Saint-Vallier, the Captain of our Archers! That strikes us nearly. This conspiracy, my lords," says Francis, advancing to where Guise, La Trémouille, Montmorenci, and the others stand somewhat apart during his conversation with Bonnivet, "is much more serious than I imagined. I must remain in France to wait the issue of events. You, Bonnivet, must take command of the Italian campaign."

Bonnivet kneels and kisses the hand of Francis.

"I am sorry for Jean de Poitiers," continues Francis, turning to Guise. "Are the proofs against him certain?"

"Sire, Saint-Vallier accompanied the Constable to the frontier."

"I am sorry," repeats the King, and he passes his hand thoughtfully over his brow and muses.

"Jean de Poitiers, my *ci-devant* Captain of the Guards, is the father of a charming lady; Madame Diane, the Seneschale of Normandy, is an angel, though her husband, De Brézè—hum—why, he is a monster. Vulcan and Venus—the old story, eh, my lords?"

There is a general laugh.

A page enters and announces a lady humbly craving to speak with his Majesty. The King smiles, his wicked eyes glisten. "Who? what? Do I know her?"

"Sire, the lady is deeply veiled; she desires to speak with your Majesty alone."

"But, by St. Denis—do I know her?"

"I think, Sire, it is the wife of the Grand Seneschal of Normandy—Madame Diane de Brézè."

There is a pause, some whispering, and a low

laugh is heard. The King looks around displeased. "I am not surprised," says he. "When I heard of the father's danger I expected the daughter's intercession. Let the lady enter."

With a **wave of** his hand he dismisses the Court, and seats himself on a chair of state under a rich canopy embroidered in gold with the arms of France.

Diane enters. She is dressed in long black robes which sweep the floor. Her head is covered **with a** thick lace veil which she raises as she approaches **the** King. She weeps, but her tears do not mar her beauty, which is absolutely radiant. She is exquisitely fair and wonderfully fresh, with golden hair and dark eyebrows—a most winsome lady.

She throws herself at the King's feet. She clasps her hands. Her sobs drown her voice.

"Pardon, Sire, pardon my father!" she at length falters. The King stoops forward, and raises her **to the** estrade **on** which he stands. He looks tenderly into her soft blue eyes, his hands are locked in hers.

"Your father, madame, my old and trusted servant, is guilty of treason."

"Alas! Sire, I fear so; but he is old, too old for punishment. He has been hitherto a true subject **of** your Majesty."

"He is blessed, madame, with a most surpassing daughter." Francis pauses and looks steadfastly at her with eyes of ardent admiration. "But I fear I must confirm the sentence of my judges, madame; your father is certain to be found guilty of treason."

"Oh! Sire, mercy, mercy! grant me my father's life, I implore you;" and again Diane falls prostrate

at the King's feet, and looks supplicatingly into his
face. Again the King raises her.

"Well, madame, you are aware that you desire
the pardon of a traitor; on what ground do you ask
for his life?"

"Sire, I ask it for the sake of mercy; mercy is the
privilege of kings," and her soft eyes seek those of
Francis and rest upon them. "I have come so **far,**
too, from Normandy, to invoke it—my poor father!"
and she sobs again. "Your Majesty will not send me
back refused, broken-hearted?" Still her eyes are fixed
upon the King.

"Mercy, Madame Diane, is, doubtless, a royal prerogative. I **am** an anointed king," and he lets go her
hands, and draws himself up proudly, "and I may use
it; but **the** prerogative of a woman is beauty. Beauty,
Madame Diane," adds Francis, with a glance at the
lovely woman still kneeling at his feet, "is more potent
than a king's word."

There is silence for a few moments. Diane's eyes
are now bent **upon the** ground, her bosom heaves.
Francis contemplates her with delight.

"Will you, **fair lady,** deign **to** exercise your prerogative?"

"Truly, Sire, I know not what your Majesty
would say," replies Diane, looking down and blushing.

Something in his eyes gives her hope, for she
starts violently, rises, and clasping her hands together
exclaims, "How, Sire! do I read your meaning aright?
can I, by my humble service to your Majesty——"

"Yes, fair lady, you can. Your presence at my
Court, where your adorable beauty shall receive due
homage, will be my hostage for your father's loyalty.

Madame Diane, I declare that the Comte de Saint-Vallier is PARDONED. Though he had rent the crown from off our head, your father is pardoned. And I add, madame, that it was the charm of his daughter that rendered a refusal impossible."

Madame Diane's face shines like April sunshine through rain-drops; a smile parts her lips, and her glistening eyes dance with joy; she is more lovely than ever.

"Thanks, thanks, Sire!" And again she would have knelt, but the King again takes her hands, and looks into her face so earnestly that she again blushes.

Did that look of the King fascinate her? or did the sudden joy of saving her father move her heart with love? Who can tell? It is certain, however, that from this time Diane left Normandy, and became one of the brightest ornaments of that beauty-loving Court. Diane was a woman of masculine understanding, concealed under the gentlest and most fascinating manners; but she was also mercenary, intriguing, and domineering. Of her beauty we may judge for ourselves, as many portraits of her are extant, especially one of great excellence by Leonardo da Vinci, in the long gallery at Chenonceau.

Diane was soon forsaken, but the ready-witted lady consoled herself by laying siege to the heart of the son of Francis, Prince Henry, afterwards Henry II.

Henry surrendered at discretion. Nothing can more mark the freedom of the times than this *liaison*. Yet both these ladies—Diane de Poitiers and her successor in the favour of the King, the Duchesse

d'Etampes—were constantly in the society of two
most virtuous queens—Claude, and Elinor of Spain,
the successive wives of Francis.

CHAPTER V.

All Lost save Honour.

THE next scene is in Italy. The French army lies
encamped on the broad plains of Lombardy, backed
by snowy lines of Alpine fastnesses.

Bonnivet, in command of the French, presumptuous
and inexperienced, has been hitherto defeated in every
battle. Bourbon, fighting on the side of Spain, is, as
before, victorious.

Francis, stung by the repeated defeat of his troops,
has now joined the army, and commands in person.
Milan, where the plague rages, has opened its gates
to him; but Pavia, distant about twenty miles, is occupied by the Spaniards in force. Antonio De Leyva
is governor. Thither the French advance in order to
besiege the city.

The open country is defended by the Spanish
forces under Bourbon. Francis, maddened by the
presence of his cousin, rushes onward. Montmorenci
and Bonnivet, flatterers both, assure him that victory
is certain by means of a *coup de main*.

It is night; the days are short, for it is February.
The winter moon lights up the rich meadow lands
divided by the broad Ticino and broken by the deep
ditches and sluggish streams which surround the city.
Tower, campanile, dome, and turret, with here and
there the grim façade of a mediæval palace, stand out
of the darkness.

Yonder among the meadows are the French, darkening the surrounding plain. Francis knows that the Constable is advancing to support the garrison of Pavia, and he desires to carry the city by assault before his arrival. Ever too rash, and now excited by a passionate sense of injury, Francis, with d'Alençon, De la Trémouille, De Foix, and Bonnivet, leads the attack at the head of his cavalry. Now he is under the very walls. Despite the dim moonlight, no one can mistake him. He wears a suit of steel armour inlaid with gold; a crimson surcoat, embroidered with gilt "F's;" a helmet encircled by a jewelled crown, out of which rises a yellow plume and golden salamander. For an instant success seems certain; the scaling-ladders thick with soldiers are already planted against the lowest walls, and the garrison retreats under cover of the bastions. A sudden panic seizes the troops beneath who are to support the assault. In the treacherous moonlight they have fallen into confusion among the deep, slimy ditches; many are drifted away in the current of the great river. A murderous cannonade from the city walls now opens on the assailants and on the cavalry. Francis falls back. The older generals conjure him to retreat and raise the siege before the arrival of Bourbon, but, backed by Bonnivet and Montmorenci, he will not hear of it. The battle rages during the night. The morning light discovers the Spaniards commanded by Bourbon and Pescara, with the whole strength of their army, close under the walls. Again the King leads a fresh assault — a forlorn hope, rather. He fights desperately; the yellow plumes of his helmet wave hither and thither as his horse dashes wildly

from side to side amidst the smoke, in the thickest of
the battle.   See, for an instant he falters,—he is
wounded and bleeding.   He recovers, however, and
again clapping spurs to his horse, scatters his surrounding foes; six have already fallen by his hand.
Look! his charger is pierced by a ball and falls with .
his rider.   After a desperate struggle the King extricates himself; now on foot, he still fights furiously.
Alas! it is in vain.   Every moment his enemies thicken
around him, pressing closer and closer.   His gallant
followers drop one by one under the unerring aim of
the Basque marksmen.   La Trémouille has fallen.   De
Foix lies a corpse at his feet.   Bonnivet in despair
expiates his evil counsel by death.*   Every shot takes
from him one of the pillars of his throne.   Francis
flings himself wildly on the points of the Spanish
pikes.   The Royal Guards fall like summer grass before the sickle; but where the King stands, still dealing desperate blows, the bodies of the slain form a
rampart of protection around him.   His very enemies
stand back amazed at such furious courage.   While
he struggles for his life hand to hand with d'Avila
and d'Ovietta, plumeless, soiled and bloody, a loud
cry rises from a thousand voices—"It is the King—
LET HIM SURRENDER—*Capture the King!*"   There is
a dead silence; the Spanish troops fall back.   A circle
is formed round the now almost fainting Francis, who
lies upon the blood-stained earth.   De Pompérant
advances.   He kneels before the master whom he has
betrayed, he implores him to yield to Bourbon.

     At that hated name the King starts into fresh
fury; he grasps his sword, he struggles to his feet.

* See Note 4.

"Never," cries he in a hoarse voice; "never will I surrender to that traitor! Rather let me die by the hand of a common marksman. Go back, Monsieur de Pompérant, and call to me the Vice-King of Naples."

Lannoy advances, kneels, and kisses his hand. "Your Majesty is my prisoner," he cries aloud, and a ringing shout is echoed from the Spanish troops.

Francis gives him **his** sword. Lannoy receives it kneeling, and replaces it by his own. The King's helmet is then removed; a velvet cap is given to him, which he places on his head. The Spanish and Italian troopers and the deadly musketeers silently · creep round him where he lies on the grass, supported by cushions, one to tear a feather from his broken plume, another to cut a morsel from his surcoat as a relic. This involuntary homage from his enemies is evidently agreeable to Francis. As his surcoat rapidly disappears under the knives **of his** opponents, he smiles, and graciously acknowledges the rough advances of **those** same soldiers who a moment before thirsted **for his blood. Other** generals with Pescara advance and surround him. He courteously acknowledges their respectful salutations.

"Spare my poor soldiers, spare my Frenchmen, generals," he says.

These unselfish words bring tears into Pescara's eyes.

"Your Majesty shall be obeyed," replies he.

"I thank you," replies Francis with a faltering voice.

A pony is now brought to bear him into Pavia. Francis becomes greatly agitated. As they raise him up and assist him to mount, he turns to his escort of generals—

"Marquis," says he, turning to Pescara, "and you, my lord governor, if my calamity touches your hearts, as it would seem to do, I beseech you not to lead me into Pavia. I would not be exposed to the affront of entering as a prisoner a city I should have taken by assault. Carry me, I pray you, to some shelter without the walls."

"Your Majesty's wishes are our law," replies Pescara, saluting him. "We will bear you to the monastery of Saint-Paul, without the gate towards Milan."

To Saint-Paul the King was carried. It was from thence he wrote the historic letter to his mother, Louise de Savoie, Regent of France, in which he tells her, "*all is lost save honour.*"

CHAPTER VI.

Broken Faith.

WE are at Madrid. Francis has been lured hither by incredible treachery, under the idea that he will meet Charles V., and be at once set at liberty.

He is confined in one of the rooms of the Alcazar, then used as a state prison. A massive oaken door, clamped and barred with iron, opens from the court from whence a flight of steps leads into two small chambers which occupy one of the towers. The inner **room** has narrow windows, closely barred. The light is dim. There is just room for a table, two chairs, and a bed. It is a cage rather than a prison.

On a chair, near an open window, sits the King. He is emaciated and pale; his cheeks are hollow, his lips are white, his eyes are sunk in his head, his dress is neglected. His glossy hair, plentifully streaked with grey, covers the hand upon which he wearily leans his head. He gazes vacantly at the setting sun opposite—a globe of fire rapidly sinking below the low dark plain which bounds his view.

There are boundless plains in front of him, and on his left a range of tawny hills. A roadway runs beneath the tower, where the Imperial Guards are encamped. The gay fanfare of the trumpets sounding the retreat, the waving banners, the prancing horses, the brilliant accoutrements, the glancing armour of the imperial troops, mock him where he sits. Around him is Madrid. Palace, tower, and garden rise out of a sea of buildings burnt by southern sunshine. The church bells ring out the Ave Maria. The fading light darkens into night. Still the King sits beside the open window, lost in thought. No one comes to disturb him. Now and then some broken words escape his lips:—"Save France—my poor soldiers—brave De Foix—noble Bonnivet—see, he is tossed on the Spanish pikes. Alas! would I were dead. My sister—my little lads—the Dauphin—Henry—Orleans—I shall never see you more. Oh, God! I am bound in chains of iron—France—liberty—glory—gone—gone for ever!" His head sinks on his breast; tears stream from his eyes. He falls back fainting in his chair, and is borne to his bed.

Francis has never seen Charles, who is at his capital, Toledo. The Emperor does not even excuse his absence. This cold and cautious policy, this death in life, is agony to the ardent temperament of Francis. His health breaks down. A settled melancholy, a morbid listlessness overwhelms him. He is seized with fever; he rapidly becomes delirious. His royal gaoler, Charles, will not believe in his danger; he still refuses to see him. False himself, he believes Francis **to be shamming.** The Spanish ministers are distracted by their master's obstinacy, for if the French King **dies** at Madrid of broken heart, all is lost, and **a** bloody war with France inevitable.

At the moment when the Angel of Death hovers over the Alcazar, a sound of wheels is heard below. A litter, drawn by reeking mules and covered with mud, dashes into the street. The leather curtains are drawn aside, and Marguerite d'Alençon, pale and shrunk with anxiety and fatigue, attended by two ladies, having travelled from Paris day and night, descends. Breathless with excitement, she passes quickly up the narrow stairs, through the ante-room, and enters the King's chamber. Alas! what a sight awaits her. Francis lies insensible on his bed. The room is darkened, save where a temporary altar has been erected, opposite his bed, on which lights are burning. A Bishop officiates. The low voices of priests, chanting as they move about the altar, alone break a death-like silence. Marguerite, overcome by emotion, clasps her hands and sinks on her knees beside her brother. Her sobs and cries disturb the solemn ordinance. She is led almost fainting away. Then the Bishop approaches the King, bearing the bread of life, and, at that moment, Francis becomes suddenly conscious. He opens his eyes, and in a feeble voice prays that he may be permitted to receive it. So humbly, yet so joyfully, does he communicate that all present are deeply moved.

In spite, however, of the presence of Marguerite in Madrid, the King relapses. He again falls into a death-like trance. Then, and then only, does the Emperor yield to the reproaches of the Duchesse d'Alençon and the entreaties of his ministers. He takes horse from Toledo and rides to Madrid almost without drawing rein, until he stops at the heavy door in the Alcazar. He mounts the stairs and enters the chamber. Francis, now restored to consciousness, prompted by a too generous nature, opens his arms to embrace him.

"Your Majesty has come to see your prisoner die," says he in a feeble voice, faintly smiling.

"No," replies Charles, with characteristic caution and Spanish courtesy, bowing profoundly and kissing him on either cheek; "no, your Majesty will not die, you are no longer my prisoner; you are my friend and brother. I come to set you free."

"Ah, Sire," murmurs Francis in a voice scarcely audible, "death will accomplish that before your Majesty; but if I live—and indeed I do not believe I shall, I am so overcome by weakness—let me implore you to allow me to treat for my release in person with your Majesty; for this end I came hither to Madrid."

At this moment the conversation is interrupted by the entrance of a page, who announces to the Emperor that the Duchesse d'Alençon has arrived and awaits his Majesty's pleasure. Glad of an excuse to terminate a most embarrassing interview with his too confiding prisoner, Charles, who has been seated on the bed, rises hastily—

"Permit me, my brother," says he, "to leave you, in order to descend and receive your august sister in person. In the meantime recover your health. Reckon upon my willingness to serve you. Some other time we will meet; then we can treat more in detail of these matters, when your Majesty is stronger and better able to converse."

Charles takes an affectionate leave of Francis, descends the narrow stairs, and with much ceremony receives the Duchess.

"I rejoice, madame," says he, "to offer you in person the homage of all Spain, and my own hearty thanks for the courage and devotion you have shown in the service of the King, my brother. He is a prisoner no longer. The conditions of release shall forthwith be prepared by my ministers."

"Is the King fully aware what those conditions are, Sire?" Marguerite coldly asks.

Charles was silent.

"I fear our mother, Madame Louise, Regent of France," continues the Duchesse d'Alençon, "may find it difficult to accept your conditions, even though it be to liberate the Sovereign of France, her own beloved son."

"Madame," replies Charles evasively, "I will not permit this occasion, when I have the happiness of first saluting you within my realm, to be occupied with state affairs. Rely on my desire to set my brother free. Meanwhile the King will, I hope, recover his strength. Pressing business now calls me back to Toledo. Adieu! most illustrious princess, to whom I offer all that Madrid contains for your service. Permit me to kiss your hands. Salute my brother, the King, from me. Once more, royal lady, adieu!"

Marguerite curtseys to the ground. The Emperor, with his head uncovered, mounts his horse, again salutes her, and attended by his retinue puts spurs to his steed and rides from the Alcazar on his return to Toledo. Marguerite fully understands the treachery of his words. Her heart swelling with indignation, she slowly ascends to the King's chamber.

"Has the Emperor departed already?" Francis eagerly asks her.

"Yes, my brother; pressing business, he says, calls him back to Toledo," replies Marguerite bitterly, speaking very slowly.

"What! gone so soon, before giving me an opportunity of discussing with him the terms of my freedom. Surely, my sister, this is strange," says Francis, turning eagerly towards the Duchess, and then sinking back pale and exhausted on his pillows.

Marguerite seats herself beside him, takes his hand tenderly within both her own, and gazes at him in silence.

"But, my sister, did my brother, the Emperor, say *nothing* to you of his speedy return?"

"Nothing," answers Marguerite drily.

"Yet he assured me, with his own lips, that I was already free, and that the conditions of release would be prepared immediately."

"Dear brother," says the Duchess, "has your imprisonment at Madrid, and the conduct of the Emperor to you this long time past, inclined you to believe what he says?"

4*

"I, a king myself, should be grieved to doubt a brother sovereign's word."

"Francis," says Marguerite, speaking with great earnestness and fixing her eyes on him, "what you say convinces me that you are weakened by illness. Your naturally acute intellect is dulled by the confusion of recent delirium. If you were in full possession of your senses you would not speak as you do. My brother, take heed of my words—you will never be free."

"How!" exclaims the King, starting up, "never be free? What do you mean?"

"Calm yourself, my brother. You are, I fear, too weak to hear what I have to say."

"No, no! my sister; suspense to me is worse than death. Speak to me, Marguerite; speak to me, my sister."

"Then, Sire, let me ask you, when you speak of release, when the Emperor tells you you are free, are you aware of the conditions he imposes on you?"

"Not accurately," replies Francis. "Certain terms were proposed, before my illness, that I should surrender whole provinces in France, renounce my rights in the Milanese, pay an enormous ransom, leave my sons hostages at Madrid; but these were the proposals of the Spanish council. The Emperor, speaking personally to a brother sovereign, would never press anything on me unbecoming my royal condition; therefore it is that I desire to treat with himself alone."

"Alas! my brother, you are too generous; you are deceived. Much negotiation has passed during your illness, and since my arrival. Conditions have been proposed by Spain to the Regent, that she—your mother—supported by the parliament of your country,

devoted to your person, has refused. Listen to me,
Francis. Charles seeks to dismember France. As
long as it remains a kingdom, he intends that you shall
never leave Madrid."

"Marguerite, my sister, proceed, I entreat you!"
breaks in Francis, trembling with excitement.

"Burgundy is to be ceded; you are to renounce
all interest in Flanders and in the Milanese. You are
to pay a ransom that will beggar the kingdom. You
are to marry Elinor, Queen Dowager of Portugal, sister
to Charles, and you are to leave your sons, the Dauphin
and the Duc d'Orléans, hostages in Spain for the ful-
filment of these demands."

Francis turns very white, and sinks back speechless
on the pillows that support him. He stretches out
his arm to his sister and fondly clasps her neck.
"Marguerite, if it is so, you say well,—I shall never
leave Madrid. My sister, let me die ten thousand
deaths rather than betray the honour of France."

"Speak not of death, dearest brother!" exclaims
Marguerite, her face suddenly flushing with excitement. "I have come to make you live. I, Marguerite
d'Alençon, your sister, am come to lead you back to
your army and to France; to the France that mourns
for you; to the army that is now dispersed and insub-
ordinate; to the mother who weeps for her beloved
son." Marguerite's voice falters; she sobs aloud, and
rising from her chair, she presses her brother in her
arms. Francis feebly returns her embrace, tenderly
kisses her, and signs to her to proceed. "Think you,"
continues Marguerite more calmly, and reseating herself, but still holding the King's hand—"think you
that councils in which *Bourbon* has a voice——" At

this name the King shudders and clenches his fist upon the bed-clothes. "Think you that a sovereign who has treacherously lured you to Madrid will have any mercy on you? No, my brother; unless you agree to unworthy conditions, imposed by a treacherous monarch who abuses his power over you, here you will languish until you die! Now mark my words, dear brother. Treaties made under *duresse*, by *force majeure*, are legally void. You will dissemble, my generous King—for the sake of France, you will dissemble. You must fight this crafty emperor with his own weapons."

"What! my sister, be false to my word—I, a belted knight, invested by the hands of Bayard on the field of Marignano, stoop to a lie? Marguerite, you are mad!"

"Oh, Francis, hear me!" cries Marguerite passionately, "hear me; on my knees I conjure you to live, for yourself, for us, for France." She casts herself on the floor beside him. She wrings his hands, she kisses his feet, her tears falling thickly. "Francis, you must, you shall consent. By-and-by you will bless me for this tender violence. You are not fit to meddle in this matter. Leave to me the care of your honour; is it not my own? I come from the Regent, from the council, from all France. Believe me, brother, if you are perjured, all Europe will applaud the perjury."

Marguerite, whose whole frame quivers with agitation, speaks no more. There is a lengthened pause. The flush of fever is on the King's face.

"My sister," murmurs Francis, struggling with a broken voice to express himself, "you have conquered. Into your hands I commit my honour and the future of France. Leave me a while to rest, for I am faint."

Treaties made under *duresse* by *force majeure* are legally void. The Emperor must be decoyed into the belief that terms are accepted by Francis, which are to be broken the instant his foot touches French soil. It is with the utmost difficulty that the chivalrous monarch can be brought to lend himself to this deceit. But the prayers of his sister, the deplorable condition of his kingdom deprived of his presence for nearly five years, the terror of returning illness, and the thorough conviction that Charles is as perfidious as he is ambitious, at length prevail. Francis ostensibly accepts the Emperor's terms, and Queen Claude being dead, he affiances himself to Charles' sister, Elinor, Queen Dowager of Portugal.

Francis was perjured, but France was saved.

CHAPTER VII.

La Duchesse d'Etampes.

RIDING with all speed from Madrid—for he fears the Emperor's perfidy—Francis has reached the frontier of Spain, on the banks of the river Bidassoa. His boys—the Dauphin and the Duc d'Orléans, who are to replace him at Madrid as hostages—await him there. They rush into their father's arms and fondly cling to him, weeping bitterly at this cruel meeting for a moment after years of separation. Francis, with ready sympathy, mingles his tears with theirs. He embraces and blesses them. But, wild with the excitement of liberty and insecure while on Spanish soil, he cannot spare time for details. He hands the poor lads over to the Spanish commissioners. Too impatient to await the arrival of the ferry boat, which is pulling across the river, he steps into the waters of the Bidassoa to meet it. On the opposite bank, among the low scrub wood, a splendid retinue awaits him. He springs into the saddle, waves his cap in the air, and with a joyous shout exclaims, "Now I am a king! Now I am free!"

The political vicissitudes of Francis's reign are as nothing to the chaos of his private life; only as a lover he was never defeated. No humiliating Pavia arrests his successful course. At Bayonne he finds a brilliant Court; his mother the Regent, and his sister Marguerite, await his arrival. After " Les embrasseurs d'usage," as Du Bellay quaintly expresses it, the King's eye wanders over the parterre of young beauties assembled in their suite, "la petite bande des dames de la Cour." Then Francis first beholds Anne de Pisselieu, afterwards Duchesse d'Etampes. No one can compare to her in the tyranny of youth, beauty, and talent. A mere girl, she already knows everything, and is moreover astute, witty, and false. In spite of the efforts of Diane de Poitiers to attract the King (she having come to Bayonne in attendance on the Regent-mother), Anne de Pisselieu prevails. The King is hers. He delights in her joyous sallies. Anne laughs at every one and everything, specially at the pretensions of Madame Diane, whom she calls "an old hag." She declares that she herself was born on Diane's wedding-day!

Who can resist so bewitching a creature? Not Francis certainly. So the Court divides itself into two factions in love, politics, and religion. One party,

headed by the Duchesse d'Etampes—a Protestant, and
mistress of the reigning monarch; a second by Madame
Diane de Poitiers—a Catholic, who, after many efforts,
finding the King inaccessible, devotes herself to his
son, Prince Henry, a mere boy, at least twenty years
younger than herself, and waits his reign. Oddly
enough, it is the older woman who waits, and the
younger one who rules.

The Regent-mother looks on approvingly. Morals,
especially royal morals, do not exist. Madame Louise
de Savoie is ambitious. She would **not** see the new
Spanish Queen—a comely princess, as she hears from
her daughter Marguerite—possess too much influence
over the King. It might injure her own power. The
poor Spanish Queen! No fear that her influence will
injure any one! The King never loves her, and never
forgives her being forced upon him as a clause in the
ignominious treaty of Madrid. Besides, she is thirty-
two years old and a widow; grave, dignified, and learned,
but withal a lady of agreeable person, though of mature
and well-developed charms. Elinor admired and **loved**
Francis when she saw him at Madrid, and all the
world thought that the days were numbered in which
Madame d'Etampes would be seen at Court. "But,"
says Du Bellay, either with perfect naiveté or profound
irony—"it was impossible for the King to offer to the
virtuous Spanish princess any other sentiments than
respect and gratitude, the Duchesse d'Etampes being
sole mistress of his heart!" So the royal lady fares no
better than Queen Claude, "with the roses in her soul,"
and only receives, like her, courtesy and indifference.

The King returns to the Spanish frontier to receive Queen Elinor and to embrace the sons, now

released, to whom she has been a true mother during the time they have been hostages at Madrid.

By-and-by the Queen's brother—that mighty and perfidious sovereign, Charles V., Emperor of Germany —passing to his estates in the Netherlands, "craves leave of his beloved brother, Francis, King of France, to traverse his kingdom on his way," so great is his dread of the sea voyage on account of sickness.

Some days before the Emperor's arrival Francis is at the Louvre. He has repaired and embellished it in honour of his guest, and has pulled down the central tower, or donjon, called "Philippine," which encumbered the inner court. By-and-by he will pull down all the mediæval fortress, and, assisted by Lescot, begin the palace known as the "Old Louvre."

Francis is seated tête-à-tête with the Duchesse d'Etampes. The room is small—a species of boudoir or closet. It is hung with rare tapestry, representing in glowing colours the Labours of Hercules. Venetian mirrors, in richly carved frames, fling back the light of a central chandelier, also of Venetian workmanship, cunningly wrought into gaudy flowers, diamonded pendants and true lovers' knots. It is a blaze of brightness and colour. Rich velvet hangings, heavy with gold embroidery, cover the narrow windows and hang over the low doors. The King and the Duchess sit beside a table of inlaid marble, supported on a pedestal, marvellously gilt, of Italian workmanship, on which are laid fruits, wines, and *confitures*, served in golden vessels worked in the Cinque-cento style, after Cellini's patterns. Beside themselves, Triboulet,* the king's fool, alone is present. As Francis holds out

* See Note 5.

his cup time after time to Triboulet, who replenishes it with Malvoisie, the scene composes itself into a perfect picture, such as Victor Hugo has imagined in *Le Roi s'amuse;* so perfect, indeed, that Francis might have sung, "La donna è mobile," as he now does in Verdi's opera of *Rigoletto.*

"Sire," says the Duchess, her voice dropping into a **most** delicious softness, "do you leave us to-morrow?"

The King bows his head and kisses her jewelled fingers.

"So you persist in going to meet your brother, the Emperor Charles, your loving brother of Spain; whom I hate because he was so cruel to you at Madrid." The Duchess looks up and smiles. Her eyes are beautiful, but hard and cruel. She wears an ermine mantle, for it is winter; her dress is of the richest green satin, embroidered with gold. On her head is a golden net, the meshes sprinkled with diamonds, from which her dark tresses escape in long ringlets over her shoulders.

Francis turns towards her and pledges her in a cup of Malvoisie. The corners of his mouth are drawn up into a cynical smile, almost to his nostrils. He has now reached middle life, and his face at that time would have made no man's fortune.

"Duchess," says he, "I must tear myself from you. I go to-morrow to Touraine. Before returning to Paris, I shall attend my brother the Emperor Charles at Loches, then at Amboise on the Loire. You will soon follow me with the Queen."

"And, surely, when you have this heartless king, this cruel gaoler in your power, you will punish him and revenge yourself? If he, like a fool, comes into Touraine, make him revoke the treaty of Madrid, or shut him up in one of Louis XI.'s oubliettes at Amboise or Loches."

"I will *persuade* him if I can to liberate me from all the remaining conditions of the treaty," said the King, "but I will never *force* him." As he speaks, Triboulet, who has been shaking the silver bells on his parti-coloured dress with suppressed laughter, pulls out some ivory tablets to add something to a list he keeps of those whom he considers greater fools than himself. He calls it "his journal."

The King looks at the tablets and sees the name of Charles V.

"Ha! ha! by the mass!—how long has my brother of Spain figured there?" asks he.

"The day, Sire, that I heard he had put his foot on the French frontier."

"What will you do when I let him depart freely?"

"I shall," said Triboulet, "rub out his name and put yours in its place, Sire."

"See, your Majesty, there is some one else who agrees with me," says the Duchess, laughing.

"I know," replies Francis, "that my interests would almost force me to do as you desire, madame, but my honour is dearer to me than my interests. I am now at liberty,—I had rather the treaty of Madrid should stand for ever than countenance an act unworthy of 'un roi chevalier.'"

Francis receives Charles V. at Amboise with ostentatious splendour. Aware of the repugnance of his royal guest to mount steps (the Spanish Emperor was early troubled by those attacks of gout that caused

him at length to abdicate and to die of premature old
age, at the monastery of San Juste), Francis caused
an inclined plane or slope to be constructed in place
of stairs within one of the round towers by which the
Castle of Amboise, standing on a precipitous pile of
rocks, is approached. Up this slope, which remains
in excellent preservation, Charles ascends to the plateau on which the castle stands, seated in his ponderous coach, drawn by heavy horses, attended by guards
and outriders. Elinor, his sister, the neglected Queen,
as well as the favourite, Madame d'Etampes, are present at the fêtes given in honour of the Emperor.
There are no secrets at Court, and Charles soon comes
to know that the *maîtresse en titre* is his enemy. One
evening, after a dance executed by Anne d'Etampes
along with the ladies of the Court, in which she displayed the graces of her person, the Emperor approaches her.

"Madame," he says, "it is only in France that I
have seen such perfection of elegance and beauty.
My brother, the King, would be the envy of all the
sovereigns of Europe could they have witnessed what
I have just seen. There is no ransom that I would
accept for such a captive, had I the power of retaining her at Madrid."

The Emperor's eyes melt with admiration as he
gazes on her.

The Duchess's countenance beams with delight at
the Emperor's high-flown compliment.

The King approaches the spot where they stand.

"Know, my brother," says the King with a slight
touch of irony in his tone, for he is displeased at the
tender glances Charles is casting on his favourite,

"know that this fair Duchess would have had me detain you here a prisoner until you had revoked the treaty of Madrid."

The Emperor starts visibly and frowns. "If you consider the advice good, your Majesty had better follow it," he replies haughtily, turning away to address some nobles standing near.

Some few days afterwards the Duchess gives a supper in her apartments, to which the Emperor and the Court are invited. After the reception, sinking on her knees, she presents his Majesty with rose water in a gold embossed basin in which to wash his hands. Charles adroitly drops a large diamond ring into the basin. The Duchess stoops and places the vessel on the ground in order to pick up the jewel.

"This ring, madame," he says, and he speaks low, and leans forward in order to catch her ear, "is too becoming to that fair hand for me to remove it. It has itself sought a new possessor," and he kisses her hand. "Keep it as a pledge of my admiration and my friendship."

The Duchess rises and makes a deep obeisance. Not only did she keep the ring, but she became so decided a partisan of this "*gaoler*," that she is popularly accused of having betrayed Francis to the Emperor; specially in the subsequent wars between England, France, and Spain.

CHAPTER VIII.

Last Days.

RAMBOUILLET is now a station on the railway between Versailles, Chartres, and Le Mans. It is a sunny little town, sloping to the south, in a sheltered hollow, over which the slanting roofs and conical turrets of the palace rise out of stately elms and spiked poplars. The principal façade of the château—which consists of two wings at right angles to each other, having at each corner a circular turret, surmounted by a spire—faces the mid-day sun. The ground lies low, and canals, extending in three directions, bordered by terraced walks and avenues, intersect the grassy lawns which lengthen into the tangled woodland of the surrounding forest. Opposite the château, on an islet, is a grotto called "La Marmite de Rabelais." To the right, the three canals flow into a river, spanned by a low bridge, known as "the accursed bridge," from some now obscure tradition foreboding evil to those who pass over it. On every other side, the trunks of venerable trees, their over-arching branches closing above like a cloister—pillars of oak, elm, and ash—wind away into grassy meads and shady dingles, intersected by long rides cut straight through the forest, proper for the stag-hunts which have been held in this ancient manor since the Middle Ages.

The château itself has now been modernised, save where one ivy-crowned round tower (the donjon of the mediæval fortress), in deep shadow, frowns an angry defiance to the stucco and whitewash of the flimsy modern façade.

It is the month of March, in the year 1547. Francis, attended by a small retinue, has arrived at the foot of this **round** tower. Coming from the south, he has crossed the river by "the accursed bridge."

During the whole past year he has wandered from place to place, revisiting all his favourite haunts as though conscious that he is bidding them farewell. The restlessness of mortal disease is upon him. Though he flies from city to hamlet, from castle to palace, vainly seeking respite from pain, death haunts and follows him. His life is agony. He is greatly changed—an internal fever consumes him. His eyes are haggard; his face is thin, and his body emaciated. Only fifty-two years old, like his great rival the Emperor Charles, he is prematurely aged. Now he is half lifted from his coach and slowly led up a winding staircase to his apartments on the second floor by his friend James d'Angennes, to whose ancestors Rambouillet belonged. Francis comes from Chambord, where Marguerite, now Queen of Navarre by her second marriage, met him. Marguerite and her brother still cling to each other, but they are both aged and full of care. Her beauty is faded and her health is broken. Even she, though devoted as ever, cannot amuse Francis or dissipate the weight that oppresses his spirit. The old topics that were wont to delight him are irritably dismissed. He no longer cares for poetry, is wearied of politics, shrinks from society, and abuses women. It is at this time he writes with the point of a diamond, on the window of his closet at Chambord, these significant lines:—

> "Souvent femme varie;
> Mal habile qui s'y fie!"

He can only talk to his sister on sorrowful subjects: of the death by plague of his favourite son Charles, who caught the infection when sleeping at Abbeville; or of his old friend, Henry VIII. of England, who has also recently died.

The death of the latter seems to affect Francis terribly:—"Our lives," he says, "were very similar—he was slightly older, but I shall not long survive him." Vainly does Marguerite combat these dismal forebodings. She laments in secret the sad change. Ever sympathetic with her brother, she, too, throws aside romance and poetry and composes "The Mirror of a Sinful Soul" to suit his altered humour. Alas! what would Marguerite say if she knew what is carefully concealed from her? That the great surgeon Paré— Paré, who was afterwards to draw the spear-point from the cheek of the Balafré—has pronounced that the King's malady is hopeless!

After a short sojourn together at Chambord, the brother and sister part never to meet again.

Francis was to have passed the carnival at Limours, says Du Bellay; now he commands the masked balls and the court ballets to be held at Saint-Germain en Laye. The King's fancy changes: he will rouse himself; he will shake off the horrible lethargy that is creeping over him; he will dismiss sinister presentiments. Disguised himself, he will dance among the maskers—the excitement will revive him.

But strong as is his will, high as is his courage, the mortal disease within him is stronger still. Suddenly he countermands all his orders. He will rather go to Rambouillet to visit his old friend, d'Angennes;

to meet Rabelais perhaps, who loves the old castle, and to hunt in the great woods.

The quiet old manor, half hunting-lodge, half fortress, buried in secluded woods just bursting into leaf, where the wild boar and the stag are plentiful, will suit him better than banquets, balls, games, and boisterous revelry. The once dauntless Francis is grown nervous and querulous, and is painfully conscious of the slightest noise. After a rapid journey he crosses the ill-omened bridge and arrives at Rambouillet. No sooner has he been laid in his bed than again his mind changes. He must rise and go to Saint-Germain, more suitable than Rambouillet in accommodation for his present condition. But the intense anguish he suffers renders this project impossible. Well, he will remain. He will rest one night here; then, he will depart. In the morning, says the same historian, he awakes at daylight, feeling somewhat better. He commands a royal hunt for stags and boars. Once more he hears the bugle of the huntsmen, the baying of the hounds, the tramp of the impatient steeds. The fresh morning air gives him fictitious strength. He rises from his bed, dresses himself, descends, forces himself on horseback and rides forth, defying disease and pain. Alas! he is soon brought back to the donjon tower and carried up the stairs speechless and in mortal agony to his bed. Fever and delirium ensue, but as the death shadows gather round him weakness clears his brain.

"I am dying," says he faintly, addressing d'Angennes, who never leaves him for an instant; "send for my son Henry."

"Sire," replies the Count, "his Highness is already here."

"Let him come to me at once; my breath fails me fast."

The Prince enters and kneels beside the dying king. He weeps bitterly, takes his father's already cold hand in his own and kisses it. Francis feebly returns the pressure. He turns his sunken eyes towards his son and signs that he would speak. Henry, the better to catch his words, rises and bends over him.

"My son, I have been a great sinner," falters the dying King, "my passions led me astray; avoid this, Henry. If I have done well, follow that, not the evil."

"Sire," replies the Prince, "we all love and honour your Majesty."

"Cherish France, my son," continues the King; "it is a noble nation. They refused me nothing in my adversity, nor will they you, if you rule them rightly. Lighten the taxes, my son,—be good to my people."

His voice grows fainter and less distinct, his face more ashen.

The Prince, seeing his lips move but hearing no sound, lays his ear close to his father's mouth.

"Commend me to Catherine, your wife; beware of the Guises; they will strip you; they are all traitors;* cherish my people." He spoke no more.

The Prince motions to d'Angennes, and the parish priest with his acolytes enter, bearing the Host. Speechless, but conscious, with a look of infinite devotion, Francis receives the sacraments. Then, turning his

* See Note 6.

dying eyes towards his son, he feebly raises his hands to bless him.

Henry, overcome by the sight of his dying father, sinks prostrate beside the bed. D'Angennes stands at the head, supporting his dying master in his arms; while he wipes the moisture from his forehead, Francis expires.

CHAPTER IX.
Catherine de Medici.

CATHERINE DE **Medici, widow of Henry** II., and mother of three kings regnant, rules France in their name. Her father, Lorenzo, Duke of Urbino, second tyrant of Florence, died before she was born; her mother, Madaleine de la Tour d'Auvergne (for Catherine had French blood in her veins), died when she was born; so fatal was this Medici, even at her birth.

The *Duchessina*, as Catherine was called, was reared by her aunt Clarice Sforza, within the mediæval stronghold of the Medici at Florence—now known as the Riccardi Palace. Although bereft of palisade **and** towers **of defence, it is** still a stately pile of Italian Gothic architecture, with pillared cortile, ornate front, and sculptured cornice, bidding a mute defiance to the encroachments of the modern buildings of the Via Cavour, the Corso of the City of Flowers.

Catherine was educated by the nuns of the "Murate" (walled up), in their convent near the Porta Santa Croce. The teaching of these lonely enthusiasts strangely contrasted with the life she afterwards led in the Florentine Court—a very hot-bed of vice, intrigue, and ambition. There did this Medea **of the** Cinque-

cento learn how to dissimulate and to betray. At
fifteen she became, by the favour of her uncle, Pope
Clement VII., the richest heiress in Europe. She was
tall and finely formed, of a clear olive complexion
(inherited from her French mother), with well-cut features, and large prominent eyes, like all the Medici.
Her manners were gracious, her countenance expressive, but there was, even in extreme youth, a fixed
and cold expression on the statuesque face that belied
these pleasant attributes. Many suitors sought her
hand, but Clement VII., outraged at the brutality of
the Spanish coalition against him under Charles V.,
which had resulted in the sack of Rome and his own
imprisonment in the Castle of St. Angelo, was glad to
spite his enemies by bestowing his wealthy niece on
the Duc d'Orléans, son of Francis I. As the heiress
of the Medici came of a republican race of merchant
princes, mere mushrooms beside the lofty antiquity of
the Valois line, the Pope, to give greater lustre to the
espousals, announced that he would himself conduct
his niece to her future husband. At Leghorn, Catherine embarked with her uncle in a sumptuous papal
galley, attended by his tonsured Court. A flotilla of
boats accompanied the vice-regent of God upon earth
and his niece the sparkling *Duchessina*. Fair winds
and smooth seas soon wafted them to the French
shore, where Francis and his sons awaited their arrival
at Marseilles.

Francis, says Brantôme, was so charmed with the
Medici bride, her intelligence and lively manners, that
he romped with her the entire evening after her arrival. When Francis found that she danced admirably,
that she shot with an arquebuse like a trooper, played

at maille like a boy, and rode boldly and gracefully, his partiality to his new daughter-in-law knew no bounds. What was the opinion of the bridegroom Orléans, and what comparison he made between a bride of fifteen and a mistress of thirty-five, is not recorded. There was nearly twenty years difference in age between Prince Henry, Duc d'Orléans, a mere **boy**, and Diane de Poitiers, yet her influence over him was still absolute. To the day of his death he **wore** her colours—white and black—upon his shield. Diane, secure in power, was rather proud of her age. She boasted to the new Duchess that she was never ill, •that she rose at six o'clock in the morning, bathed in the coldest water, and rode two hours before breakfast.

When Catherine first appeared at the Louvre as the bride of Prince Henry, she *seemed* but a clever, **facile** girl, ready to accept her humiliating position as subordinate in power, influence, and beauty to her husband's mistress, Diane de Poitiers, as well as to the Duchesse d'Etampes, the favourite of Francis. Placed among these two women and the lonely Spanish Queen, Elinor of Portugal, for fourteen years she acquitted herself with the most perfect temper and discretion. Indeed, with strange self-command in one so young, she endeavoured to flatter both the favourites, but failing to propitiate either Diane or the Duchess, and not being able to attract her husband **or** to interest the sedate Spaniard, she devoted herself wholly to charm her father-in-law, Francis. She became the constant and beloved companion of his various progresses and hunting parties to Fontainebleau, Amboise, Chenonceau, and Loches. No court pageants these, on ambling pads over smooth lawns, among limber trees, with retinue of velvet-liveried menials on the watch for any possible casualty; but hard and dangerous riding in search of boars, and wolves, and stags, over a rough country, among thick underwood, rocky hills, and precipitous uplands.

Thus Catherine *seemed*, but in her heart she despised the Duchess, abhorred Diane, and suffered all the mortification of a neglected wife. Diane did not moreover spare her feelings, but insolently and ostentatiously paraded her superior influence, especially after Prince Henry came to the throne and created her Duchesse de Valentinois.

Catherine, however, with marvellous self-command bore all meekly, brought the King ten children, and for fourteen years bided her time. And that time came sooner than either the wife or the mistress expected.

CHAPTER X.

A Fatal Joust.

IT is the wedding-day of the two princesses, Elizabeth and Marguerite; the first a daughter, the latter a sister, of Henry II. A tournament is to be held in the Rue Saint-Antoine, near the Palace des Tournelles, so called from its many towers.*

King Henry and the elder princes, his sons, are to ride in the lists and to break a lance freely with all comers. Queen Catherine and the brides—Elizabeth, the very youthful wife of the morose Philip II. of Spain,

* See Note 7.

lately husband of Mary Tudor, known as Bloody Mary, now deceased; Marguerite, wife of the Duke of Savoy, and Marguerite de Valois, second daughter of Catherine, then but a child—are seated in the centre of an open dais covered with damascened silk, and ornamented with feathers, tassels, and gaudy streamers, which flutter in the summer breeze.   Behind them are ranged the greatest ladies of the Court, among whom Diane de Poitiers, now Duchesse de Valentinois, occupies the place of honour. The ladies in waiting on the Queen and the great officers of state are ranged at the back.

It is a lovely morning in the month of July.   The summer sun lights up the gay dresses and fair faces of the Court into a glowing parterre of bright colours. At a signal from Queen Catherine bands of wind instruments burst into martial music; the combatants enter the arena and divide themselves into different squadrons.   First rides the King at the head of his knights.   His appearance is the signal for all to rise, as much out of respect to him as the better to observe his chivalrous bearing and magnificent accoutrements. He wears a suit of armour in which gold is the chief metal. His sword-handle and dagger are set with jewels, and from his shield and lance fly streamers of black and white—the colours of Diane de Poitiers. He rides a Spanish barb, caparisoned with crimson velvet, that tosses his head and curvets proudly, as if conscious of its royal burden.   Three times the King passes round the list within the barriers, preceded by pages and esquires bearing shields bound with ribbons, on which are engraven, in letters of gold or of gems, the initials of their masters' ladye-loves. The King is followed by squadrons of knights. All range themselves near the open dais occupied by the queens and the princesses.

A herald in a parti-coloured dress advances into the centre of the open space, and to the sound of trumpet proclaims that the lists are open. The barriers are then lowered by the pages and the esquires, and the tilting begins.

Catherine looks on with a troubled countenance. Her eyes incessantly follow the King and watch his every movement. As knight after knight is unhorsed and rolls in the dust, and loud cries and shouts of laughter rise at each discomfiture above the tumult of the fight, the anxious expression on her face never changes. Now and then, when the King, excited by the mimic warfare, deals and receives hard blows and vigorous lance thrusts, Catherine visibly trembles. Like the wife of Pilate, "she has suffered much because of a dream concerning him"—a dream that has shown him to her, disfigured and dabbled with blood, lying dead in a strange chamber.

In the early morning she had implored the King not to enter the lists, but Henry had laughed and had ridden forth wearing the colours of her rival.

Now the long day is drawing to a close; the sun is low on the horizon and the tournament is over. The King, who has fought like a son of Francis I., and broken the lances of the Ducs de Ferrara, Guise, and Nemours, has retired from the lists into his tent to unarm. The young princes have dismounted and ascended into the dais beside their mother and the brides. Catherine breathes again; the King is safe—her dream but the coinage of her brain! But hark! the faint sound of a trumpet is heard, proceeding from

the extremity of the long street of Saint-Antoine. The
Queen grows pale and bends her ear to listen. The
sound comes nearer; it becomes more distinct at each
fresh blast. Now it is at hand, and as the shrill and
ill-omened notes strike her ear, a herald advances
preceded by a trumpeter, and announces that a masked
knight has arrived and challenges his Majesty to break
a lance with him in honour of his lady.

The masked knight, habited entirely in black
armour, rides into the arena. Certain of the fatal
event, the Queen rises abruptly from her seat. Her
countenance expresses absolute terror. She beckons
hastily to the Comte d'O, who is in attendance. "Go,"
says she in a low voice, speaking rapidly; "go at once
to the King. Tell him that if he fights with this
stranger he will die!—tell him so from me. Haste!
for the love of the Virgin, haste!"

No sooner has the Comte d'O left her, than, leaning over the dais, Catherine, with clasped hands and
eager eyes, watches him as he crosses the enclosure.
She sees him parley with the King, who is replacing
his casque and arranging his armour. Henry laughs.
The Queen turns to the young Comte de la Molle,
who is near— "Call up hither his Majesty to me
instantly. Tell him he must come up to me here
before he enters the lists. It is for life or death—the
life of the King. Go! fly!"

This second messenger crosses to where Henry is
just mounting on horseback. "Alas! alas! he does
not heed my messenger. Let me go," cries the Queen
in the most violent agitation; "I will myself descend
and speak with his Majesty." She rushes forward
through the astonished courtiers to where a flight of

steps leads below into the enclosure. As her foot is
on the topmost stair, she sees the King gallop forth,
fully equipped, in face of the masked knight. The
Queen is ashy pale, her large eyes are fixed on the
King, her white lips tremble. She stands motionless,
supported by the balustrade. Her daughters, the brides,
and her ladies, gather round her full of wonder. By
a **great effort** she masters her agitation, and slowly
turns back into a retiring-room behind the dais, **and**
seats herself on a chair **of state.** Then with solemn
gesture she addresses herself to the princesses—

"Elizabeth, my daughter, and **you**, Marguerite,
come hither. My sons, Francis and Charles, come to
me all of you quickly." At her invitation they assemble
round her in astonishment. "Alas! my children, you
are all orphans and I am a widow. I have seen it.
It is true. Now, while I speak, the lance is pointed
that will pierce the King. Your father must die, my
children. I know it and I cannot save him."

While they all press with pitying looks around her,
trying to console yet unable to comprehend her meaning, she slowly rises. "Let us, my children," says she
in a hollow voice, "pray for the King's soul." She
casts herself on the ground and folds her hands in
silent prayer. Her children kneel around her. There
is **a** great silence. Then **a** loud cry is heard from
below— "The King is wounded; the King is unhorsed;
the King bleeds; *en avant* to the King!" Catherine
rises. She is calm now and perfectly composed. She
approaches the wooden steps leading into the arena
below. There she sees, stretched on the ground, the
King insensible, his face bathed in blood, pierced in
the eye by the lance of the masked knight who has

fled. Henry is mortally wounded, and is borne, as
the Queen saw in her dream, into a strange chamber
in the Palace des Tournelles, hard by. After some
days of horrible agony he expires, aged forty-one.
The masked knight struck but a random blow, and
was held innocent of all malice. He was the Sieur
de Montgomeri, ancestor of the present Earls of
Eglinton.

CHAPTER XI.

The Widowed Queen.

EVEN while the King lay dying, Catherine gave a
taste of her vindictive character by ordering Diane de
Poitiers instantly to quit the Louvre; to deliver up the
crown jewels; and to make over the possession of the
Château of Chenonceau, in Touraine, to herself. Chenonceau was Catherine's "Naboth's vineyard." From
a girl, when she had often visited it in company with
her father-in-law, Francis, she had longed to possess
this lovely woodland palace, beside the clear waters
of the river Cher. To her inexpressible disgust, her
husband, when he became King, presented it to "the
old hag," Diane, Duchesse de Valentinois.

When Diane, sitting lonely at the Louvre, for
Henry II. was dying at the Palace des Tournelles,
received the Queen's message, she turned indignantly
to the messenger and angrily asked, "Is the King then
dead?" "No, madame, but his wound is pronounced
mortal; he cannot last out the day."

"Tell the Queen," said Diane haughtily, "that her
reign has not yet begun. I am mistress over her and

the kingdom as long as the King lives. If he dies I care little how much she insults me. I shall be too wretched even to heed her."

As Regent, Catherine's real character appeared. She revelled in power. Gifted with a masculine understanding and a thorough aptitude for state business, she was also inscrutable, stern, and cruel. She believed in no one, and had faith in nothing save the prediction of astrologers and the course of the stars, to which she gave unquestioning belief. As in the days of her girlhood, Catherine (always armed with a concealed dagger, its blade dipped in poison) traded on the weaknesses of those around her. She intrigued when she could not command, and fascinated the victim she dared not attack. All who stood in the way of her ambition were "*removed*." None can tell how many she hurried to an untimely grave. The direful traditions of her race, the philters, the perfumes, the powders, swift and deadly poisons, were imported by her into France. Her cunning hands could infuse death into the fairest and the freshest flowers. She had poisons for gloves and handkerchiefs, for the folds of royal robes, for the edge of gemmed drinking cups, for rich and savoury dishes. She stands accused of having poisoned the Queen of Navarre, mother of Henry IV.,* in a pair of gloves; and, spite of the trial and execution of Sebastian Montecucolli, she **was** held guilty of having compassed the death of her brother-in-law, the Dauphin, in a cup of water, thus opening **the** throne for her husband and herself.

Within her brain, fertile in evil, was conceived the massacre of St. Bartholomew—to exceed the horrors

* See Note 3.

of the Sicilian Vespers under John of Procida—the
plan of which she discussed years before the event
with Philip II. and his minister, the Duke of Alva,
whom she met at Bayonne, when she visited there her
daughter, Elizabeth of Spain. Catherine was true to
no party and faithful to no creed. During her long
government she cajoled alike Catholics and Protestants.
She balanced Guise against Coligni, and Condé against
Navarre, as suited her immediate purpose. Provided
the end she proposed was attained, she cared nothing
for the means. Although attached to her children in
infancy, before supreme power had come within her
grasp, she did not hesitate to sacrifice them, later, to
her political intrigues.

For her youngest daughter—the bewitching Marguerite, frail Queen of Navarre—she cared not at all.
Her autobiography is filled with details of her mother's
falseness and unkindness. As to her sons, all—save
Francis, who died at eighteen—were initiated early
into vice. Their hands were soon red with blood.
Long before they reached manhood they were steeped
in debauchery and left the cares of government entirely
to their mother. Her Court—an oasis of delight and
artistic repose, in an age of bloodshed (for Catherine
was a true Medici, and loved artists and the arts,
splendour and expenditure)—was as fatal as the gardens of Armida to virtue, truth, and honour. She
surrounded herself with dissipated nobles, subservient
courtiers, venal nymphs, and impure enchantresses, all
ready to barter their souls and bodies in the service
of their Queen. The names of the forty noble demoi-
selles by whom Catherine was always attended, are
duly recorded by Brantôme.

"Know, my cousin," said the Queen, speaking to the Duc de Guise, "that my maids of honour are the best allies of the royal cause."

She imported ready-witted Italians, actors and singers, who played at a theatre within the Hôtel Bourbon at Paris; saltimbanques and rope-dancers, who paraded the streets; astrologers, like Ruggiero; jewellers, like Zametti; and bankers, like Gondi. These men were ready to sell themselves for any infamy; to call on the stars for confirmation of their prophecies; to tempt spendthrift princes with ample supply of ready cash; to insinuate themselves into the confidence of unwary nobles; all to serve their royal mistress as spies.

A woman of such powerful mind, infinite resource, and unscrupulous will, overawed and oppressed her children. During the three successive reigns of her sons, Francis II., Charles IX., and Henry III., Catherine ruled with the iron hand of a mediæval despot. Yet her cruelty, perfidy, and statescraft, were worse than useless. She lived to see the chivalric race of Valois degraded; her favourite child, Anjou, Henry III., driven like a dog from Paris, by Henri de Guise; and son after son go down childless to a dishonoured grave.

CHAPTER XII.

Mary Stuart and her Husband.

FRANCIS II., aged sixteen, eldest son of Henry II., is nominally King of France. He is gentle and affectionate (strange qualities for a son of Catherine), well principled, and not without understanding. Born with a feeble constitution and badly educated, he lacks vigour both of mind and body to grasp the reins of government in a period so stormy—a period when Guise is at variance with Condé, and the nation is distracted between Catholic and Protestant intrigues. Though yet a boy, Francis is married to Mary Stuart, Queen of Scotland, daughter of James V. and Mary of Lorraine, and niece to the Duc de Guise and the Cardinal de Lorraine.

Francis and Mary have known each other from earliest childhood. At the age of five the little Scottish Princess was sent to the Louvre to be educated with her royal cousins. Even at that tender age she was the delight and wonder of the Court—a little northern rose-bud, transplanted into a southern climate, by-and-by to expand into a perfect flower. Her sweet temper, beauty, and winning manners gained all hearts. She was, moreover, says Brantôme, quiet, discreet, and accomplished. Accomplished, indeed, as well as learned, for, at fourteen, the fascinating girl recited a Latin oration of her own composition in the great gallery of the Louvre, before her future father-in-law, King Henry, and the whole Court, to the effect "that women ought to rival, if not to excel, men in learning." She spoke with such composure, her voice was so melodious, her gesture so graceful, and her person so lovely, that the King publicly embraced her, and swore a great oath that she alone was fit to marry with the Dauphin. Forthwith he betrothed her to his son Francis. This marriage between a youth and a girl yet in their teens was a dream of love, short, but without alloy.

Catherine rules, and Francis and Mary Stuart, too young and careless to desire any life but a perpetual holiday in each other's company, tremble at her frown and implicitly obey her.

Now and then Mary's maternal uncles, the princes of Lorraine, Francis, the great Duc de Guise (the same who took Calais and broke the English Queen's heart), and the Cardinal de Lorraine, the proudest and falsest prelate in the sacred college,* endeavour to traverse the designs of Catherine, and to inspire their beautiful niece with a taste for intrigue—under their guidance, be it well understood. But all such attempts are useless. Mary loves poetry and music, revels in banquets and masques, hunts, and games, and toys with her boy-husband, of whose society she never wearies.

Nevertheless, the Queen-mother hates her, accuses her of acting the part of a spy for her uncles, the Guises, and, sneering, speaks of her as "une petite reinette qui fait tourner toutes les têtes."

The Court is at Amboise, that majestic castle planted on a pile of sombre rocks that cast gloomy shadows across the waters of the Loire, widened at this spot into the magnitude of a lake, the river being divided by an island and crossed by two bridges.

Over these bridges they come, a glittering procession, preceded by archers and attended by pages and

* See Note 9.

men-at-arms. Francis rides in front; he is tall, slight
and elegantly formed, and sits his horse with perfect
grace. His grey, almond-shaped eyes sparkle as he
turns them upon the young Queen riding at his side.
Mary is seated on a dark palfrey. She is dressed in
a white robe, fastened from the neck downwards with
jewelled buttons. The robe itself is studded with gold
embroidery and trimmed with ermine. A ruff of fine
lace, and a chain of gold, from which hangs a medallion, are round her slender throat. Her hair is drawn
back from her forehead, and a little pointed cap, set
with jewels, to which is attached a thin white veil
falling behind, sets off the chiselled features, the
matchless eyes, and exquisite complexion of her fair
young face.

Catherine and the Duc de Guise, the Cardinal de
Lorraine and the Duc de Nemours, follow. Behind
them the gay multitude of a luxurious Court fills up
the causeway. Francis has a prepossessing face, but
looks pale and ill. As they ride, side by side, Mary
watches him with tender anxiety. Her sweet eyes rest
on him as she speaks, and she caressingly places her
hand upon **his** saddle-bow as they ascend the rocky
steep leading to the castle.

When they dismount, the Queen-mother—her hard
face set into a frown—passes, without speaking a word,
into her own apartments. The Duc de Guise and the
Cardinal de Lorraine also retire with gloomy looks.
Not a single word do either of them address to Francis
or to Mary. The young sovereigns enter the royal
chambers, a stately suite of apartments, the lofty windows of which, reaching from ceiling to floor, overlook
the river. Folding doors open into a gallery wain-

scoted with oak richly gilt, with a carved ceiling embla-
zoned with coats of arms. The walls are covered with
crimson brocade set in heavy frames of carved gold;
chandeliers of glittering pendants hang from open
rafters formed of various-coloured wood arranged in
mosaic patterns. Beyond is a retiring-room, hung
with choice tapestry of flowers and fruit on a violet
ground, let into arabesque borders of white and gold.
Inlaid tables of marble bear statues and tazzas of ala-
baster and enamel. Clustered candelabra of coloured
Venetian glass hold perfumed candles, and the flowers
of the spring are placed in cups and vases of rarest
pottery.

Mary, with a wave of her hand, dismisses her
attendants. Francis sinks into a chair beside an open
window utterly exhausted. He sighs, leans back his
head, and closes his eyes.

"*Mon amour*," says Mary, throwing her arms round
him, and kissing his white lips, "you are very weary.
Tell me—why is the Queen-mother so grave and
silent? When I spoke she did not answer me. My
uncles, too, frighten me with their black looks. Tell
me, Francis, what have I done?"

"Done, sweetest?—nothing," answered Francis, un-
closing his eyes, and looking at her. "Our mother is
busied with affairs of state, as are also your uncles.
There is much to disquiet them." Francis draws her
closer to him, laying his head upon her shoulder
wearily, and again closing his eyes. "It is some conspiracy against her and your uncles—the Guises—
mignonne," added he, whispering into her ear.

"Conspiracy! Holy Virgin, how dreadful! Why
did you not tell me this before we left Blois?"

"I feared to frighten you, dear love, ere we were safe within the thick walls of this old fortress."

Mary starts up and seizes his hand.

"Tell me, tell me," she says, in an unsteady voice, "what is this conspiracy?"

"A plot of the Huguenots, in which Condé and the Coligni are concerned," replies Francis, roused by her vehemence into attention. "Did you not mark how suddenly our uncle, Francis of Guise, appeared at Blois, and that he was closeted with her Majesty for hours?" Mary, her eyes extended to their utmost limit and fixed on his, bows her head in assent. "Did we not leave immediately after the interview for Amboise? Did not that make you suspicious?"

"No, Francis; for you said that we came here to hold a joust and to hunt in the forest of Chanteloup. How could I doubt your word? Oh! this is horrible!"

"We came to Amboise, *ma mie*, because it is a stronghold, and Blois is an open town."

"Do you know no more? or will you still deceive me?" asks Mary eagerly, looking at him with tearful eyes.

"My mother told me that the Duc de Guise was informed by the Catholics of England (which tidings have been since confirmed), that the Huguenots are arming in force, that they are headed by Condé, that they are plotting to imprison the Queen-mother and your uncles, and to carry you and me to Paris by force."

"By force? Would they lay hands on us? Oh, Francis, are we safe in this castle?" exclaims Mary, clasping her hands. "Will our guards defend us? Are the walls manned? Is the town faithful? Are there plenty of troops to guard the bridges?"

As she speaks, Mary trembles so violently that she has slid from her chair and sinks upon the ground, clinging to Francis in an agony of fear.

"Courage, my *reinette!* rise up, and sit beside me;" and Francis raises her in his arms and replaces her on her chair. "Here we are safe. This conspiracy is not directed against us, Mary. The people say my mother and the Guises rule, not I, the anointed King. The Huguenots want to carry us off to Paris for our good. Pardieu! I know little of the plot myself as yet; my mother refused to tell me. Anyhow, we are secure here at Amboise from Turk, Jew, or Huguenot, so cheer up, my lovely queen!"

As Mary looks up again further to question him, he stops her mouth with kisses.

"Let us leave all to the Queen-mother. She is wise, and governs for us while we are young. She loves not to be questioned. Sweetest, I am weary, give me a cup of wine; let me lie in your closet, and you shall sing me to sleep with your lute."

"But, Francis," still urges Mary, gently disengaging herself from his arms as he leads her away, "surely my uncles must be in great danger; a conspiracy perhaps means an assassination. I beseech you let me go and question them myself."

"*Nenni,*" answers Francis, drawing her to him. "You shall come with me. I will not part with you for a single instant. Ah! *mignonne*, if you knew how my head aches, you would ask me no more questions, or I shall faint."

Mary's expressive face changes as the April sunshine. Her eyes fill with tears of tenderness as she leads Francis to a small closet in a turret exclusively **her** own,—a *chinoiserie*, quaint and bright as the plumage of a bird,—and seats him, supported by a pile of pillows, on a couch—luxurious for that period of stiff-backed chairs and wooden benches.

"Talk to me," says Francis, smoothing her abundant hair, which hung in dark masses on her shoulders as she knelt at his feet, "or, better still, sing to me. I love to hear your soft voice; only, no more politics —not a word of affairs of state, Marie. Sing to me those verses you showed to Ronsard, about the knight who leapt into a deep stream to pluck a flower for his love and was drowned by the spell of a jealous mermaid who watched him from among the flags."

Mary rises and fetches her lute. All expression of fear has left her face. Reassured by Francis and occupied alone by him, she forgets not only the Huguenots and the conspiracy, but the whole world, beside the boy-husband, who bends lovingly over her as she tries the strings of her instrument. So let us leave them as they sit, two happy children, side by side, bathed in the brief sunshine of a changeful day in March, now singing, now talking of country fêtes, especially of a *carrousel* to take place on the morrow in the courtyard of the castle, in which the Grand Prieur is to ride disguised as a gipsy woman and carry a monkey on his back for a child!

CHAPTER XIII.

A Traitor.

THE Queen-mother sits alone; a look of care overshadows her face; her prominent eyes are fixed and glassy. From her window she can gaze at an old familiar scene, the terrace and parterre bordered by lime walks, planted by Francis I., where she has romped in many a game of *cache-cache* with him.

Presently she rises and summons an attendant from the ante-chamber.

"Call hither to me Maître Avenelle," says she to the dainty page who waits her command.

Avenelle, a lawyer and a Huguenot, is the friend of Barri, Seigneur de la Renaudie, the nominal leader of the Huguenot plot; of which the Duc de Guise has been warned by the Catholics of England. Avenelle has, for a heavy bribe, been gained over in Paris by the Duke's secretary, Marmagne; he has come to Amboise to betray his friends "of the religion" by revealing to the Queen-mother all he knows of this vast Huguenot conspiracy, secretly headed by the Prince de Condé and by Admiral Coligni.

Avenelle enters and bows low before the Queen who is seated opposite to him at a writing-table. He is sallow and wasted-looking, with a grave face and an anxious eye; a tremor passes over him as he suddenly encounters the dark eyes of Catherine fixed upon him.

"Have you seen the Duc de Guise?" says she haughtily, shading her face with her hand the better to observe him, as he stands before her motionless and pale with fear.

"Yes, madame," replies he, again humbly bowing; "I come now from his chamber, whither I was conducted by M. Marmagne, his secretary."

"And you have confided to him all you know of this plot?"

"I have, madame, all."

"Is it entirely composed of Huguenots?"

"It is, madame."

"What are the numbers?"

"Perhaps two thousand, your Majesty."

Catherine starts, the lines on her face deepen, and her eyes glitter with astonishment and rage.

"Who is at the head of these rebels?" she asks suddenly, after pausing a few moments.

Avenelle trembles violently; the savage tone of her voice and her imperious manner show him his danger. His teeth chatter, and drops of moisture trickle down his forehead. So great is his alarm that, in spite of his efforts to reply, his voice fails him. Catherine, her eyes riveted on his, waves her hand with an impatient gesture.

"Why do not you answer me, Maître Avenelle? If you are waiting to invent a lie with which to deceive me, believe me, such deceit is useless. The torture-chamber is at hand; the screw will make you speak."

"Oh, madame," gasps Avenelle, making a successful effort to recover his voice, "I had no intention to deceive your Majesty; I am come to tell you all I know. It was a passing weakness that overcame me."

"Who, then, I again ask," says the Queen, taking a pen in her hand in order to note his reply, "who is at the head of this plot?"

"Madame, it is secretly headed by that heretic, the Prince de Condé. Coligni knows of it, as does also his brother d'Andelot, and the Cardinal de Châtillon. The nominal leader, Barri de la Renaudie, is but a subordinate acting under their orders."

"Heretics do you call them; are not you, then, yourself a Huguenot?"

"Madame, I was," replies Avenelle obsequiously, with an effort to look fearless, for Catherine's glittering eyes are still upon him; "but his Highness the Duc de Guise has induced me to recant my errors."

"Ah!" says Catherine, smiling sarcastically; "I did not know our cousin of Guise troubled himself with the souls of his enemies. But this La Renaudie, was he not your friend? Did he not lodge with you in Paris?"

"He did lodge, for a brief space, in my house in Paris, madame; but I have no friend that is not a loyal subject to your Majesty." Avenelle now speaks more boldly.

Catherine eyes him from **head** to foot with a glance of infinite contempt. "I am glad to hear this **for** your own sake, Maître Avenelle," she replies drily. "What is the precise purpose of this plot?"

"Madame, it is said by the Huguenots that your Majesty, not your son, his Majesty Francis II., governs, and that under your rule no justice will ever be done to those of 'the religion;' that your Majesty seeks counsel of the Duc de Guise and of his brother the Cardinal de Lorraine, who are even more bitterly opposed than yourself to their interests. Therefore they have addressed themselves to the Prince de Condé, who is believed to share their opinions both political and religious, for present redress. The conspirators propose, madame, to place his Highness the Prince de Condé on the throne as Regent, until such measures are taken as will insure their independence; imprison your Majesty; send the young King and Queen to some unfortified place—such as Blois or Chenonceau —and banish the noble Duke and his brother the Cardinal from France."

While Avenelle, speaking rapidly, gives these details, Catherine sits unmoved. As he proceeds her eyes never leave him, and her hands, singularly small and delicate, are clenched upon her velvet robe. When he has done speaking a look of absolute fury passes over her face. There is a lengthened silence, during which her head sinks on her breast and she remains lost in thought. When she looks up all passion has faded out of her face. She appears as impassible as a statue, and speaks in a clear metallic voice which betrays no vestige of emotion.

"Have these conspirators many adherents, Maître Avenelle?"

"I fear so, madame. Nearly two thousand are gathering together, from various points, at Nantes. On the 15th of the present month of March they would have attacked Blois. Had your Majesty not received timely warning and retreated to this fortified castle, these rebellious gentlemen would have captured your sacred person and that of our Sovereign and the young Queen. They would have kept you imprisoned until you had consented to abdicate the throne or to dismiss our great Catholic Princes of Lorraine, to whom and to your Majesty all evil influence is attributed."

"Influence? Yes, influence to punish traitors, heretics, and *spies!*" exclaims Catherine, and she darts a fierce look at Avenelle, who, though still pale as death, is now more composed, and meets her glance without flinching. He knows his life is in the balance, and he thinks he reads the Queen-mother rightly, that he may best ensure it by showing no cowardice.

"Is this all you know, Maître Avenelle?" says the Queen coldly.

"Yes, madame; and I trust you will remember that I have been the means of saving your Majesty and the young King from imprisonment, perhaps from death."

Catherine turns her terrible eyes full upon Avenelle. "Maître Avenelle, I appreciate both your disinterestedness and your loyalty," replies she, with a bitter sneer. "You, sir, will be kept a prisoner in this castle until his Majesty's council have tested the truth of what you say. We may *use* such as you, but we mistrust them and we despise them. If you have spoken the truth, **your** life shall be spared, but you will leave France **for ever**. If you have lied, you will die." As these words fall from her lips and are echoed through the lofty chamber, she strikes on a sharp metal placed before her. Two guards immediately enter and remove Avenelle in custody.

Catherine again strikes on the metal instrument, summons her attendant, and desires that Francis, Duc de Guise, and the Cardinal de Lorraine shall attend her.

In this interview between the heads of the Catholic party their plan of action is decided. A council of state is to be at once called at Amboise, to which the

Huguenot chiefs, the Prince of Condé, the Admiral
Coligni, his brother d'Andelot, the Cardinal de Châtillon, and others are to be invited to attend; and a
conciliatory edict in favour of the Calvinists, signed
by the King, is to be proclaimed.

Thus the Reformed party will be thrown completely off their guard, and La Renaudie and the
conspirators, emboldened by the apparent security
and ignorance of the government, will gather about
Amboise, the better to carry out their designs of
capturing the King, the Queen, and the Queen-mother,
and banishing or killing the Guises, her supposed evil
counsellors. But another and **secret** condition is appended to this edict which would at once, if known,
have awakened the suspicions and driven back from
any approach to Amboise both the conspirators and
the great chiefs of the Huguenot party.

This secret condition is that Francis, Duc de Guise,
shall be forthwith nominated Lieutenant-General of
the kingdom, and be invested with almost absolute
power.

CHAPTER XIV.

The Council of State.

THE council assembles in a sombre chamber
panelled with dark oak, crossed by open rafters—a
chamber that had remained unaltered since the days
of Louis XI. A long table stands in the centre surrounded with leather chairs heavily carved, on which
are seated the members of the council. Condé, who
is of royal blood, takes the highest place on the

Calvinist side. He is somewhat below middle height and delicately formed. His complexion is fair, his face comely; his dark eyes, sunk deep in his head, bright with the power of intellect, are both cunning and piercing. Nevertheless, it is a veiled face and betrays nothing. His dress is dark and simple, yet studiously calculated to display to the best advantage his supple and elegant figure. There is an air of authority about him that betrays itself unwittingly in every glance he casts around the room. He is a man born to command.

Next to him is a man older, sturdier, rougher; a powerfully built man, who sits erect and firm in his chair. His head is covered with long white hair; he has overhanging eyebrows, a massive forehead, and a firmly-closed mouth. His weather-beaten face and sunken cheeks show that he has lived a life of exposure and privation—a man this to meet unmoved peril or death. He wears a homely suit of black woollen stuff much worn, and as he sits he leans forward, plunged in deep thought. This is Admiral Coligni. Beside him is his brother d'Andelot, slighter and much younger: he is dressed with the same simplicity as the Admiral, but wants that look of iron resolve and fanatic zeal which at the first glance stamps Coligni as a hero. Châtillon has placed himself beside his brother prelate of Lorraine. Each wears the scarlet robe of a cardinal, over which falls a deep edging of open guipure lace; their broad red hats, tasselled with silken cords, lie on the table before them. Lorraine is thin and dark, with a treacherous eye and a prevailing expression of haughty unconcern. Châtillon is bland and mild, but withal shrewd and astute; a smile rests upon his thin lips as his eyes travel round the table, peering into every face, while from time to time he whispers some observation to the Cardinal de Lorraine, the Minister of State, who affects not to hear him.

A door opens within a carved recess or dais raised one step from the floor, and Francis and Mary appear. The whole council rises and salutes the young King and Queen. They seat themselves under a purple velvet canopy embroidered in gold with fleurs-de-lys and the oriflamme. They are followed by Catherine and Francis Duc de Guise, a man of majestic presence and lofty stature. He is spare, like the Cardinal, but his eager eye and sharply cut features, on which many a wrinkle has gathered, proclaim the man of action and the warrior, ardent in the path of glory, prompt, bold, and unscrupulous. At the sight of Coligni, Condé, and Châtillon, he knits his brows, and a sinister expression passes over his face which deepens into a look of actual cruelty as he silently takes his place next to Catherine de Medici.

The young King and Queen sit motionless side by side, like two children who are permitted to witness a solemn ceremony upon the promise of silence and tranquillity. They are both curious and attentive. Not all Mary Stuart's questions have elicited further information from her uncles, and Francis, too feeble in health to be energetic, is satisfied with the knowledge that the Queen-mother occupies herself with affairs of state.

The Queen-mother, with a curious smile upon her face, stands for a few moments on the estrade facing

the council-table. She coldly receives the chiefs of
the Reformed faith, but her welcome is studiously
polite. With the same grave courtesy she greets the
Guises, Nemours, and the other Catholic princes. All
are now seated in a circle of which Francis and Mary,
motionless under the canopy of state, form the centre.
Catherine rises from her chair and in a guarded
address speaks of danger to the Crown from the
Huguenot party, darkly hinting at a treasonable plot
in which some near the throne are implicated, and
she calls on those lords favourable to the Reformed
religion for advice and support in this emergency.

As she speaks an evil light gathers in her eye,
especially when she declares that she has at this time
summoned her son's trusty counsellors of the Calvinist
faith in order to consider an edict of pacification,
calculated to conciliate *all* his Majesty's subjects, and
to rally *all* his faithful servants round his throne.

Her composed and serious countenance, the grave
deliberation of her discourse, her frank yet stately
avowal of peril to the State and desire for counsel in
an hour of danger, are all so admirably simulated
that those not aware of her perfidy are completely
duped.

Francis, her son, listens with wonder to his
mother's words, believing, as he does, that she is
both indignant and alarmed at the machinations of
that very party she has called to Amboise and which
she now proposes to propitiate.

The Duc de Guise, who perfectly understands her
drift, secretly smiles at this fresh proof of the dissimulation and astuteness of his cousin who caresses
ere she grasps her prey. When she has ended he

loudly applauds her conciliatory resolutions, and by
so doing astonishes still more the unsuspicious Francis,
as well as his niece Mary whose wondering eyes are
fixed on him.

As to Coligni and the other Protestants, they
fall blindfolded into the snare spread for them by
Catherine, all save the Prince de Condé, who, crafty
and treacherous himself, is more suspicious of others.
He has marked, too, the Queen-mother's words, "some
near the throne," and thinks he knows to whom they
are applied. However he immediately rises and in a
few well-chosen phrases declares himself ready to
defend the royal cause with his life. The Admiral
next speaks, and in an eloquent harangue he un-
suspectingly dilates on his own views of the present
administration, and reproves the ambition of those
princes who usurp the government of France. "There
are two millions of Protestants in the kingdom," he
says, "who look to the heads of their own faith for
relief from the tyranny and injustice under which they
have long languished. Two millions," repeats Coligni
in a grave, sad voice, looking steadfastly round the
circle, "who seek to live at peace, industrious, tranquil,
loyal. But these two millions demand that they shall
enjoy equal privileges with the least of his Majesty's
Catholic subjects. This is now refused. They ask
to be neither suspected, watched, nor wilfully persecuted. If any conspiracy exists, such as is known to
her Majesty the Queen-mother — and I accept her
statement as true with the deepest sorrow—it can
only arise from the bitter feeling engendered by the
disgrace of these Calvinistic subjects of this realm
who are uniformly treated as aliens, and repulsed

with cruel persistency from such places of trust and honour as their **services** have entitled them to enjoy. Let these heavy grievances be removed, let his Majesty reign for himself *alone*"—and Coligni's eye rests on the Duc de Guise and the Queen-mother—"with equal favour over both parties, Catholic as well as Protestant. Let the conciliatory edict now before the council be made public, **and** I, Gaspard de Coligni, bind myself upon my plighted word as a noble and upon my conscience as a devout Calvinist, that the House of Valois will for ever live in the hearts of our people, and receive from them as entire a devotion as ever animated subject to his sovereign."

A dead silence follows Coligni's address, and the Duc de Guise and the Cardinal de Lorraine exchange glances of indignation.

Francis has become more and more mystified. Timid and inexperienced, he fears to betray his absolute ignorance of state affairs, and perhaps incense his mother by indiscreet questions. But when the parchment, heavy with seals of state, is produced **and** borne to him by the Chancellor for signature, he can no longer conceal his astonishment that he should be called on to sign an edict giving both liberty and protection to those very persons whom the Queen-mother and his uncles had represented to him as his mortal enemies. He looks so long and earnestly at Catherine, that she, fearing that by one mistaken word he is about to destroy the whole fabric of her masterly dissimulation, rises quickly from the armchair in which she sits, and advancing quickly towards him with a commanding look and imperious gesture, takes the pen from the hand of the Chancellor and presents it to him herself.

"Sign, my son," says she, "this edict which has been framed by the unanimous advice of your council in favour of your loyal subjects. Fear not to sanction this royal act of mercy. Your Majesty is still too young to understand the far-seeing wisdom of the act. Take it on my word, Sire, take it *now* on my word. You will understand it better later."

"Truly, madame," replies the King, "I call God to witness that I desire the good of all my subjects, Huguenot and Catholic." So saying he takes the pen and signs the edict. The council forthwith breaks up, with what wondering curiosity on the part of the King and of Mary, who dare ask no questions, cannot be told.

CHAPTER XV.

Catherine's Vengeance.

MEANWHILE the conspirators, emboldened by the news of the edict of Amboise, carried out their purpose exactly as the Queen-mother intended, with perfect confidence and little concealment. Catherine's object was to draw them towards Amboise and there destroy them. Band after band, in small detachments the better to avoid suspicion, rode up from Nantes where they lay, to concentrate in force on the Loire and within Amboise itself. When sufficiently strong they proposed to carry off the King and Queen by a *coup-de-main*, make away with the Jesuitical Guises, banish the Queen-mother to some distant fortress, and place Condé on the throne as Regent.

They came through the plains of Touraine, halting beside solitary farms, in the vineyards, under the willows and tufted underwood that border the rivers, and through the dark forests that lie on the hills behind Amboise. Band after band reached certain points, halted at the spots indicated to them, and met other detachments with whom they were to act; but not one of them was heard of more.

The walls of the Castle of Amboise bristled with troops, and the open country towards Loches was full of soldiers. Trusty guards stationed on the double bridge across the Loire were instructed by the Duc de Guise, who wielded absolute power and who had now gained minute knowledge of the plot, to take all suspected persons prisoners, or if needful, slay them as they stood. Crowds of prisoners poured into Amboise, tied together and driven like cattle to the shambles. Those who were known were reserved for a further purpose, the rest—the herd—were either hanged or drowned. The Loire was full of floating corpses.

Condé, wary with the wariness of his race, ventured not again to Amboise. Coligni and his brother knew not how to oppose a power exercised in the royal name, but Jean Barri de la Renaudie, the ostensible leader of the conspiracy and a bold adventurer, alarmed at the mysterious disappearance of party after party of his followers, set out in rash haste towards Amboise. He too was watched for and expected among the wooded hills of the forest of Château Renaud.

La Renaudie had encamped in the woods towards morning after advancing under cover of the night from Niort. Suddenly his detachment was approached by

two or three horsemen, who, after reconnoitring for a
few moments, retreated. These were evidently the
advance guard of the royal forces. La Renaudie immediately broke up his camp and dashed on towards
Amboise, concealed by the overhanging trees on the
banks of a stream which flowed through a wild defile.
In a hollow of the river, among beds of stone and
sand, he was fallen upon by a regiment of royal troops
who had tracked and finally caught him as in a trap.
His own cousin Pardilliac commanded the attack, he
recognised him by the flag. A deadly struggle ensued,
in which both cousins fell. La Renaudie's corpse,
carried in triumph to Amboise, was hung in chains
over the bridge.

Then Condé, Coligni, and the other Calvinists
came fully to understand what the edict of concilia-
tion really meant.

The Castle of Amboise during all this time had
been strictly guarded; every door was watched, every
gallery was full of troops; the garden and the walled
plateau, within which stands the beautiful little votive
chapel erected by Anne of Brittany, was like a camp.
Silence, suspicion, and terror were on every face. Although the Queen-mother, with her crafty smiles and
unruffled brow, affected entire ignorance and exhorted
"la petite reinette," as she called Mary, to hunt in the
adjoining forest, and to assemble the Court in the state
rooms with the usual banquets and festivities, Mary,
pale and anxious, remained shut up with Francis in
her private apartments.

"My uncle," said Francis to the Duc de Guise whom
he met leaving the Queen-mother's retiring-room, "I
must know what all these precautions mean. Why are

so many troops encamped about the castle, the guards doubled, and the gates closed? Why do you avoid me and the Queen? Uncle, I insist on knowing more."

"It is nothing, Sire—nothing," faltered the Duke, who, dissembler as he was, could scarcely conceal the confusion the King's questions caused him. "A trifling conspiracy has been discovered, a few rebels have been caught, your Majesty's leniency has been abused by some false Huguenots. These troops assembled about the castle are your Majesty's trusty guards brought here to ensure the maintenance of the terms of the edict."

"But, uncle, the Queen and I hear the clash of arms and firing on the bridges as against an enemy. I cannot sleep, so great is the tumult. What have I done that my people should mistrust me? Huguenots and Catholics are alike my subjects. Are you sure, uncle, that it is not you and my mother that they hate? I would that you would all go away for a while and let me rule alone, then my people would know me."

When all the Huguenot conspirators, about two thousand in number, were either massacred or imprisoned, Catherine threw off the mask. She called to her Francis and the young Queen. "My children," said she, "a plot has been discovered by which the Prince de Condé was to be made Regent. You and the Queen were to be shut up for life, or murdered perhaps. Such as remain unpunished of the enemies of the House of Valois are about to be executed on the southern esplanade of the castle. You are too young to be instructed in all these details, but, my son, when you signed that edict, I told you I would afterwards explain it—now come and behold the reason.

Mary, my reinette, do not turn so pale, you will need
to learn to be both stern and brave to rule your rough
subjects the Scotch."

Catherine, erect and calm, led the way to the state
apartments overlooking on either side the garden, terrace, and river. Large mullioned windows had by the
command of Francis I. taken the place of the narrow
lights of the older fortress. He had changed the esplanade and southern terraced front within the walls
and the balconied windows to the north overlooking
the town, into that union of manoir and château which
he first created.

The boy-King and Queen followed tremblingly the
steps of their mother, who strode on in front with
triumphant alacrity. Without, on the pleasant terrace
bordered by walls now bristling with guns and alive
with guards and archers, on the pinnacles and fretted
roof of the votive chapel, which stands to the right in
a tuft of trees inside a bastion, the sun shone brightly,
but the blue sky and the laughing face of nature seemed
but to mock the hideous spectacle in front. Close
under the windows of the central gallery, a scaffold
was erected covered with black, on which stood an
executioner masked, clothed in a red robe. Long lines
of prisoners packed closely together, a dismal crowd,
wan and emaciated by imprisonment in the loathsome
holes of the mediæval castle, stood by hundreds ranged
against the outer walls and those of the chapel, guarded
by archers and musketeers; as if such despairing
wretches, about to be butchered like cattle in the
shambles, needed guarding! The windows of the royal
gallery were wide open, flags streamed from the archi-
traves, and a loggia, or covered balcony, had been

prepared, hung with crimson velvet, with seats for the royal princes.

Within the gallery the whole Court stood ranged against the sculptured walls. Catherine entered first. With an imperious gesture she signed to Mary, who clung, white as death, to her husband, to take her place under a royal canopy placed in the centre of the window. Francis she drew into a chair beside herself, the Chancellor, the Duc de Guise, his brother the Cardinal, and the Duc de Nemours seated themselves near. Their appearance was the signal to begin the slaughter. Prisoner after prisoner was dragged up beneath the loggia to the scaffold and hastily dispatched. Cries of agony were drowned in the screeching of fifes and the loud braying of trumpets. The mutilated bodies were flung on one side to be cast into the river, the heads borne away to be placed upon the bridge. Blood ran in streams and scented the fresh spring breezes. The executioner wearily rested from his labour, and another masked figure, dressed like himself in red from head to foot, took his place.

Spellbound and speechless sat the young Queen. A look of horror was on her face. She had clutched the hand of Francis as she sat down, and ere a few minutes had passed, she had fainted.

Catherine, who, wholly unmoved, was contemplating the death of her enemies the Huguenots, turned with a terrible frown towards her son, handing him some strong essence with which to revive Mary. As her senses returned, even the basilisk eyes of her dreaded mother-in-law could not restrain her. One glance at the awful spectacle gave her courage; she gave a wild scream, and rushing forward, flung herself

passionately at the feet of her uncle, Francis of
Guise.

"Uncle, dear uncle, stay this fearful massacre.
Speak to the Queen, or I shall die. Oh! why was I
brought here to behold such a sight?"

"My niece," answered the Duke solemnly, raising
her from the ground, and tenderly kissing her on the
cheek, "have courage; these are but a few pestilent
heretics who would have dethroned you and your husband, the King, and set up a false religion. By their
destruction we are doing good service to God and to
the blessed Virgin. Such vermin deserve no pity. You
ought to rejoice in their destruction."

"Alas! my mother," said Francis, also rising, "I too
am overcome at this horrible sight, I also would crave
your highness's permission to retire; the blood of my
subjects, even of my enemies, is horrible to see. Let
us go!"

"My son, I command you to stay!" broke in Catherine, furious with passion, and imperiously raising
her hand to stay him. "Duc de Guise, support your
niece, the Queen of France. Teach her the duty of
a sovereign."

Again Francis, intimidated by his mother's violence,
reseated himself along with the unhappy Mary, motionless beside him. Again the steel of the axe flashed
in the sunshine, and horrible contortions writhed the
bodies of the slain. It was too much. Mary, young,
tender, compassionate—afraid to plead for mercy as
though committing a crime, again fainted, and was
again recovered. The Queen-mother, to whom the
savage scene was a spectacle of rapture, again com-

manded her to be reseated; but Francis, now fully roused by the sufferings of his wife, interposed.

"My mother, I can no longer permit your Majesty to force the Queen to be present. You are perilling her health. Govern my kingdom and slay my subjects, but let me judge what is seemly for my wife."

So, bearing her in his arms, with the assistance of her ladies, Francis withdrew.

When the butchery was over, and the headless bodies were floating in the river or strung up on the branches of the trees or piled in heaps about the castle, Catherine retired. She commanded that the remains of the chief conspirators should be hung in chains from the iron balustrades of the stone balcony which protects the windows of the royal gallery and which still remains intact, on the north front of the castle, towards the river. The remainder were to be thrown into the Loire. This stone balcony borders now, as then, the whole length of the state apartments towards the river. A fall of some hundred feet down a sheer mass of grey rock on which the castle stands makes the head dizzy. Over this precipice the headless bodies dangled, swaying to and fro in the March wind, a hideous and revolting sight. No one could pass through any of the apartments of the castle without beholding it. But despised humanity in the shape of the murdered Huguenots asserted its claim on the attention of the Court, and the stench of these bodies hung to the balcony, and of those strung up on the trees, and the rotting corpses that dammed up the river, soon became so overwhelming, that even Catherine herself was forced to retreat, and accompany her

son and the young Queen to Chenonceau. The shock
and excitement were, however, too much for the sickly
Francis. Rapidly he pined and died; no physician
was found who could cure a nameless malady.

Mary Stuart, a widow at eighteen, passionate and
romantic, clung fondly to that "pleasant land" where
she had spent such happy days with the gracious
Francis. She had been created Duchesse de Touraine
at her marriage, and craved earnestly to be allowed
to enjoy that apanage rather than be banished to reign
in a barren land, which she dreaded like a living
tomb. But her ambitious uncles, the Duc de Guise
and the Cardinal de Lorraine, who were to her as
parents, obstinately insisted on her departure for Scotland. So she sailed from Calais; and, from the deck
of the ship that bore her across the seas, as the shores
of France—which she was never more to see—gradually
faded from her view, she sang to her lute that plaintive
song, so identified with her memory:—

> "Adieu, oh plaisant pays!
> Adieu! oh ma patrie,
>   La plus chérie, qui a nourri
>   Ma belle enfance,—Adieu!"

CHAPTER XVI.

The Astrologer's Chamber.

WHEREVER Catherine chose to reside, either in
Paris or in Touraine, an observatory for the stars was
always at hand, and Cosmo Ruggiero, who had attended
her from Italy, never left her. Cosmo was the Queen's
familiar demon; he was both astrologer, alchemist,
and philosopher. He fed the glowing furnaces with
gold and silver, sometimes with dead men's bones;

concocted essences, powders, and perfumes; drew horoscopes, and modelled wax figures in the likeness of those who had incurred the Queen's enmity. These were supposed to suffer pangs from each stab inflicted on their images, and to waste away as their wax simili-tudes melted in the flames. Cosmo was also purveyor of poisons to her Majesty, and dealt largely in herbs and roots fatal to life. His apartments and the ob-servatory were always near those of the Queen and connected with them by a secret stair.

We are at the Tuileries.* It stands on a plot of ground outside Paris—where tiles were baked and rubbish shot—given by Francis I. to his mother, Louise de Savoie. Charles IX., who has succeeded his brother —Francis II.—inhabits the Louvre, now entirely rebuilt by Francis I. The Queen-mother desired to live alone. She therefore commanded Philippe de Lorme to erect a new palace for her use, consisting of a central pa-vilion, with ample wings. Catherine is now middle-aged; her complexion is darker, the expression of her face sterner and more impassive. She seldom relaxes into a smile except to deceive an enemy. In her own person she dislikes and despises the luxury of dress, and principally wears black since the death of her husband. But on fitting occasions of state she, too, robes herself in royal apparel. She stands before us in a long black dress, tightly fitting her shape. She has grown much stouter though she is still upright and majestic. Her active habits and her extraordinary ca-pacity for mental labour are the same. A stiff ruff is round her neck and a black coif upon her head. Jewels she rarely uses. Her suite of rooms at the Tuileries,

* See Note 10.

hung with sombre tapestry or panelled with dark wood, are studiously plain. She loves artists and the arts, but pictures and statues are not appropriate to the state business she habitually transacts. There is a certain consistent grandeur in her plain, unadorned *entourage;* a sense of subdued power—hidden yet apparent—that makes those who approach her tremble. Her second son Charles, now King of France, is wholly under her influence. He was only ten years old when he ascended the throne at the death of his brother Francis, and his mother has carefully stamped out every good quality in his naturally frank and manly nature. Now he is rough and cruel, loves the sight of blood, and has become a perfect Nimrod. He blows the horn with such violence, so often and so loud, that he has injured his lungs. Charles knows much more about the bears, wolves, deer, and wild boars of France, than of his Christian subjects.

The Princess Marguerite is now grown into a woman, "a noble mind in a most lovely person," says the flattering Brantôme. Her mother encourages Marguerite's taste for intrigue, and throws her into the company of women, such as Madame **de** Sauve, the court Ninon de l'Enclos of that day. Catherine contemplates her beauty, not with the proud affection of a mother, but as a useful bait to entrap those whom she desires to gain. When she was young herself **the** Queen never allowed any tender passion to stand in her way, but ruthlessly sacrificed all who were either useless or troublesome.

When the palace is quiet, and the sighing of the winter wind without, as it sweeps along the quays and ruffles the surface of the river, is **only** broken by the challenge of the sentinels on the bastion bordering **the** Seine, Catherine rises from her chair. She passes over her black dress a long white mantle, puts her feet into silken slippers, lights a scented bougie, takes from her girdle a golden key—which is hid there along with a poisoned dagger in case of need—draws aside the ta-**pestry,** unlocks a hidden door, and mounts a secret stair. Cosmo Ruggiero is seated on a folding stool in a small laboratory under the roof. He is reading an ancient manuscript. A lamp illuminates the page, and he is, or affects to be, so profoundly absorbed that he does not hear his terrible mistress enter. She glides like a ghost beside him and laying her hand on **his** shoulder rouses him. Ruggiero rises hastily and salutes her. Catherine draws a stool beside him, seats herself, and signs to him to do so also.

"Well, Cosmo! always studying; always at work **in** my service," says she, in a low metallic voice.

"Yes, madame, I have no other pleasure than in **your** Majesty's service."

"Yes, **yes**! you serve the Queen for love, and science out of interest—I understand. Disinterestedness is the custom of our country, my friend."

"**Your** Majesty mistakes; I serve her as a loyal servant and countryman should."

"La! la!" says Catherine, "we know each other, Cosmo,—no professions. Is the poison ready I ordered of you, the subtle powder to sprinkle on gloves or flowers? It is possible I may want it shortly."

Ruggiero rises and hands a small sealed packet, enclosed in satin, to the Queen, who places it in her bosom.

"Madame," he says, "beware! this poison is most powerful."

"So much the worse for those for whom it is destined," replies Catherine; and a cruel smile lights up her face for a moment. "It will serve me the quicker. But to business, Cosmo. What say the stars? Have you drawn the horoscopes?"

"Here, madame, are the horoscopes;" and he draws from his belt a bundle of papers. "Here are the celestial signs within the House of Life of all the royal persons concerned, traced by the magic pencil from the dates you furnished me."

Catherine glances at the papers. "Explain to me their import," says she, looking at him with grave attention.

"Your present design, madame, to marry Madame Marguerite to the King of Navarre appears favourable to the interests of France. A cloud now rests upon the usually brilliant star of the King of Navarre, but another night, madame, perhaps——"

"This is all very vague, Ruggiero, I want an absolute prediction," says Catherine, fixing her black eyes full upon the soothsayer. "Among all these illustrious personages is there not one whose horoscope is clear and defined?"

"Assuredly, madame; will your Majesty deign to interrogate me as to the future? I will unfold the purposes of the stars as I have read them."

"You have spoken of the Princess. Does she love the young Duc Henri de Guise?"

"Madame, her highness affects the Duke; but she is unstable in her affections."

"The Queen of Navarre—will she still forward this marriage?"

"It will cause her death."

"How?"

"By poison."

"Where?"

"At Paris."

"That is well," answers the Queen, and deep thought darkens her swarthy face. "Her son, the King of Navarre—what of him?"

"He, madame, is safe for awhile, though he will shortly be exposed to extreme peril."

"But is he destined to die violently?"

"Perhaps; but long years hence. His hair will be grey before the poniard I see hovering over him strikes. But, as I have said to-night, there is a cloud upon his star. Long he will certainly escape steel, fire, illness, or accident; he will bear a charmed life. Madame, the King of Navarre will be a proper husband for Madame Marguerite."

"But how of that bold man, the Duc de Guise, who dares without my leave to aspire to the hand of the Princess?" asked Catherine.

"Henri de Guise, madame, will die a violent death, as will his father and Coligni. The Admiral will be stabbed in his own house. This is certain."

The Queen smiles, and for a time is silent.

"Tell me," at length she almost whispers, "have you discovered anything more about myself and my sons?"

"Madame, I tremble to reply," replies Ruggiero, hesitating.

"Speak, I command you, Cosmo."

Catherine rises, and lays her hand heavily upon his arm. Her eyes meet his.

"If I must reveal the future of your Majesty and the royal princes, well, let it be done. Your Majesty can but kill me. I fear not death."

"Fool, your life is safe!"

"You, madame, will live; but the Princes, your sons——" and he stops and again hesitates.

"Speak!" hisses Catherine between her set teeth. "Speak, or, *pardieu!* I will force you," and she raises her hand aloft, as if to strike him.

"Madame," replies Ruggiero, quite unmoved by her violence, rising from his stool, and moving towards the wall, "you yourself shall see the future that awaits them." He withdraws a black curtain covering an arched recess and reveals a magic mirror. The kings your sons, madame, shall pass before you. Each shall reign as many years as he makes the circuit of that dark chamber you see reflected on the polished steel. There is your eldest son, Francis. See how feebly he moves, how pale he looks. He never lived to be a man. Twice he slowly passes round, and he is gone. The next is Charles, ninth of that name. Thirteen times he turns around, and as he moves a mist of blood gathers about him. Look, it thickens—it hides him. He shall reign thirteen years, and die a bloody death, having caused much blood to flow. Here is Henri, Duc d'Anjou, who shall succeed him. A few circuits, and then behold—a muffled figure—a monk, springs on him from behind. He falls and vanishes."

There is a pause.

"What! Cosmo," whispers Catherine, who stood supporting herself on the back of a high chair opposite the magic mirror. "Francis, Charles, Henry are gone, but do they leave **no child?**"

"None, madame."

"Where, then, is d'Alençon, my youngest boy? Let me see him."

"**Madame**," falters Ruggiero, "**his highness is** not **destined to** reign. The successor **of your sons is** before you;" and on the magic glass rises up, **clear** and distinct, **the** image **of** the King **of** Navarre. With strong, firm **steps** he circles the mystic chamber **of life** twenty times. As he passes on **the** twenty-first **round,** a **mist** gathers round him; he falls **and** vanishes.

At the sight **of** Henry of Navarre, the Queen's composure utterly **forsakes** her. She trembles from head to foot and **sinks into** a chair. A sombre fire shoots from her eyes.

"I will take **care** *that* shall never be!" gasps she, unable to speak with rage.

After a few moments she rose, took up her light, **and** without one other word descended as she had **come.**

CHAPTER XVII.

At Chenonceau.

The Château of Chenonceau, **so** greatly coveted by Catherine **de** Medici in her **youth,** still remains to us. It lies in a rural district of the Touraine, far from cities and the traffic of great thoroughfares. Spared, from its isolated position, by the First Revolution, this monument of the Renaissance, half palace half château, is as beautiful as ever—a picturesque **mass** of pointed turrets, glistening spires, perpendicular roofs, **lofty** pavilions, and pillared arches.   It is partly built over the **river Cher,** at once its defence and its attraction.

Henry II., as also his father, Francis, **who** specially **loved** this sunny plaisance **and** often visited it in company with his daughter-in-law, Catherine, and his mistress, the Duchesse d'Etampes, had both lavished unknown sums on its embellishment.

Chenonceau is approached by a drawbridge over a moat fed **by** the river.   **On** the southern side a stately bridge **of five** arches has been added by Diane de Poitiers in **order to** reach **the** opposite bank, where the high **roofs** and **pointed** turrets of **the** main building are seen to great advantage, rising out of scattered woods of oak and ash, which are divided into leafy avenues leading into fair water-meadows beside the Cher.   By Catherine's command this bridge has been recently covered and now forms a spacious wing of two stories, the first floor fitted as a banqueting hall, the walls broken by four embayed windows, opening on **either side** and looking up and down **the** stream.

A fresh-breathing **air comes from the river and** the **forest, a scent of** moss and **flowers** extremely delicious. **The** cooing of the cushat doves, the cry **of the** cuckoo, the **flutter** of the breeze among the trees, **and** the hum of insects dancing in the sunbeams **are** the voices of this sylvan solitude.   The blue sky blends into the green woods, and the white clouds, sailing over the tree-tops, make the shadows come and go among the arches of the bridge and the turrets of the château.

A sudden flourish of trumpets breaks the silence. It is Catherine, in the early summer, coming, like

Jezebel, to possess herself of her fair domain. She is habited in black and wears a velvet toque with an ostrich plume. A perfect horsewoman, she rides with a stately grace down the broad avenue leading from the high road, followed by her maids of honour—a bevy of some forty beauties, the *escadron volant de la reine*, who serve her political intrigues by fascinating alike Huguenots and Catholics.

To the right of the Queen-mother rides Madame Marguerite, her daughter—by-and-by to become infamous as Queen of Navarre, wife of Henry IV.—now a laughter-loving girl, who makes her brown jennet prance, out of pure high spirits. She is tall, like all the Valois, and finely formed. Her skin is very fair and her eyes full of expression; but there is a hard look on her delicately-featured face that belies her attractive appearance.

On the other side of the Queen-mother is her son, the young King, Charles IX. He has a weak though most engaging countenance. Naturally brave and witty and extremely frank and free, the artifices of his mother's corrupt Court have made him what he now is—cruel, violent, and suspicious. Catherine has convinced him that he is deceived by all the world except herself, and leads him at her will. He is to marry shortly the daughter of the Emperor Maximilian. Beside him is the vicious and elegant Duc d'Anjou, his next brother, of whom Charles is extremely jealous. Already Henry has been victor at Jarnac, and almost rivals Henry of Navarre in the number of battles he fights. He is to be elected King of Poland during his brother's life. Henry is handsomer than Charles, but baby-faced and effeminate. He wears rouge, and is as gay as a woman in his attire. Catherine's youngest son, d'Alençon, long-nosed, ill-favoured, and sullen, rides beside his sister.

Behind the royal Princess, is Francis, Duc de Guise, a man, as we have seen, of indomitable will and unflinching purpose; fanatical· in his devotion to the Catholic Church, and of unbounded ambition. He secretly cherishes the settled purpose of his house,— destruction of the race of Valois. Ere long he will be assassinated at Orleans, by Poltrot, a Huguenot, a creature of Coligni, who firmly believes he will ensure his salvation by this crime. Such is Christianity in the sixteenth century! There are also two cardinals mounted on mules. Lorraine, a true Guise,. most haughty and unscrupulous of politicians and of churchmen; and d'Este, newly arrived from Ferrara, insinuating, treacherous, and artistic. He has brought in his train from Italy the great poet Tasso, who follows his patron, and wears a gabardine and cap of dark satin. Tasso looks sad and careworn spite of the high favour shown him by his countrywoman, the Queen-mother. Ronsard, the court poet, is beside Tasso, and Châtelard, who, madly enamoured of the widowed Queen, Mary Stuart, is about to follow her to Scotland, and to die of his presumptuous love ere long at Holyrood.

As this brilliant procession passes down the broad avenue through pleasant lawns forming part of the park, at a fast trot, a rider is seen, mounted on a powerful black horse, who neither entirely conceals himself nor attempts to join the Court. As he passes in and out among the underwood skirting the adjoining forest, many eyes are bent upon him. The Queen-

mother specially, turns in her saddle the better to
observe him, and then questions her sons as to whether
they recognise this solitary cavalier, whose face and
figure are completely hidden by a broad Spanish hat
and heavy riding cloak.

At the moment when the Queen-mother has turned
her head to make these inquiries and is speaking
earnestly to Francis of Guise, whom she has summoned
to her side, the unknown rider crosses the path of
the Princess Marguerite (who in frolicsome mood is
making her horse leap over some ditches in the grass),
and throws a rose before her. Marguerite looks up
with a gleam of delight, their eyes meet for an instant; she raises her hand, kisses it, and waves it towards him. The stranger bows to the saddle-bow,
bounds into the thicket, and is seen no more. The
royal party cross the drawbridge through two lines of
attendants, picquers, retainers, pages, and running
footmen, and dismount at the arched entrance from
which a long stone passage leads to the great gallery,
the staircase, and the various apartments.

Leaving the young King and the Princes, his
brothers, to the care of the chamberlains who conduct
them to their various apartments, the Queen-mother
turns to the left, followed by the Princess, who is
somewhat alarmed lest her mother should have observed her recognition of the disguised cavalier. They
pass through the guard-room—a lofty chamber, with
raftered ceiling and walls hung with tapestry, on which
cuirasses, swords, lances, casques, shields, and banners
are suspended, fashioned into various devices.

Beyond is a saloon, and through a narrow door
in a corner is a small writing-closet within a turret,

Catherine, who knows the château well, has chosen this suite of rooms apart from the rest. She enters the closet alone, closes the door, seats herself beside the casement, and gazes at the broad river flowing beneath. Her eye follows the current onwards to where the stream, by a graceful bend, loses itself among copses of willow and alder. She smiles a smile of triumph. All is now her own. Then she summons her chamberlain, and commands a masque on the river for the evening, to celebrate her arrival. None shall say that she, a Medici, neglects the splendid pageantry of courts. Besides, the hunting parties, banquets, and masques are too precious as political opportunities to be disregarded.

Having dismissed her chamberlain, who with his white wand of office bows low before her, she calls for writing materials, bidding the Princess and a single lady-in-waiting, Charlotte de Pressney, her favourite attendant, remain without in the saloon.

This is a large apartment, used by Catherine as a sleeping-room, with a high vaulted ceiling of dark oak, heavily carved, the walls panelled with rare marbles, brought by the Queen's command from Italy. Busts on sculptured pedestals, ponderous chairs, carved cabinets and inlaid tables, stand around. In one corner there is a bedstead of walnut-wood with heavy hangings of purple velvet which are gathered into a diadem with the embossed initials "C. M.," and an antique silver toilet-table, with a mirror in Venetian glass set in a shroud of lace. The polished floor has no carpet, and there is not a chair that can be moved without an effort. A window, looking south towards the river and the woods, is open. The sum-

mer breezes fill the room with fragrance. Under a
ponderous mantelpiece of coloured marbles Marguerite
seats herself on a narrow settee. Her large, sparkling
eyes and animated face, her comely shape, and easy
though stately bearing, invite, yet repel, approach. She
still wears her riding-dress of emerald velvet laced with
gold, and a plumed cap lies beside her. Her luxuriant
hair, escaped from a golden net, covers her shoulders.
She is a perfect picture of youth and beauty, and as
fresh as her namesake, the daisy.

Charlotte de Pressney, at least ten years older than
the Princess, is an acknowledged belle. Her features
are regular, her complexion brilliant, and her face full
of intelligence; but there is a cunning expression
about her dimpling mouth that greatly mars her
beauty.

"Have you nothing for me, Charlotte?" whispers
the Princess, stretching out her little hand glistening
with precious rings. "I know you have. Give it me.
His eyes told me so when he passed me in the avenue."

"Your highness must not ask me. Suppose her
Majesty opens that door and sees me in the act of
giving you a letter?"

"Oh! _méchante_, why do you plague me? I know
you have something hidden; give it me, or I will
search you," and she jumps up and casts her soft arms
round the lady-in-waiting.

Charlotte disengages herself gently, and with her
eyes fixed on the low door leading into the Queen's
closet sighs deeply and takes a letter from her bosom,
bound with blue silk and sealed with the arms of
Guise.

"Ah! my colours! Is he not charming, my lover?"

mutters Marguerite, as her eager eyes devour the lines. "He says he has followed us, disguised, from Tours; not even his father knows he has come, but believes him to be in Paris, in case he should be questioned by the Queen-mother,—Charlotte, do you think her Majesty recognised him in the avenue? He was admirably disguised."

"Your highness knows that nothing escapes the Queen's eye. The sudden appearance of a stranger in this lonely spot must have created observation."

"Ah! is he not adorable, Charlotte, to come like a real knight-errant to gaze at his lady-love? How grand he looked—my noble Guise, my warrior, my hero!" and Marguerite leans back pensively on the settee as though calling up his image before her.

"Her Majesty will be very angry, madame, if she recognised him. I saw her questioning the Duke, his father, and pointing towards him as he disappeared into the wood," answers Charlotte, with the slightest expression of bitterness in her well-modulated voice.

"Henry **has** discovered," continues Marguerite, still so **lost** in **reverie** that **she** does not heed her remark, "that the Queen has a masque to-night on the river. He will be disguised, he tells me, as **a** Venetian nobleman, in a yellow brocaded robe, with a violet mantle, and a red mask. He will wear my colours —blue, heavenly blue, the symbol of hope and faith —on his shoulder-knot. Our watchword is to be 'Eternal love.'"

"Holy Virgin!" exclaims Charlotte, with alarm, laying her hand on Marguerite's shoulder, "your highness will not dare to meet him?"

"Be silent, *petite sotte*," breaks in the Princess.

"We are to meet on the southern bank of the river. Charlotte, you must help me; I shall be sure to be watched, but I must escape from the Queen by some device. Change my dress, and then—and then———" and she turns her laughing eyes on the alarmed face of Charlotte, "under the shady woods, by the parterre near the grotto, I shall meet him—and, alone."

"And what on earth am I to say to the Queen if she asks for your highness?" replies Charlotte, turning away her face that the Princess might not see the tears that bedew her cheeks.

"Anything, my good Charlotte; you have a ready wit, or my mother would not favour you. I trust to your invention, it has been often exercised," and she looks archly at her. "Tell the Queen that I am fatigued and have retired into the château until the banquet, when I will rejoin her Majesty. There is no fear, *ma mie*, especially as the Comte de Clermont is at Chenonceau. Her Majesty, stern and silent though she be, unbends to him and greatly affects his company," and she laughs softly and points towards the closed door.

"I trust there is, indeed, no fear of discovery, Princess," returns Charlotte; "for her Majesty would never forgive me." At which Marguerite laughs again.

"Princess," says Charlotte, looking very grave, and seating herself on a stool at her feet, "tell me truly, do you love the Duc de Guise?" Charlotte's fine eyes are fixed intently on Marguerite as she asks this question.

"*Peste!* you know I do. He is as great a hero as Rinaldo in the Italian poet's romance of 'Orlando.'

Somewhat sedate, perhaps, for me, but so handsome, spite of that scar. I even love that scar, Charlotte."

"Does the Duke love you?" again asks Charlotte, with a trembling voice.

"*Par exemple!* do you think the man lives who would not return my love?" and the young Princess colours, and tosses the masses of waving brown curls back from her brow, staring at her companion in unfeigned astonishment.

"I was thinking," continues Charlotte, avoiding her gaze and speaking in a peculiar voice, "I was thinking of that poor La Molle, left alone in Paris. How jealous he was! You loved him well, madame, a week ago."

"Bah! that is ancient history—we are at Chenonceau now. When I return to Paris it is possible I may console him. Poor La Molle! one cannot be always constant. Charlotte," said the Princess, after a pause, looking inquisitively at her, "I believe you are in love with the Balafré yourself."

Charlotte colours, and, not daring to trust her voice in reply, shakes her head and bends her eyes on the ground.

Marguerite, too much occupied with her own thoughts to take much heed of her friend's emotion, pats her fondly on the cheek, and proceeds—

"You are dull, *ma mie;* amuse yourself like me, now with one, then with another. Be constant to none. Regard your own interest and inclination only. But leave Guise alone; he is my passion. His proud reserve pleases me. His stately devotion touches me. He is a king among men. I love to torment the hero of Jarnac and Moncontour. He is jealous too

—jealous of the very air I breathe; but in time, that may become wearisome. I never thought of that," adds she, musing.

"Your highness will marry soon," says Charlotte, rising and facing the Princess, "and then Guise must console himself——"

"With you, *par exemple, belle des belles?* You need not blush so, Charlotte, I read your secret. But, *ma mie*, I mean to marry Henri de Guise myself, even if my mother and the King, my brother, refuse their consent. They may beat me—imprison me—or banish me; I will still marry Henri de Guise."

"Her Majesty will never consent to this alliance, madame."

"You are jealous, Charlotte, or you would not say so. Why should I not marry him, when my sister-in-law, the young Queen of Scots, is of the House of Lorraine?"

"Yes, madame, but the case is altogether different; she is a Queen-regnant. The house of Lorraine is already too powerful."

"Ah!" exclaims the volatile Marguerite, starting up, "I love freedom; freedom in life, freedom in love. Charlotte, you say truly, I shall never be constant."

"Then, alas, for your husband! He *must* love you, and you will break his heart."

"Husband! I will have no husband but Henri de Guise. Guise or a convent. I should make an enchanting nun!" And she laughs a low merry laugh, springs to her feet, and turns a pirouette on the floor. "I think the dress would suit me. I would write Latin elegies on all my old lovers."

"You will hear somewhat of that, madame, later

from the Queen," Charlotte replies, with a triumphant air. "A husband is chosen for you already."

"Who? Who is he?"

"You will learn from her Majesty very shortly."

"Charlotte, if you do not tell me this instant, I will never forgive you;" and Marguerite suddenly becomes grave and reseats herself. "Next time you want **my** help I won't move a finger."

"I dare not tell you, madame."

"Then I will tell Guise to-night you are in love with him," cries she, reddening with anger.

"Oh, Princess," exclaims Charlotte, sinking at her feet, and seizing her **hand**; "you would not be so cruel!"

"But I will, unless you tell me."

At this moment, when Marguerite was dragging **her** friend beside her on the sofa, determined to obtain an avowal from her almost by force, the low door opens, and Catherine stands before them.

CHAPTER XVIII.
A Dutiful Daughter.

THE two girls were startled and visibly trembled; **but,** recovering from their fright, rose and made their obeisance. For a moment Catherine gazed earnestly at them, as if divining the reason of their discomposure; then beckoning to the Princess, she led her daughter into her writing room, where she seated herself beside a table covered with dispatches and papers.

"My daughter," said **the** Queen, contemplating Marguerite with satisfaction, as the Princess stood before her, her cheeks flushed by the fright that Catherine's sudden entrance had occasioned. "I have commanded a masque to-night on the river, and a banquet in the water-gallery, to celebrate my return. You will attend me and be careful not to leave me, my child. Strangers have been seen among the woods. Did you not mark one as we approached riding near us?" And Catherine gave a searching glance at Marguerite. "I have given strict orders that all strangers (Huguenots, probably, with evil designs upon his Majesty) shall be arrested and imprisoned."

Again Catherine turned her piercing eyes upon Marguerite, who suddenly grew very pale.

"My daughter, you seem indisposed, the heat has overcome you—be seated."

Marguerite sank into a chair near the door. She knew that her mother had recognised the Duke, and that it would be infinitely difficult to keep her appointment with him that evening. Neither mother nor daughter spoke for some moments. Catherine was studying the effect of her words on Marguerite, and Marguerite was endeavouring to master her agitation. When the Queen next addressed her, the Princess was still pale but perfectly composed.

"My daughter, you passed much of your time before you left the Louvre with the Comte la Molle. I know he is highly favoured by my son, Anjou. Does his company amuse you?"

Marguerite's cheeks became scarlet.

"Your Majesty has ever commanded me," replied she in a firm voice, "to converse with those young nobles whom you and my brother, the King, have called to the Court."

"True, my child, you have done so, I acknowledge freely, and, by such gracious bearing you have, doubtless, forwarded his Majesty's interests." There was again silence. "Our cousin, the young **Duc** Henri de Guise, is also much in your company," Catherine said at length, speaking very slowly and turning her eyes full upon Marguerite who, for an instant, returned her gaze boldly. "I warn you, Marguerite, that neither the King my son, nor I, will tolerate more **alliances** with **the** ambitious House of Lorraine. They stand too near the throne already."

Marguerite during this speech did not look up, **not** daring to meet the steadfast glance of the Queen.

"Surely," said she, speaking low, "your Majesty has been prejudiced against the Duke by my brother Charles. His Majesty hates him. He is jealous of him."

"My child, speak with more respect of his Majesty."

"Madame, the King has threatened to beat me if I dared to love the Duc de Guise. But I am your Majesty's own child," and Marguerite turned towards Catherine caressingly. "**I fear** not threats." Catherine smiled and curiously observed her. "But your Majesty surely forgets," continued Marguerite warmly, "that our cousin of Guise is the chief pillar of the throne, a hero who, at sixteen, vanquished Coligni at Poitiers; **and** that at Massignac and Jarnac, in company with my brother Anjou, he performed prodigies of valour."

"My daughter, I forget nothing. You appear to

have devoted much time to the study of the Duke—our cousin's life. It is a brilliant page in our history. I have, however, other projects for you. You must support the throne by a royal marriage."

"Oh! madame!" exclaimed Marguerite, heaving a deep sigh, and clasping her hands as she looked imploringly at her mother, who proceeded to address her as though unconscious of this appeal.

"Avoid Henri de Guise, Princess. I have already remonstrated with his father on his uninvited presence here, of which he professes entire ignorance—for he *is here*, and you know it, Marguerite"—and she shot an angry glance at the embarrassed Princess. "Avoid the Duke, I say, and let me see you attended less often by La Molle, or I must remove him from the Court."

"Madame!" cried Marguerite, turning white, and looking greatly alarmed, well knowing what this *removal* meant; "I will obey your commands. But whom, may I ask, do you propose for my husband? Unless I can choose a husband for myself"—and she hesitated, for the Queen bent her eyes sternly upon her and frowned—"I do not care to marry at all," she added in a low voice.

"Possibly you may not, my daughter. But his Majesty and the council have decided otherwise. Your hand must ultimately seal a treaty, important to the King, your brother, in order to reconcile conflicting creeds and to conciliate a powerful party."

All this time Marguerite had stood speechless before the Queen. At this last sentence, fatal to her hopes of marrying the Duc de Guise, the leader of the Catholic party, her lips parted as if to speak, but she restrained herself and was silent.

"The daughters of France," said Catherine, lifting her eyes to the ceiling, "do not consider personal feelings in marriage, but the good of the kingdom. My child, you are to marry very shortly the King of Navarre. I propose journeying myself to the Castle of Nérac to conclude a treaty with my sister, Queen Jeanne, his mother. Henri de Béarn will demand your hand. He will be accepted when an alliance is concluded between the Queen of Navarre and myself."

"But, my mother," answered Marguerite, stepping forward in her excitement, "he is a heretic. I am very Catholic. Surely your Majesty will not force me——"

"You will convert him," replied Catherine.

"But, madame, the Prince is not to my taste. He is rough and unpolished. He is a mountaineer—a Béarnois."

"My daughter, he will be your husband. Now, Marguerite, listen to me. This marriage is indispensable for reasons of state. The King, your brother, and I myself like the King of Navarre as little as you do. That little kingdom in the valleys of the Pyrenees is a thorn in our side which we must pluck out. Those pestilent and accursed heretics must be destroyed. We call them to our Court; we lodge them in the Louvre—not for love, Marguerite—not for love. Have patience, my daughter. I cannot unfold to you the secrets of the council; but it is possible that Henry of Navarre may not live long. Life is in the hands of God,—and of the King." She added in a lower voice. "Console yourself. A day is coming that will purge France of Huguenots; and if Henry do not accept the mass——"

"Madame," said Marguerite archly (who had eagerly followed her mother's words), "I trust that the service of his Majesty will not require me to *convert* the King of Navarre?"

"No, Princess," said Catherine, with a sinister smile. "My daughter," continued she, "your dutiful obedience pleases me. The King may, in the event of your marriage, create new posts of honour about the King of Navarre while he lives. Monsieur La Molle, a most accomplished gentleman, shall be remembered. *Au revoir*, Princess. Send Charlotte de Presney to me. Go to your apartments, and prepare for the masque on the river I have commanded to-night in honour of our arrival."

So Marguerite, full of thought, curtseying low before her mother, kissed her hand, and retired to her apartments.

As the sun sets and the twilight deepens, torch after torch lights up the river and the adjacent woods. Every window in the château is illuminated, and great beacon-fires flash out from the turrets. The sound of a lute, the refrain of a song, a snatch from a hunting-chorus, are borne upon the breeze, as, one by one, painted barges shoot out from under the arches of the bridge along the current.

As night advances the forest on both sides of the river is all ablaze. On the southern bank, where the parterre is divided from the woods by marble balustrades, statues and hedges of clipped yew, festoons of coloured lamps hang from tree to tree, and fade away into sylvan bowers deep among the tangled coppice. The fountains, cunningly lit from below, flash up in streams of liquid fire. Each tiny streamlet that crosses the mossy lawns is a thread of gold. Tents of satin and velvet, fringed with gold, border broad alleys and marble terraces of dazzling whiteness. The river, bright as at midday with the light of thousands of torches, is covered with gondolas and fantastic barques. Some are shaped like birds—swans, parrots, and peacocks; others resemble shells, and butterflies whose expanded wings of glittering stuff form the sails. All are filled with maskers habited in every device of quaint disguisement. Not a face or form is to be recognised. See how rapidly the fairy fleet cleaves the water, now dashing into deep shadows, now lingering in the torchlight that glances on the rich silks and grotesque features of the maskers. Yonder a whole boat's crew is entangled among the water lilies that thickly fringe the banks under the over-arching willows. Some disembark among the fountains, or mount the broad marble steps leading to the arcades; some descend to saunter far away into the illuminated woods. Others, tired of the woods, are re-embarking on the river. In the centre of the stream is a barge with a raised platform covered with velvet embroidered in gold, on which are placed the Queen's musicians, who wake the far-off echoes with joyous symphonies. Beyond, in the woods, are maskers who dance under silken hangings spread among the overhanging branches of giant oaks, or recline upon cushions piled upon rich carpets beside tables covered with choice wines, fruit and confectionery. The merry laughter of these revellers mixes

with strains of voluptuous music from flutes and
flageolets, played by concealed musicians placed in
pavilion-orchestras hidden among the underwood,
tempting onwards those who desire to wander into
the dark and lonely recesses of the forest.

Among the crowd which thickly gathers on the
parterre, a tall man of imposing figure, habited in a
Venetian dress of yellow satin and wrapped in a cloak
of the same colour, paces up and down. He is alone
and impatient. He wears a red mask; conspicuous
on his right shoulder is a knot of blue and silver ribbons. As each boat approaches to discharge its gay
freight upon the bank he eagerly advances and mixes
with the company. Then, as though disappointed, he
returns into the shadow thrown by the portico of a
shell grotto. Wearied with waiting, he seats himself
upon the turf. "She will not come!" he says, and
then sinks back against a tree and covers his face
with his hands. The fountains throw up columns of
fiery spray; the soft music sighs in the distance;
crowds of fluttering maskers pace up and down the
plots of smooth grass or linger on the terrace—still
he sits and waits.

A soft hand touches him, and a sweet voice whispers "Eternal love!" It is the Princess, who, disguised
in a black domino procured by Charlotte de Presney,
has escaped from the Queen-mother and stands before
him.

For an instant she unmasks and turns her lustrous
eyes upon him.

Henri de Guise (for it is he) leaps to his feet. He
kneels before her and kisses her hands. "Oh! my
Princess, what condescension!" he murmurs in a low

voice. "I trembled lest I had been too bold. I feared that my letter had not reached you."

A gay laugh answers his broken sentences.

"My cousin, will you promise to take on your soul all the lies I have told my mother in order to meet you?"

"I will absolve you, madame."

"Ah, my cousin, I have ill news! My mother and the King are determined to marry me to the King of Navarre."

"Impossible!" exclaims the Duke; "it would be sacrilege!"

"Oh, Henry!" replies the Princess in a pleading voice and laying her hand upon his arm, "my cousin, bravest among the brave, swear by your own sword you will save me from this detestable heretic!"

The Duke did not answer, but gently drew her near the entrance of the grotto. It was now late, and the lights within had grown dim. "Marguerite," he says, in a voice trembling with passion, "come where I may adore you as my living goddess—come where I may conjure you to give me a right to defend you. Say but one word and to-morrow I will ask your hand in marriage; the King dare not refuse me."

"Alas! my cousin, my mother's will is absolute."

"It is a vile conspiracy!" cries the Duke, in great agitation. "The House of Lorraine, my Princess, save but for the Crown, is as great as your own. My uncle, the Cardinal, shall appeal to the Holy See. Marguerite, do but love me, and I will never leave you! Marguerite, hear me!" He seizes her hands—he presses her in his arms, drawing her each moment deeper into the recesses of the grotto. As they disappear, a voice is heard without, calling softly—

"Madame! Madame Marguerite! for the love of heaven, come, come!"

In an instant the spell is broken. Marguerite extricates herself from the arms of the Duke and rushes forward.

It is Charlotte de Presney, disguised like herself in a black domino. "Not a moment is to be lost," she says hurriedly. "Her Majesty has three times asked for your highness. She supposes I am in the château seeking you." Charlotte's voice is unsteady. She wore her mask to conceal her face, for it was bathed in tears.

In an instant she and the Princess, followed by the Duke, cross the terrace to where a boat is moored under the shade of some willows and are lost in the crowd.

The Duke dashes **into** the darkest recesses of the forest, and is seen no more.

CHAPTER XIX.

Before the Storm.

HENRY, King of Navarre, accompanied by the Prince de Condé and his wife and attended by eight hundred Huguenot gentlemen dressed in black (for his mother, Queen Jeanne, had died suddenly at Paris, while he was on the road), had just arrived at the Louvre to claim the hand of the Princess Marguerite. The two Princes and the Princesse de Condé are received with royal honours and much effusion of compliments by King Charles and Catherine; they are

lodged in the Palace of the Louvre. Whatever Marguerite's feelings are, she carefully conceals them. Insinuating, adroit, clever, gifted with a facile pen and
a flattering tongue, she is too ambitious to resist, too
volatile to be constant. She lives in a world of intrigue, as she tells us in her memoirs, and piquing herself on being "so Catholic, so devoted to the 'sacred
faith of her fathers,'" and she pendulates between
Henri de Guise and La Molle, amid a thousand other
flirtations. She lives in a family divided against itself.
Sometimes she takes part with the Duc d'Anjou and
watches the Queen-mother in his interests, in order to
report every word she says to him; or she quarrels
with d'Anjou and swears eternal friendship with her
youngest brother, d'Alençon—all his life the puppet of endless political conspiracies; or she abuses
the King (Charles) because he listens to her enemy,
De Gaust, and tells her that she shall never marry the
Duc de Guise, because she would reveal all the
secrets of state to him and make the House of Lorraine more dangerous than it is already. This greatest
princess of Europe, young and beautiful, a "noble
mind in a lovely person," as Brantôme says of her, is
agitated, unhappy, and lonely. "Let it never be said,"
writes she, "that marriages are made in heaven; God
is not so unjust. All yesterday my room echoed with
talk of weddings. How can I purge it?"

The Duc de Guise no longer whispers in her ear
"Eternal love." The great Balafré, stern in resolve,
firm in affection, is disgusted at her *légèreté*. He has
ceased even to be jealous. His mind is now occupied
by those religious intrigues which he developed later
as leader of the Holy Catholic League. Guise dis-

likes and distrusts the Valois race. He especially ab-
hors their unholy coquetting with heretics in the matter of Marguerite's approaching marriage. He has now
adopted the motto of the House of Lorraine, "Death
to the Valois! Guise upon the throne!" Moreover
he looks with favour on a widow—the Princesse de
Porcian, whom he marries soon after. Guise only remains at Court to fulfil the vow of vengeance he has
sworn against Coligni for his suspected connivance in
the murder of his illustrious father, Francis of Guise,
of which accusation Coligni could never clear himself.* The great Admiral is now at Court. He is
loaded with favours. Charles IX. has requested his
constant attendance at the council to arrange the details of a war with Spain. He has also made him a
present of a thousand francs. The friends of Coligni
warn him to beware. His comrade and friend Montmorenci refuses to leave Chantilly. The Admiral,
more honest than astute, is completely duped. It is
whispered among the Catholics that revenge is at
hand, and that the Protestant princes and Coligni are
shortly coming to their death. It is said also that the
marriage liveries of the Princess will be "crimson,"
and that "more blood than wine will flow at the marriage feast."

And the Queen? Serene and gracious, she moves
with her accustomed majesty among these conflicting
parties. She neither sees, nor hears, nor knows aught
that shall disarrange her projects. Silent, inscrutable,
her hands hold the threads of life. Within her brain
is determined the issue of events. Her son Charles
is a puppet in her hands. This once frank, witty,

* See Note 11.

brave, artistic youth, who formerly loved verses and literature,—when not a roaring Nimrod among the royal forests,—is morose, cruel, and suspicious; convinced that the whole world is playing him false, all perjured but his mother. She has told him, and she has darkly hinted in the council, that events are approaching a crisis. She has secured the present support of the young Duc de Guise and the powerful House of Lorraine, ever foremost when Catholic interests are at stake. She can now sit down calmly and marshal each act in the coming drama, as a general can marshal those regiments which are to form his battle-front. Fifteen hundred Protestants were slaughtered at Amboise alone, but there are thousands upon thousands remaining, and she has promised Philip II., her awful son-in-law, and his minister the Duke of Alva, that she will cut off the head of heresy within the realm of France. She has tried both parties, intrigued with both—with Coligni and the Condés, with Guise and the Cardinal de Lorraine, and she finds that at present orthodoxy answers her purpose best.

Besides, there is personal hatred, fear, and offence towards the Huguenots. Did not Coligni dare to criticize her government at the Council of Amboise? Did not Condé (that cautious Bourbon) escape her? The King of Navarre, too, her future son-in-law, is he to be lured to Court and married to the fascinating Marguerite for *nothing?* Has not Ruggiero shown her that his life crossed the life of her sons? Does she not hate him? Is he not adored by the people, who, grown cold towards the House of Valois, extol his vigour, courage, and ability? Yes, he shall marry. Then he shall die along with all rebels, heretics, and traitors!

A general massacre of the Huguenots throughout France can alone satisfy her longings and secure Charles on the throne.

Thus came to be planned that most tremendous crime, fixed for the festival of St. Bartholomew, ostensibly for the triumph of the Catholic Church, but in reality to compass the death of the Queen's political enemies—Navarre, Condé, and Coligni—and to crush the freedom of thought and opinion brought in by liberty of conscience and a purer faith.

This was the Court to which Henry of Navarre came, to be lodged under the roof of the Louvre, and to marry the Princess Marguerite!

The marriage took place on the 18th of August, 1572, at Notre-Dame.* The outspoken Charles had said that, in giving his sister *Margot* to the King of Navarre, he gave her to all the Huguenots in his kingdom. The Princess tells us she wore a royal crown and a state mantle of blue velvet, wrought with gold embroidery, four yards long. It was held up by three princesses; and she further wore a corset, forming the body of her dress, covered with brilliants and the crown jewels. The streets through which she passed were dressed with scaffoldings, lined with cloth of gold, to accommodate the spectators, all the way from the Archbishop's palace to Notre-Dame.

A few nights after, Admiral Coligni was shot at, with an arquebuse, by a man standing at a barred window in the street of the Fossés Saint-Germain, as he returned from playing a game of rackets with the King, at the Louvre, to his lodgings at the Hôtel de Saint-Pierre, in the Rue Béthisy. He was walking

* See Note 12.

along slowly, reading a paper; the finger of his right hand was broken, and he was otherwise grievously wounded. The assassin, Maurévert, was a fellow known to be in the pay of Henri, Duc de Guise. The house from which the shot was fired belonged to the Duke's tutor. The King of Navarre and Condé were overcome at the news. Charles IX., along with the Queen-mother, visited the Admiral next day and stayed an hour with him. Before leaving, Charles folded him in his arms and wept. "You, my father," he said, "have the wound, but I suffer the pain. By the light of God, I will so avenge this act that it shall be a warning as long as the world lasts."

A few hours after the shot was fired, the Huguenot chiefs assembled in Navarre's apartments to deliberate what means should be taken to punish the assassin. About the same time a secret council was called by the Queen-mother, to decide whether or no Navarre and Condé should be massacred. Charles IX., the Duc de Guise—who, however hostile otherwise, join issue to destroy Navarre and Condé—Anjou, Nevers, and d'Angoulême were present. It was resolved that the King of Navarre and the Prince de Condé should **die,** and that the massacre should take place that very night, before the Huguenots—alarmed by the attempt on Coligni—had time to concert measures of defence. Under pretence of protecting them from further violence, all hotels and lodging-houses were diligently searched, and a list made of the name, age, and condition of every Protestant in Paris. Orders were also given for the troops to be under arms, during the coming night, throughout the city. Every outlet and portal of the Louvre were closed and guarded by

Swiss Guards, commanded by Cossein. The Hôtel de Saint-Pierre, in the Rue Béthisy, where Coligni lay, was also surrounded by troops, "for his safety," it was said. No one could go in or out. At a given signal, the tocsin was to sound from all places where a bell was hung. Chains were to be drawn across the streets and bonfires lighted. White cockades, stitched on a narrow white band to be bound round the right arm, were distributed, in order that the Catholics might be recognised in the darkness. The secret, known to hundreds, was well kept; the Huguenots were utterly unprepared. "No one told me anything," said Marguerite.* "They knew that I was too humane. But the evening before, being present at the coucher of my mother the Queen, and sitting on a coffer near my sister Claude, who seemed very sad, the Queen, who was talking to some one, turned round and saw I was not gone. She desired me to retire to bed. As I was making my obeisance to her, my sister took me by the arm and stopped me. Then sobbing violently she said, 'Good God, sister, do not go!' This alarmed me exceedingly. The Queen, my mother, was watching us, and, looking very angry, called my sister to her and scolded her severely. She peremptorily desired her to say no more to me. Claude replied that it was not fair to sacrifice me like that, and that danger might come to me.

"'Never mind,' said the Queen. 'Please God, no danger will come to her; but she must go to bed at once in order to raise no suspicions.' But Claude still disputed with her, although I did not hear their words. The Queen again turned to me angrily and

* See Note 13.

commanded me to go. My sister, continuing her sobs, bade me 'good night.' I dared ask no questions. So, cold and trembling, without the least idea of what was the matter, I went to my rooms and to my closet, where I prayed to God to save me from I knew not what. The King, my husband, who had not come to bed, sent word to me to do so." (They occupied the same room, she tells us, but separate beds.) "I could not close my eyes all night," she adds; "thinking of my sister's agitation, and sure that something dreadful was coming. Before daylight my husband got up. He came to my bed-side, kissed me, and said that he was going to play a game of rackets before the King was awake. He said he would have justice in the matter of the attempt on the Admiral's life. Then he left the room. I, seeing the daylight, and overcome by sleep, told my nurse to shut the door, that I might rest longer."

This took place on Saturday evening, the 23rd of August, being the eve of St. Bartholomew.

CHAPTER XX.
St. Bartholomew.

A SIGNAL sounded from the belfry of Saint-Germain l'Auxerrois. It was answered by the great bell of the Palace of Justice on the opposite bank of the Seine. Catherine and her two sons, Charles IX. and the Duc d'Anjou, had risen long before daylight. Catherine dared not leave Charles to himself. He was suddenly grown nervous and irresolute. He might yet countermand everything. Within a small closet over the gate of the Louvre, facing the quays, the mother and her two sons stood huddled together. Charles was tallest of the three. The window was open; it was still dark; the streets were empty; not a sound was heard save the crashing of the bells. They listened to the wild clamour without; but not a word was spoken. Catherine felt Charles tremble. She clutched him tightly, and, dreading to hear the echo of her own voice, she whispered in his ear, "My son, God has given your enemies into your hands. Let them not escape you."

"*Mort de Dieu*, mother, do you take me for a coward?" whispered back Charles, still trembling.

Suddenly a shot was fired on the Quays. The three conspirators started as if the weapon had been levelled against themselves.

"Whence this pistol shot came, who fired it, or if it wounded any one, I know not," writes the Duc d'Anjou, who as well as his sister has left an account of the massacre; "but this I know, that the report struck terror into our very souls. We were seized with such sudden dread at the horrors we had ourselves invoked, that even the Queen-mother was dismayed. She dispatched one of the King's gentlemen who waited without, to command the Duc de Guise to stay all proceedings and not to attack Admiral Coligni." This counter order came too late. The Duke had already left his house.

All the bells in Paris were now ringing furiously; the quays and streets were rapidly filling with citizens bearing flambeaux. Multitudes came pouring in from every opening, every window was filled with persons holding lights, and the cracking of firearms, loud curses, piercing screams and wild laughter were heard

on every side. In the midst of this uproar, Henri de
Guise, thirsting for revenge upon the supposed murderer of his father, accompanied by Nevers and d'Angoulême, and a company of Catholic nobles, made his
way to the Hôtel Saint-Pierre, in the Rue Béthisy,
where Coligni lodged.

Coligni, who had the night before been embraced
by his sovereign, lay asleep on his bed. Some of his
Protestant friends, Guerchi, Teligny, with Cornaton
and Labonne his gentlemen, who had hastened to him
upon the news of the attempted assassination, lingered
in the ante-room. Paré, the surgeon who had dressed
his wounds, had not yet left the hotel. The Admiral
had been conversing with him and with his chaplain
Merlin, who had offered up a thanksgiving for his
deliverance. Within the court five Swiss Guards stood
behind the outer doors; without, in the darkness of
the night, crouched Cossein with fifty arquebusiers,
who had been gained over by the Duc de Guise.

Suddenly, out of the stillness of the night a voice
is heard calling from without, "Open the door—open
in the name of the King!" At the King's name the
street-door is immediately unbarred; Cossein and his
men rush in, poniard the five guards, break open the
inner door, and dash up the stairs. The noise dis-
turbs Cornaton, who descends the stairs; he is pushed
violently backwards amid cries of *"De par le Roi!"*
Now the whole house is aroused, Merlin has risen, and
Coligni awakened from his sleep, calls loudly from the
door of his room, "Cornaton, what does this noise
mean?" "My dear Lord," cries Cornaton hurrying up
to him, wringing his hands, "it means that it is God
who summons you! The hall below is carried by your

enemies—Cossein is a traitor—we cannot save you—
we have no means of defence!"

"I understand," replies Coligni unmoved. "It is
a plot to destroy me now that I am wounded and
cannot defend myself. I have long been prepared
to die. I commend my soul to God. Cornaton,
Merlin, and the others, if the doors are forced, you
cannot save me, save yourselves." Coligni returns to
his room.

By this time the Admiral's retainers are aroused
and enter his chamber, but no sooner does he repeat
the words, "Save yourselves, you cannot save me,"
than they lose not a moment in escaping to the leads
of the house. One man only remains with his master;
his name is Nicolas Muso. The door is then shut,
barred, and locked.

Meanwhile Cossein, heavily mailed and sword in
hand, having slain all he has found in his way, is on
the landing. Besme, a page of the Duc de Guise,
Attin, and Sarbaloux are with him; they force open
the door of Coligni's room.

The Admiral, his long white hair falling about
his shoulders, is seated in an arm-chair. There is
a majesty about him even thus wounded, unarmed
and alone, that daunts his assailants. The traitor
Cossein falls back. Besme advances brandishing his
sword.

"Are you Admiral Coligni?" he cries.

"I am," replies the veteran, following with his eyes
the motion of the sword. "Young man, respect my
grey hairs and my infirmities," and he signs to his
arm bound up and swathed to his side. Besme makes
a pass at him. "If I could have died by the hands

of a gentleman and not of this varlet!" exclaims the Admiral. Besme for answer plunges his sword up to the hilt into Coligni's breast.

A voice is now heard from without under the window—"Besme, you are very long; is all over?"

"All is over," answers Besme, thrusting his head out and displaying his bloody sword.

"Sirrah, here is the Duc de Guise, and I, the Chevalier d'Angoulême. We will not believe it until we see the body. Fling it out of the window, like a good lad."

With some difficulty the corpse is raised and thrown into the street below. The gashed and bleeding remains of the old hero fall heavily upon the pavement. Henri de Guise stoops down to feast his eyes upon his enemy. The features are so veiled with blood he cannot recognise him. He takes out his handkerchief and wipes the wrinkled face clean. "I know you now—Admiral Coligni," says he, "and I spurn you. Lie there, poisonous old serpent that murdered my father. Thou shalt shed no more venom, reptile!" and he kicks the corpse into a corner, amidst the dirt and mud of the thoroughfare. (Coligni's dead body* is carried to the gallows at Montfaucon, where it hangs by the feet from a chain of iron.) Guise then turns to the fifty arquebusiers behind him. "En avant—en avant, mes enfants!" he shouts; "you have made a good beginning—set upon the others—slaughter them all—men, women—even infants at the breast—cut them down." Sword in hand Guise rushes through the streets with Nevers, d'Angoulême, and

---

* See Note 14.

Tavannes, as well as Gondi and De Retz, who have now joined him, at his back.

Meanwhile, Marguerite de Valois is awakened by some one beating violently with feet and hands against her door crying out, "Navarre! Navarre!" "My nurse," writes she, "thinking it was the King, ran and opened the door; but it was M. de Séran, grievously wounded and closely pursued by four archers, who cried out, 'Kill him! kill him! spare no one.' De Séran threw himself on my bed to save himself. I, not knowing who he was, jumped out, and he with me, holding by me tightly. We both screamed loudly; I was as frightened as he was, but God sent M. de Nançay, Captain of the Guards, who finding me in this condition, could not help laughing. He drove the archers out and spared the life of this man, whom I put to bed in my closet and kept there till he was well. I changed my night-dress, which was covered with blood. M. de Nançay assured me that my husband was safe and with the King. He threw over me a cloak, and took me to my sister Claude, in whose room I arrived more dead than alive; specially so when, as I set my foot in the ante-chamber, a gentleman named Bourse dropped, pierced by a ball, dead at my feet. I fell fainting into the arms of M. de Nançay, thinking I was killed also. A little recovered, I went into the small room beyond where my sister slept. While I was there, two gentlemen-in-waiting, who attended my husband, rushed in, imploring me to save their lives. So I went to the King and to the Queen, my brother and my mother, and falling on my knees begged that these gentlemen might be spared, which was granted to me."

"Having," continues Marguerite, "failed in the principal purpose, *which was not so much against the Huguenots as against the Princes of the blood—the King my husband, and the Prince of Condé*—the Queen, my mother, came to me and '*asked me to break my marriage.*' But I replied that I would not; being sure that she only proposed this in order to murder my husband."*

The magic mirror of Ruggiero had revealed the truth; Henry of Navarre led a charmed life. Of his escape, against the express command of the all-powerful Catherine, various accounts are related. He is said to have been saved by his wife, but of this *she* says nothing. It is believed on good authority that, with the Prince de Condé, he went out unusually early, before daybreak even, in order to prepare for playing that identical game of rackets, of which he spoke to Marguerite and which probably saved his life. When it is discovered that these two princes, Condé and Navarre, are both alive, they are summoned to the King's presence. They find Charles, arquebuse in hand, within the same small closet over the gate of the Louvre. He has been there since daybreak. A page stands by him, ready to reload his weapon. He is mad with exultation and excitement; he leans out of window to watch the crowds of fugitives rush by and to shout to the Swiss Guards below—"Kill—kill all—cut them all in pieces!" "*Pardieu!* see," he roars out pointing to the river, "there is a fellow yonder escaping. By the mass, look—one, two, three —they are swimming across the Seine—at them, at

* See Note 15.

them—take good aim—shoot them down, the carrion!"
Volleys of shot **are** the **reply.** Charles had recovered
his nerves; he now looks on Huguenots as game, and
has been potting them with remarkable precision from
the window. With hideous mirth, he boasts to Navarre
and Condé how many heretics he has brought down
with his own hand. He counts upon his fingers the
names of the Huguenot chiefs already slaughtered.
He yells with fiendish laughter when he describes how
Coligni, whom the night before he had called "father,"
looked when dead. "By the light of God, it is a royal
chase!" shrieks Charles, as the page quickly reloads
his arquebuse. "That last shot was excellent. Not a
heretic shall be left in France." Again he points his
gun and shoots; a piercing cry follows. Charles nods
his head approvingly. "We will have them all—
babies and their mothers. 'Break the eggs and the
nest will rot.' Our mother says well—we must reign.
We will no longer be contradicted by our subjects.
We will teach them to revere us as the image of the
living God. You, Princes,"—and as he turns to address the King of Navarre and Condé, his tall, gaunt
figure, distorted countenance, bleared and bloodshot
eyes, and matted hair are repulsive to look upon—
"You, Princes, I have called hither, out of compassion **for** your youth, to give you a chance for your
lives, *as you are alive*,—but by **the** holy Oriflamme, *I
thought you were both dead already.* You are, both of
you, rebels, and sons of rebels. You must instantly
recant and enter **the true** Church or you must die.
So down on your knees, both of you. Purge yourselves from your accursed sect. Give me your parole,
and your swords too, Princes, **that** you will not leave

10*

the Louvre; or, *Dieu des Dieux*, you shall be massacred like the rest!"

Thus did Henry IV. and the Prince de Condé escape death, unknown to, and contrary to the express orders of Catherine.

Without, Paris is a charnel-house. The streets are choked up by murdered Huguenots. Carts and litters full of dead bodies, huddled together in a hideous medley, rumble along the rough causeways, to be shot into the Seine. The river runs red with blood; its current is dammed up with corpses. But the Court is merry. Catherine triumphs. Her ladies—*la petite bande de la Reine*—go forth and pick their way in the gory mud, to scrutinise the dead, piled in heaps against the walls and in the courts of the Louvre, to recognise friends or lovers.

On the 6th September the news of the massacre reaches Rome by letters from the Nuncio. Gregory XIII. commands solemn masses and thanksgivings to God for the event. The cannon of St. Angelo booms over the papal city; *feux de joie* are fired in the principal streets; a medal is struck; a jubilee is published; a legate is sent into France; a procession, in which the Pope, Cardinals, and Ministers to the See of Rome appear, visit the great Basilicas; the Cardinal de Lorraine, uncle to the Balafré, then at Rome, is present, and in the name of his master, Charles IX., congratulates his Holiness on the efficacy of his prayers these *seventeen years past* for the destruction of heretics.

Blood calls for blood!* Charles IX., whose royal mandate authorised the massacre (which lasted seven

---

* See Note 16.

days and seven nights), falls sick two years after at the Castle of Vincennes. "I know not what has befallen me," he says to his surgeon, Ambrose Paré; "my mind and body both burn with fever. Asleep or awake, I see the mangled Huguenots pass before me. They drip with blood; they make hideous faces at me; they point to their open wounds and mock me. Holy Virgin! I wish, Paré, I had spared the old and the infirm and the infants at the breast." Aged twenty-four, Charles died, abhorring the mother whose counsels had led him to this execrable deed—abhorring her so intensely that he could not even bear her in his sight. In her place he called for the King of Navarre, and confided to him his last wishes. He died, poor misguided youth, piously thanking God that he left no children. The blood actually oozed from the pores of his skin. His cries and screams were horrible.

Thus another King of France passed into the world of spirits, bringing Henry of Navarre one step nearer the throne. Charles, according to the prediction of Ruggiero, had died young, bathed in his own blood.

And Catherine? Calm, undaunted, still handsome, she inaugurated a new reign—that of her third and best beloved son, Henri, Duc d'Anjou and King of Poland, popularly known by the style and title of Henry III., "*by the favour of his mother inert King of France.*"

CHAPTER XXI.

The End of Catherine de Medici.

FIFTEEN years have passed. The Queen-mother is now seventy. She suffers from a mortal disease, and lies sick at the Château of Blois.

Hither her son Henry III. and his Court have come to meet the States-General. Trouble is in the kingdom; for the great Balafré, supported by Rome and Spain, is in rebellion; Henry totters on his throne.

And what a throne! What a monarch! Henry, who in his youth was learned, elegant, sober, who fought at Jarnac and Moncontour * like a Paladin, has become effeminate, superstitious, and vicious. His sceptre is a cup-and-ball; his sword, a tuft of feathers; he paints and dresses like a woman, covers himself with jewels, and passes his time in arranging ecclesiastical processions, or in festivals, pageants, masques, and banquets. His four favourites ("minions" they are called, and also "beggars," from their greed and luxury), De Joyeuse, d'Epernon, Schomberg, and Maugiron, govern him and the kingdom. They are handsome and satirical, and think to kill the King's enemies with ridicule and *jeux de mots*. But Henri de Guise, who sternly rebukes their ribaldry and ab-hors their dissolute manners, is not the man to be conquered by such weapons as words. He has placed himself at the head of the Catholic League, negotiates with Spain, and openly aspires to the throne.

For a moment there is peace. Henry, before leav-

* See Note 17.

ing Paris, by the advice of his mother summoned the
Duc de Guise from Nancy to Paris. The Balafré
enters the capital in disguise. The cry, "The Duke is
with us!" spreads over the city like lightning. The
populace, who adore Guise and detest Henry, tear off
his mask and cloak and lead him through the streets
in triumph. Catherine, although very ill, is so alarmed
at the threatening aspect of affairs, that she causes
herself, to be carried out to meet him, borne in a
chair, and so brings him to the Louvre into the presence of the King. His insolent bearing transports
Henry with rage. The citizens, not to be pacified, fall
out with the King's guards, and there is a fearful uproar in the city. The Louvre is besieged. Henry,
haughty and obstinate, is no longer safe in Paris.
Maréchal d'Ornano offers to assassinate the Duc de
Guise, but the King, by advice of d'Epernon, affects
to yield to the policy of his mother, and to accept the
supremacy of Guise. Under pretence, however, of a
walk in the Tuileries Gardens, then newly planted, he
orders his horses to be saddled, and escapes out of
Paris, by way of Montmartre, attended only by his
favourites. He reaches Chartres in safety. At Chartres
he is joined by Catherine, and a treaty is signed—a
treaty of false peace, for already d'Epernon and
Joyeuse are whispering into the King's ear that "the
Duc de Guise must die."

The treaty stipulates that Henry be declared Head
of the Catholic League; that all Huguenots be
banished—notably the King of Navarre, heir-pre-
sumptive to the throne; and that the Duc de Guise be
Lieutenant-General of the kingdom. The States-
General are to be immediately assembled; and Henri

de Guise, once the poetic lover, now hardened into
the cold, ambitious bigot—ready to usurp the throne
of France to ensure the triumph of the Catholic party,
and exclude the King of Navarre—canvasses France,
to insure a majority for the Holy League against
those pertinacious enemies of orthodoxy, Condé and
Navarre.

The King, meanwhile, overridden and humiliated,
agrees to everything, and listens complacently to
d'Epernon, who tells him, "He will never be king
while Guise lives." So, for the moment, there is
peace.

Now the King has left Chartres, and is at Blois.
The Balafré and his brother the Cardinal are also
there to attend the Parliament, which is summoned,
and to make known their grievances. So the sunny
little town of Blois, sloping sweetly downwards to the
Loire, with its superb castle marked by towers, turrets, broad flat roofs, painted windows, and ample
courts, is the theatre on which the great battle is to
be fought between the rival houses of Guise and
Valois. All the chiefs on either side are to be present at a council which is to precede the meeting of
the Assembly. Henry—at the instigation of d'Epernon—the better to play his perfidious game has communicated at the same altar with the Balafré and his
brother the Cardinal, and given them the kiss of peace
to seal their reconciliation.

Catherine's apartments are on the first floor of the
château,—a gallery-saloon, the diamonded windows
set in painted arches overlooking the town, the dark
walls, decorated with a crowned C and a monogram
in gold; her oratory, with a large oval window where

an altar stands; her writing-closet, with many concealed drawers and *secrets* in the walls—a hidden
stair leading to an observatory, and a sleeping-room
with a recess for her bed. So unaltered are these
rooms that the presence of Catherine still haunts
them; she faces one at every step.

In her bed within that recess the great Queen lies
dying. She is old and broken, and her mind wanders
at times through excess of pain. But she cannot die
in peace, for she knows that her son Henry—the last
of her race—meditates a hideous crime; a crime in
which she would have gloried once, but now, racked
with bodily suffering and mental anguish, with remorse for the past and terror for the future, she shudders at the very thought.

She calls him to her. Henry, her beloved Anjou!
As he enters her chamber, she struggles upright on
her bed. No one would have recognised the majestic
Queen in the hideous skeleton that now speaks.

"What are you about to do, my son?" she asks in
a tremulous voice; "answer me, Henry. I fear I know
too well what is on your mind. God grant you may
succeed, but I fear evil will come of it. The Duke
and his brother are too powerful."

"The very reason they should die, my mother. I
shall never be King of France while they live."

"But, Henry," gasps Catherine, trembling from
weakness and excitement, as she clasps her son's hand,
"have you taken measures to assure yourself of the
cities? Have you communicated with the Holy Father?
Do this, do it at once!"

"Madame, good measures have been taken; trouble
not yourself further."

"But, my son," continues Catherine with increasing agitation, "the Cardinal de Guise has been here to visit me; they are full of suspicion. The Cardinal says that I have betrayed them. I replied, 'May I die, my cousin, if I have anything to do with any treason whatever.' My son, I am in great agony," and she groans and turns her eyes glowing with fever full upon him; "do not listen to d'Epernon; let there be peace while I live, and after."

"What!" cries Henry, disengaging himself from her and striding up and down the room. "What! spare, when Guise, triumphant among the citizens of Paris, dared to lay his hand on the hilt of his sword in our very presence at the Louvre! Spare him who drove me a fugitive from the capital! Spare the chief of the League, who, assisted by Spain, is dismembering France! Spare them, when they will both be within this castle to-night, to attend the council! Spare *them* who never spared ME! No, my mother, I will NOT spare them! Your sickness has weakened your courage. 'A nut for a nut' was once your motto. It is mine. If the Balafré and the Cardinal enter these doors to-morrow they shall not go hence alive; they shall die like rebels as they are."

"Alas! my son," says the Queen in a very low voice,—she has fallen back exhausted upon the bed, —"alas! it is easy to cut the thread of life; but once cut, can you mend it? Shed no more blood, Henry, for my sake, for I am dying. Let my last hour be undisturbed. I have much that troubles me," and she heaves a deep sigh. "Too much blood has flowed already. Spare them, Henry, spare them."

"My mother, *you* never spared an enemy when

within your power, nor will I. Either Guise or I must die. You have taught me that all means are good to save the sovereign and support his authority. My brother Charles, by your order, spared not Coligni and massacred the Huguenots at the festival of St. Bartholomew. *I helped him.* The Guises, madame, **must die.**"

"**But, my son,**" replies Catherine, wringing her bony **hands, and** struggling again to raise herself upright, "it **is** sacrilege. You have sworn peace upon the altar; you have eaten together the body of the Lord."

Catherine's voice is so feeble, that the King either does not hear, or does not heed her. He still strides up and down the room, speaking from time to time as if to himself.

"Every **detail is** arranged; **we cannot** fail. To-morrow the guards **within** the **walls will be** doubled; a hundred Swiss will be posted at the entrance in **the** courtyard **and** on the grand staircase. When the Duke arrives, Crillon will see that the outer gates are closed. As soon as Guise enters the council-chamber, I will send for him into my closet. When he has passed **through the guard**-room to **reach** it, Nambre will bar **the door,** that he may not return. My trusty Dalahaide **and the** guards—the 45th—who will be hidden on the secret stair behind **the** arras, will then rush down, fall upon the traitor as **he** passes through the guard-room, and finish him."

Catherine, with haggard eyes, listens breathlessly. **When** the King has ceased speaking and looks round for a reply, she has fainted.

*   *   *   *   *

The next morning the sky was black with clouds. The month was December. It rained violently, and the wind howled round the corners of the château. Catherine, lying in the uneasy slumber of disease, was awakened at eight o'clock by the sound of heavy footsteps overhead. The state apartments are on the second floor, immediately over and corresponding with those of the Queen-mother. They still remain, gloomy and ill-omened, haunted by evil memories. Every plank has its history—each corner a ghastly detail. There is the hidden stair within the wall, concealed by tapestry, where Dalahaide and the guards hid; the door against which the great Balafré fell, stabbed by Malines in the breast, where he was spurned by the heel of the King, as he himself had spurned Coligni, and where he long lay uncovered, until an old carpet was found in which to wrap his corpse.

*   *   *   *   *

Catherine, listening breathlessly, hears the council assembling. Heavy footsteps are passing backwards and forwards through the guard-room overhead to the royal gallery where the council is to meet. Then all is hushed, and the face of the dying queen flushes with hope, and her hands clasp themselves in prayer, if, perchance, at the last moment Henry has relented and listened to her entreaties to spare the Duke.

A moment after a door closes violently. She hears a single footstep—a powerful and firm footstep. It crosses the floor. Then come loud tramplings, as of a rush of armed men, a clash of weapons, a fall as of a heavy body; then a terrible cry—

"A moi, mes amis!—trahison!—à moi, Guise,—je me meurs."

The dying woman knows that all is over; she sinks back on her bed raving in delirium. In a few days she was dead.

CHAPTER XXII.

The Last of the Valois.

WE are at Saint-Cloud. The time, the wars of the League. At the head of the Leaguers is the Duc de Mayenne, only living brother of the Guises. Henry III. commands the royal forces. With him is Henry of Navarre. Since the Queen-mother's death the King of France has become reconciled to his brother-in-law. He shows himself almost a hero. They are both defending the Crown to which Mayenne aspires. Eight months have passed since the murder of the Balafré. That treacherous deed has done the King no good; Mayenne lives to avenge his brother's death, and the Catholic party is still more alienated from the King since he has called a heretic into his councils. The royal troops are lying encamped among the hilly woodlands of the park towards Ville d'Avray and Meudon, then, as now, pleasant to the eye.

On the 1st August, 1589, Henry sat in the long gallery of the palace (until lately lined with pictures and gorgeously decorated), playing at cards with his attendants. He holds himself so upright, that he moves neither his head nor his feet, and his hands as little as possible. A hood hangs upon his shoulders; a little cap, with a flower stuck in it, is placed over one ear; round his neck, suspended by a broad blue ribbon, is a basket of gold wickerwork, full of little puppies.

Monsieur d'O, Seigneur of Fiesnes and Maillebois, first gentleman of the bed-chamber, and Governor of Paris, has been joking him about the predictions of an astrologer, named Osman, who has arrived that evening at Saint-Cloud in company with some noblemen.

"By our Ladye-mother! let us have him in and hear what he can say," cries the King. "These fellows are diverting. I will question him myself."

Osman is sent for; but startled at so sudden and unexpected an interview with the King himself in such a whimsical attire, scarcely knows how to reply to the gibes his Majesty addressed to him.

"Come, come," says the King, "let us hear what you can do. They tell me you draw horoscopes. Let me have a specimen of your skill."

"Sire," replies Osman, somewhat recovered from his confusion, "I will obey you; but, as sure as fate, the heavens this night are unpropitious. The light of the moon is veiled; there are signs of mourning among the stars; lamentations and woe are written in the planets; a great misfortune hangs over you—Beware!"

"By St. Denis!" cries the King, "the fellow is glib enough with his tongue; but tell me, good heathen, are the stars in mourning for a king or for an emperor?"

"Sire, they mourn over the approaching extinction of your race."

"Heaven preserve us!" answers the King, with affected consternation, caressing his puppies. "But tell me now, if you have any knowledge, what do the celestial powers think of those accursed rebels, the Leaguers, and their chief, the Duc de Mayenne? Is that bold traitor in favour among the stars?"

Osman does not at once reply; but, advancing to the window, throws open the sash, and silently observes the heavens.

"Sire, I see one star shining brightly in the firmament."

"Where?" asks the King.

"Just over the Camp of Meudon, where Henry of Navarre lies this night. But look, your Majesty, at that other star there over the woods. It blazes for a moment; and now, see—it falls; it has disappeared behind the palace!"

"By the mother of God," says the King, reddening either with terror or passion; "I have had enough of this gibberish. Hark ye, you wandering Jew! no more of these ugly portents, or, by St. Louis, the guardian of our race, we will hold you warrant for all that may happen to our person."

Osman shrunk back from the window, trembling with fright. He does not wait for permission to depart, but as the King rises to address some gentlemen he glides from the gallery.

"If ever I heard a voice hoarse with blood, it is his," mutters the astrologer, pointing to the King as he crept away. "By the brightness of the celestial bodies, there will be evil this night. I will never draw horoscope more, if to-morrow's sun finds Henry of Valois alive. There is blood on him, but he sees it not. His star has fallen, he beheld it; but he understood not the portent."

As Osman crosses the circular hall opening from the gallery and leading to the principal staircase, he meets the Comte d'Auvergne* conversing with a

* See Note 18.

Dominican monk, whose sinister countenance expressed every evil passion. A crowd of attendants had assembled and are listening to the conversation.

"Good father," says M. d'Auvergne, addressing the Dominican, "you must not, at this late hour, insist on seeing his Majesty; he is engaged."

"But, indeed, monseigneur, I do insist upon seeing him without a moment's delay, and alone. It is on a matter of life and death." The monk's bold words and determined bearing evidently impress M. d'Auvergne in his favour.

"Are you the bearer of any dispatches for his Majesty?" he asks. "Those might be delivered, although his Majesty has just retired and is at this moment in his oratory, busy with his devotions."

As he spoke, d'Auvergne scans him curiously; the monk perceives the look, draws his cowl closer over his face, and withdraws from the full glare of the lights on the staircase.

"I am the bearer of letters of the greatest importance, monseigneur—letters from the President Harlay, now a prisoner of the League; but I am charged to deliver them in person, and into the hand of his Majesty alone. Nor is that all; I have a secret communication to make, which it behoves the King to hear without delay. Good gentlemen," and he faces round to the courtiers who are gathered about him "I pray you, one of you, go to the King and tell him what I say."

"Impossible," replies the Count d'O, who came from the gallery at that moment, and hears the last few words; "impossible. His Majesty is now alone;

I have just left him. He is fatigued, and desired **not** to be disturbed."

"Good God!" cries the monk, clasping his hands, "if I do not see him to-night, I shall never see him."

"And why not, I pray?" asks the Comte d'Auvergne. "Come and sup with my people to-night; and to-morrow, **as early as** you please, I will take **you** to **his** Majesty. **Follow me.**"

"I wash my hands of all the **evil** this delay will cause," exclaims the **monk**, following him reluctantly. **"On** your head be **it,** monseigneur." They quitted the hall together.

All this time Osman had stood near watching them. He had not lost a syllable of the conversation. "Did I not say that there was blood?" he mutters half aloud; "is it not true? The knowledge of it came to me in **a vision.** Now I have read it also in the stars. The **blood** of the King is on that monk. His robes are **spotted** with it. In his hand, while he spoke, there **was a** dagger. None else beheld it; but I saw it, and **the** point streamed with the King's life-blood. Woe! woe! woe! Would that I could speak! Would that they would listen! Before many hours, death will be within **these walls.** Alas! it is given to me to avert it if they **would but** hear me."

The astrologer slowly follows the steps of the Comte d'Auvergne and the Dominican, descending the stairs after them. They enter a suite of rooms on the ground floor of the palace. The monk had now thrown back his cowl and displayed a face yet young, but seamed and wrinkled with deep lines. His eyes are dull and bloodshot; his thin hair scarcely shades his projecting forehead. He stands in the centre of the apartment, silent, sullen, and preoccupied.

"What is your name?" asks the Count sternly, turning towards him.

"Jacques Clément," is the short rejoinder.

"You say you are the bearer of letters to the King?"

"Yes," replies he, "from Monsieur de Brienne and the President Harlay, now both prisoners in the Bastille. There is my passport; you see it is signed by Monsieur de Brienne."

"Show me the President's letter," says d'Auvergne; "his writing is as familiar to me as my own. If you are a spy, you will meet with no mercy here," and he measured him from head to foot with eyes full of doubt and suspicion.

The monk draws forth a parcel of unsealed letters, which the Count reads and examines.

"It is well," he says. "These are proofs that you are a messenger from the King's friends. But how did you, carrying such dangerous credentials, contrive to pass the gates of Paris? Answer me that, my father."

"My habit protected me," replies the monk, devoutly crossing himself, "our Blessed Lady gave me courage and address to escape from those Philistines. Once past the gates, I came here in company with Monsieur de la Guesle's people."

"You say, then, that you will answer with your head that two gates of Paris will open to the King if he advances?"

"I swear before God that this is the truth," replies the monk, again crossing himself; "and my God is not that false one worshipped by the Huguenot dogs under Henry of Navarre, but the true God of the Holy Catholic Church. Let the King trust to his loyal Catholic subjects, and beware of the heretics that are in his council and amongst his troops." And the monk scowls around. His eyes meet those of Osman the astrologer, which are fixed on him with the intensity of a cat ready to spring. Jacques Clément trembles. For an instant his courage forsakes him and he turns pale.

"Well, **father**," says d'Auvergne, laughing, "you are true to your trade—a steady Catholic. We understand; you can smell a heretic a mile off, I'll be sworn."

The monk makes no reply, and to avoid further discussion turns to a table on which supper is spread, and sitting down, begins to eat.

The Attorney-General de la Guesle having been told of the arrival of a mysterious monk, enters the room and confirms what he had said of their meeting outside the gates of Paris.

The Comte d'Auvergne, after scrutinising Jacques Clément for some minutes, turns aside to Monsieur de la Guesle, and whispers—

"I do not know why, but I have a strange suspicion of that fellow. All he says seems fair enough and his papers are properly signed; but there is something about his dark, sinister face and surly answers that alarms me."

Osman, seeing them converse apart, advances eagerly from the bottom of the room, and addresses them in a low voice, "If monseigneur will only listen to me, he will not admit this monk within a hundred miles of his Majesty. The stars, Count, are——"

"Confound the stars!" interrupts Monsieur de la Guesle. "Do you take us for a parcel of fools? Go prate elsewhere."

The noblemen seat themselves at the upper end of the supper-table. The Comte d'Auvergne, Monsieur de la Guesle, and other gentlemen are served by an old valet who, after pouring out the wine all round, stands behind the chair of his master, the Count. His eyes are fixed on Jacques Clément, who had drawn forth from the folds of his sleeve a large dagger with which he cuts up his meat.

"May it please, monseigneur," the valet whispers into the Count's ear, "the reverend father knows how to travel in these stormy times. He has not forgotten to bring a goodly dagger with him; though perhaps the breviary, being less useful, is forgotten."

"Not so, brother," answers the monk who, over-hearing his whisper, draws out a missal from his bosom; "I never travel without the one and the other—defences for the body and the soul—whichever may most need it."

But the garrulous old servant, once set talking, is not to be silenced. He begins a long account, in a low voice, addressed to the Count, of how the monk, on arriving, had entertained him and his fellows in the courtyard with a history of the death of Holofernes the tyrant, by the hands of a Jewish maiden Judith, the saviour of her country.

"A bloody tale, forsooth," says M. de la Guesle, eyeing the monk.

"Ay, blood, blood!" mutters Osman, who is seated

below the salt, next the Comte d'Auvergne. "See you not, my lord," he continues, half aloud to the Count, holding up his hand warningly, "that this monk is a mad fanatic? Admit him to no speech with the King, I entreat you; he is mad, monseigneur."

"Oh," answers the Count, in a low voice, "I will watch over his Majesty. As the bearer of letters of importance I cannot refuse him an audience, but I will answer that no mischief comes of the meeting."

Soon after, supper being ended, the party separates. The monk is conducted to a bed; and Osman, heaving many heavy sighs, retires to the room appropriated to him, where he consults the stars, until the dawn of day obliterates them and ends his labour.

The next day is the 2nd of August, and the King, who has been informed of the arrival of a monk with letters over night, commands his early attendance in his bed-chamber. The Comte d'Auvergne conducts Jacques Clément into the presence of Henry, who sits in an arm-chair, only partially dressed, close to the bed. As the communication is to be private, the King signs to d'Auvergne, Clermont, and the other attendants present, to retire to the farther end of the room; then he stretches out his hand to receive the packet from Jacques Clément, who in presenting it bows his head, and stands motionless, his arms crossed on his breast.

As Henry's attention is absorbed and his eyes are bent upon the page, Jacques Clément suddenly draws out the dagger he carried concealed in his sleeve, springs forward, and plunges it up to the hilt in the King's abdomen.

"Help!" groans the King, with difficulty plucking

out the weapon and flinging it on the floor. "Help! the wretch has stabbed me. I am killed—kill him!"

D'Auvergne rushes forward. The pages and gentlemen in attendance, the guards outside, and Monsieur de la Guesle, who is waiting for an audience, all burst into the room.

The King is lying back in the arm-chair; a pool of blood stains the floor from a deep wound; Jacques Clément still stands immovable before him. Swords flash in the air; some fly to support the dying monarch, some to raise an alarm over the palace; others, transported with fury, fall upon the monk, who offers no resistance. He is speedily dispatched. Osman, hearing the uproar, enters. "What!" cries he, "is the King dead?"

"Not quite," is the reply.

"Who did it?"

"Jacques Clément."

"Sainte Marie!" groans the astrologer, wringing his hands, "If you had listened to me this would never have happened. Did I not say there was blood on that monk? Did I not say that the star of the House of Valois had fallen? Alas! alas! If you had but listened!"

At this moment M. d'O and the Comte d'Auvergne leave the King's room to send for a surgeon.

"Why did you kill the assassin? We might have tortured him, and discovered his accomplices," says M. d'O, while they await the messenger whom they had dispatched.

"I did not kill him," answered the Comte d'Auvergne. "The King was seated when he entered, and, taking the wretch's papers in his hands, was busy reading them. M. Clermont and I were present, but had retired a little to leave his Majesty more at liberty. As he rose from his seat and was addressing the monk, the traitor drew a dagger from his sleeve and plunged it into the King's stomach. The King cried out, "Kill him—he has killed me!" and, drawing forth the dagger from the wound, gave two or three cuts at the assassin, and then fell. We rushed to his aid, and smote the fellow, who was unarmed, right and left. At the noise, the doors burst open, and the gentlemen and pages in their rage finished him with a hundred blows. Seeing that he was dead, I ordered him to be stripped and thrown out of the window, in order to be recognised if possible."

"What does it matter who recognises him?" answers M. d'O. "Have the papers that he showed the King disappeared also?"

Before the Count could reply the surgeon appears. He desires that every one shall be turned out of the King's bedroom whilst he examines him. He pronounces the wound mortal; the dagger was poisoned. Henry, after great anguish, expires in a few hours. The letters were forgeries. The body of Jacques Clément, having first been drawn by four horses through the streets of Saint-Cloud, is burned by the common hangman. He is much lauded, however, at Rome, where Sixtus V. reigns as Pontiff; at Paris his effigy is placed upon the altars beside the Host.

Meanwhile the King of Navarre is within his quarters at Meudon. His minister Sully lodges a little way down the hill, in the house of a man called Sauvat. Sully is just sitting down to supper, when his secretary enters and desires him to go instantly to his master.

Henry of Navarre tells him that an express has arrived from Saint-Cloud, and that the King is already dead, or dying. "Sully," he says, "for what I know, I may be at this very instant King of France. Yet, who will support me? Half my army will desert if Henry be really dead. Not a prince of the blood—not a minister will stand by me. I am here as it were in the midst of an enemy's country, with but a handful of followers. What is to be done?"

"Stay where you are, Sire, is my advice," answers Sully. "If you are indeed now King of France, remain with such as are faithful to you. A monarch should never fly. But let us go to Saint-Cloud and hear the truth."

"That is just what I desire," answers Henry. "We will start as soon as our horses are saddled."

As they enter the gates of Saint-Cloud, a man rushes by them, shouting "The King is dead—the King is dead!" Henry reins up his horse. The Swiss Guard, posted round the château, perceive him. They throw down their arms and cast themselves at his feet. "Sire," they cry, "now you are our King and master, do not forsake us." Biron, the Duc de Bellegarde, the Comte d'O, M. de Châteauvieux, and De Dampierre come up; they all warmly salute Henry as their sovereign.

But the bonfires that already blaze in the streets of Paris at the news of the death of the King, warn Henry of Navarre that he must fight as many battles to gain the Crown as he has already done to secure his personal liberty.

CHAPTER XXIII.

Don Juan.

THE wars of the League rage fiercer than ever. By the death of the last Valois, Henry III., Henry IV., a Bourbon, is King of France.* But **he** is only acknowledged by his Protestant subjects. To the Catholics he is but a rebel, and still only King of Navarre. The Duc de Mayenne (a Guise, brother of the Balafré), subsidised with money and troops by Spain, is the orthodox pretender to the throne. The capital, Paris, is with him. The two Henries, reconciled after the death of Catherine de Medici, encamped with their respective forces at Saint-Cloud, were about to invest the city. But now Henry III. is dead. His successor, Henry of Navarre, weakened in influence, troops, and money, is forced to raise the siege and retire. Henry IV. had at this time but 3,000 troops, while the army of Mayenne numbered 32,000 men. Then came help from England. The victory of Ivry was gained, Henry again invested Paris and encamped on the heights of Montmartre. It was now he uttered that characteristic *mot:* — "I am like the true mother in the judgment of Solomon,—I would rather not have Paris at all than see it torn to pieces."

At this time the fortune of war called the King in many places. He loved an adventurous life. Brave to a fault, he rode hither and thither like a knight-errant, regardless of his personal safety, accompanied only by a few attendants.

Although a warrior and a statesman, Henry was

* See Note 19.

a true child of the mountains. Born under the shadow
of the Pyrenees, he would as soon encamp under a
hedge as lie on a bed of down; would rather eat
dried ham spiced with garlic than **dine** sumptuously
at Jarnet's Palace, at the Marais or at "Le Petit
More," the polite *traiteur* of that day; would quaff the
petit cru of his native grape with more relish than the
costliest wines from the vineyards of Champagne or
Bordeaux. Henry was not born upon the banks of
the Garonne, but a more thorough Gascon never lived,
—his hand upon his sword, his foot in the stirrup,
his gun slung across his shoulder, the first in assault,
the last in retreat, ready to slay the wild boar of his
native forests, or lute in hand to twang a roundelay
in honour of the first Dulcinea he encountered.
Boastful, fearless, capricious; his versatility of accomplishments suited the changing aspects of the times.
He was plain **of** speech, rough in manner—with a
quaint jest alike for friend or foe; irregular in his
habits, eating at no stated times, but when hungry
voraciously devouring everything that pleased him,
especially fruit and oysters; negligent, not to say dirty,
in his person, and smelling strong of garlic. A man
who called a spade a spade, **swore like** a trooper,
and hated the parade of courts; was constant in
friendship, fickle in love, promised anything freely,
especially marriage, to any beauty who caught his eye;
a boon companion among men, a libertine with women,
a story **teller**, cynical in his careless epicureanism, and
so profound a believer in "the way of fate," that reckless of the morrow he extracted all things from the
passing hour.

He is now thirty-three years old, **of** middle height,

broad-shouldered, and coarsely made. His swarthy skin is darkened by constant exposure; he looks battered, wrinkled, and dissipated. His long nose overhangs his grizzly moustache, and a mocking expression lurks in the corners of his mouth. The fire of his eyes is unquenched, and the habit of command is stamped on every motion.

He is with his army at Mantes. It is evening; he is surrounded by a few friends, and from talk of war the conversation turns to women. The Duc de Bellegarde, captain of light horse, the close friend and constant companion of the King, sits beside him. He has a noble presence, is supple, graceful, gentle in speech and generous in nature.

Bellegarde speaks boastingly of the beauty of a certain lady whom he is engaged to marry, Gabrielle d'Estrées, daughter of the Marquis d'Estrées.

"*Cap de Dieu!*" exclaims Henry, after listening to Bellegarde in silence; "I have heard of the lady, one of the daughters of our brave general of artillery, Antoine d'Estrées; but I will back my bewitching Abbess of Montmartre, Marie de Beauvilliers, against your Gabrielle."

"Not if your Majesty saw her, believe me," replies Bellegarde warmly.

"You are a boaster, Bellegarde. You dare not produce your paragon."

"On the contrary, Sire, I only desire that Mademoiselle d'Estrées should be seen, for then alone she can be appreciated."

"Say you so, Bellegarde? That is fair; will you bet a thousand crowns on Gabrielle against Marie?"

"I accept, Sire; but how can we decide?"

"You see the lady. It is easily managed. Do you visit her often?"

"Your Majesty seemingly forgets I am engaged to marry her."

"I understand. Now, Bellegarde, I forbid you, as your sovereign and master, to see this fair lady, except in my company. *Par Dieu!* I will refuse you leave of absence."

Bellegarde's heart misgave him. The King's vehemence alarms him. He saw too late the mistake that he has made.

"Now, Bellegarde, don't look like a doctor of the Sorbonne in a fix; Mademoiselle d'Estrées will not object if I go in your company?"

"Your Majesty must consider that I have no excuse for introducing you," replies he, with some hesitation. "Besides, consider, Sire, the roads are unsafe and skirmishers are abroad."

"Tut! tut! man; when did I ever care for that when a fair lady was in the way? I insist upon going, or you shall not either. Both or none. Listen how it shall be managed. I will disguise myself as—well, let me see—a Spaniard; no one will suspect me in that character. You shall introduce me as an Hidalgo, Don Juan, we will say;" and a wicked leer lights up his countenance. "Don Juan, your prisoner,—taken in a *mêlée*, now on parole; and my poor Chicot* shall go with us, too, for company."

Gabrielle was then living at the paternal Castle of Cœuvres, which stood on a wooded height between Soissons and Laon, with her father and her sisters. She was passionately attached to the seductive Belle-

* See Note 20.

garde, and anticipated their speedy union with all imaginable happiness.

One evening, while she was indulging in those agreeable musings proper to the state called "being in love," Bellegarde was abruptly announced. He was accompanied by two gentlemen: one, short in stature, with a comical expression of countenance, was introduced as Monsieur Chicot; the other, by name "Don Juan," neither tall nor short, but with very broad shoulders, had greyish hair, highly coloured cheeks, a swarthy skin, and was remarkable for a prominent nose and exceedingly audacious eyes.

Gabrielle rose in haste and was about to fling her arms round Bellegarde, but, on seeing his two companions, she drew back, welcoming them all with a more formal courtesy.

Gabrielle was eighteen, tall, slim, and singularly graceful. The severity of her aquiline features was relieved by the bluest eyes and a most delicate pink and white complexion; webs of auburn hair flowed over her shoulders. She cast a curious glance at her lover's singular companions; she was surprised and vexed that Bellegarde had not come alone, and to find him cold and reserved. However, any shortcomings on his part were amply made up by the cordial accolade of the Spanish Don, who extolled her beauty to her face, and, without asking permission, kissed her on the cheek.

Gabrielle's delicacy was hurt at this freedom; she reproached herself for the frankness with which she had received strangers, believing them to be friends of her lover. Casting a helpless glance at him, she looked down, blushed and retreated to a distant part of the room, where she seated herself.

"Pray, madame, excuse our friend," said Chicot, seeing the confusion of Gabrielle at such unexpected familiarity; "he is a Spaniard, only newly arrived in France; he is quite unacquainted with the usages of the country."

"By the mass!" cried Bellegarde, evidently ill at ease, and placing himself in front of his love, "Spaniard, indeed! I, for my part, know no country in the world where gentlemen are permitted, thus uninvited, to salute the ladies—at least, in civilised latitudes. It is well Mademoiselle's father was not present."

His annoyance was, however, quite lost on the Don, who, his eyes fixed in bold admiration on Gabrielle, did not heed it.

"Bellegarde," said Gabrielle, blushing to her forehead, seeing his deeply offended look, "excuse this stranger, I entreat, for my sake; I am sure he meant no offence. Let not the joy I feel at seeing you be overcast by this little occurrence." And she rose, advanced to where he stood, looked fondly at him, and took his hand in both of hers.

This appeal was enough. Bellegarde, though anxious, was no longer angry, and, upon Gabrielle's invitation, the party seated themselves, Gabrielle placing herself beside Bellegarde.

"This gentleman, madame," said Chicot, turning towards Gabrielle, "whose admiration of you has led him to offend, is our prisoner; he surrendered to us yesterday in the _mêlée_ at Marly, and, his ransom paid, to-morrow morning he will start to join the army of the Duke of Parma. Though somewhat hot-headed and wilful he is an excellent soldier; he knows how to behave in the battle-field, if his manners are otherwise too free;" and Chicot turned round his head and winked at Don Juan, who laughed.

"At least, gentlemen, now you are here," said Gabrielle, "by whatever chance—and the chance must be good that brings you to me" (and her blue eyes turned towards Bellegarde)—"you will partake of some refreshment. I beg you to do so in the name of Monsieur de Bellegarde, my affianced husband, my father being absent."

"Fair lady," said the Spaniard, breaking silence for the first time, and speaking in excellent French, "I never before rejoiced so much in being able to understand the French tongue as spoken by your dulcet voice; this is the happiest moment of my life, for it has introduced me to the fairest of your sex. I repeat it deliberately—the fairest of your sex;" and he looked significantly at Bellegarde. "I accept your invitation, readily. Were I fortunate enough to be your prisoner instead of the Captain's, my ransom would never be paid, I warrant."

"*Cap de Dieu!*" exclaimed Chicot, grinning from ear to ear, "the Spanish Dons well merit their reputation for gallantry, but our friend here, Don Juan, outdoes them all, and, indeed, every one of his nation."

"Madame," broke in the Spaniard, very red in the face and speaking with great vehemence, not appearing to hear this remark, and still addressing Gabrielle, on whom his eyes were riveted, "I declare if any one, be he noble or villein, knight or king, dare to say that any woman under God's sun surpasses you in beauty or grace, I declare him to be false and disloyal, and with fitting opportunity I will prove, in more than words, that he lies to the teeth."

"Come, come, my good friend," interrupted Belle-garde, much discomposed, "do not, I beseech you, go into these heroics; you will alarm this lady. If you heat yourself in this way, the night air will give you cold. Besides, remember, Señor, this lady, Mademoi-selle d'Estrées, is my affianced bride, and that certain conditions were made between us before I introduced you, which conditions **you** swore to observe;" and Bellegarde looked reproachfully **at** him.

Don Juan felt the implied reproof, and, for the first time since he had entered, moved his eyes to some other object than the smiling face of Gabrielle.

Her sisters now joined them. Although they much resembled her, and would have been comely in any other company, Gabrielle so far exceeded them as to throw them altogether into the shade. They were both immediately saluted with nearly equal warmth by the Spanish Don, who evidently would not reform his manners in this particular. Like Gabrielle, they were **quite abashed and** retreated to the farther side of the room.

"Let me tell you, ladies," said Chicot, advancing towards them, "if you were to see our friend, Don Juan, in a justaucorps of satin and glittering with gold and precious stones, with a white panache in his velvet cap, you would not think he looked so much amiss. But are you going to give us nothing to eat? What has the Don done that he is to be starved? Though he be a Spaniard, and serves against Henry of

Navarre, he is a Christian, and has a stomach like any other."

On this hint the whole party adjourned to the eating-room. Gabrielle carefully avoided the Don and kept close to Bellegarde, who looked the picture of misery. Her sisters clung to her, Chicot was bursting with ill-suppressed laughter, and the Don was fully occupied in endeavouring to place himself beside Gabrielle, on whom his eyes were again intently fixed. At table, spite of Bellegarde's manœuvres, he contrived to place himself beside her. He eat and drank voraciously; perpetually proposed toasts in Gabrielle's honour, and confused her to such a degree, that she heartily repented having invited him to remain, particularly as the annoyance of Bellegarde did not escape her. In this state of general misunderstanding, the merry Chicot again came to the rescue.

"Let us drink to the health of the King of France and Navarre!" cried he. "Come, Don Juan, forget your politics and join us: here's prosperity and success to our gallant Henry—long may he live!"

"This is a toast we must drink standing and in chorus," said Bellegarde, rising.

The Spaniard smiled.

"But why," observed Gabrielle, "does Don Juan bear arms against the King of France if he is his partisan?"

"Fair lady, your remark is just," replied the Don, "but the fortune of war drives a soldier into many accidents; however, I only wish all France was as much the King's friend as I am."

Chicot now took up a lute which lay near, tried the strings, and in a somewhat cracked voice sang the

following song, wagging his head and winking at the
Spaniard as he did so:—

> "Vive Henri Quatre,
> Vive ce roi vaillant;
> Ce diable à quatre,
> A le triple talent
> De boire et de battre
> Et d'être vert galant."

"Long live the King! Vive Henri Quatre!" was
drunk, with all the honours, in a chorus of applause.
The Spaniard wiped a tear from his eye, and sat down
without speaking.

"*Cap de Dieu!*" cried Chicot, "the right cause will
triumph at last."

"Yes," replied Bellegarde, "sooner or later we
shall see our brave King enter Paris and his noble
palace of the Louvre in state; but meanwhile he must
not fool away his time in follies and amours while
the League is in strength."

"There you speak truth," said Chicot; "he is too
much given to such games; he's a very Sardanapalus:
and," continued he, squinting at the Don with a most
comical expression, "if report speak true, at this very
moment his Majesty is off on some adventure touching **the rival beauty** of certain ladies, to the manifest
neglect of his Crown and the ruin of his affairs."

"Ah!" exclaimed Gabrielle, her eyes sparkling
with enthusiasm, "if some second Agnes Sorel would
but appear, and, making like her a noble use of the
King's love and her influence, incite him to conquer
himself, to forsake all follies, and to devote his great
talents in fighting heart and soul against the rebels
and the League!"

"Alas!" sighed Don Juan, "those **were** the early

ages; such love as that is not to be found now—it is
a dream, a fantasy. Henry will find no Agnes Sorel
in these later days."

"**Say** not so, noble Don," replied Gabrielle; "I for
my part adore the King—I long to know him."

The Spaniard's eyes flashed, and Bellegarde started
visibly.

"Love," continued Gabrielle, flushing with excitement, "love is of all times and of all seasons. True
love is immortal. But I allow that it is rare, though
not impossible, to excite such a passion."

"If it is a science to be learnt, will you teach me,
fair lady?" asked the Spaniard tenderly.

At this turn in the conversation Bellegarde again
became painfully agitated, and the subject dropped.
The Don now addressed his conversation to the sisters
of Gabrielle, and at their request took up the lute and
sang an improvised song with considerable taste, in a
fine manly voice, which gained for him loud applauses
all round. The words were these:

> "Charmante Gabrielle,
> Percé de mille dards,
> Quand la gloire m'appelle
> A la suite de Mars,
> Cruelle départie.
> Que ne suis-je sans vie
> Ou sans amour?"

Gabrielle looked, perhaps, a trifle too much pleased
at the somewhat **free** admiration expressed in these
verses, and spite of Bellegarde, approached the Don
to thank him after he had finished.

"Lady, did my **song** please you?" said he softly,
trying to kiss her hand. "If it had any merit you inspired me."

"Yes," replied she musingly. "You wished just

12*

now you were my prisoner. Had you been, I should long ago have freed you if you had sung to me like that, I am sure."

"And why?" asked he.

"Because you have something in your voice I should have feared to hear too often," said she in a low voice, lest Bellegarde should hear her.

"Then in that case I would always have remained your voluntary captive, *ma belle*."

How long this conversation might have continued authorities do not state; but Bellegarde, now really displeased, approached the whispering pair, giving an indignant glance at Gabrielle and a look full of reproach at the Don.

"Come, come, Don Juan!" said he. "It is time to go. Where are our horses? The day wears on, we shall scarce reach the camp ere sundown."

"*Ventre Saint Gris!*" said the Spaniard, starting, "there is surely no need for such haste."

"Your promise," muttered Bellegarde in his ear.

"Confound you, Bellegarde! You have introduced me into paradise, and now you drag me away just when the breath of heaven is warming me." Don Juan looked broken-hearted at being obliged to leave, and cast the most loving glances towards Gabrielle and her handsome sisters.

"I opine we ought never to have come at all," said Chicot, winking violently and looking at Gabrielle, who with downcast eyes evidently regretted the necessity of the Don's departure.

"*Mère de Dieu!*" muttered the latter to Bellegarde, "you are too hard thus to bind me to my cursed promise."

"Gabrielle," said Bellegarde, drawing her aside, and speaking in a low voice, "one kiss ere I go. You are my beloved—my other self, the soul of my soul. Adieu! This has been a miserable meeting. You have grieved me, love; but perhaps it is my own fault. I ought to have come alone. That Spaniard is disgusting"—Gabrielle turned her head away—"But I will soon **return**. In the meantime, a caution in your ear. **If this same Don** Juan comes again during my absence to pay you a second visit, send him off I charge you, by the love I know you bear me. Give him his *congé* without ceremony; hold no parley, I entreat you; he is a sad good-for-nothing, and would come with no good intentions. I could tell you more. He is—— but next time you shall hear all. Till then, adieu!"

"I will obey you, Bellegarde," replied Gabrielle somewhat coldly; "but the Spaniard seems to me an honest gentleman, and looks born to command."

The whole party then proceeded to the courtyard, where the three horses were waiting.

"Adieu, most adorable Gabrielle!" cried **the** Spaniard, vaulting first into the saddle. "Would to heaven I had never set eyes on you, or that, having seen you, I might gaze to eternity on that heavenly face."

"**Well,**" said Bellegarde gaily, for his spirits rose as he **saw** the Spaniard ready to depart, "you need only wait until peace be made, and then I will present you at Court, Don Juan, where Madame la Duchesse de Bellegarde, otherwise La Belle Gabrielle, will shine fairest of the fair."

"You are not married yet, Duke, however," rejoined the Spaniard, looking back; "and remember, you must

first have his Majesty's leave and license—not always
to be got. Ha, ha, my friend, I have you there!"
laughed the Don. "Adieu, then, once more, most
beautiful ladies, adieu to you all! Bellegarde, *you have
gained your bet.*"

CHAPTER XXIV.
Charmante Gabrielle.

AFTER this meeting Don Juan soon contrived to
return, and the lady, forgetful of her lover's advice,
received him. This was sufficient encouragement for
so audacious a cavalier, and an intimacy sprang up
between them ending in a confession of his being the
King. Gabrielle was charmed, for she had always
been his devoted partisan. What at first appeared
bold and free in his manner she now ascribed to a
proper sense of his own rank, born as he was to command and to be obeyed. Their romantic introduction
and the disguise he had condescended to assume on
that occasion captivated her imagination almost as
much as his unbounded admiration of her person
flattered her vanity. Henry, too, was a fit subject for
devoted loyalty at that time, closely beset as he was
by the troops of the League, unable to enter Paris,
and only maintaining his ground by prodigies of
valour and the most heroic perseverance.

Should she, then, be unkind, and repulse him,
when he vowed to her, on his knees, that his only
happy moments were spent in her society? The image
of Bellegarde grew fainter and fainter; their meetings
became colder and more unsatisfactory. He reproached
her for her unbecoming encouragement of a libertine

monarch; Gabrielle defended herself by declaring that
her heart was her own, and that she might bestow it
where she thought proper. As yet, however, there had
been no formal rupture between them. Bellegarde
loved the fascinating girl too fondly to renounce her
lightly; and she herself, as yet undecided, hesitated
before resigning a man whose attachment was honourable and legitimate, and whose birth and position
were brilliant, to receive the dubious addresses of a
married monarch. True, the shameful excesses of
Marguerite de Valois, his Queen, excused and almost
exonerated the King; Henry urged this circumstance
with passionate eloquence, promising Gabrielle, spite
of state reasons, to marry her as soon as, settled on
the throne, he had leisure legally to prove the scandalous conduct of his wife and to obtain a papal
divorce. This, to a vain and beautiful woman like
Gabrielle, was a telling argument.

Still, Gabrielle had not broken with Bellegarde;
she delighted to irritate the passion of the King by
yet professing some love for her old admirer. At
times she refused to see Henry at all, and actually
went on a visit to her aunt, Madame de Sourdis, without even bidding him adieu. This coquetry made
the King desperate. He was so overcome at her
sudden departure, that he was ready, according to his
habit, to promise anything she asked. The difficulty
was how to reach her, for he must start from Mantes,
at the gravest risk, passing through two outposts and
seven leagues of open country occupied by the League.
But now he was wrought up to such a pass that he
was ready to sacrifice his Crown or his head to win
her. As soon, therefore, as he ascertained that Gabri-

elle had returned to Cœuvres he swore a solemn oath **to** see her or die. The country was covered with troops; alone he dared not venture; with attendants he compromised his beloved. Such obstacles were maddening. At last he decided to set forth on horseback, accompanied only by a few devoted followers. With this escort he rode four leagues through the most dangerous part of the route, then left them at a certain spot to await his return. Towards Cœuvres he wandered on alone until he found a roadside house. There he offered a peasant some gold pieces to lend him a suit of clothes, in order, as he told the man, the more safely to deliver some letters of importance to the Seigneur of Cœuvres. The peasant readily consented to his proposal. In those boisterous days of internecine warfare nothing of this kind caused astonishment, spies, in every species of disguise, continually passing to and fro between the two armies. So Henry IV., in the garb of a peasant, pushed on alone.

The day was fast falling, deep shadows gathered in the forest and around the castle. Gabrielle sat within in the twilight embroidering a scarf. She was thinking over all the difficulties of her position, divided as she was between regard for the generous Bellegarde and her passion each day growing stronger for the King. Suddenly her maid Louise came into the room and begged her, as she had passed all day in the house, to take a little fresh air.

"Come, madame, while there is yet a little light; come, at least, to the balcony that looks out over the terrace, where the breeze is so pleasant, and see the sun set over the tree-tops."

"No, no," replied Gabrielle, shaking her head sadly. "Leave me alone. I have enough to think about, and I want to finish my scarf, or it will not be done by the time I promised Bellegarde. Besides, I do not fancy open balconies in the month of November; it is too cold."

"Oh! but," pleaded Louise, "the day has been so splendid—like summer in the forest. Pray come, madame."

"Why do you plague me so? I never remember your great desire for open air before." And Gabrielle rose. She was no sooner on the balcony, watching the last streaks of golden light glittering among the branches and lighting up the plain beyond in a ruddy mist, than all at once she heard a rustling noise, and on looking down saw, just under the balcony, on the grass-plot, a peasant on a horse, laden with a bundle of straw.

The peasant stopped and gazed at her for some time, then, throwing away the straw, he flung himself from his horse and fell on his knees before her, clasping his hands, as if about to worship at some shrine.

Juliette, Gabrielle's sister, now joined her on the balcony. Readier-witted than she, Juliette whispered—

"Gabrielle, it is the King—he is disguised!"

Louise burst into a loud laugh at their surprise and ran away. It was now apparent why she was so anxious to make Gabrielle go on the balcony to see the sun set. Gabrielle had not dreamt of seeing the King, who was reported to be encamped at some distance. Her first feeling was one of anger for his utter want of dignity. To kneel on the wet grass, and in the dress of a peasant! Besides, this disguise was most unbecoming to him. He looked positively hideous.

Juliette retired, and Gabrielle was left standing alone on the balcony before the King. As yet she had not spoken.

"What! not a word to greet me?" cried Henry, rising. "Why, *vrai Dieu*, many a lady of our Court would have flung herself down headlong to welcome me, and never cared if she broke her neck! Come, *belle des belles*, look down graciously upon your devoted slave, whose only desire is to die at your feet."

"Sire," replied Gabrielle, "for heaven's sake go away. Return to Mantes, and never let me see you again so vilely dressed. Always wear your white panache and your scarlet mantle when you come. Without it you are not Henri Quatre. Better stay away altogether, for you know well your enemies are prowling about in this neighbourhood. Besides, who can tell? Bellegarde may come. Pray, I entreat you, go away directly."

"*Ma foi!*" replied the King, "let them come, Leaguers or Spaniards, Bellegarde or the devil, what care I, if La Belle Gabrielle looks kindly on me? Come down to me, Gabrielle."

"Kind I will certainly not be if your Majesty do not at once depart. Kneeling in that manner is too ridiculous. I will not come down. I shall go away. I am no saint to be prayed to, heaven knows. If your Majesty won't remount, I shall really go away."

"You could not have the heart, Gabrielle," replied

Henry, "when I have run such risks to see you for a moment."

His horse stood by cropping the grass. The King leaving the bundle of straw on the ground, sprang into the saddle without even touching the stirrup, and again addressed her. She was terrified at the idea of being surprised by any one, especially Bellegarde, who would have been so incensed, that he might have forgotten himself towards his Majesty.

For a moment Gabrielle was overcome. Tears came into her eyes out of sheer vexation and fear of consequences, both to him, who might fall into an ambuscade, and to herself. As she lifted up her hands to wipe the tears away, the scarf she had been embroidering, and which she still held, slipped out of her hand, and borne by the wind, after fluttering for a few moments, dropped on the King, who, catching it, exclaimed—

"*Ventre Saint Gris!* what have we here?"

"Oh, Sire!" cried Gabrielle, "it is my work—a scarf; it is all but finished, and now I have dropped it."

"By all the rules of war, fair lady," said Henry, "what falls from the walls of a besieged city belongs to the soldier; so, by your leave, dear Gabrielle, the scarf is mine; I will wear it."

"Oh!" replied she, leaning over the balcony, "do give it me back; it is for Monsieur de Bellegarde, and he knows it. Should he see your Majesty with it, what will he think? He would never believe but that I gave it to you."

"By the mass! it is too good for him; I will keep it without any remorse, and cover with a thousand kisses these stitches woven by your delicate fingers."

"But, indeed, Sire, it is promised—Monsieur de Bellegarde will ask me for it; what am I to say?"

"Bellegarde shall never have it, I promise you. Tell him that, like Penelope, you undid in the night what you worked in the day. Come, come, now, Gabrielle, confess you are not in reality so much attached to Bellegarde as you pretend, and that if I can prove to you he is unworthy of your love and inconstant into the bargain, you will promise to give me his place in your heart. Besides, his position is unworthy of your beauty; there is but one ornament worthy of that snowy brow—Bellegarde cannot place it there; but I know another able and willing, when the cursed League is dispersed, to give that finishing touch to your loveliness."

"Sire," replied she, "I must not listen to what you say. I cannot believe anything against Bellegarde; I have known him all my life, and he has never deceived me. Nothing but the most positive evidence shall convince me that he is false."

"How now? *Saints et Saintes!* you doubt my word —the word of a king! But, Gabrielle, I can give you proofs, be assured."

"Oh, Sire, it is not for me to talk of proofs or to reproach him. Poor Bellegarde! my heart bleeds when I think of him." Her head fell upon her bosom; again the tears gathered in her eyes. Then she looked up, and becoming aware all at once that it had grown quite dusk, she forgot every other feeling in fear for the King's safety. "Sire, go away, I implore you, return to your quarters as fast as your horse can carry you. If I have been cold, remember what you are risking—your life and my good name! for you will be seen by some one."

"Gabrielle, do you drive me away thus, when to leave you costs me such a pang! Heaven knows when this war will allow us again to meet! I never know from day to day but that some rebel of a Leaguer may finish me by a stray shot; much less do I know where or how I may be. The present is all I have—let me enjoy it."

"Ah, Sire! only put down that atrocious League, and we will meet when you please. I shall offer up no end of prayers that it may be so."

"Whatever comes out of those ruby lips will not fail of being heard; as to your slave Henry, the very knowledge that such a divinity stoops to interest herself in his fate will serve as a talisman to shield him from every danger."

"Your Majesty speaks like a poet," and a soft laugh was heard out of the darkness. "Now adieu, Sire! I wish you a safe journey wherever you go, and may you prevail against your foes. When you see Monsieur de Bellegarde, assure him of my love."

"Ungrateful Gabrielle! thus to trifle with me. But I have proofs, *vrai Dieu!* I have proofs that shall cure you of that attachment."

"Sire, why should you seek to make me unhappy? You know that for years I have been engaged to Bellegarde, and that I look forward to my marriage with the utmost delight. Why, then, endeavour to separate us?"

"*Par exemple, ma belle*, you give me credit for being vastly magnanimous, upon my word! What then, Gabrielle, would you have me resign you without a struggle?—nay, am I expected to bring about your marriage with a rival? That is a little too much, forsooth!"

"*Nenni*, Sire; I only ask you **not to** prevent it. Such artifice would be unworthy so generous a monarch to a faithful servant like poor Bellegarde, to whom I am"—and she could not help again laughing, so dismal was the look of the King—"to whom I am bound in all honour. Then there is your Majesty's wife, the Queen of Navarre—for, Sire, you seem to forget that you have a wife."

"Yes, as I have a Crown, which I am never to wear. That infernal Marguerite is keeping her state with a vengeance, and forgetting, *par Dieu, she has a husband*. The people of Usson, in Auvergne, call shame on her; they know what she is better than I do."

"Sire, I beg of you to speak at least with respect of Madame Marguerite de France."

"Why should I not be frank with you, *ma belle*, at least? Ah, *Margot, la reine Margot, à la bonne heure!* I only wish she were in her coffin at Saint-Denis along with her brothers. I shall be quit of a wife altogether until I enter Paris, and then we shall see—we shall see who will be crowned with me. But, *mignonne*, I must indeed bid you adieu. *Morbleu!* my people will think I am lost, and besiege the château. Adieu until I can next come. I will write to you in the meantime. Remember to forget Bellegarde, as you value the favour of your Sovereign."

And kissing the scarf he had stolen from her, the King put spurs to his horse and galloped away into the darkness.

Gabrielle d'Estrées followed his pernicious counsel but too readily, as the sequel will show. Unable to resist the continued blandishments of the King, and silencing her conscience by a belief in his promise of marriage, she sacrificed her lover, the Duc de Belle-garde, sincerely and honourably attached to her for many years and whom she had once really loved, for the sake of the gallant but licentious Henry. She followed the King to Mantes, in company with her father, whom the King made General of Artillery and loaded with honours. After this Henry would not hear of her returning to the Château of Cœuvres, a place, he said, too remote and difficult of access. He finally prevailed on her to accompany him to the camp at Saint-Germain.

The Duc de Bellegarde was banished.

In the autumn she was still at Saint-Germain, where the King, in his brief intervals of leisure, showed more and more delight in her society.

One day he entered Gabrielle's apartment, and dismissing his attendants sank into a chair without saying a word. He heaved a deep sigh. Gabrielle looked up at him, wondering at his silence—she perceived that he was weeping. Surprised at his emotion, she asked him, with an offended air, if the sight of her had caused those tears, for if such were the case she would go back to the Castle of Cœuvres, if it so pleased his Majesty.

"*Mignonne*," replied Henry very gravely, taking her hand and kissing it, "it is indeed you who are partly the cause of my grief, but not because you are here. Seeing you makes me envy the happiness of the poorest peasant in my dominions, living on bread and garlic, who has the woman he loves beside him, and is his own master. I am no king, I am nothing but a miserable slave, jostled between Calvinists and Catholics, who both distrust me."

"Come, come Sire, dismiss these fancies, at least while you are with me," answered she.

"On the contrary, Gabrielle, it is the sight of you that recalls them. You have escaped from the control of a father to live with me, while my chains press about me tighter than ever. I cannot, I dare not break them,—and be wholly yours. You gain and I lose—that is all."

"Sire," said she sadly, "I am not sure of that. Women, I believe, are best in the chains you speak of. I shall **see**. If I have gained, you will keep your promise **to me**. I am not so certain of it; all I know is, whatever has been or is to be, that I love you," and she turned her languishing blue eyes full upon him.

"Gabrielle, I swear I will keep my promise. Does not every act of my life prove my devotion?"

"Well then, Sire, succeed in putting down that odious League, march on Paris, and I shall be happy. To see you crowned and anointed at Rheims I would give my life!"

"Never fear, sweet; this will come about shortly, I am certain. There are, however, more difficulties than you are aware of. If I become a Catholic, as all my nobles wish me to do—and beautiful France is well worth a mass—then the Calvinists will at once reorganise this cursed League; and, if I persist in my faith, which my poor mother reared me up to love sincerely—why then I shall be forsaken by all the Catholics; a fact they take care to remind me of every day of my life. *Vrai Dieu!* I only wish I were once again Prince of Navarre, free and joyous, fighting and hunting, dancing and jousting, without an acre of land, as I was formerly."

"Sire, all will be well; be more sanguine, I entreat you. If my poor words have any power over you," she added encouragingly, "dismiss such gloomy thoughts. Believe me, the future has much in store for you and for me."

"Ah! dear Gabrielle, when I am far away over mountains and valleys, separated from those lovely eyes that now beam so brightly on me, I feel all the torments of jealousy. Away from you, happiness is impossible."

"Well, Sire, if it is only my presence you want, I will follow you to the end of the world—I will go anywhere;" Gabrielle spoke with passionate ardour.

"*Ma mie!* it is this love that alone enables me to bear all the anxieties and troubles that surround me on every side. I value it more than the Crown of France; but this very love of yours, entire as I believe it to be, is the one principal cause of my misery."

"How can that be?" answered she caressingly; "I love you — I will ever be constant, I swear it solemnly, Henry."

"Yes," replied he thoughtfully, "but I have promised you marriage—you must sit beside me as Queen of France. Do you forget that I have the honour of being the husband of a queen—the sister of three defunct monarchs—the most abandoned, the most disgraceful, the most odious——"

"Sire, you need not think about her; you are not

obliged to be a witness of her disorders. Let her
enjoy all her gallantries at the Castle of Usson. You
can easily divorce her when you please——and then
nothing can part us."

"*Ventre Saint Gris!* cursed be **the** demon who
dishonours me by calling herself my wife! that **wretch**
who prevents my marrying the angel whom I love so
entirely—your own sweet self!"

"Henry, my heart at least is yours."

"Yes, dearest; but not more mine than I am yours
eternally—and I would recompense your love as it
deserves. But know, Gabrielle, that Marguerite de
Valois absolutely refuses to consent to a divorce that
I may marry you. She declares she acts in my interests;
but I believe her odious pride is offended at being
succeeded by a gentlewoman of honest and ancient
lineage, a thousand times better than all the Valois
that ever lived, a race born of the devil, I verily believe. I have threatened her with a state trial; the
proofs against her are flagrant. She knows that she
would in that case be either beheaded or imprisoned
for life. Not even that shakes her resolve, so invete-
rate is she against our union."

"Alas! poor lady—did she ever love you?"

"**Not a** whit; she **was false** from the beginning.
Let us speak of her no more," said the King, rising
and walking up and down the room. Then stopping
opposite Gabrielle, who, dismayed at what she heard,
sat with her face buried in her hands, he asked her,
"How about Bellegarde?"

Gabrielle shrank back, then looked up at him.

"Are you sure he is entirely banished from your
remembrance?"

"As much as if I had never known him," replied she promptly.

"I depend upon your pledge of meeting him no more, because, good-natured as I am—and I am good natured, *par Dieu!*—I am somewhat choleric and hot (God pardon me), and if by chance I ever surprised you together, why, *Vrai Dieu*, if I had my sword I might be sorry for the consequences."

"Sire, there is no danger; you may wear your sword for me. If such a thing ever occurred, it is I who would deserve to die."

"Well, *ma mie*, I must draw the trenches nearer the walls of Paris. In my absence remain at Mantes," said Henry. "Then I must advance upon Rouen. I expect a vigorous resistance, and God only knows how it will end. I leave all in your care, and invest you, fair Gabrielle, with the same power as if you were really queen. Would to heaven you were—confound that devil of a Margot! I will return to you as often as I can, and write constantly. Now I must say that sad word, adieu. Adieu! adieu! *ma mie.*"

Gabrielle consoled the King as best she could, and after much ado he took his departure, always repeating, "*adieu, ma mie.*"

After he had passed down the great gallery, Gabrielle rushed to one of the windows overlooking the entrance, to catch the last sight of him. She saw him vault on horseback, and ride down the hill with a brilliant retinue; that excellent creature, Chicot the jester, as faithful as Achates, but whom he had the misfortune soon after to lose, close at his side.

CHAPTER XXV.

Italian Art.

YEARS have passed. The wars of the League are over, and Henry is undisputed master of France. He has proved himself a hero in a hundred battles, but has acquired nothing heroic in his appearance. Still in the prime of life, he has the keenest sense of enjoyment, the warmest heart, the old love of danger and contempt of consequences. His time is divided between hunting in the forest of Fontainebleau and the society of Gabrielle d'Estrées, and her little son Cæsar, created Duc de Vendôme.

• Gabrielle has nominally been married to the Sieur de Liancourt, in accordance with court etiquette, which did not permit a single lady permanently to form part of a Court without a Queen. Henry has been severely commented on for this marriage mockery, for husband and wife parted at the church door. Gabrielle, who has been created Duchesse de Beaufort, is exceedingly unpopular. The divorce from "la reine Margot" is still incomplete, that obstinate princess objecting to conclude the needful formalities on the ground that Gabrielle is not of royal blood. Conquered by her prayers, her sweetness, and her devotion, Henry is still resolved to marry his lovely duchess. In vain he urges, threatens, and storms; the tyrant Queen will not consent. By Gabrielle's advice he has become a Catholic. "Ma Gabrielle," he writes from Paris, "I have yielded to your entreaties. I have spoken to the bishops; on Sunday I make *the perilous leap*. I kiss my angel's hand."

A strong political party opposed the marriage.
Sully was dead against it. Gabrielle, it was argued,
however fascinating and correct in conduct, was no
match for Henry the Great. Besides, as being already
the mother of two children by the King, a disputed
succession would be certain. The Court of Rome had
plans of its own, too, about the King's marriage, and
already the name of Marie de Medici had been mentioned as a fitting consort. The Pontiff himself
favoured the match, and he alone could solve every
difficulty with regard to the divorce. Sully looked
askance at the excessive influence Gabrielle exercised
over his master. The Florentine marriage was approved
by him, and negotiations had already begun. Marie
de Medici fulfilled every requirement. She was young,
beautiful, rich, and allied to the throne of France by
her relative, Catherine de Medici. As long as Gabrielle
lived there was no chance of inducing the King to
consider seriously any other alliance. Must she die?
Poor Gabrielle! there were not wanting foreign noblemen like Maréchal d'Ornano, besides a host of low
Italian usurers and Jews brought to France by Catherine
de Medici—mere mushrooms who had acquired enormous wealth by pillaging the Court—who lent the
King money and pandered to his desires, ready and
willing to forward his marriage with a richly dowered
princess, their countrywoman, even by a crime.

Gabrielle is at Fontainebleau. She expects the
King, who is in Paris. An extraordinary depression,
a foreboding of evil, overwhelms her. She knows but
too well of the powerful party arrayed against her,—
that Sully is her enemy, that the Pope is inflexible
about granting the divorce, even if Marguerite de

Valois should consent, which she will not whilst
Gabrielle lives; she knows that all France is reluctant
to receive her as its queen. But there is the King's
promise of marriage, repeated again and again with
oaths of passionate fondness. Will he keep that promise of marriage? That is the question. She knows
he loves her; but love is but an episode in the
chequered life of a soldier-king. How many others
has he not loved? How many promises of marriage
has he not broken? True, she is always treated as
his wife. She lodges in the apartments assigned to
the Queen of France in the "Oval Court." She is
seated beside him on occasions of state; every favour
she asks is granted, all who recommend themselves to
her intercession are pardoned. The greatest ladies of
the Court — the Duchesse de Guise and her witty
daughter, the Duchesse de Retz, even the austere
Duchesse de Sully—are proud to attend upon her.
Bellegarde, the faithful Bellegarde, restored to favour,
now her devoted servant, watches over her interests
with ceaseless anxiety. Yet her very soul is heavy
within her; her position is intolerable. After all, what
is she but the mistress of the King? She shudders at
the thought.

The season is spring. The trees are green; their
tender foliage but lightly shades the formal walks
ranged round a fountain in a little garden (still remaining) that Henry has made for her under the
palace walls. The fountain, in the centre of a parterre of grass and flowers, catches the rays of the April
sun, glitters for an instant in a flood of rainbow tints,
then falls back in showers of spray into a marble
basin supported by statues.

Gabrielle is dressed in a white robe; the long folds trail upon the ground. Her auburn hair, drawn off her face, is gathered into a coronet of gold; rich lace covers her bosom, and a high ruff rises from her shoulders; on her neck is a string of pearls, to which is attached a miniature of the King. With the years that have passed the bloom of youth is gone; the joyous expression of early days has died out of those soft pleading eyes. Lovely she is still; her complexion is delicately fair, and the pensive look in her face is touching to the last degree. Graceful and gracious as ever, there is a sedate dignity, a tempered reserve in her address, befitting the royal station which awaits her.

She stops, sighs, then listens for the sound of horses' feet. There is not a breath stirring, save the hum of insects about the fountain and the murmur of the breeze among the trees. She takes from her bosom a letter. It is in the King's handwriting and shows manifest signs of having been often handled. She kisses the signature, and reads these words:—

"You conjured me to take with me as much love for you as I know I leave with you for me. Now in two hours after you receive this you shall behold a knight who adores you. People call him King of France and of Navarre, but he calls himself your subject and your slave. No woman can compare to you in judgment or in beauty. I cherish and honour you beyond all earthly things."

A dreamy smile comes over her face. Again she raises her head to listen, and again hears nothing. Wearily she paces round and round the fountain, holding the letter still in her hands. Then she re-enters the palace by an arcaded corridor, and mounting a flight of steps, seats herself in the vestibule to await the King's arrival. At length he enters the court named "The White Horse." Gabrielle is on the terrace to receive him.

"You are late, Sire."

"Yes, sweetheart. I thought I should **never** get here. The Seine was swollen and we had a saucy ferryman. Çome hither, Gabrielle, and I will tell you what he said, while he pulled us across the river. He was a funny rogue."

"Did he **not** know you then, Sire?"

"No. How should he in this grey **doublet and** with only a single gentleman? He asked me if **we** were gallants for the Court. I said Yes, we were bound to Fontainebleau to hunt with the King. 'People say we have a hero for a King,' he said; 'but, *morbleu!* this hero taxes everything. Even the very boat your excellency sits in is taxed. We will pray for him nevertheless; he is an honest King. But it is his mistress, folks say, who wants the money to pay for her fine gauds and dresses. She is but a plain gentlewoman born, after all. If she were a princess now, why then I'd forgive her.' So you see, Gabrielle, when you are a queen, the people will love you and pay the taxes willingly." And Henry laughs and looks at Gabrielle, who has changed colour; but the King does not observe it and continues his story. "'Sirrah,' I said to him, 'you malign a charming lady.' 'Devil take her!' replied the churlish ferryman; 'I wish she were in heaven.' So I rode away without paying my toll. The fellow bellowed after me, and ran, but could not catch me. We will call this *drôle* hither, and divert ourselves with him."

As Henry proceeds with his story, Gabrielle's look of pain has deepened.

"I pray your Majesty to do nothing of the kind," she answers sharply; "I do not love coarse jokes." Henry looks at her with surprise.

"I am wretched enough already, heaven knows, without being mocked by the ribaldry of a low barge-man, who, after all, has reason for what he says. Why did you tell me this story, Henry?" she adds in a plaintive tone, bursting into tears. "Am I not degraded enough already?"

"How, Gabrielle, this from you? when, spite of every obstacle, within a few weeks you will be crowned my queen?"

A knock is now heard at the door, and Sully enters. He looks hot and surly. He barely salutes the King, and scowls at Gabrielle, who instantly retreats to the farther corner of the room. Sully wears a threadbare doublet, his grey hair is uncombed over his forehead, and he carries some papers in his hand.

"Sire," he says, addressing the King abruptly and unfolding these papers, "if you pass this document, you had better declare yourself at once the husband of her grace there, the Duchesse de Beaufort." Sully points at Gabrielle, who cowers in the corner.

Poor Gabrielle is thunderstruck, and trembles at the certainty of a violent scene. She had often had to bear at different times roughness, and even rudeness, from Sully, but such language as this she had never heard. What does it mean?

The King takes the papers in his hand.

"What are these, Sully?" he says, looking grave. "Bills for the entertainment given by the Duchesse de Beaufort for the baptism of my second son, Alexander, son of France, eight thousand francs! Impossible! Baptismal fees for a son of France? There is no son of France. I wish to God there were! What does all this mean, Sully?"

"It means, Sire, that if you sign that paper, I shall leave the Court."

"Come, come, my good Rosny, you forget that the Duchess is present;" and he glances at Gabrielle, who lay back on the arm-chair, weeping bitterly.

"No, Sire; I mean what I say. My advice is disregarded; I am superseded by a council of women;" and he turns fiercely towards the Duchess. "The nation groans under heavy taxes. Complaints reach me from every quarter. What am I to do, if the revenues are squandered like this?"

Gabrielle's sobs had now become audible. Henry, still holding the paper, looks greatly perplexed.

"The amount is certainly enormous. Some enemy of her grace must have done this. Tell me, Gabrielle, you cannot have sanctioned it? There are no 'sons of France.' Say to me, Gabrielle, that you were ignorant of all this."

Gabrielle neither speaks nor moves, save that she shakes with sobs. Sully gazes at her with a cynical air as of a man who would not be deceived.

"You see, Rosny," whispers the King into his ear, "that she does not govern me, much as I love her. You do me wrong to say so." Sully shrugged his shoulders. "No, she shall not control you, who only live for my service. I must make her feel that I am displeased. Speak, Gabrielle," he continues aloud, in a voice which he endeavours to make severe, "speak." Receiving no answer he turns away with affected unconcern. Yet in spite of his words, he glances over his shoulder to watch her. Had Sully not been present, he would have flown to her on the spot and yielded. This Sully well knew; so he did not stir.

There is an awkward pause. Horrible suspicions rush into Gabrielle's mind. That strange story of the ferryman and the taxes; Sully's audacious language; the King's coldness: it could only mean one thing, and as this conviction comes over her, her heart dies within her.

"Sire," she answers at last, suppressing her sobs as she best could and approaching where Henry stood, affecting not to notice her, "I see that you have permitted the Duc de Sully to come here in order to insult me. You want to abandon me, Sire. Say so frankly; it is more worthy of you. But remember that I am not here by my own wish, save for the love I bear you." As she utters these words her voice nearly failed her; but by a strong effort she continues, "No one can feel more forlorn than I do. Your Majesty has promised me marriage against the advice of your ministers. This scene is arranged between you to justify you in breaking your sacred word, else you could never allow the lady whom you design for so high an honour to be thus treated in your very presence."

Henry, placed between Sully and Gabrielle, is both angry and embarrassed. Her bitter words have stung

him to the quick. He knows that she has no cause
to doubt his loyalty.

"*Pardieu*, madame, you have made me a fine
speech. You talk all this nonsense to make me dismiss
Rosny. If I must choose between you, let me tell you,
Duchesse, I can part with you better than with him."
Gabrielle turns very pale, and clings to a chair for
support. "Come, Rosny, we will have a ride in the
forest, and leave the Duchesse to recover her usually
sweet temper;" and without one look at her, Henry
strode towards the door.

These bitter words are more than his gentle mistress
can bear. With a wild scream she rushes forward,
and falls flat upon the floor at the King's feet. Henry,
greatly moved, gathers her up tenderly in his arms.
Even the stern Sully relents. He looks at her sorrowfully, shakes his head, collects his papers, and departs.

The Holy-week is at hand. Gabrielle, who is to
be crowned within a month, is to communicate and
keep her Easter publicly at Paris, while the King
remains at Fontainebleau. An unaccountable terror
of Paris and a longing desire not to leave the King
overwhelm her. Again and again she alters the hour
of her departure. She takes Henry's hand and wanders
with him to the Orangery, to the lake where the carp
are fed, to the fountain garden, and to the Salle de
Diane, which he is building. She cannot tear herself
from him. She speaks much to him of their children,
and commends them again and again to his love.
She adjures him not to forget her during her absence.

"Why! *ma belle des belles!*" exclaims the King, "one
would think you were going round the world; remember,
in ten days I shall join you in Paris, and then my

Gabrielle shall return to Fontainebleau as Queen of France. I have ordered that *bon diable* Zametti, to receive you at Paris as though you were already crowned."

Now Zametti was an Italian Jew from Genoa, who had originally come to France in the household of Catherine de Medici, as her shoemaker. He had served her and all her sons in that capacity, until Henry III., amused by his jests, and perceiving him to be a man of no mean talents, gave him a place in the Customs. Zametti's fortune was made, and he became henceforth usurer and money-lender in chief to the reigning monarch.

"I love not Zametti," replies Gabrielle, shuddering. "I wish I were going to my aunt, Madame de Sourdis, she always gives me good advice. Cannot your Majesty arrange that it should be so still?"

"It is too late, sweetheart. I do not like Madame de Sourdis; she is not a fitting companion for my Gabrielle. Zametti has, by my orders, already prepared his house for your reception, and certain *parures* for your approval; besides, what objection can you have to Zametti, the most courteous and amusing of men?"

"Alas! Henry, I cannot tell; but I dread him. I would I were back again. I feel as though I were entering a tomb. I am haunted by the most dismal fancies."

She drives through the forest accompanied by the King, who rides beside her litter, attended by the Ducs de Retz, Roquelaure, Montbazon, and the Maréchal d'Ornano, to Mélun, where a royal barge awaits her, attended by a flotilla of boats decorated with flags and streamers in the Venetian style. Here they take a tender farewell; again and again Gabrielle throws herself upon the King's neck and whispers through her tears that they will never meet again. Henry laughs, but, seeing her agitation, would have accompanied her and have braved the religious prejudices of the Parisians, had it not been for the entreaties of d'Ornano. Almost by force is he restrained. Gabrielle embarks; he stands watching her as the barge is towed rapidly through the stream; one more longing, lingering look she casts upon him, then disappears from his sight. Downcast and sorrowful the King rides back to Fontainebleau.

All night long Gabrielle is towed up the river. She arrives at Paris in the morning. Zametti, the Italian usurer and jeweller, with a numerous suite of nobles and attendants, is waiting on the quay to receive her. She is carried to Zametti's house or rather palace, for it was a princely abode, near the Arsenal, in the new quarter of Paris then called the Marais.

Here unusual luxuries await her, such as were common only in Italy and among Italian princes: magnificent furniture, embroidered stuffs, delicious perfumes, rich dishes. She rests through the day (the evening having been passed in the company of the Duchesse de Guise and her daughter), and the first night she sleeps well. Next day she rises early and goes to church. Before she leaves the house, Zametti presents her with a highly decorated filigree bottle, containing a strong perfume.

Before the service is over she faints. She is carried back and placed, by her own desire, in Zametti's garden, under a tuft of trees. She calls for refreshments. Again in the garden she sinks back insensible. This time it is very difficult to revive her. When she recovers, she is undressed and orders a litter to be instantly prepared to bear her to her aunt's house, which is situated near Saint-Germain l'Auxerrois, close to the Louvre.

In the meantime her head aches violently, but she is carried to her aunt's, where she is put to bed. Here she lies with her sweet eyes wide open and turned upward, her beautiful face livid, and her mouth distorted. In her anguish she calls incessantly for the King. He cannot come for it is Holy-week, which he must pass out of her company. She tries to write to him, to tell him of her condition. The pen drops from her hand. A letter from him is given her; she cannot read it. Convulsions come on, and she expires insensible.

That she died poisoned is certain. Poisoned either by the subtle perfume in the filigree bottle, or by some highly flavoured dish of Zametti's Italian *cuisine.*

CHAPTER XXVI.

Biron's Treason.

THE scene is again at Fontainebleau. Henry's brow is knit. He is gloomy and sad. With slow steps he quits the palace by the Golden Gate, passes through the parterre garden under the shadow of the lime *berceau* which borders the long façade of the palace, and reaches a pavilion under a grove of trees overlooking the park and the canal. This pavilion is the house he has built for Sully. The statesman is seated writing in an upper chamber overlooking the avenues leading to the forest.

The King enters unannounced; he throws his arms round Sully, then sinks into a chair. Sully looks at him unmoved. He is accustomed to outbreaks of passion and remorse caused by the King's love affairs, and he mentally ascribes his master's present trouble to this cause. "Sully," says Henry, speaking at last, "I am betrayed, betrayed by my dearest friend. *Ventre de ma vie!* Maréchal Biron has conspired against me, with Spain."

"How, Sire?" cries Sully, bounding from his chair; "have you proofs?"

"Ay, Sully, only too complete; his agent and secretary Lafin has confessed everything. Lafin is now at Fontainebleau. I have long doubted the good faith of Biron, but I must now bring myself to hold him as a traitor."

"If your Majesty has sufficient proofs," said Sully, re-seating himself, "have him at once arrested. Allow him no time to communicate with your enemies."

"No, Sully, no; I cannot do that: I must give my old friend a chance. Of his treason, there is, however, no question. He has intrigued for years with the Duke of Savoy and with Spain, giving out as his excuse that the Catholic faith is endangered by my heresy, and that I am a Calvinist. He has entered into a treasonable alliance with Bouillon and d'Auvergne; and worse, oh, far worse than all, during the campaign in Switzerland he commanded the battery of St. Catherine's Fort to be pointed against me.— God knows how I was saved."

"Monstrous!" cries Sully, casting up his hands. "And your Majesty dallies with such a miscreant?"

"Yes, I can make excuses for him. He has been irritated against me by the base insinuations of the Duke of Savoy. Biron is vain, hot-tempered, and credulous. I know every detail. He shall come here to Fontainebleau: I have summoned him. The sight of his old master will melt his heart. He will confide in me; he will confess, and I shall pardon him."

"I trust it may be as your Majesty wishes," answers Sully; "but you are playing a dangerous game, Sire. God help you safe out of it."

Biron, ignorant of the treachery of Lafin, arrives at Fontainebleau. He reckons on the King's ignorance and their old friendship, and trusts to a confident bearing and a bold denial of all charges. They meet —the Maréchal and the King—in the great parterre, where, it being the month of June, sweetly scented herbs and gay flowers fill the diamonded beds—under the lime berceau surrounding the garden. Biron, perfectly composed, makes three low obeisances to the King, then kisses his hand. Henry salutes him. His eyes are moist as he looks at him. "You have done well to confide in me," he says; "I am very glad to see you, Biron," and he passes his arm round the Maréchal's neck, and draws him off to describe to him the many architectural plans he has formed for the embellishment of the château, and to show him the great "gallery of Diana" which is in course of decoration. He hopes that Biron will understand his feelings, and that kindness will tempt him to confess his crime. Biron, however, is convinced that if he braves the matter out, he will escape; he ascribes Henry's

clemency to an infatuated attachment to himself. He
wears an unruffled brow, is cautious and plausible
though somewhat silent, carefully avoids all topics
which might lead to discussion of any matters touching his conduct, and pointedly disregards the hints
thrown out from time to time by the King. Henry
is miserable; he feels he must arrest the Maréchal.
Sully urges him to lose no time. Still his generous
heart longs to save his old friend and companion in
arms.

Towards evening the Court is assembled in the
great saloon. The King is playing a game of primero.
Biron enters. He invites him to join; Biron accepts,
and takes up the cards with apparent unconcern. The
King watches him; is silent and absent, and makes
many mistakes in the game. The clock strikes eleven,
Henry rises, and taking Biron by the arm, leads him
into a small retiring-room or cabinet at the bottom of
the throne-room, now forming part of that large apartment. The King closes the door carefully. His
countenance is darkened by excitement and anxiety.
His manner is so constrained and unnatural that Biron
begins to question himself as to his safety; still he
sees no other resource but to brave his treason out.
"My old companion," says the King, in an unsteady
voice, standing in the centre of the room, "you and I
are countrymen; we have known each other from boyhood. We were playfellows. I was then the poor
Prince de Béarn, and you, Biron, a cadet of Gontaut.
Our fortunes have changed since then. I am a great
king, and you are a Duke and Maréchal of France."
Biron bows; his confident bearing does not fail him.

"Now, Biron," and Henry's good-natured face

grows stern—"I have called you here to say, that if you do not instantly confess the truth (and all the truth, instantly mind), you will repent it bitterly. I was in hopes you would have done so voluntarily, but you have not.—Now I can wait no longer."

"Sire, I have not failed in my duty," replies Biron haughtily; "I have nothing to confess; you do me injustice."

"Alas, my old friend, this denial does not avail you. I know *all!*"—and Henry sighs and fixes his eyes steadfastly upon him. "I conjure you to make a voluntary confession. Spare me the pain of your public trial. I have kept the matter purposely secret. I will not disgrace you, if possible."

"Sire," answers Biron, with a well-simulated air of offended dignity, "I have already said I have nothing to confess. I can only beseech your Majesty to confront me with my accusers."

"That cannot be done without public disgrace—without danger to your life, Maréchal. Come, Biron," he adds, in a softer tone, and turning his eyes upon him where he stands before him, dogged and obstinate; "come, my old friend, believe me, every detail is known to me; your life is in my hand."

"Sire, you will never have any other answer from me. Where are my accusers?"

"Avow all, Biron, fearlessly," continues Henry, in the same tone, as if not hearing him. "Open your heart to me;—I can make allowances for you, perchance many allowances. You have been told lies, you have been sorely tempted. Open your heart,—I will screen you."

"Sire, my heart is true. Remember it was I who

14*

first proclaimed you king, when you had not a dozen
followers at Saint-Cloud," Biron speaks with firmness,
but avoids the piercing glance of the King; "I shall
be happy to answer any questions, but I have nothing
to confess."

"*Ventre Saint Gris!*" cries Henry, reddening, "are
you mad? Confess at once—make haste about it.
If you **do** not, I swear by the crown I wear to convict
you publicly as a felon and a traitor. But I would
save you, Maréchal," adds Henry in an altered voice,
laying his hand upon his **arm**, "God knows I would
save you, if you will let me. *Pardieu!* I will forgive
you all!" he exclaims, **in an outburst** of generous
feeling.

"Sire, **I can** only reply—confront me with my
accusers. I am your Majesty's oldest friend. I have
no desire but the service of your Majesty."

"Would to God it were so!" exclaims the King,
turning upon Biron a look of inexpressible compassion. Then moving towards the door he opens it,
and looks back at Biron, who still stands where he
has left him, with his **arms** crossed, in the centre of
the **room**. "Adieu, *Baron* **de** Biron!"—and the King
emphasises the word "Baron," his original title before
he had received titles and honours—"adieu! I would
have saved you had you let me—your blood be on
your own head." The door closed—Henry was gone.

Biron gave a deep sigh of relief, passed his hand
over his brow, which was moist with perspiration, and
prepared to follow.

As he was passing the threshold, Vitry, the Captain
of the Guard, seized him by the shoulder, and wrenched

his sword from its scabbard. "I arrest you, Duc de Biron!"

Biron staggered, and looked up with astonishment. "This must be some jest, Vitry!"

"No jest, monseigneur. In the King's name, you are my prisoner."

"As a peer of France, I claim my right to speak with his Majesty!" cried Biron loudly. "Lead me to the King!"

"No, Duke; the King is gone—his Majesty refuses to see you again."

Once in the hands of justice, Biron vainly solicited the pardon which Henry would gladly have granted. He was arraigned before the parliament, convicted of treason, and beheaded at the Bastille *privately*, the only favour he could obtain from the master he had betrayed.

* * * * *

The pleasant days are now long past when Henry wandered, disguised as a Spaniard or a peasant, together with Bellegarde and Chicot in search of adventures—when he braved the enemy to meet Gabrielle, and escaped the ambuscades of the League by a miracle. He lives principally at the Louvre, and is always surrounded by a brilliant Court. He has grown clumsy and round-shouldered, and shows much of the Gascon swagger in his gait. He is coarse-featured and red-faced; his hair is white; his nose seems longer —in a word, he is uglier than ever. His manners are rougher, and he is still more free of tongue. There is a senile leer in his eyes, peering from under the tuft of feathers that rests on the brim of his felt hat, as, cane in hand, he passes from group to group of

deeply curtseying beauties in the galleries of the **Louvre.** He has neither the chivalric bearing of Francis I., nor the refined elegance of the Valois princes. Beginning with his first wife, "la reine Margot," the most fascinating, witty, and depraved princess of her day, **his** experience of the sex **has** been various. The only woman who really loved him was poor Gabrielle, and to her alone he had been tolerably constant. Her influence over him was gentle and humane, and, although she sought to legalise their attachment by marriage, **she** was singularly free from pride or personal ambition.

Now she **is** dead. **He** has wedded a new wife, Marie de Medici, whose ample charms and imperious ways are little **to his** taste. "We have married you, Sire," said Sully to him, entering his room one day, bearing the marriage contract in his hand; "you have **only** to affix **your** signature." "Well, well," Henry had replied, "so be it. If the good of France demands it, I will marry." Nevertheless, he had bitten his nails furiously and stamped up and down the room for some hours, like a man possessed. Ever **reckless** of consequences, **he** consoles himself by plunging deeper than ever into a series of intrigues which compromise his dignity and create endless difficulties and dangers.

What complicated matters was his readiness to promise marriage. He would have had more wives than our Henry VIII. could he have made good all his engagements. Gabrielle would have been his queen **in a** few weeks had not the subtle poison of Zametti, **the** Italian usurer, cleared her from the path of the Florentine bride. Even in the short interval between

her death and the landing of Marie de Medici at
Marseilles, he had yielded to the wiles of Henriette
de Balsac d'Entragues, half-sister to the Comte
d'Auvergne, son of Charles IX., and had given her a
formal promise of marriage.

Henriette cared only for the sovereign, not for the
man, who was old enough to be her father. In the
glory of youth and insolence of beauty, stealthy, clever,
and remorseless, a finished coquette and a reckless
intrigante, she allured him into signing a formal contract of marriage, affianced though he was to a powerful princess proposed by the reigning Pontiff, whose
good-will it was important to the King, always a cold
Catholic, to secure.

The new favourite claimed to be of royal blood
through her mother, Marie Touchet, and therefore a
fitting consort for the King. She showed her "marriage lines" to every one—did not hesitate to assert
that she, not Marie de Medici, was the lawful wife;
that the King would shortly acknowledge her as such,
and send the Queen back whence she came, together
with the hated Concini, her chamber-woman and
secretary, along with all the jesters and mountebanks
who had come with her from Italy. Endless complica-
tions ensued with the new Queen. Quarrels, recrimi-
nations, and reproaches ran so high that Marie on
one occasion struck the King in the face. Henry was
disgusted with her ill-temper, but was too generous
either to coerce or to control her. Her Italian con-
fidants, Concini and his wife, however, made capital of
these dissensions to incense Marie violently against
her husband, and at the same time to gain influence
over herself. Henry was watched,—no very difficult

undertaking, as he had assigned a magnificent suite of rooms in the Louvre to his new mistress, between whose apartments and those of the wife there was but a single corridor.

Henriette meanwhile lived with all the pomp of a sovereign; there were feasts at Zametti's, balls, and jousts, and hunting-parties at Saint-Germain and Fontainebleau. Foreign ambassadors and ministers scoured the country after the King; so engaged was he in pleasure and junketing.

CHAPTER XXVII.

A Court Marriage.

THE great gallery of the Louvre is just completed. It is on the first floor, and approached through a circular hall with a fine mosaic floor; it has painted walls and a vaulted ceiling. The gallery is lighted by twelve lofty windows looking towards the quays and the river, which glitters without in the morning sun. Every inch of this sumptuous apartment is painted and laden with gilding; the glittering ceiling rests upon a cornice, where Henry's initials are blended with those of the dead Gabrielle. A crowd of lords-in-waiting and courtiers walk up and down, loll upon settees, or gather in groups within the deep embrasures of the windows, to discuss in low tones the many scandals of the day, as they await his Majesty's lever. Presently Maréchal Bassompierre enters. Bassompierre, the friend and confidant of Henry, as great a libertine as his master, who has left behind him a minute chronicle of his life, is a tall, burly man; his face is bronzed by the long campaigns against the League, and his bearing as he moves up and down, his sword clanging upon the polished floor, has more of the swagger of the camp than the refinement of the Court. He wears the uniform of the Musketeers who guard the person of the King, and on his broad breast is the ribbon of the Order of the "Saint-Esprit." He is joined by the Duc de Roquelaure. Now Roquelaure is an effeminate-looking man, a gossip and a dandy, the retailer of the latest scandal, the block upon which the newest fashions are tried. He wears a doublet of rose-coloured Florence satin quilted with silk, stiff with embroidery and sown with seed-pearls. The sleeves are slashed with cloth of silver; a golden chain, with a huge medallion set in diamonds, hangs round his neck. Placed jauntily over his ear is a velvet cap with a jewelled clasp and white ostrich plume. Broad golden lace borders his hose, and high-heeled Cordovan boots—for he desires to appear tall—of amber leather, with huge golden spurs, complete his attire. Being a man of low stature —a pigmy beside the Marshal—as the sun streams upon him from the broad window-panes, he looks like a gaudy human butterfly.

"Well, Bassompierre," says the Duke eagerly, standing on the points of his toes, "is it true that your marriage with the incomparable Charlotte de Montmorenci is broken off?"

Bassompierre bows his head in silence, and a sorrowful look passes over his jovial face.

"*Pardieu!* Marshal, for a rejected lover you seem well and hearty. Are you going to break your heart, or the Prince of Condé's head—eh, Marshal?"

A malicious twinkle gathers in Roquelaure's eye,

for there is a certain satisfaction to a man of his inches in seeing a giant like Bassompierre unsuccessful.

"Neither, Duke," replies Bassompierre drily. "I shall in this matter, as in all others, submit myself to his Majesty's pleasure."

"Mighty well spoken, Marshal; you are a perfect model of court virtue. But how can a worshipper of 'the great Alexander,' at the court of 'Lutetia,' in the very presence of the divine Millegarde, the superb Dorinda, and all the attendant knights and ladies, tolerate the affront, the dishonour of a public rejection?" And Roquelaure takes out an enamelled snuff-box, taps it, and with a pinch of scented snuff between fingers covered with rings awaits a reply. "Not but that any gentleman," continues he, receiving no answer, "who marries the fair Montmorenci will have perforce to submit to his Majesty's pleasure—eh, Marshal, you understand?" and Roquelaure takes his pinch of snuff and dusts his perfumed beard.

"I cannot allow the lady to be made a subject for idle gossip, Duke," replies Bassompierre, drawing himself up to his full height and eyeing the other grimly. "Although I am not to have the honour of being her husband, her good name is as dear to me as before."

"But, *morbleu!* who blames the lady?"

"Not I—I never blamed a lady in my life, let her do what she may—it is my creed of honour."

"But his Majesty's passion for her is so unconcealed. Perhaps, Marshal, the King understood that this marriage must break up your ancient friendship?"

Bassompierre scowls, but makes no reply.

"The King has grown young again," continues

Roquelaure. "Our **noble** Henri Quatre,—he orders new clothes every day, wears embroidered collars, sleeves of carnation **satin**—(I brought in the mode)" and he glances at his own— "and scents and perfumes his hair and beard. We are to have another tournament to-morrow in honour of the marriage of the Prince de Condé—in reality to show off a suit of armour his Majesty has received from Milan. Will you have the heart to be present, Marshal?"

"**Yes, Duke,** I shall attend his Majesty as usual," replies Bassompierre, turning away with an offended air.

"Come, Marshal, between such old friends as you and I these airs of distance are absurd;" and the Duke lays his hand on the other's arm to detain him. "Own to me honestly that this marriage with the Prince de Condé gives you great concern———"

Bassompierre hangs down his head and plays with his sword-knot. "I should have desired a better husband for her, truly," answers he in a low voice. "The Prince is a shabby fellow, with an evil temper. I fear Mademoiselle de Montmorenci can never affect him," **and a** deep sigh escapes him.

"Never, never," rejoins Roquelaure, looking round to note who arrives, "it is an ill-assorted union. You, Bassompierre, would have loved her well. It was possible she might have reformed your manners. Ha! I have you there, Marshal. Pardon my joke," adds he, as he sees a dark scowl again gathering on the Marshal's face. "But Condé, the *rustre*, he hates women—I never saw him address one in his life; a cold, austere fellow, as solitary as an owl; a miser, and silent too— if he does speak he is rude and ungracious; and with

the temper of a fiend. If he does right, it is only
through obstinacy. I am told he suspects the lady already, and has set spies to watch her. A pretty match
for the fair Montmorenci truly, who has lived with a
sovereign at her feet."

"Duke," cries Bassompierre fiercely, secretly writh-
ing under the Duke's malicious probing of a heart-
wound which still bled, "I have already observed that
any inuendoes touching Mademoiselle de Montmorenci
displease me."

"Inuendoes! why, Marshal, even Condé confessed
the other day that rich as was the prize, and surpassing the lady, he hesitated to accept 'one whom the
King's attention had made so notorious!'"

Bassompierre's eyes flash. He is about to make an
angry rejoinder when a page approaches and summons
them to attend his Majesty.

The marriage between Charlotte de Montmorenci
and the Prince de Condé was, as had been anticipated,
a failure. Condé, devoured by jealousy, shut up his
wife at Chantilly, or at the still more remote Château
of Muret. The petted beauty, accustomed to the incense of a Court and the avowed admiration of an
infatuated sovereign, scolded and wept, but in vain.
The more bitterly they quarrelled, the more deep and
dangerous became Condé's enmity to Henry. Dis-
loyalty was the tradition of his race, rebellious practices
with Spain the habit of his house. We have seen how
a Condé was ready to usurp the throne under pretence
of a Regency, during the conflict with the Huguenots
at Amboise. His son, "the great Condé," is by-and-by
to head the standard of revolt, and at the head of
Spanish troops to bring France to the brink of ruin.

Avarice had led him to accept the hand of Charlotte de Montmorenci—avarice and poverty—and he had counted upon constant espionage and absence from Court as sufficient precautions. But he was young: he had yet to learn the wilfulness of his wife and the audacity of the King. As he gradually discovered that the Princess was neither to be soothed nor coerced, his rage knew no bounds. Sully, seriously alarmed at the rumours that reached him respecting the Prince's language, requested a visit from him at the Arsenal.

Sully is seated in a sombre closet—looking towards the towers of Notre-Dame—at a table covered with papers. Condé is tall, thin, and slightly made. He is singularly ill-favoured, with dark hair and swarthy skin, a nose quite out of proportion with the rest of his face, and a sinister expression in his eyes. On entering he cannot conceal his uneasiness.

"Be seated, monseigneur," says Sully, scanning him from under his heavy eyebrows. "I have no time to spare—therefore I must use plain words. You speak of the King my master in terms that do you little credit. You are playing the devil, Prince. The King's patience is well-nigh exhausted. I am commanded to keep back the payment of the pension you receive to mark his Majesty's displeasure. If this has no effect upon you, other means must be tried."

While Sully speaks, Condé sits opposite to him unmoved, save that his dark face hardens, and he fixes his sullen eyes steadfastly upon Sully.

"If I am what you say," replies he at last doggedly, "if I speak ill of his Majesty, am I not justified? He is determined to ruin me. He persecutes me because

I choose to keep my wife in the country. It is my desire to leave France—then I shall no longer give his Majesty offence."

"Impossible, monseigneur! As a Prince of the blood your place is at Court, beside the Sovereign."

"What! have I not liberty even to visit my own sister, the Princess of Orange, at Breda, in company with the Princess, my wife? That can be no affront to his Majesty. Surely, Monsieur de Sully, you cannot advise the King to refuse so reasonable a request?"

"I shall advise him to refuse it, monseigneur, nevertheless. Persons of your rank cannot leave the kingdom—the very act is treason."

Condé casts up his eyes, and his hands—

"Was ever a man so ill used? My personal liberty denied me! My very allowance stopped!"

"It is said, Prince, that you have plenty of Spanish doubloons at Chantilly," returns Sully significantly.

"It is false—tales to ruin me. Ever since my marriage I have been pursued by informers. It was by his Majesty's command I married. Now he desires to seduce my wife—that is the truth. If I appear ungrateful, there is my reason."

"His Majesty assures me, Prince," breaks in Sully, "that his sentiments towards your illustrious consort are those of a father."

"A father! Why, then, does he come disguised to Chantilly? He has been seen hiding in the woods there and at Muret. A pretty father, indeed! By the grace of God, I will submit to the tyranny of no such a father. It is a thraldom unbecoming my birth, my position, and my honour! While the King acts thus I will not come to Court, to be an object of pity and contempt!"

"You speak of tyranny, Prince, towards yourself. It may be well for your highness to consider, however, that the King, my master, has to a certain extent justified your accusation." Condé looks up at him keenly. "But it is tyranny exercised in your favour, Monsieur le Prince, not to your prejudice."

Sully's eyes are bent upon the Prince. While he speaks a half smile flitters about his mouth.

"I do not understand you, Duke. Explain yourself," replies Condé, with real or affected ignorance; but something in the expression of Sully's face caused him to drop the tone of bravado he had hitherto assumed.

"His Majesty, Prince, has justified your accusation of tyranny by having hitherto insisted, nay even compelled, those about him to acknowledge you—well—*for what you are not!*"

Condé almost bounds from his seat. There was a horrible suspicion that his mother had shortened his father's life, and this suspicion had cast doubts upon his legitimacy.

Sully sits back in his chair, and contemplates Condé at his ease.

"Your highness will, I think, do well for the future to consider how much you owe to his Majesty's bounty in many ways." And these last words are strongly emphasised. Condé is silent. "Again, I say, as your highness is fortunately accepted as a Prince of the blood, you must bear the penalties of this high position."

Condé, who has turned ashy pale, rises with difficulty—he even holds the table for support.

"Have you more to say to me, Duc de Sully, or is our interview ended?"

He speaks in a suppressed voice, and looks care-worn and haggard.

"Monseigneur, I have now only to thank you for the honour you have done me in coming here," replies Sully, rising, a malicious smile upon his face. "I commend to your consideration the remarks I have had the honour to make to you. Believe me, you owe everything to the King, my master."

CHAPTER XXVIII.
The Prediction fulfilled.

HENRY was seated in his closet playing at cards, with Bassompierre, the Comtes de Soissons, Cœuvres, and Monseigneur de Lorraine. It was late, and the game was almost concluded, when Monsieur d'Ellène, a gentleman-in-waiting, entered hurriedly, and whispered something in the King's ear. In an instant Henry's face expressed the utmost consternation. He threw down his cards, clenched his fists with passion, and rose hastily; then, leaning over upon Bassompierre's shoulder, who sat next to him, he said in a low voice—

"Marshal, I am lost. Condé has fled with his wife into the woods. God knows whether he means to murder her, or carry her out of France. Take care of my cards. Go on playing. I must learn more particulars. Do the same, and follow me as soon as you can." And he left the room.

But the sudden change in the King's face and manner had spread alarm in the circle. No one would play any more, and Bassompierre was assailed with eager questions. He was obliged to reply that he believed the Prince de Condé had left France. At this astounding news every tongue was let loose. Bassompierre then retired, and after having made himself master of every particular, joined the King, in order to inform him. Henry listened with horror to Bassompierre's narrative. Meanwhile, late as it was (midnight), he commanded a council of state to be called. The ministers assembled as quickly as was possible. There were present the Chancellor, the President Jeannin, Villeroy, and the Comtes de Cœuvres and de Cremail. Henry hastily seated himself at the top of the table.

"Well, Chancellor, well — you have heard this dreadful news," said he, addressing him. "The poor young Princess! What is your advice? How can we save her?"

Bellièvre, a grave lawyer, looked astounded at the King's vehemence.

"Surely, Sire, you cannot apprehend any personal danger to the illustrious lady?" said he, with hesitation. "The Princesse de Condé is with her husband, he will doubtless act as is fitting."

"*Ventre Saint Gris!*" cried the King, boiling with passion. "I want no comments — the remedy. What is the remedy? How can we rescue her?"

"Well, Sire, if you have reason to misdoubt the good faith of the Prince de Condé, if her highness be in any danger, you must issue edicts, proclaim fines, and denounce all persons who harbour and abet him; but I would advise your Majesty to pause."

Henry turned away with a violent gesture.

"Now, Villeroy, speak. If the Princess is out of the kingdom, what is to be done?"

"Your Majesty can do nothing then but through your ambassadors. Representation must be made to the Court of the country whither the Prince has fled. You must demand the Prince's restitution as a rebel."

The King shrugged his shoulders with infinite disgust. Such slow measures little suited his impetuous humour.

"Now, President Jeannin," said Henry, "let us hear your opinion. These other counsels are too lengthy. God knows what mischief may ere this have happened."

"I advise your Majesty," replied the President, "to send a trusty officer after the Prince and bring him back along with his wife, if within the realm. He is doubtless on his way to Flanders. If he has passed the frontier, the Archduke, who would not willingly offend your Majesty, will, doubtless, dismiss the Prince at your desire."

Henry nodded his head approvingly, and turned quickly round to issue orders at once to follow this advice, which suited the urgency of the case; all at once he remembered that Sully **was** not present, and he hesitated.

"Where is Sully?" cried he.

"Monsieur de Praslin," replied Bassompierre, who had just left him, "has been again dispatched to fetch him from the Arsenal; but he is not yet arrived."

At this moment the door opened, and Sully appeared. It was evident that he was in one of his surliest moods. Henry, preoccupied as he was, observed this, and, fearing some outburst, dismissed the Council and Bassompierre, and carefully shut the door.

"Sully, what am I to do? By the mass! that monster, my nephew, has fled, and carried off my dear Charlotte with him."

This was not, as has been seen, the first time that the grave statesman Sully had been consulted in his master's love affairs. He had passed very many hours in endeavouring to cajole Henriette d'Entragues to give up the fatal marriage contract signed by the King; he had all but quarrelled with his master in opposing his marriage with Gabrielle d'Estrées; and he had been called up in the dead of night to remonstrate with the Queen when, in consequence of a violent quarrel, she had sworn that she would leave the Louvre. Sully, like the King, had grown old, and was tired of acting adviser to a headstrong master, whose youthful follies never seemed to end. Now he gave a grunt of disapproval.

"I am not surprised, Sire. I told you the Prince would go. If he went himself, it was not likely he would leave his wife behind him—was it? That would have been too complaisant in his highness. If you wanted to secure him, you should have shut him up in the Bastille."

"Sully, this raillery is ill-timed. I am distressed beyond all words. The Princess is in an awful predicament. Laperrière's son brought the news. His father was their guide. He left them in the middle of a dismal forest. He shall be paid a mine of gold for his information."

Sully shook his head and cast up his hands.

15*

"God help us!" muttered he.

"Never was anything more dreadful," continued the King. "My beloved Charlotte. was lured from Muret under the pretence of a hunting-party. She was to be carried to the rendezvous in a coach. The dear creature started before daylight, says Laperrière's son, and as the morning broke, found herself in a strange part of the country—in a plain far from the forest. She stopped the coach, and called to Virrey, who rode by the door, and asked him whither they were going? Virrey, confused, said he would ride on and ask the Prince, who was in advance, leading the way, the cowardly scoundrel!" and Henry shook his fist in the air. "My nephew came up, and told her she was on her road to Breda, upon which the sweet soul screamed aloud, says Laperrière, and lamented, entreating to be allowed to return. But that ruffian, Condé, rode off and left her in the middle of the road, bidding the driver push forward. At last they came to Coucy, where they changed horses. Just as they were about again to start the coach broke down."

"Praised be God!" ejaculated **Sully**. "I hope no one was found to mend it."

"Sully, I believe you are without heart or feeling," cried the King reproachfully.

"Not at all Sire; but my heart and my feelings also are with your Majesty, not with the Princess. Proceed, Sire, with this touching narrative."

"Condé then, says Laperrière, the night beginning to fall, purchased a pillion at Coucy, and mounted his wife behind him on horseback." Sully shook with laughter; but fearing to offend his master, suppressed

it as well as he could. "Her two attendants mounted
behind two of the suite, the guides being in advance.
It rained heavily. *Pardieu!* I can hardly bear to speak
of it. My dear Charlotte in such a condition! The
night was dark; but Condé rode on like a devil in-
carnate to Castellin, the first village across the frontier.
When she was taken down, Charlotte fainted." The
tears ran down Henry's cheeks as he said this. "She
fainted; and then Laperrière, convinced of some treason on the part of my nephew, dispatched his son to
tell me these particulars. Now, Sully," and the King
rose suddenly and seized his hand, shaking off the
sorrow that had overcome him during the narrative,
"now tell me, what am I to do? I would lose my
Crown rather than not succour her."

"Do nothing, Sire," replied Sully quietly.

"How, Sully! Do nothing?"

"Yes, Sire; I advise you—I implore you, do nothing. If you leave Condé to himself he will be
laughed at. Even his friends will ridicule his escapade.
In three months he will be back again at Court with
the Princess, ashamed of himself. Meantime Madame
la Princesse will see foreign Courts, acquire the Spanish manner from the Archduchess, and return more
fascinating than ever. On the other hand, if you
pursue him, you will exalt him into a political victim;
all your Majesty's enemies will rally round him."

Excellent advice, which the King was too infatuated to follow! Forgetting all decency, and even
the law of nations, he insisted on punishing Condé as
a rebel, and called on the Spanish Government formally to release the Princess. Spain refused; and this
ridiculous passion may be said to have been the ap-

proximate cause of that formidable alliance against
Spain in which, at the time of his death, Henry was
about to engage.

The favour which Henry had shown his Protestant
subjects had long rankled in the minds of the Catholics. He was held to be a renegade and a traitor. It
was affirmed that his conversion was a sham, to which
he lent himself only the more effectually to advance
the interests of the reformed faith. While he gave
himself up to amorous follies and prepared for foreign
wars, a network of hate, treachery, and fanaticism was
fast closing around him. Enemies and spies filled the
Louvre, and dogged his every movement. Already
the footsteps of the assassin approached.

After the birth of the Dauphin a strong political
party had gathered round Marie de Medici. Her constant dissensions with the King, her bitter complaints,
and the scandal of his private life, afforded sufficient
grounds for elevating her into a kind of martyr.

The intrigues of Concini, whose easy manners,
elegant person, and audacious counsels had raised him
from a low hanger-on at Court into the principal adviser of his royal mistress, gradually contrived to
identify her interests with those of the great feudal
princes, still absolute sovereigns in their own territory.
The maintenance of the Catholic Church against
heresy, and the security of the throne for her son,
were the ostensible motives of this coalition. But the
bond between Marie and her chief supporters, the
powerful Ducs de Bouillon and d'Epernon, was in
reality a common hatred of Henry and a bitter jealousy of Sully, whose clear intellect and firm hand had

directed with such extraordinary sagacity the helm of state throughout Henry's long and stormy reign.

Evil influences, which displayed themselves in predictions, warnings, and prophecies, were abroad. The death of the King would at once raise Marie, as Regent for her son, to sovereign power, and throw the whole control of the State into the hands of her adherents. How far Marie was implicated in the events about to happen can never be known, and whether she listened to the dark hints of her Italian attendants, *that by the King's death alone* she could find relief. But undoubtedly the barbarous cruelty with which Concini and his wife were afterwards murdered by Henry's friends had regard to this suspicion. Whether the Duc d'Epernon knew beforehand of the conspiracy, and insured his master's death by a final thrust when he had already been struck by the assassin, or whether Henriette d'Entragues, out of revenge for the King's passion for the Princesse de Condé, herself instigated Ravaillac to the act, must ever remain a mystery.

Marie de Medici, urged by the Concini, and advised by her friend the Duc d'Epernon, was at this time unceasing in her entreaties to the King to consent to her coronation at Saint-Denis. According to her varying mood she either wept, raved and stamped about the room, or kissed, coaxed, and cajoled him. And there was cause for her pertinacity. Henry's weak compliances with Henriette d'Entragues' pretensions, her residence in the Louvre, and her boastings of that unhappy promise of marriage, had given occasion for questions to arise touching the legitimacy of the Dauphin. Those who were politically opposed to the King would be ready, at any moment after his death, to justify rebellion on the pretence of a prior contract invalidating his present marriage.

Such an idea drove the Queen frantic. There was no peace for Henry until he consented to her coronation. Yet he was strangely reluctant to comply. An unaccountable presentiment of danger connected with that ceremony pursued him. He had never been the same since the loss of the Princesse de Condé. Now he was dull, absent, and indifferent, eat little and slept ill. Nothing interested or pleased him, save the details of his great campaign against Spain, which was about to convulse all Europe.

"Ah, my friend," said he to Sully, "how this ceremony of the coronation distresses me. Whenever I think about it I cannot shake off sinister forebodings. Alas! I fear I shall never live to head my army. I shall die in this city of Paris. I shall never see the Princesse de Condé again. Ah, cursed coronation! I shall die while they are about it. Bassompierre tells me the maypole, which was set up in the court of the Louvre, has just fallen down. It is an evil omen."

"Well, Sire," returned Sully, "postpone the ceremony."

"No, Sully, no; it shall not be said that Henry IV. trembled before an idle prophecy. For twenty years, Sully, I have heard of predictions of my death. After all, nothing will happen to me but what is ordained."

"My God, Sire!" exclaimed Sully, "I never heard your Majesty speak so before. Countermand the coronation, I entreat you. Let the Queen not be crowned at all rather than lose your peace of mind. What does it matter? It is but a woman's whim."

"Ah, Sully, what will my wife say? I dare not

approach her unless I keep **my** word;—her heart is so set upon being crowned."

"Let her say what she pleases, Sire; never heed her. Allow me to persuade her Majesty to postpone the ceremony."

"Try, Sully; try, **if** you please:—**you** will find what the Queen is. **She** will **not consent to** put it off."

The King spoke truly. Marie **de** Medici flew into a violent rage, and positively refused to listen to any postponement whatever. The coronation was fixed to take place on Thursday, the 13th of May.

It is certain that the King was distinctly warned of his approaching death. The very **day** and hour were marked with a cross of blood **in** an almanack sent to him anonymously. A period of six hours on the 14th of May was marked as fatal to him. If he survived that time, on that day—**a** Friday—he was safe. The day named for his death was that preceding the public entry of the Queen into Paris, after her coronation at Saint-Denis. He rose at **six** o'clock in the morning on that day Friday, the 14th of May. On his **way** down-stairs, he was met by the Duc de Vendôme, his son by Gabrielle d'Estrées. Vendôme held in his hand a paper, which he had found lying on **his** table. It was a horoscope, signed by an astrologer called La Brosse, warning the King that the constellation under which he was born threatened him with great danger **on** the 14th of May. "My father," said Vendôme, standing in his path, "do not go abroad; spend this day at home."

"La Brosse, my boy," replied Henry, looking at the paper, "is an old fox. Do you not see that he

wants money? You are a young fool to mind him.
My life is in the hands of God, my son,—I shall live
or die as he pleases,—let me pass."

He heard mass early, and passed the day as usual.
At a quarter to four o'clock in the afternoon he ordered his coach, to visit Sully at the Arsenal, who was
ailing. The streets were much crowded. Paris was
full of strangers, assembled for the coronation, and to
see the spectacle of the Queen's public entry. Stages
and booths blocked up the thoroughfares. Henry was
impatient for the arrival of his coach, and took his
seat in it immediately it arrived. He signed to the Duc
d'Epernon to seat himself at his right hand. De Liancourt and Mirabeau, his lords in waiting, placed themselves opposite to him. The Ducs de Lavardin,
Roquelaure, and Montbazon, and the Marquis de la
Force, took their places on either side. Besides these
noblemen seated inside, a few guards accompanied
him on horseback, but when he reached the hôtel of
the Duc de Longueville, the King stopped and dismissed all his attendants, save those lords in the coach
with him. From the Rue Saint-Honoré, which was
greatly crowded, they entered the Rue de la Ferron-
nière, on the way to the Arsenal. This was a narrow
street, and numbers of wooden stalls (such as are still
seen on the boulevards in Paris) were ranged along a
dead wall, on one of the sides. There was a block
of carts about these booths, and the royal coach was
obliged to draw up close against the dead wall. The
running footmen went forward to clear the road; the
coach halted close to the wall. Ravaillac now slipped
between the wall and the coach, and jumping on one
of the wheels, stabbed the King twice in the breast

and ribs. The knife passed through a shirt of fine
cambric, richly embroidered *à jour*. A third time the
assassin raised his hand to strike, but only ripped up
the sleeve of the Duc de Montbazon's doublet, upon
whom the King had fallen. "I am wounded," gasped
Henry, "but it is nothing—" Then the Duc d'Epernon raised his royal master in his arms. Henry made
a convulsive effort to speak, he was choked by blood,
and fell back lifeless. He was brought back dead to
the Louvre. There he lay in state, clothed in his
coronation robes, the crown upon his head.

The bloody almanack had told true. Henry had
circled twenty times the magic chamber of life!

CHAPTER XXIX.
Louis XIII.

It is related that the night after the assassination
of Henri Quatre by Ravaillac, and while his body lay
in the Louvre, his little son, Louis XIII., screaming
with terror, cried out that he saw the same men who
had murdered his father coming to kill him. Louis was
not to be pacified until he was carried to his mother's
bed, where he passed the rest of the night.

To this infantine terror, this early association with
death and murder, may be traced the strange character of Louis; weak in body and mind, timid, suspicious, melancholy, superstitious, an undutiful son, a bad
husband, and an unworthy king. The fame of his great
father, and the enthusiasm his memory inspired, instead of filling him with emulation, crushed and de-
pressed him. He became a complete "*Roi fainéant*."
His reign was the reign of favourites, and nothing

was heard of the monarch but in connection with them, save that, with a superstition worthy of the Middle Ages, he formally placed France "under the protection of the Virgin."

His early favourite, Albret the Gascon, created Duc de Luynes and Constable of France, was his tyrant. As long as he lived Louis both hated and feared him. He hated his mother, he hated Richelieu, he hated his wife, Anne of Austria. Louis, surnamed "the Just," had a great capacity for hatred.

Poor Anne of Austria, to whom he was married at fifteen, she being the same age, what a lot was hers!

Her personal charms actually revolted the half-educated, awkward boy, whom all the world thought she would govern despotically. He could not help acknowledging her exceeding loveliness; but she was his superior, and he knew it. He shrank back, terrified, at her vivacity and her talents. Her innocent love of amusement jarred against his morbid nature. Melancholy himself, he disliked to see others happy, and from the day of their marriage he lived as much apart from her as state etiquette permitted.

Marie de Medici, ambitious and unprincipled as ever, widened the breach between them. She still sat supreme in the council, and regulated public affairs. Richelieu, her favourite and minister during the Regency, in continual dread of a possible reconciliation between Louis and his wife, and in love with the young Queen himself, was rapidly rising to that dictatorship which he exercised over France and the King until he died. Both he and the Queen-mother roused Louis's jealousy against his wife, and dropped dark hints of danger to his throne, perhaps to his life.

They succeeded only too well; the King and Queen became more and more estranged.

Anne of Austria uttered no complaint. She showed no anger, but her pride was deeply wounded, and amongst her ladies and her friends her joyous raillery did not spare the King. Reports of her flirtations also, as well as of her *bon mots* and her mimicry, heightened by the malice of **those** whose interest it was to keep them asunder, reached Louis, and alienated him more and more. Anne, too young **to** be fully aware of the growing danger of her position, vain of her success, and without either judicious friends or competent advisers, took no steps to reconcile herself to her husband. Coldness and estrangement rapidly grew into downright dislike and animosity; suspicions were exaggerated into certainty, until at last she came to be treated as a conspirator and a criminal.

The age was an age of intrigue, treachery, and rebellion. The growing power of the nobles narrowed the authority of the throne. The incapacity of the King strengthened the pretensions of the princes. Spain, perpetually at war with France, sought its **dis**-memberment by most 'disloyal conspiracies. Every disaffected prince or rebellious noble found a home at the Court of Philip, brother of Anne of Austria.

Thus Louis knew nothing of royalty but its cares and dangers. As a boy, browbeaten and overborne by his mother, when arrived at an age when his own sense and industry might have remedied defects of education, he took it for granted that his ignorance was incapacity, his timidity constitutional deficiency.

A prime minister was absolutely indispensable to such a monarch, and Louis at least showed some dis-

cernment in selecting for that important post the
Bishop of Luçon (Cardinal Richelieu), the protégé of
his mother.

Estranged from his wife, pure in morals, and correct in conduct, Louis, still a mere youth, yearned for
female sympathy. A confidante was as necessary as
a minister—one as immaculate as himself, into whose
ear he could, without fear of scandal, murmur the
griefs and anxieties of his life. Such a woman he
found in Mademoiselle de Hautefort, maid of honour
to the Queen. Her modesty and her silence first attracted him. Her manners were reserved, her speech
soft and gentle. She was naturally of a serious turn
of mind, and had been carefully educated. She took
great apparent interest in all the King said to her.
Her conversation became so agreeable to him, that he
dared by degrees to confide to her his loneliness, his
misery, and even his bodily infirmities, which were
neither few nor slight. This intimacy, to a solitary
young King who longed for affection, yet delicately
shrunk from the slightest semblance of intrigue, was
alluring in the highest degree.

Long, however, ere Louis had favoured her with
his preference she had given her whole heart to her
mistress, Anne of Austria. Every word the King
uttered was immediately repeated to the Queen, with
such comments as caused the liveliest entertainment
to that lovely princess, who treated the *liaison* as an
admirable joke, and entreated her maid of honour to
humour the King to the very utmost, so as to afford
her the greatest possible amount of amusement.

The Court is at Compiègne. Since the days of
Clotaire it has been a favourite hunting-lodge of the

Kings of France. One vast façade stretches along
verdant banks sloping to the river Oise, across which
an ancient bridge (on which Jeanne d'Arc, fighting
against the English, was taken prisoner) leads into the
sunny little town. On the farther side of the château
a magnificent terrace, bordered by canals, links it to
the adjoining forest. So close to this terrace still press
the ancient trees and woodland alleys, backed by rising hills crowned with lofty elms, and broken by deep
hollows where feathery beeches wave, that even to this
day the whole scene faithfully represents an ancient
chase. So immense is the château that the two
Queens, Marie de Medici and Anne of Austria, could
each hold distinct Courts within its walls. Marie, in
the suite called the "Apartments of the Queens-dow-
ager of France," then hung with ancient tapestry and
painted in fresco, looking over the grassy lawns beside the river and the town; Anne, in the stately
rooms towards the forest and the woodland heights.

Within a vaulted room, the walls hung with Cor-
dova leather stamped in patterns of gorgeous colours,
Anne of Austria is seated at her toilette. Before her
is a mirror, framed in lace and ribbons, placed on a
silver table. She wears a long white *peignoir* thrown
over a robe of azure satin. Her luxuriant hair is un-
bound and falls over her shoulders; Doña Estafania,
her Spanish dresser, who has never left her, assisted
by Madame Bertant, combs and perfumes it, drawing
out many curls and ringlets from the waving mass,
which, at a little distance, the morning sunshine turns
into a shower of gold. Around her stand her maids
of honour, Mademoiselles de Guerchy, Saint-Mégrin,
and De Hautefort. The young Queen is that charm-

ing anomaly, a Spanish *blonde*. She has large blue
eyes that can languish or sparkle, entreat or command, pencilled eyebrows, and a mouth full-lipped
and rosy. She has the prominent nose of her family;
her complexion, of the most dazzling fairness, is heightened by rouge. She is not tall, but her royal presence, even in youth, lends height to her figure. When
she smiles her face expresses nothing but innocence
and candour; but she knows how to frown, and to
make others frown also.

There is a stir among the attendants, and the
King enters. He is assiduous in saluting her Majesty
at her lever when Mademoiselle de Hautefort is present.
Louis XIII. has inherited neither the rough though
martial air of his father, nor the beauty of his Italian
mother. His face is long, thin, and sallow; his hair
dark and scanty. He is far from tall, and very slight,
and an indescribable air of melancholy pervades his
whole person. As Louis approaches her, Anne is
placing a diamond pendant in her ear; her hands are
exquisitely white and deliciously shaped, and she loves
to display them. She receives the King, who timidly
advances, with sarcastic smiles and insolent coldness.
While he is actually addressing her, she turns round
to her lady in waiting, the Duchesse de Chevreuse,
who stands behind her chair, holding a hand-mirror
set in gold, whispers in her ear and laughs, then points
with her dainty finger, bright with costly rings, to the
King, who stands before her. Louis blushes, waits
some time for an answer, which she does not vouchsafe
to give; then, greatly embarrassed, retreats into a corner
near the door, and seats himself.

The Duchesse de Chevreuse, the friend and confidante of Anne of Austria, widow of the King's favourite the Duc de Luynes, now a second time Duchess, as wife of Claude Lorraine, Duc de Chevreuse, an adventuress and an *intrigante*, is a gipsy-faced, bewitching woman, dark-skinned, velvet-eyed, and enticing; her cheeks dimpling with smiles, her black eyes dancing with mischief.

The King sits lost in thought, with an anxious and almost tearful expression, gazing fixedly at Mademoiselle de Hautefort who stands behind the Queen's chair among the maids of honour. Suddenly he becomes aware that all eyes are turned upon him. He rises quickly, and makes a sign to Mademoiselle de Hautefort to approach him; but the eyes of the maid of honour are fixed upon the ground. With a nervous glance towards the door, he reseats himself on the edge of his chair. The Queen turns towards him, then to Mademoiselle de Hautefort, and laughs, whilst the maid of honour busies herself with some lace. A moment after she advances towards the Queen, carrying the ruff in her hand which is to encircle her Majesty's neck.

Anne leans back, adjusts the ruff, and whispers to her— "Look, mademoiselle, look at your despairing lover. He longs to go away, but he cannot tear himself from you. I positively admire his courage. Go to him, *ma belle*—he is devouring you with his eyes. Have you no mercy on the anointed King of France?"

Mademoiselle de Hautefort colours, and again turns her eyes to the ground.

"Duchess," continues Anne in a low voice, addressing the Duchesse de Chevreuse, "tell mademoiselle what you would do were you adored by a great king.

Would you refuse to look at him when he stands before you—red, white, smiling, almost weeping, a spectacle of what a fool even a sovereign may make of himself?" And the Queen laughs again softly, and, for an instant, mimics the grotesque expression of the King's face.

"Madame," says Mademoiselle de Hautefort, looking up and speaking gravely, "the opinion of Madame la Duchesse would not influence me. We take different views of life. Your Majesty knows that the King is not my lover, and that I only converse with him out of the duty I owe your Majesty. I beseech you, Madame," adds she in a plaintive voice, "do not laugh at me. My task is difficult enough. I have to amuse a Sovereign who cannot be amused—to feign an interest I do not feel. Her grace the Duchesse de Chevreuse would, I doubt not, know how to turn the confidence with which his Majesty honours me to much better account;" and Mademoiselle de Hautefort glances angrily at the Duchess, who smiles scornfully, and makes her a profound curtsey.

"You say true, mademoiselle," replies she; "I should certainly pay more respect to his Majesty's exalted position, and perhaps I should feel more sympathy for the passion I had inspired. However, you are but a mere girl, new to court life. You will learn in good time, mademoiselle—you will learn."

Mademoiselle de Hautefort, about to make a bitter reply, is interrupted by the Queen.

"Come, *petite sotte*," says Anne, still speaking under her breath, "don't lose your temper. We all worship you as the modern Diana. Venus is not at all in the line of our royal spouse. Look, he can bear it no longer; he has left the room. There he stands in the ante-room, casting one last longing look after you; I see it in the glass. Go, mademoiselle; I dismiss you— go and console his Majesty with your Platonic friendship."

Mademoiselle de Hautefort left the room, and was instantly joined by Louis, who drew her into the embrasure of an oriel window.

CHAPTER XXX.

The Oriel Window.

"You have come at last," said Louis eagerly. "Why would you not look at me? I have suffered tortures; I abhor the Queen's ladies, a set of painted Jezebels, specially the Duchesse de Chevreuse a dangerous intriguer, her Majesty's evil genius. I saw them all mocking me. Why did you not look at me? you knew I came for you," repeated he querulously.

"Surely, Sire, I could not be so presumptuous as to imagine that a visit to her Majesty from her husband concerned me."

"Her husband! would I had never seen her, or her friend the Duchess. They are both—well, I will not say what, certainly spies, spies of Spain. My principles forbid me to associate with such women. You look displeased, mademoiselle—what have I done?"— for Mademoiselle de Hautefort showed by her expression the disapproval she felt at his abuse of the Queen. "It is your purity, your sweetness, that alone make the Court bearable. But you are not looking at me— cruel, selfish girl! would you too forsake me?"

The maid of honour feeling that she must say

16*

something, and assume an interest she did not feel,
looked up into the King's face and smiled. "I am
here, Sire, for your service. I am neither cruel nor
selfish, but I am grieved at the terms in which you
speak of my gracious mistress. Let me pray your
Majesty, most humbly, not to wound me by such
language."

Her look, her manner, softened the irritable Louis.
He took her hand stealthily and kissed it. He gazed
at her pensively for some moments without speaking.

"How beautiful you are, and wise as you are
beautiful!" exclaimed he at length. "I have much
to say to you, but not about my Spanish wife. Let
us not mention her." His eyes were still riveted on
the maid of honour; his lips parted as if to speak,
then he checked himself, but still retained her hand,
which he pressed.

"You hunted yesterday, Sire," said she, confused
at the King's silence and steadfast gaze; "what number
of stags did you kill? I was not present at the *curée*."
She gently withdrew her hand from the King's grasp.

"I did not hunt yesterday; I was ill," replied Louis.
"I am ill, very ill."

This allusion to his health instantly changed the
current of his thoughts, for Louis was a complete
valetudinarian. He became suddenly moody, and sank
heavily into a seat placed behind a curtain, the thick
folds of which concealed both him and the maid of
honour.

"I am harassed, sick to death of everything. I
should die but for you. I can open my heart to you."
And then suddenly becoming conscious that Mademoiselle de Hautefort still stood before him, he drew

a chair close to his side, on which he desired her to seat herself.

Mademoiselle de Hautefort, knowing well that the King would now go on talking to her for a long time, assumed an attitude of pleased attention. Louis looked pale and haggard. His sallow cheeks were shrunk, his large eyes hollow. As he spoke a hectic flush went and came upon his face.

"Will you not let me take your hand, mademoiselle?" said he timidly. "I feel I could talk much better if I did, and I have much to say to you."

She reluctantly placed her hand in his. The King sighed deeply.

"What is the matter, Sire?"

"Ah, that is the question! I long to tell you. I sigh because I am weary of my life. My mother, who still calls herself Regent, and pretends to govern the kingdom, quarrels perpetually with Richelieu. The council is distracted by her violence and ill-temper; affairs of state are neglected. She reproaches Richelieu publicly for his ingratitude, as she calls it, because he will not support her authority rather than the good of the kingdom. The Duc d'Epernon supports her. He is as imperious as she is. Her ambition embitters my life, as it embittered that of my great father."

"Oh, Sire, remember that the Queen-dowager of France is your mother. Besides, Richelieu owes everything to her favour. Had it not been for her he would have remained an obscure bishop at Luçon all his life. She placed him at Court."

"Yes, and he shall stay there. *Par Dieu!* he shall stay there. If any one goes it shall be my mother. I

feel I myself have no capacity for governing; I shrink
from the tremendous responsibility; but I am better
able to undertake it than the Queen-mother. Her
love of power is so excessive she would sacrifice me
and every one else to keep it—she and the Duc
d'Epernon," he added bitterly. "Richelieu is an able
minister. He is ambitious, I know, but I am safe in
his hands. He can carry out no measures of reform,
he cannot maintain the dignity of the Crown, if he is
for ever interfered with by a fractious woman,—vain,
capricious, incompetent."

"Oh, Sire!" and Mademoiselle de Hautefort held
up her hands to stop him.

"It is true, madame. Did not the Queen-mother
and her creatures, the Concini and the Duc d'Epernon, all but plunge France into civil war during her
regency? She was nigh being deposed, and I with
her. What a life I led until De Luynes rescued me!
He presumed upon my favour, *le fripon*, and brought
boat-loads of Gascon cousins to Court from Guienne.
I never knew a man have so many cousins! They came
in shoals, and never one of them with a silken cloak
to his back—a beggarly lot!"

"But, Sire," said Mademoiselle de Hautefort, sitting upright in her chair, and trying to fix the King's
wandering mind, "why do you need either her
Majesty the Queen-mother or the Cardinal de Richelieu? Depend on no one. Govern for yourself,
Sire."

"Impossible, impossible. I am too weak. I have
no capacity. I have none of my great father's genius."
And the King lifted his feathered hat reverently from
his head each time he named his father. "Richelieu

rules for me. He has intellect. He will maintain the honour of France. The nation is safe in his hands. As for me, I am tyrannized over by my mother, laughed at by my Spanish wife, and betrayed by my own brother. I am not fit to reign. Every one despises me—except you." And the King turned with an appealing look towards Mademoiselle de Hautefort. "You, I hope, at least, understand me. You do me justice."

There was a melting expression in the King's eyes which she had never seen before. It alarmed her. She felt that her only excuse for the treacherous part she was acting was in the perfect innocence of their relations. A visible tremor passed over her. She blushed violently, a look of pain came into her face, and her eyes fell before his gaze.

"You do not speak? Have I offended you?" cried Louis, much excited. "What have I said? Oh, mademoiselle, do not lose your sympathy for me, else I shall die! I know I am unworthy of your notice; but —see how I trust you. The hours I spend in your society give me the only happiness I enjoy. Pity, pity the King of France, who craves your help, who implores your sympathy!"

Mademoiselle de Hautefort, speaking in her usual quiet manner, entreated him to be calm.

"Am I forgiven?" said he in a faltering voice, looking the picture of despair. "Will you still trust me?"

"Yes, yes, Sire. I am ashamed to answer such a question. Your Majesty has given me no offence."

Louis reseated himself.

"It is to prepare you for an unexpected event that

I wish to talk to you. It is possible I may shortly leave Compiègne suddenly and secretly. I must tear myself away from you for a while."

"Leave the Court, Sire! What do you mean?"

"The quarrels between my mother and Richelieu are more than I can endure. They must end. One must go—I will not say which. You can guess. I am assured by Richelieu, who has information from all parts of France, that her Majesty is hated by the people. She is suspected of a knowledge of my great father's death; she has abused her position. No one feels any interest in her fate."

"But, surely, your Majesty feels no pleasure in knowing that it is so, even if it be true, which I much doubt."

"Well, her Majesty has deserved little favour of me," replied he with indifference. "Richelieu tells me that her exile would be a popular act——"

"Her exile, Sire! You surely do not contemplate the exile of your own mother?"

"Possibly not—possibly not; but a sovereign must be advised by his ministers. It is indispensable to the prosperity of the State."

Mademoiselle de Hautefort was silent, but something of the contempt she felt might have been seen in her expressive eyes.

"I do not feel disposed," continued he, "to face the anger of the Queen-mother when she hears my determination. She would use violent language to me that might make me forget I am her son. Richelieu must break it to her. He can do it while I am away. Agitation injures my health, it deranges my digestion. I have enough to bear

from my wife, from whom it is not so easy to
escape——"

Again he stopped abruptly, as if he were about to
say more than he intended.

Mademoiselle de Hautefort, ever on the look out
for all that concerned her mistress the Queen, glanced
at him with sudden curiosity. Her eyes read his
thoughts.

"Your Majesty is concealing something from me?"
she said.

"Well, yes,"—and he hesitated—"it is a subject
too delicate to mention."

"Have you, then, withdrawn your confidence
from me, Sire?" asked she, affecting the deepest
concern.

"No, no—never. I tell you everything—yet, I
blush to allude to such a subject."

"What subject, Sire? Does it concern her Majesty?"

"By heaven it does!" cried the King, with unwonted excitement, a look of rage on his face. "It is
said——" and he stopped, and looked round suspiciously,
and became crimson. "Not here—not here," he muttered,
rising. "I cannot speak of it here. It is too public.
Come with me into this closet."

Mademoiselle de Hautefort, foreboding some misfortune to the Queen, followed him, trembling in every
limb, into a small retiring-closet opening from the
gallery where they had been seated. He drew her
close to the window, glanced cautiously around, and
placed his hand on her arm.

"It is said,"—he spoke in a low voice—"it is said
—and appearances confirm it—that"—and he stooped,

and whispered some words into Mademoiselle de
Hautefort's ear, who started back with horror. "If
it be so," he added coolly, "I shall crave a dispensation from the Pope, and send the Queen back to
Madrid."

"For shame, Sire! you are deceived," cried Mademoiselle de Hautefort, an expression of mingled disgust, anger, and terror on her face. She could hardly
bring herself to act out the part imposed upon her for
the Queen's sake. She longed to overwhelm the un-
manly Louis with her indignation; but she controlled
her feelings. "On my honour, Sire," said she firmly,
"they do but converse as friends. For the truth of
this I wager my life—my salvation."

"Nothing of the kind," insisted Louis doggedly.
"It is your exalted virtue that blinds you to their
wickedness. My mother, who hates me — even
my mother pities me; she believes in the Queen's
guilt."

"Sire," broke in the maid of honour impetuously,
her black eyes full of indignation, "I have already
told you I will not hear my royal mistress slandered;
this is a foul slander. To me she is as sacred
as your Majesty, who are an anointed king."
Louis passed his hand over his brow, and mused in
silence. "I beseech you, Sire, listen to me," continued
she, seeing his irresolution. "I speak the truth; before God I speak the truth!" Louis looked fixedly at
her. Her vehemence impressed, if it did not convince
him. "Your Majesty needs not the counsel of the
Queen-mother in affairs of state; do not trust her, or
any one else, in matters touching the honour of your
consort." And she raised her eyes, and looked boldly

at him. "Promise me, Sire, to dismiss this foul tale
from your mind."

"All your words are precious, mademoiselle," replied Louis evasively, and he caught her hand and
kissed it with fervour.

Mademoiselle de Hautefort dared not press him
further. She withdrew her hand. They were both
silent, and stood opposite to each other. As Louis
gazed into her eyes, still sparkling with indignation,
his anger melted away.

"When I am gone, mademoiselle," said he tenderly, "do not forget me. You are my only friend.
I will watch over you, though absent. Here is a piece
of gold, pure and unalloyed as are my feelings towards you," and he disengaged from his neck a medallion delicately chased. "See, I have broken it. One
half I will keep; the other shall rest in your bosom;"
and he pressed it to his lips, and placed it in Mademoiselle de Hautefort's hands. "As long as you hold
that piece of gold without the other half, know that
as the token is divided between us, so is my heart—
the better half with you."

Her conscience smote her as she received this
pledge. Louis had such perfect faith in her integrity,
she almost repented that her duty to the Queen forced
her to deceive him.

"Your Majesty overwhelms me," said she, making
a deep reverence.

"The Court is full of intrigues," continued Louis.
"I have no wish to control my minister; but remember this—obey no order, defy all commands, that are
delivered to you without that token." The maid of
honour bowed her head. A tear stole down her

cheek; the King's simplicity touched her in spite of herself. "Adieu, mademoiselle," said he, "my best, my only friend. I humbly crave your pardon for aught I may have said or done to wound your delicacy. We will meet at Saint-Germain: then, perhaps, you will fear me less. We will meet at Saint-Germain."

He hesitated, and approached dangerously near to the handsome maid of honour, whose confusion made her all the more attractive. As he approached, she retreated.

Suddenly the curtain was drawn aside, and a page entered the closet, and announced—

"The Queen-dowager, who demands instant admittance to her son, the King."

Mademoiselle de Hautefort disappeared in an instant through a door concealed in the arras. The King, pale as death, put his hand to his heart, sank into a chair, and awaited the arrival of his mother.

CHAPTER XXXI.

An Ominous Interview.

Louis had not long to wait, scarcely a moment passed before Marie de Medici appeared. She entered hastily; marks of violent agitation were on her countenance; her brows were knit; her eyes flashed. She was in the prime of middle life, but grown stout and unwieldy; her delicate complexion had become red and coarse, and her voice was loud and harsh; but her height, and the long habit of almost absolute command, gave her still an imposing presence. Louis involuntarily shuddered at her approach; he had been long accustomed to tremble at her frown. His first impulse was to fly by the same door through which Mademoiselle de Hautefort had vanished. He rose, however, bowed low before her, and offered her a seat.

"My son," she cried in a husky voice, walking straight up to him, "I have come to request you instantly to banish Richelieu. If you do not, I shall return to Florence. The insolence of that villain whom I have made your minister is intolerable. He has disobeyed my express commands!"

"What has Richelieu done, Madame?"

"Is it not enough that I, your mother, who have governed France almost from your birth, should declare to you my pleasure? Would you prefer a lackey to your own mother?* Let it suffice that Richelieu has offended me past forgiveness. Sit down, my son" —and she seized on the terrified Louis, and almost forced him into a chair beside the table—"here are my tablets; write instantly an order that within twenty-four hours Richelieu leaves France for ever."

Louis took the tablets, but his trembling hands could not hold them. The jewelled leaves of ivory, set in gold, fell on the ground with a crash. There was a pause.

"What! Louis, you hesitate to obey me?" and the Queen's fierce eyes darted a look of fury at the King, whose slender figure positively seemed to shrink as she laid her hand upon him.

"My mother," he said, in a faltering voice, "you have told me nothing. A great minister like Richelieu cannot be dismissed on the instant."

"Yes, he can, if there be another to replace him,

* Words used by Marie de Medici to Louis XIII.

a better than he; one who knows the respect due to the Queen-dowager of France, the widow of Henry the Great, your mother, and still Regent of the kingdom."

"But, Madame, what has Richelieu done to offend you?" and the King had the courage to meet his mother's glance unmoved.

"He has dared to disobey my positive orders. I had appointed the Duc d'Epernon governor of Poitiers. He has placed there a creature of his own. After this insult, you will understand, I can never again sit at the council with Richelieu."

"Well, Madame, and suppose you do not!" rejoined the King, whose nervous dread was rapidly giving place to resentment at his mother's arrogance. "I shall be still King of France, and Richelieu will be my minister."

"Undutiful boy!" exclaimed Marie de Medici, and she raised her hand as if to strike him; "you forget yourself."

"No, Madame, it is you who forget that, if I am your son, I am also your king. You may strike me, if you please, Madame," added he in a lower voice, "but I will not sign the exile of Richelieu." The countenance of Louis darkened with growing passion; the threatening aspect of his mother standing before him with upraised arm, roused him to unwonted courage. "I will not exile Richelieu. I leave him to settle his differences with you and your favourites— their claims do not concern me. I will have no more *Concini*, madame; I would rather abdicate at once." And turning on his heel, without another word, or even saluting the Queen, he left the room.

A sudden dizziness, an overwhelming conviction of something new and strange in her position, sobered the passion of Marie de Medici the instant the King was gone. She stood motionless where he had left her, save that her uplifted arm dropped to her side. A mournful look—the shadow of coming misfortunes—clouded her face. Silent and dejected, the tears streaming from her eyes, she withdrew. When she had reached her own apartments, she commanded that no one should be admitted.

That same day the King left Compiègne, taking with him only two attendants. No one knew whither he was gone.

Early the next morning the Queen-mother's ladies were startled by the appearance of Cardinal Richelieu in her ante-room. It was long since he, who was wont never to be absent from her service, had been seen there.

"Tell her Majesty," he said to the Duchesse d'Epernon, "that I am come on urgent state business, by the express command of the King, and that I must speak with her in person."

After some delay he was admitted into the Queen's apartment.

Marie de Medici wears a long robe of black velvet, and a widow's coif upon her head. She looks old, worn, and anxious; she is neither imperious nor angry. She begins to realise that power is passing from her; she is intensely curious, not to say alarmed, as to what the intelligence may be, of which the Cardinal is the bearer; and she now secretly repents that she has quarrelled with him.

The Cardinal wears a close-fitting black *soutane* bound with purple, and a *beretta* of the same colour on his head; he has nothing of the churchman in his appearance. He is still a young man, upright in figure and easy in manner, attractions which he owes to his early military training. He has piercing black eyes, light brown hair that lies straight upon his fore-head, and a pale, thoughtful face, already lined with wrinkles. His closely shutting mouth, thin-lipped and stern, expresses inflexible determination. His manners are composed, almost gentle; his voice melodious. He has not yet become the imperious autocrat—the merci-less butcher of the chivalrous nobles of France—of after years. Chalais and Montmorenci have not yet fallen by his order on the scaffold; and Cinq-Mars is a precocious lad, living with his mother on the banks of the Loire. Without vanity he knows that he has genius to conceive great deeds, and industry to ela-borate every necessary detail. Already the conscious-ness of growing greatness forces itself upon him. The incompetence of the King, his indolent acquiescence in all his measures, the jealousy between Louis and his mother whom the King has hitherto not dared to check, his alienation from the young Queen his wife, open before Richelieu's mental vision a vista of al-most boundless power. Now he stands in the presence of his early benefactress, the sovereign to whom he would have been faithful, had such fidelity been con-sistent with the welfare of France and his own ambi-tion. Spite of habitual self-control, he is greatly moved at her forlorn condition. He still hopes that he may save her from an overwhelming calamity.

Richelieu advances to where the Queen-mother is

seated beside the hearth, and after making a profound obeisance waits for her to address him.

"You bear to me a message from my son. What can he have to say to me, that he cannot speak himself?" Marie asks with dignity.

"Nothing, my most gracious mistress," replies Richelieu, almost submissively, "if your Majesty will deign to be guided by my counsel."

"You call me your mistress, Cardinal," says Marie bitterly; "but you have left my service, and you disobey my positive commands. How can I treat with such a hypocrite?"

"Madame, I beseech you, let not personal animosity towards myself—be I innocent or guilty of what you accuse me—blind you to the danger in which you now stand."

"Danger! What do you mean? To what danger do you allude?"

"The danger that threatens you, Madame, in the displeasure of his Majesty."

"Ah, I perceive. My son strikes through you, my creature, that he may crush me. I congratulate your eminence on your triumphant ingratitude."

"Madame," and the Cardinal wrings his hands and advances a step or two nearer the Queen with an air of earnest entreaty, "hear me, I implore you. Let us not lose precious time in mere words. I have come here in a twofold character, as your friend and as minister of state. Permit me first to address you as the former, Madame, your counsellor and your sincere friend." As he speaks his voice trembles, his manner is almost humble as he seeks to allay the stormy passions that gather on the brow of his royal mistress.

Marie de Medici is so much taken aback at this unusual display of feeling in the stern Cardinal, that though her eyes glisten with anger she makes no reply.

"Your Majesty, in honour and greatness," continues Richelieu, "stands next to the throne. Be satisfied, Madame, with the second place in the kingdom. Your own age, Madame"—Marie starts—"and the increased experience of his Majesty, justify you in committing the reins of government into his hands and into the hands of such ministers as he may appoint."

"Yourself, for instance," breaks in Marie bitterly.

"Madame, I implore you, by the respect and the affection I bear you, not to interrupt me. Withdraw, graciously and cheerfully, from all interference with state affairs. Resign your place at the council. Dismiss those nobles who, by their rebellious conduct, excite his Majesty's displeasure, specially the Duc d'Epernon."

"Never!" exclaims Marie passionately. "I will not resign my place at the council, nor will I sacrifice my supporter, the Duc d'Epernon. My son is incapable of governing. He has ever been the tool of those about him. I am his best substitute. This is a miserable plot by which you basely seek to disgrace me by my own act—to rise by my fall."

"Oh, Madame, to whom I owe so much," pleads Richelieu, "whom I would now serve while I can, hear me. I speak from my heart—I speak for the last time. Be warned, I beseech you." His hands are still clasped, his voice falters, tears flow down his cheeks. Any one less obstinately blind than the Queen would have been warned by the evidence of such unusual emotion in a man ordinarily so cold and impassible as the Cardinal.

"Ha, ha, you are an admirable actor, Cardinal!" cries she. "But what if I refuse to listen to a traitor? Who named me* 'Mother of the kingdom?' Who vowed to me 'that the purple with which I invested him would be a solemn pledge of his willingness to shed his blood in my service?' I know you, Armand de Plessis."

For some minutes neither utters a word. When he addresses the Queen again, Richelieu has mastered his feelings and speaks with calmness, but his looks express the profoundest pity.

"I am no traitor, Madame, but the unwilling bearer of a decision that will infinitely pain you, if you drive me to announce it. But if you will condescend to listen to my counsel, to conciliate your son the King, and disarm his wrath by immediate submission, then that terrible decision never need be revealed. That you should be wise in time, Madame," adds he, in a voice full of gentleness, contemplating her with the utmost compassion, "is my earnest prayer."

Before he had done speaking the Cardinal sinks on his knees at her feet, and draws forth from his breast a paper, to which are appended the royal seals. Marie, whose usual insolence and noisy wrath have given place to secret fear, still clings to the hope that she is too powerful to be dispensed with, and that by a dauntless bearing she will intimidate Richelieu, and, through him, the King, replies coldly—

"I have given you my answer. Now you can withdraw." Then, rising from her chair, she turns

* Richelieu used these precise words in speaking of Marie de Medici.

her back upon Richelieu—who still kneels before her
—and moves forward to leave the room.

"Stay, Madame!" cries Richelieu, rising, stung to
the quick by her arrogant rejection of his sympathy,
and ashamed of the unwonted emotion the forlorn
position of his royal mistress had called forth; "stay,
and listen to this decree, in the name of his Majesty."
And he unfolds the parchment. "Once more, Madame,
understand. Unless you will on the instant resign
your seat in the Council of State and dismiss the Duc
d'Epernon—a man suspected of a hideous crime,
which you at least, Madame, ought never to have forgotten—from his attendance on your person, I am
commanded by his Majesty——"

"Dismiss d'Epernon!—my only trusty servant,
d'Epernon, who has defended me from your treachery!"
—breaks in Marie passionately, her voice rising higher
at every word—"Never—never! Let me die first! How
dare you, Cardinal Richelieu, come hither to affront
the mother of your King? I will NOT dismiss the Duc
d'Epernon. It is you who shall be dismissed"—and
she glares upon him with fury—"despised, dishonoured,
blasted, as you deserve."

"If you refuse, Madame—and let me implore you
to reflect well before you do," continues the Cardinal,
quite unmoved by her reproaches—"I have his Majesty's
commands to banish you from Court, and to imprison
you during his pleasure within this palace."*

No sooner has he uttered these words than the
Queen, who stands facing the Cardinal, staggers backwards. A deadly pallor overspreads her face. She
totters, tries to grasp the arm of the chair from which

* See Note 21.

she has risen, and before Richelieu, who watches her agony with eyes rather of sorrow than of anger, can catch her, she has fallen fainting on the floor.

At his cries the Queen's ladies appear. He leaves her to their care, and proceeds to the apartments of Anne of Austria, whom, through Madame de Chevreuse, he informs of what has occurred.

Anne of Austria on hearing that the Queen-mother was disgraced, saw in her unfortunate mother-in-law, who had never ceased to persecute her and to arouse the jealousy of the King, only an unhappy parent. She flew to her, threw herself into her arms, and readily promised to employ all the influence she possessed to mitigate the royal wrath.

CHAPTER XXXII.

Love and Treason.

ANNE OF AUSTRIA has left Compiègne, and the royal prisoner and is now at Saint-Germain. The château stands upon the crest of a hill, backed by a glorious forest that darkens the heights encircling Paris.

It is spring; the air is warm and genial, the sky mildly blue; light clouds temper the bright sunshine that plays upon the southern façade of the palace, and glistens among the elms which form magnificent avenues in the surrounding park.

The King has not yet returned, and the Queen and her ladies, relieved of his dreary presence, revel in unusual freedom. Concerts, suppers, dances, repasts in the forest, and moonlight walks on the terrace, are their favourite diversions. Anne of Austria has not positively forgotten the lonely captive at Compiègne, but is too much engrossed with her own affairs to remember more than her promise to assist her. That atmosphere of flattery a woman loves so well and accepts as an offering exacted by her beauty breathes around her. Monsieur Gaston, Duc d'Orléans, the King's only brother, is always by her side. Monsieur is gay, polished, gallant; tall and slight like his brother, and pale-faced, but not, as with Louis, with the pallor of disease. He has much of his mother's versatile nature without her violent temper. Like her he is fickle, weak, and treacherous, incapable of any deep or stable feeling. Monsieur talks to the Queen of Madrid, and sympathizes with her attachment to her brother, to whom Anne writes almost daily long letters in cipher (always committed to the care of the Duchesse de Chevreuse), notwithstanding the war between France and Spain. The chivalrous Duc de Montmorenci, more formal and reserved than Monsieur, but equally devoted; the Duc de Bellegarde, no longer the ideal of manly beauty dear to the heart of poor Gabrielle d'Estrées, but grey-headed and middle-aged, though still an ardent servant of the fair, with the chivalric manners and soldier-like freedom of the former reign; gallant, rough, generous Bassompierre, who was to pay so dearly by twelve years' imprisonment in the Bastille his opposition to the Cardinal; and Maréchal d'Ornano, the *beau sabreur* of that day, were also in attendance, each one the object of the King's morbid jealousy.

Mademoiselle de Hautefort rarely leaves the Queen. She rejoices almost more than her mistress in the King's absence. The Duchesse de Chrevreuse,

bewitching and spiteful, closely attended by the
Comtes Chalais and Louvigni, whom she plays one
against the other; the Duchesse de Montbazon, her
step-mother, whose imperious eyes demand worship
from all who approach her, ever in the company of
De Rancé,*—by-and-by to found the order of La
Trappe,—are some of the ladies who form the Queen's
Court.

One moonlit night the Queen and her ladies had
lingered late on the stately terrace, built by Henry
IV., which borders the forest and extends for two
miles along the edge of the heights on which the
château stands. The Queen and her brother-in-law,
Monsieur Duc d'Orléans, have seated themselves
somewhat apart from the rest on the stone balustrade
that fronts the steep descent into the plains round
Paris. Vineyards line the hill-side, which falls rapidly
towards the Seine flowing far beneath, its swelling
banks rich with groves, orchards, villas, and gardens.
Beyond, the plain lay calm and still, wrapped in dark
shadows, save where the moonbeams fall in patches
and glints of silvery light. Of the great city which
spreads itself beyond, not a vestige is to be seen. All
human lights are extinguished, but the moon rides
high in the heavens in fields of azure brightness, and
the stars shine over the topmost heights, where, on the
very verge of the horizon, and facing the terrace, the
towers of the Cathedral of Saint-Denis break the
dusky sky-line.

A range of hills links this far-off distance with the
sombre masses of the adjoining forest. Great masses
of trees surge up black in front, swaying hither and

* See Note 22.

hither in the night breeze; the rustling of their leaves
s the only sound that breaks the silence. For a time
the Queen sits motionless.

"What a lovely night," she says at last, as she
casts her eyes out over the broad expanse of earth
and sky. "Oh that the world could be ever as calm
and peaceful!"

A sad look comes into her eyes,—she heaves a
deep sigh, throws back her head and gazes upwards.
The softened rays of the moon shine upon her face,
light up the masses of her golden hair, and play
among the folds of a long white robe which encircles
her to the feet. She sits framed, as it were, in a
circle of supernatural lustre. Monsieur is beside her,
rapt in admiration. The beautiful vision before him
intoxicates his senses. The landmarks of social re-
striction, of tyrannous etiquette, have vanished, gone,
with the sun and the daylight. He forgets that she is
a great queen, the wife of his brother—his Sovereign;
he forgets that their attendants, though invisible, are
at hand, that a glittering palace lies hid among the
woods, with its attendant multitudes; he forgets all
save that she is there before him, a dazzling presence,
sprung, as it seems, out of the darkness of the night.
He gazes at her with speechless rapture. Words
which had often before trembled on his lips must
now be uttered. He is about to speak, when the
Queen, unconscious of what is passing within him,
awakes from her reverie and points to the forest.

"See, Gaston, how the moon plays upon those
branches. I could almost believe that some fantastic
shapes are gliding amongst the trees. Let us go back;

the forest is horribly dark, it frightens me." And she shudders.

"I can see nothing but you, my sister," answers Monsieur softly. "You are the very goddess of the night." And his eyes rest on her with an impassioned gaze.

Anne of **Austria** still looks fixedly into the thicket, as if fascinated by the mystery of the great woods. Again she shudders and wraps the light mantle she wore closer around her.

"It is late, my brother," she says, rising. "If I stay longer I shall have evil dreams. Let us go."

"Oh, my sister! oh, Anne!" cries the Duke, "let us stay here for ever." And he caught one of the folds of her white robe, kissed it, and gently endeavoured to draw her, again, toward the balustrade.

"By no means," replied the Queen, startled, for the first time meeting his eyes. "Ah, my brother," adds she, becoming suddenly much confused, "are **you** sure you do not frighten me more than the strange shapes among the trees?"

"Trust me," cries Monsieur ardently, retaining her **robe almost by** force. "Tell me you will trust me— **now, always.** Ah, my sister, my heart bleeds for you. **Never, never** will you find one so devoted to you **as I——**"

There was a certain eloquence in his words, a truth in his protestings, that seemed to touch her. Anne flushes from head to foot.

"Monsieur—Gaston—let me go." And she disengages herself with difficulty. Monsieur now rose. "Where is the Duchesse de Chevreuse?" asks Anne, not knowing what to say.

"No fear for her: she is well attended," replies Monsieur in a voice full of vexation. "Every one is in good luck but me. I never saw a man so madly in love as poor Chalais, and the Duchess returns it."

The Queen is now walking onwards, at as rapid a pace as the uncertain light permitted, along the terrace. Monsieur follows her.

"Yes—in love,"—and Anne laughs her silvery laugh; "but that is not the way I would give my heart if I gave it at all, which I don't think I am tempted to do." And she looked back archly at Monsieur, whose countenance fell. "Chalais is one among so many," continues the Queen, trying to resume her usual manner. "The Duchess is very benevolent."

"Alas, my poor Henry!" answers Monsieur, "with him it is an overwhelming passion. Louvigni and the others admire and court the Duchess; but they are not like Chalais—he worships her. The Duchess is a coquette who uses him for her own purposes. She is now inciting him to head a dangerous conspiracy against the Cardinal. Chalais has opened the matter to me; but they go far—dangerously far. I cannot pledge myself to them as yet."

"Oh, Gaston!" exclaims the Queen, stopping, and laying her hand eagerly on his arm; "if you love me as you say you do, join in any conspiracy against the Cardinal."

The Queen speaks with vehemence. A sudden fire shot into her eyes, as she turns towards Monsieur. Her delicate hand still rests for an instant upon him, and is then withdrawn.

"Fair sister," replies the Duke, "you cannot pretend to misunderstand me. For your service I would risk anything—how much more a tussle with an arrogant minister, who has outraged me—as much as he has you. Perhaps, Anne, I would risk too much for your sake." And the enamoured look again comes into his eyes. But the Queen draws back, and turns her head away. "Deign to command me, sister—Queen," he adds, "only to command me, and I will obey."

Anne is now walking onwards. For a few moments she does not reply.

"If you would serve me—let Richelieu be banished," says she at last imperiously. "I care not whither. Nothing is too bad for him. He has dared to insult me. You, Gaston, are safe, even if you fail. My brother will receive you at Madrid; I will take care of that."

"I am overcome by your gracious consideration for my welfare," cries Monsieur, catching at her words. "But, my sister," continues he gravely, "do you know what this plot means? Assassination is spoken of. At this very moment I wager my life the Duchess is employing all her seductions to draw Chalais into a promise of stabbing the Cardinal."

"Stabbing the Cardinal? Impossible! Chalais would not commit a crime. You make me tremble. The Duchess told me nothing of this. She must have lost her head."

"I know that Chalais is fiercely jealous. He is jealous of every one who approaches the Duchess, and we all know that the Cardinal is not insensible to her charms——"

"Odious hypocrite!" breaks in the Queen.

"As long as Richelieu lives," continues Monsieur,

"my mother will not be set at liberty. He dreads her influence. He knows she has a powerful party."

"It is infamous!" exclaims Anne of Austria.

"The Cardinal persuades the King that he alone can govern France, and that our mother desires to depose him and appoint a regency, which I am to share with her; that you, my sister, conspire against him with Spain. My brother, weak, irresolute, insensible to you, believes all that is told him. I, my mother's only friend, dare not assist her. You, his wife, the loveliest princess in Europe—nay, in the whole world,"—and his kindling eyes fix themselves upon her—"he repulses. You might as well be married to an anchorite. Thank God, his Majesty's health is feeble, his life very uncertain. If he dies I shall be King of France, and then——" He pauses, as if hesitating to finish the sentence. "Ah, my sister!" he exclaims, stopping and trying to detain her. "Had I been blessed with such a consort I would have passed my life at her feet. Would that even now I might do so! The dark canopy of these ancient trees —the silence, the solitude, make all possible. Speak to me, Anne; tell me—oh, tell me that I may hope. Do not turn away from me——"

The Queen had stopped. She stands listening to him with her face turned towards the ground.

The moon is fast sinking behind the distant tree-tops, and the deepest shadows of the night darken their path which had now left the terrace, and lay beneath the trees. The wind sighs and moans in the adjoining forest, and an owl hoots from an ivy-covered tree. For some minutes the Queen moves not. Her whole figure is in shadow. Was she listening to the voices of the night? or was she deeply musing on what she had heard? Who can tell?

Some sudden resolve seemed, however, to form itself in her mind. She roused herself, and motions to Monsieur with her hand to go onwards. "Alas, my brother," she says with a deep sigh, "do not press me, I beseech you. You know not what you say. Such words are treason." And she hurries onwards into the gloom. "Head the conspiracy against the Cardinal," she continues, moving quickly forward as if afraid to hear more; "restrain the violence of Chalais, who loves you well and will obey you. I will temper the indiscretion of the Duchess. She is an excellent lieutenant, inspired in her readiness of resource and ingenuity in intrigue; but—she is a bad general. We must be careful, Gaston, or we shall all find ourselves prisoners in the Bastille."

"No, by Saint Paul! not so, my sister," and Monsieur laughs gaily, for his facile nature dwelt upon nothing long, and his thoughts had now been diverted into other channels. "No; but we will have Richelieu there! Bassompierre and d'Ornano are with us; they swear that they will shut him up in an iron cage—as Louis XI. did Cardinal Balue—for life, and feed him on bread and water. *Corps de Dieu!* I should like to see it."

"But I will have no blood shed," rejoins the Queen; "remember that."

"My sister, your word is law. When I have learnt more from Chalais, I will inform you of every detail."

They had now reached the château. The windows

shone with light. Torches fixed in the ground burnt round the great quadrangle, and a guard of musketeers, assembled near the entrance, presented **arms** as the Queen passed.

A page appeared, and handed a dispatch to Mademoiselle de Mérigny, who had now joined the Queen. She presented it to her Majesty. Anne broke the seals. As she read she coloured, then laughed. "Gaston," whispered she, turning to Monsieur, "this is the most extraordinary coincidence. We have been talking of the Cardinal, and here is a letter from him in which he craves a private audience. You shall learn by-and-by what it means."

"*Par Dieu!*" exclaimed Monsieur, full of wonder.

"Tell no one of this but Chalais," again whispered the Queen. Then she lightly laid her small hand within that of Monsieur; they mounted the grand staircase together, and passed through the long suite of the royal apartments. All were blazing with light; on either side of the great gallery stood the Court, ranged in two lines, waiting her Majesty's pleasure. As she passed, led by Monsieur, she bowed slightly, and, with a wave of the hand, dismissed the assembly. At the door leading to her private apartment Monsieur pressed her hand, raised it to his lips, and, glancing at her significantly, bowed and retired.

CHAPTER XXXIII.

The Cardinal Duped.

ANNE OF AUSTRIA seated herself beside a fire which burnt on the hearth. She signed to her attendants to withdraw.

"Send hither to me the Duchesse de Chevreuse, if she has returned to the château," said she to one of the pages in waiting. Then Anne drew from her bosom the letter she had just received. "It is incredible," said she, speaking to herself, "that he should so compromise himself! Pride has turned his brain. Now it is my turn, Monsieur le Cardinal." The Duchess entered hastily. "Read, *ma belle*, read," cried Anne, holding out the dispatch to her, "the fates favour us. Let us lay a trap for this wicked prelate."

"*Ma foi*," replied the Duchess, after having reperused the letter contained in the dispatch, "even I could not have contrived it better. Here is the Cardinal craving a private audience of your Majesty in the absence of the King. It will be a declaration in form—such as he made to me."

"A declaration to me, Duchess? He would not dare——"

"Madame he has been a soldier, and has passed his life along with a great queen. He believes himself irresistible. Who knows if Marie de Medici did not tell him so?" Anne of Austria looked displeased. "Pardon me, Madame, this saucy Cardinal, whom I call the *Court-knave*, makes me forget myself. Your Majesty must receive him graciously."

"Yes, he shall come," cried Anne; "he shall come

and pay for his audacity, the hypocrite! But tell me, Duchess, tell me instantly, how can I best revenge myself? I have a long account to settle. Shall I command my valets, Laporte and Putange, to hide behind the arras and beat him until he is half dead?"

"No, Madame, that would be too dangerous; he might **cut** your head **off** in revenge, *à la reine Anne Boleyn*. We must mortify him—wound his vanity: no vengeance equal to that with a man like the Cardinal. He is intensely conceited, and proud of his figure. He imagines that he is graceful and alluring —perhaps he has been told so by her Majesty—I beg your pardon, Madame"—and the Duchess stopped and pursed up her lips, as if she could say more but dared not.

"Did Marion de l'Orme betray him?" asked the Queen slily, "or do you speak on your own knowledge?"

"I have it!" cried Madame de Chevreuse—not noticing the Queen's question—and her mischievous eyes danced with glee. "I will meet him when he comes to-morrow, and persuade him to appear in the dress of a Spaniard, out of compliment to you. Stay, he shall dance, too, and we will provide a mandoline to accompany his voice. I will tell him that you have long admired him in secret, and that if he appears in so becoming a costume he is sure to be well received. A Spanish costume, too, for he knows how you adore Spain, the spy—then he shall dance a *sarabande*, a *bolero à l'Espagnol*, or sing——"

"Ha! ha! Duchess, you are *impayable*," and the Queen laughed until the tears ran down her cheeks. "But will he be fool enough to believe you? If he

does, I will kill him with scorn, the daring Cardinal!"
and Anne of Austria drew herself up, looked into an
opposite mirror, shook her golden curls, and laughed
again.

The next morning, at the hour of the Queen's
lever, the Cardinal arrived. The Duchesse de Chevreuse met him and conducted him to a room near
the Queen's saloon. She carefully closed the door,
begged him to be seated, and, with an air of great
mystery, requested him to listen to her before his
arrival was announced to her Majesty. The Cardinal
was greatly taken aback at finding himself alone with
the Duchess. She looked so seductive; the dark tints
of her luxuriant hair, hanging about her neck and
shoulders, harmonized so well with her *brunette* complexion, her brown eyes bent smilingly upon him, her
delicate robe clinging to her tall figure, that he was
almost tempted to repent his infidelity to her, and that
he had come for any other than for her.

"Your eminence is surprised to see me," said she,
smiling, and speaking in the softest voice, and with
the utmost apparent frankness, "but I am not in the
least jealous," and she shook her finger at him.

The Cardinal reddened, and looked confused.

"Do you, then, Duchess, guess on what errand I
have come?"

"Perfectly, perfectly; when I heard you had requested a private audience in the absence of the King,
I understood the rest."

"Perhaps I have been indiscreet," said Richelieu,
and he sighed, "but I was anxious to explain my
position to the Queen. I fear that she misconceives
me; that she looks on me as her enemy; that she

imagines that I prejudice the King against her. I
desire to explain my feelings to her; they are of a
mixed nature."

"So I should suppose," answered Madame de
Chevreuse primly, almost bursting with suppressed
laughter.

"Do you think, then, madame, that her Majesty
might be induced to lay aside her silence, her reserve?
Are you authorised to admit me to her presence?"

"I am, Cardinal."

Richelieu's face flushed deep, his eyes glistened.

"To a certain extent," continued the Duchess, "the
Queen is gratified by your homage. Her Majesty has
noted your slim yet manly form, your expressive eyes.
She admires your great talents."

"Do I dream?" exclaimed Richelieu. "You, madame, are indeed magnanimous. I feared that you
might be indignant at what you might consider my
inconstancy."

"No, Cardinal, you could not be inconstant, for
you were never loved."

Richelieu started.

"By me—I mean to say, your eminence. You
really should spare me," added she affectedly; "but I
suppose I must speak. Anne of Austria, the daughter
of a hundred kings, the wife of your Sovereign,
secretly loves you, monseigneur. It is astonishing
your extraordinary penetration never discovered this
before. Since you went into the Church you must
have grown modest; but love is blind, says the motto,"
and the Duchess was obliged to hold her handkerchief to her face to hide her laughter.

"What words of ecstasy **do** you utter, adorable

Duchess! But you must be aware of the coldness, the insulting scorn which the lovely Queen has hitherto shown towards me. How could I venture to guess——?"

"Ah, Cardinal, it is easy to see you are not so advanced in the art of love as of politics. Let me advise you to read Ovid—a little of 'The Art of Love' —*pour vous remettre*. Did you learn so little, then, from her late Majesty, Marie de Medici, as not to know that where most Cupid triumphs he most conceals his wicked little person? That very coldness and scorn you speak of are but proofs of the Queen's passion. But let me tell you one thing: the Queen fears you may deceive—betray her; and you must excuse her in this, when you remember, monseigneur, certain tales of treachery—all utterly false, of course—but then pardon a woman's fears. You must, to speak plainly, give her some undoubted proof of your love."

"Madame, you cannot doubt after what I have just heard that I can hesitate in promising to do all and everything my royal mistress can desire."

The Duchess confessed afterwards to the Queen, that it was with the utmost difficulty she could keep her countenance, so absolutely farcical were his transports.

"Have a care what you promise," said the Duchess to the Cardinal; "the Queen is very *bizarre*, and perhaps may require something impracticable."

"Madame," replied Richelieu, "to *me* nothing in this realm is impracticable; speak only her Majesty's wishes, and I hasten to obey them."

"Well, then, to-night you must come at dusk to her apartments." The Cardinal bounded from his chair with delight. "To-night; but not in this sombre,

melancholy dress; you must wear a toilette a little
convenable to the part you hope to act—something
brilliant, gaudy—*un pantalon vert, par exemple.*" The
Cardinal started. "At your knees little bells must be
fastened. You must have a velvet jacket, scarlet scarf,
and, in fact, all the *et cæteras* of a Spanish dress. It
will please the Queen, and pay her a delicate compliment, to which, believe me, she will not be insensible."

All this time Richelieu had listened to the Duchess
in an agony of surprise and amazement. "But,
madame," said he, at length, "this is impossible. I, a
dignitary of the Church, a Cardinal. Much as I desire
to show my devotion to the Queen, she herself cannot
expect from me so strange, so extraordinary a
proof——"

"Certainly, monseigneur, it is an extreme proof
of your devotion, and as such the Queen will regard
it. She will be gratified and at the same time will
be thoroughly convinced of your sincerity. However, pray do as you please," and the Duchess shrugged her shoulders; "I merely mention her Majesty's
wishes; you are quite at liberty to refuse. I shall
therefore," and she rose, "report your refusal."

"Stop, Duchess, stop, I entreat you!" interrupted
Richelieu, "you are so precipitate! I will—I must!
(But what a fearful degradation! I, the prime minister
of France, a prince of the Church, to appear in the
disguise of a mountebank!) Ah, madame, her Majesty
is too hard on me; but I adore, I worship her too
much to refuse. Yes,—her wishes are my law; I
cannot, I dare not refuse. Tell the Queen, at twilight
this evening, I will present myself in her apartments."

The Duchess waited no longer, but flew to acquaint the Queen with her success. Neither could for a long time articulate a single syllable, they were so overcome with laughter. Music was introduced behind the arras, for the Cardinal was to be prevailed 'on to dance a *sarabande*. Then they impatiently awaited the moment of his arrival. At last, enveloped in a Spanish cloak that entirely concealed his dress, the Cardinal entered. He was hastily rushing towards the Queen—Heaven only knows with what intentions —when Madame de Chevreuse interposed:

"Not yet, Cardinal—not yet; you must show us your dress first, then you must dance a *sarabande*, a *bolero*—something. Her Majesty has heard of your accomplishments and insists on it."

"Yes," cried Anne of Austria, "I insist on it, monseigneur, and have provided the music accordingly."

The violins now struck up. Richelieu looked confounded. He was almost on the point of rushing out, when a few words whispered to him by the Duchess arrested him; they acted like a charm. Casting one deep, impassioned glance at the Queen, who sat at a little distance reposing on a couch, ravishing in beauty, her rosy lips swelling with ill-suppressed scorn, he threw down his cloak, displaying his extraordinary dress, bells, scarlet scarf and all, and began to dance —yes, to dance!

Poor man! he was no longer young, and was stiff from want of practice; so after a few clumsy *entrechats* and *pirouettes*, he stopped. He was quite red in the face and out of breath. He looked horribly savage for a few moments. The music stopped also, and there **was** a pause. Then he advanced towards the Queen, the little bells tinkling as he moved.

"Your Majesty must *now* be convinced **of** my devotion. Deign, most adorable Princess, to permit **me** to kiss that exquisite hand."

The Queen listened to him in solemn silence. The Duchess leaned behind her couch, a smile of gratified malice on her face. The Cardinal, motionless before them, awaited her reply. Then Anne of Austria rose, and, looking him full in the face, measured him from head to foot. **Anger,** contempt, and scorn flashed in her eyes. At **last** she spoke—ineffable disgust and disdain in her tone—"Your eminence is, I rejoice to see, good for something better than a *spy*. I had hitherto doubted it. You have diverted me immensely. But take my advice; when you next feel inclined **to** pay your addresses to the Queen of France, get yourself shut up by your friends **for** an old fool. Now you may go."

Richelieu, who had gradually turned livid while the Queen spoke, waited to hear no more. He covered himself with his cloak and rushed headlong from the room.

CHAPTER XXXIV.

The Maid of Honour.

THE King returns to Saint-Germain as suddenly as he had departed; he commands a hunt in the forest at noon. The château wears an air of unusual gaiety. The King and Queen start together from the quadrangle, but they do not address each other. Anne, who rides on in front, attended by Monsieur, is positively dazzling in her sunny beauty. Her delicate cheeks are flushed with excitement. A small velvet cap, with a heron's plume, rests on her head, and an emerald-coloured riding-dress, bordered with gold, sets off her rounded figure. She is followed by her ladies, many of whom wear masks to protect their complexions. The maids of honour are in blue, with large hats overtopped by enormous feathers.

Near them rides the King. He is much too shy to address Mademoiselle de Hautefort before such an assemblage; but his eyes constantly follow her, and he is infinitely gratified by the reserve of her manner towards the young gallants of the Court. Behind him rides the Grand Falconer, followed by the huntsmen, the *piqueur*, the whippers-in, and the falcons, hooded and chained to the wrists of their bearers. Last come the dogs—the sad King's special favourites. The brilliant cavalcade flashes among the glades, which intersect the forest in every direction. The gaily caparisoned steeds, and their still gayer riders, the feathers, the lace, the embroidery, flutter in and out among the openings of the wood, and are lost in the many paths, where every turn is so like the other, yet each marked by some special beauty. Most of the ladies are mounted on palfreys, but some prefer litters; others are drawn up and down in cumbrous coaches, that threaten each moment to overturn on the gnarled roots of beech and oak that break the sward. On the riders dash between the giant tree-trunks, unhidden by the luxuriant foliage that masses the woods in summer— for the season is spring—and the trees are covered with but a slight shade of green leaves just bursting from the grey boughs. Yonder they dart under a pine-tree that darkens the ground, its spiky branches casting forth an aromatic perfume. Then beneath a cherry-tree, white with snowy blossoms, on among a maze of goss and yellow broom that streak the underwood with fire.

The birds sing in the bushes, the bees buzz among the blossoms, and the horses' hoofs crush the tender mosses and the early flowers that carpet the ground. At the approach of the hunters hares and rabbits run lightly away, and timid does, with their young at their side, scamper far into the deepest recesses of the woods. Now the bugles sound, the dogs bay loudly; they spread themselves from side to side and disappear among the coppice, and the whole glittering company, gilded coaches, litters and all follow them, and dash out of sight and are hidden among the trees.

It was arranged that the hunt should lead towards a noble mansion lying on the confines of the forest, in the direction of Bondy, where the host, apprized of the intended honour, had prepared an ample collation.

Etiquette demanded that the King and Queen

should be served apart **from** the rest. After their repast was finished and their attendants had withdrawn, the Queen approached nearer to the King. He started up and turned towards the door. Anne followed him. The long ride in the forest had flushed her cheeks. She looked brilliant. "Your Majesty will not refuse to speak to me, surely," said she in the softest tones **of her** naturally **sweet** voice, and she raised her glorious eyes, which would have melted any other man but Louis, beseechingly.

The King shook his head sullenly.

"What have I done that your Majesty should scorn me?" said she, stretching out her beautiful hand with the most winning gesture to detain him.

Louis shrank from **her** touch, and turned his back upon her.

"Sire, will **you not at** least hear me, as **you** would hear the least of your subjects?" and **the** Queen's eyes filled with tears and her hand dropped to her side.

"What **have you to say to** me?" asked Louis harshly, not looking at her.

"When I last saw your Majesty at Compiègne," replied she with a faltering voice, "your mother, the Queen-dowager"—at her name Louis shuddered— "was **mistress of** the palace and of France. She sat at the royal board; she presided at the Council of State; your Majesty obeyed and loved her as a son. She is now a prisoner—disgraced, forsaken, ill." The Queen's voice became so unsteady that she was obliged to stop, and unbidden tears rolled down her cheeks. "What has this great Queen done to deserve your Majesty's displeasure?" she added after a pause.

"Madame, it is no affair of yours," answered Louis gruffly. "I refuse to give you my reasons. I act according to the advice of my council. Do not detain me," and he turned again to leave the room. Anne placed herself in front of him; her head was thrown back, her figure raised to its full height, the tears on her eyelids were dried; she was no longer timid, but exasperated.

"If I have ventured to intercede for the Queen-mother," said she with dignity, "it is because she implored me to do so. She wept upon my bosom. Her heart was all but broken. I comforted her as a daughter. I promised her to use such feeble powers as I had, to soften your heart, Sire. It is a sacred pledge I am discharging."

"You are a couple of hypocrites!" exclaimed Louis with great irritation, facing round upon her. "You hate each other. From my mother I have freed myself; but you"—and he surveyed her savagely from head to foot—"you, Madame Anne of Austria, you remain."

"Yes, I remain," returned Anne, "until, as I am told, you crave a dispensation from the Pope and send me back to Madrid." These last words were spoken slowly and with marked emphasis. "I am a childless queen," and she shot a bitter glance at Louis, who now stood rooted to the spot and listened to her with an expression of speechless amazement.

"Who told you, Madame, that I sought a dispensation from the Pope, and to send you back to Madrid?" asked Louis sharply. Then, without waiting for an answer he put his hand to his forehead as if some sudden thought had struck him, knit his brows, and was lost in thought.

"I have heard so, no matter how," answered the Queen coolly, "and on excellent authority. Sire," she cried passionately, no longer able to restrain her feelings, "you use me too ill—rather than suffer as I do I will leave France for ever; I will not bear the mockery of being called your wife—I would rather bury myself in a convent at Madrid."

Louis was so completely abstracted, that although he had asked her a question, he had forgotten to listen to her reply. Now he caught at her last word.

"Madrid? Yes, madame, I believe it. Your heart is there. I know it but too well. Would you had never left Madrid! Ever since you came into France you have desired my death that you might wed a comelier consort."

Louis could scarcely articulate, so violently was he excited. Anne did not stir, only her glowing eyes followed, as it were, each word he uttered.

"You talk of the Queen-mother, do you know that she warned me long ago that you were dishonouring me?"

"Oh, Sire, if you forget who I am," exclaimed the Queen, "remember at least that I am a woman!" and she burst into tears, and for a few moments sobbed bitterly.

"Can you deny it, Madame," continued the King, with rising fury, his mouth twitching nervously, as was his wont when much agitated—"can you deny it? Am I not become a jest among my own courtiers? You, the Queen of France, openly encourage the addresses of many lovers. You are wanting, Madame, even in the decency of the reserve becoming your high station," and Louis clenched his fist with rage.

"I deny what you say," returned the Queen boldly; "I have discoursed with no man to the dishonour of your Majesty." She was trembling violently, but she spoke firmly and with dignity. "If I am wanting in concealment," added she, "it is because I have nothing to conceal."

"I do not believe you," answered the King rudely.

"No, Sire, you do not, because you are my enemy. Your mind is poisoned against me. You encourage the lies of Richelieu, you slander me to my own attendants. Worse than all, you dare to couple my name with that of the Duc d'Orléans, your own brother. It is a gross calumny."

Her voice rose as she spoke; the power of truth and innocence was in her look—it was impossible not to believe her. For an instant the King's suspicions seemed shaken. He followed eagerly every word she uttered; but at the name of Monsieur a livid paleness overspread his face; for a moment he looked as if he would have swooned. Then recovering himself somewhat he came close up to her, and with a wild look he scanned her curiously, as though to read some answer to his suspicions. "Who can have told her? who can have told her?" he muttered half aloud— "a secret of state too. It is not possible that—" The last words were spoken so low that they were lost. Louis was evidently struggling with some painful but overwhelming conviction. His head sunk on his breast. Again he became lost in thought. Then, looking up he saw that the Queen was watching him. She was waiting for him to speak. This awakened him suddenly to a consciousness of what was passing, and his anger burst forth afresh.

"You say I am your enemy—yes, I am, and with reason. Are you not devoted to the interests of Spain, now at war with France? Do you not betray me in letters to your brother? Answer me." It was now the Queen's turn to falter and turn pale. The King perceived it. "I have you there, Madame Anne; I have you there;" and he laughed vindictively. "My life is not safe beside you. Like my great father, I shall die by an assassin whose hand will be directed by my wife!" A cold shiver passed over him. "Richelieu has proofs. *Vrai Dieu*, Madame, he has proofs. It is possible," he added with a sardonic smile, which made him look ghastly, "that you may return to Madrid sooner than you imagine — you and the Duchesse de Chevreuse, your accomplice."

"Not sooner than I desire, Sire, after your unworthy treatment," exclaimed Anne proudly, her anger overcoming her fears that her letters might have been really deciphered. "I come of a race that cannot brook insult; but I can bear disgrace."

Louis, who felt that the Queen was getting the better of him, grew furious—"I will have no more words, Madame," shouted he; "we will deal with facts. I shall appeal to my minister and to my council. For myself, I am not fit to govern," he added in an altered voice, and with the forlorn air of a man who cannot help himself.

"Speak not to me, Sire, of Richelieu and the council over which he presides," cried Anne, goaded beyond endurance. "Richelieu is a traitor, a hypocrite, a libertine—not even his sovereign's wife is sacred to him!"

"Ah, Madame, it is natural that you and Richelieu should disagree," retorted the King, with an incredulous sneer. "He is a match for you and for the Duchess your counsellor—the Duchess whose life disgraces my Court."

Anne had now thrown herself into a chair, her hands were crossed on her bosom, her eyes bent steadily on the King, as if prepared for whatever fresh extravagance he might utter. Even the enraged Louis felt the influence of her fixed, stern gaze. He ceased speaking, grew suddenly confused, paced up and down hurriedly, stopped, essayed again to address her—then abruptly strode out of the room.

*　　*　　*　　*　　*

The Queen and her ladies are seated on a stone balcony that overlooks the parterre and the park of Saint-Germain. Below, the King's violins are playing some music of his composition, set to words in praise of friendship, full of covert allusions to Mademoiselle de Hautefort. The Queen's fair young face is clouded with care; she leans back listlessly in her chair, and takes no heed of the music or of what is passing around her. The Chevalier de Jars approaches her. There is something in his air that alarms her; she signs to him to place himself beside her.

Mademoiselle de Hautefort, conscious that every one is watching the effect of the music and the words upon her, sits apart at the farther end of the gallery, from which the balcony projects, almost concealed from view. A door near her opens noiselessly and the King puts in his head. He peers round cau-

tiously, sees that no one has perceived him, and that
Mademoiselle de Hautefort is alone, then he creeps
in and seats himself by her side. He looks saddened
and perplexed.

"Why do you shun me?" he asks abruptly.

"You have been absent, Sire."

"Did you miss me?" His voice sounds so strange
and hollow that Mademoiselle de Hautefort looks up
into his face. Something had happened; what could
it be? Some misfortune to the Queen is always her
first thought. Before she can reply, Louis sighs profoundly, so profoundly that he almost groans, contemplating her, at the same time, with looks of
inexpressible sorrow. "Alas!" exclaims he at last, "I
had hoped so much from this interview when we parted
at Fontainebleau; I have lived upon the thought, and
now—my dream is ended; all is over!" The maid of
honour grows alarmed: either he is gone mad, she
thinks, or something dreadful has happened.

"I cannot conceive what you mean, Sire?" she
replies, not knowing what to say.

"Are you, too, false?" he continues, "with those
eyes so full of truth? Yet it must be you, it can be
no other. False like the rest; a devil with an angel's
face!" The maid of honour is more and more amazed.
"Yet I trusted you; with my whole heart I trusted you,"
and he turns to her with a piteous expression, and
wrings his hands. "I unfolded to you my forlorn and
desolate condition. It might have touched you. Tell
me," he continues, in a tone of anguish, "tell me the
truth; was it you who betrayed me?"

Mademoiselle de Hautefort is terribly confused.
She understands now what the King means; a mortal

terror seizes her; what shall she say to him? She is too conscientious to deny point-blank that she has told his secret, so she replies evasively, "that she is his Majesty's faithful servant."

"But, speak," insists the King, "give me a plain **answer.** How does the Queen know a state secret, that I confided to you alone, that I **even whispered in** your ear?"

"Sire, I—I do not know," falters the maid of honour.

"Swear to me, mademoiselle, that you have not betrayed me to the Queen; swear, and I will believe you. *Pardieu!* I will believe you even if it is not true!" Louis's eyes shine with hidden fire; his slight frame quivers.

Mademoiselle de Hautefort, trembling for her mistress, with difficulty controls herself. "Your Majesty must judge me as you please," she replies, struggling to speak with unconcern. "I call God to witness I have been faithful to my trust."

"I would fain believe it," replies the King, watching her in painful suspense; he seems to wait for some further justification, but not another syllable passes her lips. Still the King lingers; his looks are riveted upon her.

At this moment the music ceases. The maid of honour starts up, for the Queen has left the balcony. The King had vanished.

Anne of Austria, quitting those around her, advances alone to the spot where Mademoiselle de Hautefort had been talking with the King. "I am going at once to the Val de Grâce," she whispers in great agitation.

"Indeed, Madame; so suddenly?"

"Yes, at once. I have just heard from the Chevalier de Jars that Chalais is arrested at Nantes. He accuses me and the Duchess de Chevreuse of conspiring with him. Richelieu meditates some *coup de main* against me. I shall be safe at the Val de Grâce. You and the Duchess will accompany me. Here is a letter I have written in pencil to my brother; it is most important. I dare not carry it about me; take care to deliver it yourself to Laporte."

The Queen drew from her pocket a letter, placed it in the maid of honour's hand, and hastened back to rejoin the company. Mademoiselle was about to follow her, when Louis suddenly rose up before her, and barred her advance.

"Mademoiselle de Hautefort," he said, "I have heard all. I was concealed behind that curtain. Give me that letter, written by my wife, I command you."

"Never, Sire, never!" and Mademoiselle de Hautefort crushed the letter in her hand.

"How—dare you refuse me? Give it to me instantly?" and he tried to tear it from her grasp. She eluded him, retreated a few steps, and paused for a moment to think; then, as if a sudden inspiration had struck her, she opened the lace kerchief which covered her neck, thrust the letter into her bosom, and exclaimed:—

"Here it is, Sire; come and take it!"

With outstretched arms she stood before him; her cheeks aglow with blushes, her bosom wildly heaving. Wistfully he regarded her for a moment, then thrust out his hand to scize the letter, plainly visible beneath the gauzy covering. One glance from her flashing eye, and the King, crimson to the temples, drew back;

irresistibly impelled, he advanced again and once more
retreated, then with a look of baffled fury shouted,
"Now I *know* you are a traitress!" and rushed from
the gallery.

CHAPTER XXXV.

At Val de Grâce.

THE ancient Benedictine abbey of the Val Profond,
near Bièvre le Châlet, three leagues from Paris, was
founded by Robert, son of Hugh Capet. Soon after
her arrival in France, Anne of Austria bought the
ground upon which the then ruined abbey stood,
moved the nuns to Paris, and placed them in a convent
called the Val de Grâce,* under the Mont Parnasse,
near the Luxembourg Gardens. To this convent of
the Val de Grâce the Queen often resorted to seek in
prayer and meditation (for she was eminently pious),
consolation and repose. On these occasions she
occupied a suite of rooms specially set apart for
her use.

It is a bright morning, and the sunshine streams
through the painted windows, and streaks the marble
floor of the Queen's oratory with chequered colours.
To the east, under a lofty window, stands an altar,
covered with a costly cloth, on which, in golden
sconces, burn many votive candles. Anne of Austria
is seated in a recess, on a carved chair of dark oak.
She is dressed in black, her golden curls are gathered
under a sober coif; she looks pale, and ill at ease;

* See Note 23.

her eyes, dulled by want of sleep, are anxious and restless, but there is a resolution in her bearing that shows she is prepared to meet whatever calamity awaits her with the courage of her race. Mademoiselle de Hautefort sits on a low stool at her feet. She is weeping bitterly.

"Ah! Madame," she sobs, "this is Richelieu's revenge. It is all his doing. How could your Majesty listen to the advice of that wild Duchess, and affront him so cruelly at Saint-Germain? Alas! he will persecute you as long as he lives."

"I cannot recall the past," answers Anne sadly.

"Had you reposed confidence in me, Madame, this would never have happened. Madame de Chevreuse has sacrificed you to her love of intrigue."

"My poor Chevreuse, she is no more to blame than I am. Where is the Duchess, mademoiselle?"

While the Queen speaks a sound of wheels entering the courtyard from the street of Saint-Jacques breaks the silence. A moment after Madame de Chevreuse rushes into the oratory, so hidden in a black hood and a long cloak that no one would have recognized her. She flings herself on her knees before the Queen, and grasps her hands.

"Ah, my dear mistress, you are saved!" she cries breathlessly. Anne raises her and kisses her tenderly. "I am just come from the Bastille. I went there disguised as a priest. I have seen Chalais. The Cardinal interpreted what Chalais said—purposely, of course— into meaning an attempt upon the life of the King."

"Great God!" exclaims Anne, turning her glistening eyes to heaven, "what wickedness!"

"The King has joined the Cardinal in a purpose to prosecute your Majesty for treason. His Majesty is furious. He declares that he will repudiate you, and send you back into Spain. He has commanded the Chancellor Séguier and the Archbishop of Paris to repair here to the Convent of the Val de Grâce to search your private papers for proofs of your guilt and of your treasonable intrigues with Spain. They are close at hand. I feared lest they had already arrived before I could return and apprise your Majesty."

"But what of Chalais?" cries Anne. "Why did you visit him in the Bastille?"

"To learn what had passed between him and the Cardinal. We must all tell the same story. Chalais confesses to me that in the confusion of his arrest at Nantes he did let fall some expressions connecting your Majesty, Monsieur, and myself with the plot against Richelieu, and that when questioned he avowed that he acted with your knowledge."

"Ah, the coward!" cries Mademoiselle de Hautefort bitterly. "And you love him."

"No, mademoiselle, Chalais is no coward. He is a noble gentleman, whose fortitude will yet save her Majesty. He has been betrayed by Louvigni, the traitor, out of jealousy. Do not interrupt me, mademoiselle," continues the Duchess, seeing that Mademoiselle de Hautefort is again about to break forth into reproaches against Chalais. "No sooner had Chalais arrived at the Bastille than Richelieu visited him in his cell. He offered him his life if he would consent to inculpate your Majesty in the plot. Chalais refused, and declared that the plot of which you were informed by Monsieur the Duc d'Orléans, was directed against himself; and he told the Cardinal he might tear him in pieces with wild horses before he would say one word to your Majesty's prejudice."

"Generous Chalais!" exclaims the Queen, clasping her hands. "Can he not be saved?"

"No, Madame, my noble friend must die. He knows it, and places his life at your feet."

Anne sobs violently.

"Horrible! Oh, that I should cost those who love me so dear! Proceed, Duchess."

"The Cardinal had in the meantime, as soon as your Majesty left Saint-Germain, sent to force your drawers and cabinets for papers." Anne rises to her feet, white with terror. "Never fear, Madame; I had thought of that. Laporte had destroyed everything by my order. Only one letter to your brother the King of Spain was found. It was written the day you left, and confided by you, Mademoiselle de Hautefort, to Laporte," and the Duchess gives a spiteful glance at the maid of honour. "Before he dispatched it, Laporte was seized and searched."

"There was nothing in that letter derogatory to me as Queen of France," says the Queen quickly. "I spoke of Richelieu's insane passion for me, and described the scene at Saint-Germain, and I told him I was about to leave for the Val de Grâce; nothing more. The Cardinal will not show that letter."

"Yes, Madame, God be praised! it is so. But it was absolutely necessary that I should tell Chalais that but one letter had been found, and that perfectly innocent, before he was examined by the Cardinal. I have told him. He knows he can save his Queen. He is content to die!" As the Duchess speaks, the sound of wheels again interrupts them. "Hark! The Chancellor and the Archbishop have arrived. Courage, your Majesty! All now depends on your presence of mind. Nothing will be found in this convent, and Laporte waits at the door without. He will suffer no one to enter."

Anne flings herself into the arms of the Duchess.

"You have saved me!" she cries, and covers her with kisses.

*　　*　　*　　*　　*　　*

An hour has passed. Laporte knocks at the door, and enters. His looks betray the alarm he tries to conceal.

"The Chancellor, Madame, has arrived, in company with the Archbishop of Paris," he says, addressing the Queen. "The Archbishop has commanded the Abbess, the venerable Louise de Milli, and all the sisterhood, who went out to meet him, to return each one within her cell, and not to exchange a single word together during the time he remains in the convent, under pain of excommunication." The Queen and the Duchess exchange anxious glances. Laporte speaks again with much hesitation, "I regret to say that the Chancellor then proceeded to search all the cells. No papers were found." The Duchess clasps her hands with exultation. "How can I go on?" Laporte groans, the tears coming into his eyes. "Forgive me, Madame; I cannot help it." The Queen makes an impatient gesture, and Laporte continues: "The Chancellor craves your Majesty's pardon, but desires me to tell you that he bears a royal warrant, which he must obey, to search your private apartment, and this oratory also."

"Let him have every facility, my good Laporte,"

answers the Queen collectedly. "Mademoiselle de Hautefort, deliver up all my keys to Laporte."

"The Chancellor and the Archbishop desire to speak also to the lady-in-waiting on your Majesty, the Duchesse de Chevreuse," Laporte adds.

"What new misfortune is this?" cries Anne of Austria, turning very pale. "Go, dear Duchess; all is not yet over, I fear."

Madame de Chevreuse leaves the oratory with Laporte. The Queen casts herself on her knees before the sacred relics exposed on the altar. She hides her face in her hands.

It was not long before the Duchess returns. Her triumphant air has vanished. She tries to appear unconcerned, but cannot. Anne rises from her knees, and looks at her in silence.

"Speak, Madame de Chevreuse; I can bear it," she says meekly.

"Alas! my dear mistress, Richelieu's vengeance is not yet complete. The Chancellor has announced to me that a Council of State is about to assemble in the refectory of the convent. You are summoned to appear, to answer personally certain matters laid to your charge."

Mademoiselle de Hautefort utters a loud scream. The Queen, her eyes riveted on the Duchess, neither moves nor speaks for some moments.

"You have more to say. Speak, Duchess," she says at last in a low voice.

"Nothing whatever has been found—no line, no paper. I took care of that," and the Duchess smiles faintly.

"You have not yet told me all. I must hear it. Conceal nothing," again insists the Queen.

"Alas! it is indeed as you say. The Chancellor"— and her voice falls almost to a whisper—"has express orders under the King's hand to search your Majesty's *person*."

"Search an anointed Queen!" exclaims Anne of Austria. "Never!" **and** she stretches out her **arms** wildly towards the altar. "Holy Virgin, help me!" she cries.

At this moment the sound of many footsteps are heard without in the stone passage, approaching the door. Anne of Austria has risen; she stands in the centre of the oratory; an unwonted fire glows in her eyes, a look of unmistakable command spreads itself over her whole person. Never had she looked more royal than in this moment of extreme humiliation. The Duchess rushes to the door and draws the ponderous bolts. "Now let them come," cries she, "if they dare!" They all listen in breathless silence. The voice of Laporte, who has returned to his post outside the door, is heard in low but angry altercation. Then he is heard to say, in a loud voice—

"No one **can be** admitted to her Majesty, save only the King, without her permission."

"We command you in the name of the law. Stand aside!" is the reply.

Then another voice speaks:—

"We are the bearers of an order from the King and the Council of State to see her Majesty." It is the Chancellor's voice, and his words are distinctly audible **within.**

"I know of no order but from the Queen my mistress. Your Grace shall not pass. If you do, it shall be across my body," Laporte is heard to reply.

"We enter our solemn protest against this breach of the law; but we decline to force her Majesty's pleasure." It was still the Chancellor who spoke. Then the sound of receding footsteps told that he was gone.

"Where will this end?" asks Anne in a hollow voice, sinking into a chair.

The Duchess and Mademoiselle de Hautefort fling their arms round her.

"Bear up, Madame, the worst is over. Be only firm; they can prove nothing," whispers the Duchess. "There is not a tittle of evidence against you."

"Ah, but, my friend, you forget that the King is eager to repudiate me. Mademoiselle de Hautefort knows it from his own lips."

"He cannot, without proofs of your guilt," the Duchess answers resolutely. "There are none. And if he does, *qu'importe?* Why mar that queenly brow with sorrow, and wrinkle those delicate cheeks with tears? Be like me, Madame, a citizen of the world—Madrid, Paris, London—what matters? The sun shines as brightly in other lands as here. Life and love are everywhere. You are young, beautiful, courageous. To see you is to love you. Swords will start from their scabbards to defend you. Your exile in your brother's Court will be a triumph. You will rule all hearts; you will still be the sovereign of youth, of poetry, and of song!"

As she speaks the Duchess's countenance beams

with enthusiasm. Anne of Austria shakes her head sorrowfully, and is silent.

"You are happy, Duchess, in such volatile spirits," says Mademoiselle de Hautefort contemptuously, her eyes all the while fixed on her royal mistress; "but I cannot look on the disgrace of the Queen of France as though it were the finale to a page's roundelay."

The sound of many heavy coaches thundering into the inner court of the convent puts a stop to further conversation.

"The council is assembling!" exclaims the Duchess.

At these words the Queen rises mechanically; her large eyes, dilated and widely open, are fixed on vacancy, as though the vision of some unspoken horror, some awful disaster, had risen before her. She knows it is the crisis of her life. From that chamber she may pass to banishment, prison, or death. For a moment her mind wanders. She looks round wildly. "Spare me! spare me!" she murmurs, and she wrings her hands. "Alas! I am too young to die!" Then collecting her scattered senses, she moves forward with measured steps. "I am ready," she says, in a hollow voice. "Unbar the door."

CHAPTER XXXVI.
The Queen before the Council.

THE refectory of the convent of the Val de Grâce
is a vast apartment, dimly lit by rows of small lancet
windows placed along the side walls. These walls
are bare, panelled with dark wood; great oaken rafters
span the tented roof. At the eastern end hangs a large
crucifix of silver. In the centre is a table, round
which the three principal members of the council are
assembled. Alone, at the head, is the King, uneasily
seated on the corner of a huge chair. His whole body
is shrunk and contracted, as though he were under-
going some agonizing penance. He never raises his
eyes; his pallid face works with nervous excitement.
His hat is drawn over his brow; his hands are clasped
upon his knees. That he had come in haste is apparent, for he wears his usual dark hunting-dress.

At his right hand is the Cardinal, wearing a long
tightly fitting *soutane* of purple silk, with a cloak of
the same colour. His countenance is perfectly impassive, save that when he moves, and the light from
above strikes upon his dark eyes, they glitter. In his
delicate hands he holds some papers, to which he refers
from time to time; others lie on the table near him.
Opposite the Cardinal are the Archbishop of Paris and
the Chancellor Séguier. At the farther end of the
council-table, facing the King, Anne of Austria is
seated. The colour comes and goes upon her downy
cheeks; but otherwise no sovereign throned in fabled

state is more queenly than this golden-haired daughter of the Cæsars.

The Cardinal turns towards her, but, before addressing her, his eyes are gathered fixedly upon her. Then, in a placid voice, he speaks—

"Your Majesty has been summoned by the King here present to answer certain matters laid to your charge."

Anne of Austria rises and makes an obeisance, looking towards the King, then reseats herself.

"I am here to answer whatever questions his Majesty sees good to put to me," she replies, in a clear, firm voice.

"His Majesty, Madame, speaks through *my* voice," answers Richelieu significantly, observing her pointed reference to the King's presence; "I am here as his *alter ego*. It is said," he continues, in the same impassive manner with which he had at first addressed her, "that you, Madame Anne of Austria, consort of the King, hold a treasonable correspondence in cipher with your brother, Philip, King of Spain, now waging war against this realm of France, and that therein you betray to him secrets of state to the manifest hurt and danger of the King's armies, by affording treacherous foreknowledge of their movements and of the measures of his Government. What answer does your Majesty make to so grave a charge?"

"If it be so, let these letters be produced," answers the Queen boldly. "I declare that beyond the natural love I bear my brother and his consort, Elizabeth of France, sister to the King,—which love surely is no crime,—I have never, by word or deed, betrayed aught that I might know to the prejudice of the King, my husband, or of **this** great country of which I am the Queen."

"Why, then, Madame, if these letters were harmless did you write in a cipher unknown to the King's ministers?" asks the Cardinal, bending his piercing eyes keenly upon her.

"Because," replies the Queen, "I knew that spies were set, by the King's order, at *your* instance," and she points to the Cardinal, "to waylay these letters, the writing of which has been to me, next to God, my greatest comfort in much sorrow and persecution which I have suffered wrongfully since I came into France."

"Madame," continues Richelieu, speaking with the same unmoved voice and manner, "do you know Henry de Talleyrand, Comte de Chalais, Master of the Robes to his Majesty, and once esteemed by him as his faithful subject?"

"I do know him," answers the Queen.

"Do you also know that this gentleman, the Comte de Chalais, has been lately arrested at Nantes, and is now lying in the prison of the Bastille, accused of having treacherously conspired against the sacred person of his Majesty, with the design of placing on the throne, at his death, Monseigneur, Duc d'Orléans— brother of the King; and that the Comte de Chalais avers and declares, before witnesses, that he acted by your order and by your counsel? What answer have you to make to this, Madame?"

"That it is false, and unsupported by any evidence whatever, and that you, Cardinal Richelieu, know that it is false." Then Anne of Austria raises her hands towards the crucifix hanging before her—"By the blessed wounds of our Lord Jesus, I swear that I never

knew that the life of the King, my husband, was threatened; if it were so, it was concealed from me." A stifled groan is heard from the King. Both the Chancellor and the Archbishop appear greatly impressed by the Queen's solemn declaration, and whisper together. Richelieu alone is unmoved.

Then the Queen rises, and, for the first time, turns her large eyes full upon the Cardinal, over whose frame a momentary tremor passes. "It was of another plot that the Comte de Chalais spoke; and of another assassination, not that of the King. His Majesty himself—if I mistake not—knew and did not disapprove of *this other* project, and of removing *him* whom I mean. Nevertheless I shrank from the proposal with horror; I expressly forbade all bloodshed, although it would have removed a deadly enemy from my path." And the Queen, while she speaks, fixes her undaunted gaze full on the Cardinal, who casts down his eyes on the papers he holds in his hands. "Let his Majesty confront me with Chalais; he will confirm the truth of what I say." Anne of Austria stops to watch the effect of her words. Something like a groan again escapes from the King; he pulls at his beard, and moves uneasily in his chair, as the Cardinal's lynx eyes **are** directed, for an instant, towards him with a malignant glare. The Cardinal stoops to consult some documents that lie upon the table, and for a few moments **not a** word was uttered. Then resuming his former placid voice and manner, Richelieu faces the Queen, and proceeds:—

"Further, Madame, it is averred, and it is believed by his Majesty, that you, forgetting the duty of a wife, and the loyalty of a Queen, have exchanged love-tokens with the said prince of the blood, Gaston, Duc d'Orléans, now for his manifest treason fled into Spain,"—at these words, to which she listens with evident horror, Anne clasps her hands;—"further, that you, Madame, and your lady of the bedchamber, Marie de Lorraine, Duchesse de Chevreuse, **did** conspire, with Chalais and others, for this unholy purpose."

Anne's **face is** suffused with a deep blush of shame while the Cardinal speaks; for a moment her courage seems to fail her—then, collecting herself, she stretches out her arms towards the King, and says solemnly, "I call on his Majesty, Louis—surnamed the Just— my husband, to confront me with my accusers: I am innocent of this foul charge."

At this appeal the King half rises, as if with **an** intention to speak, then sinks back again **into** his chair. His features twitch convulsively; he never raises his eyes.

"Is that all you have to reply to the wicked and murderous project said to be entertained by you of wedding, *from inclination*, with the King's brother, at his death, if by feeble health, or any other accident, his Majesty had been removed?" and the Cardinal bends his glassy eyes earnestly upon the Queen.

"I reply that I should have gained nothing by **the** change. The Duc d'Orléans is as fickle and unworthy as his Majesty, who sits by unmoved, and hears his consort slandered by her enemies." Anne's eyes flash fire; her indignation had carried her beyond fear; she stands before the council more like a judge than a criminal. "Have a care, Armand de Plessis, Cardinal Minister and *tyrant* of France, that you question me not too closely," the Queen adds in a lower voice, addressing herself directly to Richelieu. As she speaks she puts her hand to her bosom, and discloses, between the folds of her dark velvet robe, a portion of a letter, bound with purple cord, which Richelieu instantly recognises as the identical one he had addressed to her at Saint-Germain, asking for a private audience. The Cardinal visibly shudders; his whole expression changes; his impassive look is turned to one of anxiety and doubt; he passes his hands over his forehead, as if to shade his eyes from the light, but in reality to give his fertile brain a few moments' time in which to devise some escape from the danger that threatens him should the Queen produce that letter before the council. So rapid has been the Queen's action that no one else has perceived it. Something peculiar, however, in the tone of her voice attracts the notice of the King, who, rousing himself from the painful abstraction into which he has fallen, gazes round for the first time, and bends his lustreless grey eyes suspiciously on the Cardinal, and from him on the Queen; then shaking his head doubtfully, he again resumes his former weary attitude. Meanwhile the Queen, imagining that she perceives some compassion in that momentary glance, rises and advances close to the edge of the council-table. Grief, anger, and reproach are in her looks. With a haughty gesture she signs to the Cardinal to be silent, clasps her small hands so tightly that the nails redden her tender skin, and, in a plaintive voice, addresses herself directly to the King. "Oh, Sire, is not your heart moved with pity to behold a great princess, such as I, your wife, and who might have been the mother of your children, stand before you here like a criminal, to suffer the scorn and malice of her enemies?"—she is so overcome that her voice falters, and she hastily brushes the starting tears from her eyes. "I know," she continues, with her appealing eyes resting on the King, "I know that you are **weary of me, and that** your purpose is, if possible, to repudiate **me and send** me back into Spain; **you have** confessed as much to one of my maids of honour, who, shocked at the proposal, **repeated** it to me. I appeal **to** yourself, Sire, **if** this **be not** true?" and laying one hand on the table she leans forward towards Louis, waiting for **his** reply; but, although **he** does not answer her **appeal**, he whispers a few words into the ear **of** the Archbishop, standing next to him, who bows. **Then** he falls back on his chair, **as** if weary and exhausted by a hopeless struggle. "My **lords,** the King cannot deny it," says Anne of Austria triumphantly, addressing the council; "My lords, I **have never,** since I came into **France, a girl of fifteen, been** permitted **to** occupy my legitimate place in his Majesty's affections. The Queen-dowager Marie de Medici, poisoned his mind against me; and now Cardinal Richelieu, *her creature*," —and Anne casts a look of ineffable disdain at Richelieu—"continues the same policy, because he dreads my influence, and desires wholly to possess himself of the King's confidence, the better to rule him and France."

The Queen's bold words had greatly impressed the council in her favour. The Archbishop and the Chancellor consult anxiously together. At length the Archbishop of Paris interposes.

"Her Majesty the Queen appears to have explained most satisfactorily all the accusations made against her. I was myself present at the examination of her private apartments within this convent of the Val de Grâce. Nothing was found but proofs of her pious sentiments and devout exercises, such as scourges, girdles spiked with iron to mortify the flesh, books of devotion and missals. **It is to** be desired that all royal ladies could disarm suspicion like her Majesty. If, therefore, the evidence which the Cardinal holds be in accordance with her Majesty's declarations, all the charges may be withdrawn, and her Majesty be returned to those royal dignities and honours which she so fitly adorns. Speak, Cardinal Richelieu, do you hold counter evidence—yea, or nay?"

The Cardinal does not at once answer. He shuffles some papers in his hands, then turns towards the King, and whispers in his ear. Louis makes an impatient gesture of assent, and resumes his despondent attitude.

"I have his Majesty's commands for replying," answers Richelieu, "that no letters implicating the Queen in treasonable correspondence with her brother have been at present actually found, although his Majesty has reason to believe that such exist. Also that the Comte de Chalais's statements are in accordance with those of her Majesty. Also that the King acquits Madame Anne, his consort, of the purpose of marrying with his brother, Monsieur Duc d'Orléans, on whom *alone* must rest the onus of such a crime. Usher of the Court, summon the Queen's ladies-in-waiting to attend her. Your Majesty is free," adds Richelieu, and the mocking tone of his voice betrays involuntarily something of the inward rage he labours to conceal. "Madame Anne of Austria, you are no longer a prisoner of state under examination by the council, **but** are, as before, in full possession of the privileges, powers, immunities and revenues belonging to the Queen Consort of France."

Anne of Austria leaves her chair, salutes his Majesty with a profound obeisance, of which Louis takes no other notice than to turn his eyes to the ceiling, and then advances towards the door. The Chancellor and the Archbishop rise at the same time from the council-table, and hasten to open the door by **which she is** to pass out, bowing humbly before her.

"The royal carriages are in waiting, Madame," whispered the Duchesse de Chevreuse, who, with Mademoiselle de Hautefort, was waiting outside; **and** she wrung the Queen's hand. "My dear, dear **mistress,** I know you are free!"

"Praised be God!" replied Anne, "I have escaped," and she kissed her on both cheeks, as also her maid of honour, who was so overcome she could not say one word of congratulation.

"Come, Madame," cried the Duchesse de Chevreuse, "let us leave this dreadful place, I beseech you, lest the Cardinal should concoct some fresh plot to detain you."

"Duchess," replied Anne gaily, "you shall command me. It is to **you I owe** my liberty. But for your forethought those unhappy letters, wrung from **me in** moments of anguish—ah! of despair, would **have** been found, and I should at this moment have **been** on my way to the Bastille. My good Hautefort, you have not spoken to me. You look sad. What is it?" and the Queen took her hand.

"It is because I have contributed nothing towards your Majesty's freedom. Besides, a foreboding of coming evil overpowers me," and she burst into tears.

She again kissed her, and led her by the hand towards the cumbrous coach which was to bear her to Paris. As Anne was preparing to mount into it, assisted by her page and Laporte, who had reappeared, the Chevalier de Jars approached hastily, and bowed before her.

"How now, Chevalier! any more ill news? What is your business here?" asked Anne.

"It is with this lady," said he, turning to the maid of honour. "Mademoiselle de Hautefort, you cannot accompany her Majesty to Paris."

"Why, Chevalier?" demanded Anne impatiently, still holding her hand.

"Because I am commanded to make known to you that Mademoiselle de Hautefort is exiled from France during his Majesty's pleasure. I am charged, mademoiselle, to show you this token," and he produced the other half of the golden medallion which Louis had broken during their interview at Fontainebleau. "The King bid me say that by this token he himself commands your instant departure."

The Queen clasped her in her arms.

"My poor Hautefort, is it indeed so? Must I lose my trusty friend?"

Mademoiselle de Hautefort threw herself, weeping bitterly, at the Queen's feet.

"Alas! Madame," sobbed she, "I am banished because I have been faithful to you!"

"Have you got another order—for my arrest, *par exemple*, Chevalier?" asked the Duchess archly. "I have also committed the awful crime of faithfulness to her Majesty. I suppose I shall go next."

The Chevalier shook his head.

"No, madame. You will accompany the Queen to the Louvre."

The Duchesse de Chevreuse did accompany the Queen to the Louvre; but, on arriving there, she found a *lettre de cachet* banishing her from France within twenty-four hours. A similar order was also served on the Chevalier de Jars.

The Queen was free, but her friends were exiled.

CHAPTER XXXVII.

Louise de Lafayette.

LOUISE DE LAFAYETTE—the only child of Comte Jean de Lafayette, of Hauteville, and of Margaret de Boulon-Busset, his wife—was the young lady selected to fill the vacant post of maid of honour to the Queen, *vice* De Hautefort, banished.

So long a time had elapsed since the departure of the latter that it seemed as though Anne of Austria never intended to replace her; however, the new mistress of the robes, the Duchesse de Sennécy, a distant relative of Mademoiselle de Lafayette, urged the Queen so strongly in her favour, that the appointment was at last announced.

Louise de Lafayette had passed many years of her

girlhood in a convent, and was somewhat *dévote*, but she was sincere in her piety, and good-natured to excess. Not only was she good-natured, but she was so entirely devoid of malice that it actually pained her to be made acquainted with the faults of others. Perhaps her chief characteristic was an exaggerated sensibility, almost amounting to delusion. She created an ideal world around her, and peopled it with creatures of her own imagination, rather than the men and women of flesh and blood among whom she lived—a defect of youth which age and experience would rectify. She possessed that gift, so rare in women, of charming involuntarily—without effort or self-consciousness. When most attractive and most admired, she alone was unconscious of it; **envy itself** was disarmed **by** her ingenuous humility.

Louise **was** twenty-three years **old when she** was presented **to** the Queen at Fontainebleau **by the** Principessa di Mantua, during her morning reception. The saloon was filled with company, and great curiosity was felt to see the successor of Mademoiselle de Hautefort. The most critical observers were satisfied. The new maid of honour, though modest and a little abashed, comported herself with perfect self-possession. She was superbly **dressed, had a** tall and supple figure, good features, and a complexion so exquisitely fair and fresh, and **such** an abundance of sunny hair, as to remind many in the circle of her Majesty when, in the dazzling beauty of her fifteenth year, she came a bride into France. But Anne of Austria never had those large appealing grey eyes, beaming with all the confidence of a guileless heart, nor that air of maiden reserve which lent an unconscious charm to every movement,

nor that calm and placid brow, unruffled by so much
as an angry thought.

Why had not Mademoiselle de Lafayette married?
was the general question which passed round the
circle.

"Because she has found no one **worthy of** her,"
was the reply of her friend and cousin, **the D**uchesse
de Sennécy.

After the new maid of honour had made her curtsey to the Queen, who received her very graciously, ·
the King (who had as usual placed himself almost out
of sight, near the door, in order **to** ensure a safe retreat if needful) emerged, and timidly addressed her.

Since the scene at the monastery of the Val de
Grâce, and the discovery of Mademoiselle de Hautefort's treachery, Louis **had** never once appeared at the
Queen's lever until this morning. At the few words
of compliment he found courage to say **to** her, Louise
blushed and curtsied, but made no reply.

The next day the King **was** again present at her
Majesty's lever. **He** did not speak, **but his** eyes never
for an instant left the new maid of honour.

The Court was at this time greatly agitated by
political events. The Spaniards were making the most
alarming progress in France; they had penetrated in
the north as far as Corbie, in Picardy; in **the south**
they were overrunning Provence. Troops and money
were both wanting. The position of the ministry was
so critical that even Richelieu was at fault. Louis,
roused from his habitual apathy, suddenly remembered
that he was the son of a great warrior, and electrified
the Council of State by announcing that he intended
at once to take the field in person. A resolve so con-

trary to his usual habits excited great discussion and
general interest.

*   *   *   *   *   *

The Saloon of Saint-Louis, at Fontainebleau, opens
from the royal guard-room. It is a noble apartment,
divided into a card-room and a *with*-drawing, or, as
we say, drawing-room. The decorations are the same
as those in the Gallery of Francis I.; the walls, painted
in fresco after designs by Primaticcio, are divided by
sculptured figures, in high relief, entwined by wreaths
of flowers, fruit, and foliage. The ceiling is blue, sown
with golden stars. Lights blaze from the chandeliers
disposed on marble tables and in the corners of the
room, and display the artistic beauty of the various
paintings and frescoes that cover the walls.

The Queen is playing cards with the Bishop of
Limoges. The Court groups itself about the double
rooms, and at the other card-tables. Near the Queen
are her favourites of the hour, the Principesse di Gonzaga and di Mantua; the Duchesse de Sennécy is in
attendance. The King is seated on a settee in the
darkest and most distant corner. Anne dares not now
treat him either with impertinence or *hauteur*. If she
cannot bring herself actually to fear him, she knows
that he is capable of revenge. She has learnt, however, both to fear and to dread his minister, Richelieu,
under whose insolent dominion Louis's life is passed.
Madame de Chevreuse is no longer at hand to tempt
her into rebellion, and she has learnt to submit quietly,
if not contentedly, to her lot. She has perceived the
impression made upon the King by her new maid of
honour, and looks on amused and indifferent. Of the
absolute goodness and perfect rectitude of Louise de

Lafayette, **no one,** and certainly not the Queen, could **entertain a** doubt.

As she pushes the cards towards the Bishop of Limoges to deal for her, which he does after making her a low bow, she turns round, the better to observe his Majesty. He has moved from the settee, and is now seated in earnest conversation with Mademoiselle de Lafayette. A sneer gathers about the corners of her rosy **mouth, and her** eyes dwell upon him **for an** instant with an expression of intense contempt; then she shrugs **her** snowy shoulders, leans back in **her chair,** takes up the cards that lie before her, and rapidly sorts them. The conversation between Louis and Mademoiselle de Lafayette is low and earnest. His naturally dismal face expresses more lively interest, **and** his lack-lustre eyes are more animated than they have been for years. As to the maid of honour, she listens to him with **every faculty of** her being, and hangs upon his words **as though, to her** at least, they are inspired.

"The condition of France," the King is saying, "overwhelms **me.** Would that I could offer up my life **for** my beloved country! Would that I possessed my great **father's** military genius to defend her! I go, perhaps never to return! Alas! no one will miss me," and he heaves a heavy sigh, **and** the tears gather in his eyes.

The maid of honour longs to **tell him all the in-**terest she feels for him, **her** genuine **admiration,** her devotion, her pity for his desolate condition; but she is new to court life, and, like himself, she is too timid as yet to put her feelings into words. She sits beside him motionless as a statue, not daring even to lift up her eyes, lest **they may** betray her.

"Happy, ah! happy beyond words is the man who feels he is beloved, who feels that he is missed!"—here Louis stops, casts a reproachful glance at the Queen, whose back was towards him, then a shy, furtive look at Mademoiselle de Lafayette, whose heightened colour and quickened breathing betrays the intensity of her feelings: "such a one," continues the King, "has a motive for desiring fame; he can afford to risk his life in the front of the battle. Were I"—and his voice sinks almost into a whisper—"were I dear to any one, which I know I am **no**t, I should seek to live in history, like my father. As **it is**," and he sighs, "I know that I possess no quality that kindles sympathy. I am betrayed by those whom I most trust, and hated and despised by those who are bound by nature and by law to love and honour me. My death **would** be a boon to some"—again his eyes seek out the Queen —"and a blessing to myself. **I am a** blighted and a miserable man. Sometimes I ask myself why I should live at all?" It was not possible for the human countenance to express more absolute despair than does the King's face at this moment.

"Oh, Sire!" was all Mademoiselle de Lafayette dare trust herself to reply; indeed, she is so choked by rising sobs that it is not possible for her to say more.

The King is conscious that her voice trembles; he notices also that her bosom heaves, and that she had suddenly grown very pale. Her silence, then, was not from lack of interest. Louis feels infinitely gratified by the discovery of this mute sympathy. All that was suppressed and unspoken had a subtle charm to his

morbid nature. After a few moments of silence, Louis,
fearful lest the Queen's keen eyes should be turned
upon them, rises. "I deeply deplore, mademoiselle,
that this conversation must now end. Let me hope
that it may be again resumed before my departure for
the army." Louise does not reply, but one speaking
glance tells him he will not be refused.

At supper, and when she attends the Queen in her
private apartments, she is so absent that her friend,
Madame de Sennécy, reprimands her sharply.

The next morning the Duchess went to her young
cousin's room. Madame de Sennécy had a very decided
taste for intrigue, and would willingly have replaced
the Duchesse de Chevreuse in the confidence of Anne
of Austria, but she wanted her predecessor's daring
wit, her adroitness, witcheries, and beauty; above all,
she lacked that generous devotion to her mistress,
which turned her life into a romance. Now Madame
de Sennécy thought she saw a chance of advancing
her interests by means of her cousin's growing favour
with the King. She would gain her confidence, and
by retailing her secrets excite the jealousy and secure
the favour of the Queen.

"My dear child," said she, kissing Louise on both
cheeks, a bland smile upon her face, "will you excuse
my early visit?" She seated herself opposite to Mademoiselle de Lafayette, the better to observe her.
"Excuse the warmth with which I spoke to you last
night in the Queen's sleeping-room; but really, whatever attention the King may pay you, *ma chère*, you
must not allow yourself to grow careless in her Majesty's service. As mistress of the robes I cannot permit
it. All the world, my dear cousin, sees he is in love

with you"—Louise blushed to the roots of her hair,
shook her head, and looked confused and unhappy
—"of course he loves you in his fashion. I mean,"
added Madame de Sennécy quickly, seeing her distress,
and not giving her time to remonstrate, "a perfectly
Platonic love, nothing improper, of course. He loves
you timidly, modestly, even in his most secret thoughts.
I am told by his attendants that the King shows every
sign of a great passion, much more intense than he
ever felt for Mademoiselle de Hautefort, who, after
all, trifled with him, and never was sincere."

"I do not know the King well enough, Duchess,
to venture an opinion on his character," replied Mademoiselle de Lafayette, with diffidence, "but I may say
that if I had any prepossessions against his Majesty, I
have lost them; I am sure he is capable of the tenderest
friendship; he longs to open his heart to a real friend.
His confidence has been hitherto abused."

"My dear child, I have come here to advise you
to be—well—that friend."

"Oh! madame, I fear I am too inexperienced to be
of use to him; but if the King does ask my advice,
which seems very presumptuous in me to suppose, I
shall conceal nothing that I think, neither facts nor
opinions."

"Ah, my cousin, try to rouse him; make him reign
for himself; tell him to shake off that dreadful Cardinal."

"That is, I fear, impossible; I am too ignorant of
politics. Besides, what can I do now? he is going
away to the war."

"Well, but, *petite sotte*, he will return, and you will
meet again,"

"Oh, no," replied Louise, again colouring under the scrutinizing eye of the mistress of the robes, "he will forget me long before that."

"Nothing of the kind, Louise," replied the Duchess, "the King never forgets anything."

"Dear Duchess, you really are talking nonsense. What on earth could make the King care for me?" and she sighed deeply, and fell into a muse. "I do pity him, though," she added, speaking with great feeling; "I pity him, I own. He is naturally good— brave—confiding," and she paused between each word.

"I am glad you find him so," answered the Duchess drily.

"Yet he ill fulfils his glorious mission," continued Louise, as if speaking to herself. "He is conscious of it, and it pains him. I am sure he suffers acutely."

"Heal his wounds, then," said the Duchess with a cynical smile, but speaking in so low a voice that Mademoiselle de Lafayette did not catch the words.

"Ah! if he had but one true friend, he might emulate his great father! Did you hear, Duchess, with what firmness he addressed the deputies yesterday, who had refused to register the royal edicts for raising the necessary funds for the army? 'This money,' he said, 'is not for myself, but for the nation, and to maintain the national honour. Those who refuse it, injure France more than her enemies the Spaniards. I will be obeyed,' he said. There was energy! Oh, it was noble!" and her eyes glistened and her cheeks glowed.

"I suppose the Cardinal had composed this neat little speech for him beforehand," replied the Duchess

with a sneer, contemplating her cousin with amused
inquisitiveness. "You do not believe he ever spoke
like that himself? You do not know him as well as I
do, else you would not be so enthusiastic. However,
it is all as it should be. I do not desire to disenchant
you, I am sure. *Au revoir*," and the Duchess left the
room.

The next morning, before his departure for the
campaign, Louis went to bid the Queen farewell. It
was only a formal visit, and he stayed scarcely a minute.
The Queen did not affect to care what might become
of him. On leaving her audience-chamber he lingered
in the ante-room in which her attendants were assembled. Mademoiselle de Lafayette was seated, with
another maid, in a recess; she,—Mademoiselle de
Guerchy,—seeing the King's anxious looks, at once
rose and retired. He immediately took her place, and
signed to Louise to seat herself beside him. Separated
from her companion, and sitting apart with Louis,
Louise suddenly remembered that it was precisely thus
the King had conversed *tête-à-tête* with Mademoiselle de
Hautefort; she became greatly embarrassed.

"I come," said the King, turning towards her,
and speaking in a plaintive voice, "I come to bid you
adieu."

Louise bent her head, and put her handkerchief
to her eyes. Louis started at seeing the big tears roll
down her cheeks.

"I have enjoyed few moments of happiness in the
course of my dreary life," continued he, pressing her
hand, "but this is one."

He broke off, overcome apparently by his feelings.
Louise wiped the tears from her eyes.

"Sire, believe me, I only feel the same emotion as thousands of your faithful subjects at a moment when you are about to lead the campaign against Spain. If you would condescend to inform yourself of general opinion you would find it as I say."

"It may be, mademoiselle; but I only wish now to know *your* feelings. If you will indeed be to me the devoted **friend** I have so long sought in vain, my entire confidence shall be yours. I go to-morrow, but the most tender recollections will cling to me." As he spoke he took her hand in his and kissed it with fervour. "Think of me, I implore you, with the same interest you now display. Believe me, my heart echoes **all** you feel. If I am spared, please God, your sympathy will be the consolation of my life."

At this moment the Duchesse de Sennécy opened the door, in order to cross the ante-room. The King started up at the noise, and walked quickly towards another door opposite. The Duchess stopped; looked first at Mademoiselle de Lafayette seated alone, covered with blushes, then at the retreating figure of the King. She took in the whole situation at a glance. It was too tempting an opportunity to throw away. There was a favour she specially desired to ask. This was the very moment. In his present state of confusion **the** King, only to get rid of her, was sure to grant it. She rushed after him, and before Louis could reach the door, she had seized upon him and spoken.

When he had gone the Duchess ran up to Louise, who was now stitching at some embroidery to hide her blushes, and burst out laughing.

"You are merry, Duchess," said the maid of

honour, glad that anything should divert attention from herself.

"I am laughing, Louise, at the admirable presence of mind I have just shown. As you are only a *débutante*, I will explain what I mean for your special instruction. His Majesty does not exactly hate me, but something very like it. No love is lost between us. He dreads my making capital of all I see and hear to the Queen. He dreads my turning him into ridicule —which is so easy. Of all the persons about Court whom he would least have liked to have surprised him in the tender conversation he was holding with you, I am the one. He tried to reach the door. I saw my advantage, and pursued him. I knew he wanted to shake me off, so I seized the opportunity to ask a favour—of great importance to me. It is granted! Is not this clever? I am grateful, and will not repeat one word of this little adventure to her Majesty."

Louise shook her head, and affected not to understand her. "You are altogether mistaken, Duchess. His Majesty simply honours me with such friendship as he might feel towards any loyal subject devoted to his interests. It is because the Court affects to despise him that I appear singular in estimating him at his true value; nothing else."

"You are a prude," exclaimed the Duchess bluntly. "I hate affectation, especially of that kind." Louise hung her head down, and played with some pearls with which the grey silk dress she wore was trimmed. "Besides, my little cousin, you must not sacrifice the interest of your friends, who have a right to look to you for favour and patronage."

"Oh, Duchess, what a vile thought!" cried Louise, reddening. "Do you think I would make his Majesty's friendship a matter of barter?"

"Oh, bah!" replied the Duchess, growing angry. "Louise, you are not so simple as you pretend. If you ask me the question, I reply, certainly your friends have a right to look to you—especially myself, who never let the Queen rest until she appointed you her maid of honour. She had almost made a vow never to fill up the place of her dear Mademoiselle de Hautefort." Louise stared at the Duchess with a troubled look. Worldliness and meanness was a new and unpleasant experience—a fresh page in the history of the Court—that pained and revolted her.

"When the King returns," continued Madame de Sennécy, not condescending to notice her disapprobation, "I shall expect you to give me all your confidence. You shall have excellent advice in return. If you follow it, in six months' time you will revolutionise the Court, and banish Cardinal Richelieu. You will by that one act secure the King's friendship and her Majesty's favour. Eh, Louise? a brilliant position for a little *provinciale* like you! You must mind what you are about, or the Queen will grow jealous. I will take care, on the first opportunity, to assure her you are only acting in her interests."

"Jealous of me! Impossible!" cried Louise. "Such a great Queen!—so beautiful, so fascinating! Oh, Duchess, you are joking."

"Nothing of the kind. I warn you not to imagine that there is any joking at Court, or you will find yourself mistaken. Now I shall leave you, Louise. Think over what I have said. Remember what you

owe to those friends whose influence has placed you
in your present high position."

*   *   *   *   *   *

As soon as the Duchess left her, Mademoiselle de
Lafayette hastened to her room, locked the door and
sat down to reflect calmly upon all that had passed.
She was disgusted with the coarse selfishness of the
Duchess, whom she determined for the future to avoid.
Then her heart melted within her as she recalled the
King's tender farewell. How eagerly his eyes had
sought hers! How melodious was his tremulous voice!
How tenderly he had pressed her hand! He had spoken
out: he wanted a friend; he had made choice of her;
he had promised her all his confidence! Delicious
thought!

No one had ever dreamed of attaching the slightest blame to his intimacy with Mademoiselle de Hautefort. It would be therefore absurd to reject his advances. She was safe, she felt, entirely safe in his
high principles, his delicacy, and his honour. If she
could only teach him to be as firm as he was winning,
release him from the bondage of favourites, emancipate
him from the tyranny of Richelieu, and deserve his
gratitude—perhaps his affection! With what energy
she would address him on his return, and remonstrate
with him on his indolence, his indifference! With his
courage, his powers of mind (in which she sincerely
believed), his sensibility and gentleness, guided by her
devoted far-seeing friendship, might he not equal his
father as a sovereign—surpass him, perhaps, as much
as he now does in morals, as a man? All these vague
ideas floated through the brain of the simple-minded girl
as she sat musing within the solitude of her chamber.

NOTES TO VOL. I.

NOTE 1, p. 18.

Francis I., born at Cognac, was the only son of Charles d'Orléans, Duc d'Angoulême. After the death of two sons, born to Louis XII. by his wife, Anne de Bretagne, he created his relative, Francis, Duc de Valois, married him to his daughter, Claude, and selected him as his successor to the throne.

NOTE 2, p. 34.

Saint-Germain l'Auxerrois, one of the oldest churches in France, dedicated to St. Germain, Bishop of Paris, by Chilperic. Saint-Germain l'Auxerrois, Saint-Etienne du Mont, the Hôtel de Clugny, and the Hôtel de Sens, all dating from a very early period, still remain.

NOTE 3, p. 35.

Gentille Agnès plus de loy tu mérite,
La cause était de France recouvrir;
Que ce que peut dedans un cloître ouvrir,
Close nonnaine? ou bien dévot hermite?

NOTE 4, p. 44.

The Duc d'Alençon, husband of Marguerite de Valois, sister of Francis, who commanded the left wing of the French army, was the only man who showed himself a coward at Pavia. He turned and fled, with his whole division.

NOTE 5, p. 58.

Triboulet had been court fool to Louis XII., who first discerned his good qualities, and rescued him from a most forlorn position. Triboulet's sayings are almost a chronicle of the time, so much was he mixed up with the life of the two sovereigns he served. Brusquet, who compiled the " Fools' Calendar," succeeded him in the office of **jester to** Francis.

NOTE 6, p. 67.

Francis's exact words, according to Du Bellay, were—"Les Guises mettront mes enfans en pourpoint et mon pauvre peuple en chemise." This prophecy was poetised into the following verse;—

" François premier prédit ce mot,
Que ceux de la maison de Guise,
Mettraient ses enfans en pourpoint
Et son pauvre peuple en chemise."

21 *

NOTE 7, p. 71.

The Palace des Tournelles (so named from **its many towers) stood in** the Rue Saint-Antoine, opposite the Hôtel de Saint-Paul, **upon** the site of the Place Royale. Charles VI. was confined here when insane, by his wife, Isabeau de Bavière. The Duke of Bedford, Regent of France for Henry VI., a minor, lodged here. After the expulsion **of** the English from Paris, Charles VII. made it his residence. Louis XI. **and** Louis XII. inhabited it. The latter monarch died here.

NOTE 8, p. **77.**

Another cotemporary **says that** the Queen **of Navarre** was invited **to** Marcel's, **the** Prévôt of Paris, **where,** having **eaten** some *confitures*, she **fell** sick, and died five days afterwards.

NOTE 9, p. 81.

Charles **de Guise,** Cardinal de Lorraine, was Minister under Francis II. and Charles IX. **He** endeavoured, without success, to introduce the Inquisition into France.

NOTE 10, p. **107.**

No sooner had Catherine de Medici built the Tuileries, than she left it to **inhabit** the Hôtel de Soissons (then called Hôtel **de** la Reine), in the parish of Saint-Eustache, in consequence of a prediction that she would die at Saint-Germain. The Hôtel de Soissons, as well as the Hôtel de Nesle, is now amalgamated into the Halle aux Blés. At the Hôtel de Soissons, Catherine lived for some years before her death.

NOTE 11, p. 135.

Coligni was prosecuted as accessory to the murder of Francis, Duc de Guise, by his widow, Anna di Ferrara, but no sentence was pronounced.

NOTE 12, **p. 137.**

Henri de Navarre then went to *le prêche*, **Marguerite to mass.**

NOTE 13, p. 139.

"Memoirs and Letters of Marguerite de Valois," published by the Société de l'Histoire de France, by M. Guessand, 1842.

NOTE 14, **p. 144.**

Coligni's **head was** cut off, embalmed, and sent to Rome as a trophy His remains were collected and buried by his friend, Montmorenci, at Chantilly. Before their removal from Montfaucon, Charles and all his Court rode to see them. One of the courtiers observed "that the body smelt foul." "Nay," replied Charles, "the body of an enemy always smells sweet."

NOTE 15, p. 146.

SULLY'S ACCOUNT **OF THE** MASSACRE **OF** ST. BARTHOLOMEW.

"I felt myself awakened at three hours after midnight by the loud ringing of all the bells, and the confused cries of the populace. My governor, Saint-Just, and my valet went out. I never heard any more of them. I continued alone in my chamber, dressing myself, when in a few moments I saw my land-lord enter, pale and astonished. He was of the reformed religion. He came to persuade me to go with him to mass. I did not think proper to follow him, but resolved **to try** if I could gain the College of Burgundy, where I studied, notwithstanding the **distance** it was from the house **where I** lodged, which made the attempt very perilous. I put **on** my scholar's robe, and taking **a** large prayer-book under my arm, I went out. Upon entering the street, I was seized with horror at the sight of the furies who rushed from all parts, and **burst** open the houses, bawling out 'Slaughter, slaughter—massacre the Huguenots!' the blood which I saw shed before my eyes redoubled my terror I fell into the midst of a body of guards; they stopped me, questioned me, and were beginning to use me ill, when, happily for me, the book that I carried was perceived, and served me as a passport. At last **I** arrived at the College of Burgundy, when a danger far greater than **any I had yet** met with awaited me. The porter having twice refused **me entrance, I remained** in the midst of the street, at the mercy of the Catholic furies, whose numbers increased every moment, and who were evidently **in** quest of their prey, when I bethought myself of calling for the principal of the college. La Faye, a good man, who loved me tenderly. The porter, gained by some small pieces of money which I put into his hand, did not fail **to** make him come at once. This honest man led me into his chamber. Here **two** inhuman priests, whom I heard make mention of the Sicilian Vespers, wanted to force me from him, that they might cut me in pieces, saying, 'The order was **to kill to the very** infants at the brea t!' All that La Faye could do was **to conduct me secretly** to a remote closet, where he locked me up. I was there confined **three days,** uncertain of my destiny, receiving succour only from **a** domestic belonging to this charitable man, who brought me from time to time something to preserve **my life.**"

NOTE 16, p. 148.

According to Dufresnay, "Tables Chronologiques," vol. II., seventy thousand Huguenots perished in the massacre of St. **Bartholomew,** which lasted seven days and seven nights. One **man boasted that he** had killed four hundred with his own hand.

NOTE 17, p. 150.

It was the renown of these victories that gained for Henry the crown of Poland.

NOTE 18, p. 159.

Comte d'Auvergne, son of Charles IX. by Marie Touchet, illegitimate nephew of Henry III. and half-brother of Henriette d'Entragues.

NOTE 19, p. 169.

Henry **IV. was the** son of Antoine de Bourbon, **Duc de Vendôme, and of** Jeanne d'Albret, only daughter of Henri d'Albret, **King of Navarre, married** to Marguerite d'Alençon, sister of Francis I., the widow **of the Duc d'Alençon.**

NOTE 20, p. 172.

Chicot was a Gascon, jester to Henry IV. His *specialité* **was intense** hatred to the Duc de Mayenne, whom he constantly attempted **to** attack. During an engagement at Bures, **he** made prisoner the Comte **de** Chaligny, and carried him into Henry's presence. "*Tiens!*" said he, "this is my prisoner." Chaligny was **so enraged** at having **been** captured **by a** buffoon, that he poniarded Chicot on **the spot.**

NOTE 21, p. 260.

Marie de Medici died **in poverty at** Cologne, aged sixty-nine.

NOTE 22, p. 263.

The Duchesse de Montbazon died suddenly at Paris of measles. De Rancé was in the country at the time; no one dared tell him what had happened. On his return to Paris he ran up the stairs into her rooms, expecting to find her. There he found an open coffin, containing the corpse of Madame de Montbazon. The head was severed from the body (the coffin having been made too short), and lay outside on the winding sheet. Such is the story according to the "Véritable Motifs de la Conversion de l'Abbé de la Trappe." Other authorities contradict these details.

NOTE 23, p. 290.

Now the military hospital of the Val de Grâce, 277, Rue Saint-Jacques. Anne of Austria having been married twenty-two years without issue, vowed that she would build a new church within the convent, if she bore an heir to the throne. After the death of her husband, Louis XIII., she fulfilled her vow. The first stone of the present church was laid in 1645, by her son, Louis XIV.

END OF VOL. I.

OLD COURT LIFE

IN FRANCE.

BY

FRANCES ELLIOT,

AUTHOR OF

"DIARY OF AN IDLE WOMAN IN ITALY," "PICTURES OF OLD ROME."

REVISED COPYRIGHT

EDITION.

IN TWO VOLUMES.—VOL. II.

LEIPZIG

BERNHARD TAUCHNITZ

1873.

CONTENTS

OF VOLUME II.

OLD COURT LIFE IN FRANCE.

CHAPTER I.

Tempted.

NEWS came from the army announcing brilliant success. The valour of the King was specially extolled; he was no longer a bashful, feeble prince, victimised by feminine cabals, tyrannized over by Richelieu. He had suddenly become a warrior, foremost in danger, leading his troops in person into the hottest of the fray. Each day his absence lasted, and every fresh intelligence that arrived, added to the excitement of Louise de Lafayette. The danger to which he was exposed made her tremble.

She eagerly desired his return, not for the mere pleasure of seeing and conversing with him (though that was very dear to her), but because she was sure that the time had come when he would himself hold the reins of government, and display all that nobleness of character with which her romantic fancy had invested him. Such, at least, was the conviction, however delusive, of the pretty maid of honour, who, lost in contemplation of the King's virtues, failed to perceive the state of her own heart.

At length the campaign terminated. Louis had re-taken all the places conquered by the Spaniards,

They were in full retreat. The King returned to Paris, which, not having been considered out of danger from the attacks of the enemy, received him with transports of joy. Mademoiselle de Lafayette, a witness of the universal enthusiasm, saw in Louis the worthy successor of Henry the Great, and the inheritor of all his glory. Intoxicated by these dreams, she imagined that even her advice would be in future needless—that the King of his own accord would suppress the arrogance of Richelieu, and from henceforth exercise the royal authority alone.

The following day, the Court being at the Louvre, Louis visited the Queen at her lever. As he returned into the ante-room, he approached Louise de Lafayette. She was too much agitated even to welcome him. That Louis was also greatly moved was evident. The pallor that always overspread his face when excited, was almost death-like, and every feature worked convulsively. For some moments they stood opposite each other, without saying a word. Then, overmastering his agitation, Louis spoke to her in a low voice: —"I know not, mademoiselle, when we shall be able to resume those conversations which were so infinitely delightful—I am overwhelmed with business." Then, after glancing round, and seeing that every one had retired, he seized her hand and kissed it tenderly.

"Ah! so much the better," said Louise, beaming with smiles. "May you, Sire, ever be thus occupied."

"Do you want to banish me, then, just as I am returned?" said he, retaining her hand in both of his.

"No, Sire; but I want to see you reign."

"You have heard me blamed for my indolence? I am sure you have. All I ask is, that you will wait and judge for yourself. The Court is filled with my enemies." He spoke with animation.

"Sire, I need not wait," replied the maid of honour eagerly, her liquid eyes, full of faith and affection, turned upon him, "I have long ago decided in your favour."

"May you never change!" ejaculated Louis fervently. "It would console me for a world of injustice. I must now leave you," and he pressed her hand again and raised it to his lips.

The eagerness with which Louis applied himself to state affairs after his return, evoked much mirth and ridicule among the ladies of the Court. Louise de Lafayette was pained. When Madame de Sennécy declared that his Majesty's industry could not possibly last, she was offended in the highest degree. The Cardinal too was openly abused for the military appointments he had made during the war by these fair critics, whereupon Louise, who dared not openly defend the King, endeavoured to justify him by exonerating the Cardinal. One morning, when both King and minister had been bitterly attacked in the anteroom, before the Queen had left her apartments, Louise remarked to those around her that the Cardinal, though unpopular, was undeniably great; that he had founded the Académie Française, rebuilt the Sorbonne, established the Royal Printing Press, founded the Jardin des Plantes, and that as a minister he was brave, daring, and wise.

These sentiments caused great surprise, for Mademoiselle de Lafayette had hitherto by no means spared Richelieu. The Duchesse de Sennécy openly rebuked her for what she styled her "hypocrisy," and sent her in tears to her room. Her words, however, were immediately reported to the Cardinal by Chavigny, a gentleman of the bedchamber, who was present, one of the many salaried court spies in his pay. Chavigny particularly dwelt upon the earnestness of the maid of honour, and assured the Cardinal that she could only have so expressed herself in order to gain his favour.

No sooner had Chavigny left the Palais Royal than the Comte de la Meilleraye, a distant relation of Richelieu, requested an audience. La Meilleraye was also in attendance on the King. He had come, as he said, to ask a great favour of his all-powerful cousin. Would the Cardinal assist him to a most advantageous marriage with a lady to whom he was devoted—Mademoiselle de Lafayette? From the first moment he had seen her, he said, her beauty, her elegance, her modest bearing and simplicity—qualities so rare in the Court circle—had enchanted him. Thus spoke the Comte de la Meilleraye. Richelieu listened graciously. He liked by all legitimate means to advance his family, and if the maid of honour was his partisan, as Chavigny had reported, nothing could be more expedient than such a marriage. He promised therefore to consult the King at once, and to endeavour to obtain his permission, warning La Meilleraye to do nothing in the matter until he had heard again from him.

The morning Council of State over, Richelieu accompanied the King into his writing-closet, to discuss in private some important matters.

As the Queen's coterie had predicted, Louis soon wearied of business; everything was now replaced, as before, in the hands of the minister.

Louis leant back in his chair. He scarcely heard the Cardinal's remarks.

From time to time, when specially appealed to, he bowed his head in acquiescence. Then turning away his eyes abstractedly towards the windows, which faced the inner court, he anxiously watched the driving clouds that scudded across the sky. He had fixed a hunting-party at Rambouillet, and longed to start as soon as the weather cleared, and Richelieu had left him.

The mellow voice of the Cardinal, who, however imperative in action, never startled his feeble master by any outward display of vehemence, had continued speaking for some time in a monotonous tone, when the King, seeing the sunshine appear, suddenly rose.

"Your eminence has, I imagine, done with me for to-day," said he, looking eagerly towards the door.

"Yes, Sire; but there is still a trifling matter upon which I would ask your decision."

"Pray mention it," replied Louis, tapping his boots with a riding-whip he had taken off a table.

"My relative, the Comte de la Meilleraye, begs your permission to marry."

"Willingly," replied Louis; "who is the fair lady, Cardinal?"

"It is Mademoiselle Louise de Lafayette, Sire, maid of honour to the Queen."

If a thunderbolt had fallen at his feet, Louis could not have been more overcome. He turned perfectly livid, took a long breath, tottered backwards and sat down again. The all-seeing eyes of the Cardinal were fixed upon him; he did not speak but watched his master. Louis for some moments did not raise his head; then he heaved a deep sigh, and with much effort, in a strangely different voice, asked faintly—

"Does Mademoiselle de Lafayette herself desire this marriage?"

Richelieu had turned away, and affecting to be busied with some books and papers lying on the table, replied in an indifferent manner—

"As yet, Sire, we are unacquainted with the lady's sentiments; but, as I am informed she has no other attachment, I cannot but believe such an alliance as that of my cousin will be acceptable to her."

The nervous spasm with which it was evident the King had awaited this reply instantly relaxed. The colour returned to his cheeks, his eyes brightened, and he stood up—

"Before I can decide anything," said he, "I must know Mademoiselle de Lafayette's feelings; acquaint me with them speedily."

He spoke in a firm, decided way, very unusual with him.

The Cardinal drew his own conclusions.

*   *   *   *   *   *

By-and-by Chavigny informed Richelieu that Mademoiselle de Lafayette had at once, and unhesitatingly, refused the hand of the Count. Richelieu only smiled. "I knew it. The King, my good Chavigny, is in love with her himself. She returns it. They understand each other. Chavigny, I must see this foolish girl, who ventures to mix herself up with his Majesty. I must personally acquaint myself with her feelings."

"Your Eminence will find it most difficult to speak with her in private. The Duchesse de Sennécy proposes giving a masked ball, at which her Majesty and the Court will be present; would that suit your plans?"

"Not at all," replied Richelieu. "When I speak there must be no mask. I must study her countenance. She is young and disingenuous. I shall read her inmost thoughts. She has not been long enough at Court to have learnt dissimulation. I must see her before the King leaves Paris. We can meet at my niece's, the Duchesse de Combalet."

"Mademoiselle de Lafayette could only feel honoured by such a summons from your Eminence," replied Chavigny.

"Yes, I fancy she will accept the offers I shall make her, unless she is an absolute idiot."

Mademoiselle de Lafayette was duly invited to a *déjeûner* at the Palais Cardinal by the Duchesse de Combalet, who received her alone. During breakfast her hostess said everything that could flatter and please her. She praised her dress and her appearance. She was so simple, so unselfish, so different from the other maids of honour, the Duchess said. Then she went on to inform her that she knew the Cardinal had the highest opinion of her; that he had often expressed his admiration of her character and her person to herself, the Duchess. "It is very unusual with him, mademoiselle, to speak to me about the Queen's ladies; he is too much engrossed with state affairs, too serious to notice them. But you are an exception; you have made a deep impression on my uncle."

Louise bowed, grew red and white by turns, and listened in wondering silence.

Suddenly the door opened, and Cardinal Richelieu appeared, followed by two favourite cats. Smiling benignly, he received the maid of honour with great condescension. Mademoiselle de Lafayette rose at his entrance, and was about to withdraw, when he took her hand and insisted on her reseating herself.

The Duchesse de Combalet spoke with him on general subjects, and constantly appealed to Louise for her opinion. She gave it with her usual modest frankness. Everything she said was applauded by the Cardinal. He put forth all his powers to please her.

In about half an hour a servant entered and whispered to the Duchess. She affected great annoyance at the interruption, and begged the Cardinal and her guest to excuse her for a quarter of an hour, while she gave some directions. "Besides," said she, and she turned with a meaning look to the maid of honour, "I know that his Eminence wants to have a little private conversation with you about our cousin De la Meilleraye, whom you have so cruelly refused. Poor man! he is in despair. I shall return in a few minutes." Saying which she kissed Mademoiselle de Lafayette on both cheeks, and withdrew.

Richelieu and the maid of honour were now alone. The Cardinal was no longer the dissolute prelate of other days, the adorer of two queens of France, the slave of Madame de Chevreuse, the lover of Marion de l'Orme. The life of labour he led would have long ago killed any but a man of his iron will and

calm temperament. He never slept more than three
hours at a time, and literally worked day and night.
At eight o'clock in the morning he was astir, ready to
receive spies, generals, and ministers, suppliants, and
princes, who were already waiting in the ante-room.
He was as active as a Roman senator, with a hundred
clients assembled in his portico. His cheeks were
pinched and sunken; his face sallow; his thin lips
colourless; his brow, a network of those fine wrinkles
that come of excessive thought. Even his eyes were
dull, and half concealed by his eyelids, though on occasions they would still shoot forth sparks of fire. The
straight hair that lay upon his forehead, under his red
calotte, was scanty and almost white. Altogether, his
appearance was that of a man physically worn-out, and
indicative of his painful illness and somewhat premature death. But the spirit of the man was strong
within him, and a consciousness of latent power dis-
closed itself in every feature.

As he leant back in a spacious arm-chair, the two
cats nestled on his knees, he bent his half-closed
eyes upon Louise with almost feline cunning. Those
half-closed eyes alone betrayed his nature; otherwise, his countenance expressed nothing but tranquil
enjoyment.

"Mademoiselle de Lafayette," he said in a soft,
musical voice that struck pleasantly upon the ear, "I
have both to reproach you and to thank you." Louise
looked at him with surprise. "Yes, I thank you for
the favour with which I hear you speak of me; and I
reproach you for having hitherto concealed from me
your good opinion. I am desirous to see you become
a member of my family. I hope you will marry my

cousin. But, believe me, the ties of gratitude are stronger with me than those of blood. Mademoiselle, I wish to be your friend." Louise bowed her head with great respect, but felt bewildered.

Richelieu piqued himself on being a great physiognomist. He had made a special study of the human countenance. He saw that the face of Mademoiselle de Lafayette was totally untroubled. Her perfect self-possession astonished him. The phrase he had uttered—"I wish to be your friend," solemn words, indeed, from the mouth of Richelieu—had caused in her no change of expression! Her composed demeanour was, in the eyes of the Cardinal, an additional reason for securing her as a partisan. He had before much desired to gain her to himself, but he now came to attach an immense importance to success.

"I am very grateful for your Eminence's kind expressions," said Louise at last, with great modesty, but with equal firmness; "but I do not wish to marry. If the offer of your friendship involves any sacrifice of my freedom, I must, with sorrow, decline it. I seek nothing, your Eminence. I need no protection." There was a quiet dignity in her words and manner that took the Cardinal aback. He said nothing; but his eyes, now fully open and glistening, rested on the maid of honour with surprise and displeasure.

Yet the real loftiness of soul she displayed, the indifference with which she ignored his offers, appeared to him so unaccountable that he could only imagine she wished to extract from him some terms more definite and decided. This idea gave him courage to recommence the attack.

"Let us be frank," said he, smiling. "I know all."

"What do you mean, monseigneur?"

"The King loves you. The purity of his heart and his high principles may allow you to confess it. He loves you. And his interest, as well as your own, requires that we should be friends."

Mademoiselle de Lafayette grew very pale; she trembled, but did not for a moment lose her presence of mind. "To what sort of friendship does your Eminence allude?"

"An entire confidence on your part, and an active acknowledgment on mine."

The Cardinal was on the point of promising her titles, estates, and pensions; but Mademoiselle de Lafayette, who, with downcast eyes, listened to him in silence, all at once looked up fixedly into his face. This look stopped him short.

"Your Eminence," said she, "can only wish me to give my personal confidence. In honour I could promise no other. But I *have* no secrets, no concealments. I am without ambition, I desire no favour. Besides, I am sure that your Eminence will at once understand me when I say—that, if ever it were the pleasure of his Majesty to repose confidence in me— *there is no temptation, no power upon earth*, that would induce me to betray it." As she spoke, she looked straight at the Cardinal. The colour returned to her cheeks, and she sat erect—gentle, yet infinitely bold.

Richelieu reddened, but he suppressed his rising indignation. "The confidence of a great King," replied he solemnly, a dark fire darting from his eyes, "can only be properly accepted when the person to whom it is addressed is capable of offering real assistance to the sovereign. I propose, Mademoiselle de Lafayette, to render you capable of imparting such assistance. Whatever may be your natural sense and penetration, this is an occasion in which experience alone is valuable."

"But does not your Éminence think that rectitude of purpose——"

"It is evident that you are little versed in the intrigues of courts, mademoiselle," answered he loftily, eyeing her with haughty disdain. "Perhaps some day you will discover that the offer I have made you of my esteem and assistance is not to be despised."

"No one can attach a higher value **than** I do to the good opinion of your Éminence," interposed Mademoiselle de Lafayette with warmth; "but I do not think you have at all proved it in what you have just said. Although I think I deserve it," she added timidly.

The Cardinal contemplated **her** attentively for some moments. His face was set, his eyes flashed, and his hands which were clenched rested on his knees. "I have only one word m**ore** to add," said he in an angry voice. "Any idea of favour with the King without my support is a delusion." He was rapidly losing self-restraint. This girl had lashed him into a fury. She saw it, but felt no fear.

"Your Eminence, I think only of my duty," she replied with firmness. "I fear no threats. I can make no promise."

At these words the Cardinal rose. His face was swollen with passion; a wicked fire gleamed in his eyes; her coolness transported him beyond endurance. "Once more, Mademoiselle de Lafayette, remember

what I say.—My resolutions are unalterable; I trample
down everything.   Without my assistance, beware!
Think of the future.   Recall the past.   My enemies
are rotting in their graves—my friends rule France."
Then, speaking more calmly, he added, "You are too
great a fool to understand what you are doing.   I
can pardon your presumption, however, because I
know how to cure it.   Mademoiselle de Lafayette, you
may withdraw."

CHAPTER II.

The Keeper of the Royal Conscience.

RICHELIEU, thoroughly exasperated, determined to
crush the girl who had dared to brave him.   He called
to his aid his creature Chavigny.   Chavigny was intriguing, acute, and superficial; an admirable tool—
for he originated nothing.   Years ago he had sold
himself to Richelieu, but as he always went out of his
way to abuse him, the connection was not suspected.
Under the direction of the Cardinal, he had entirely
gained the King's confidence.   His easy goodnature
encouraged the shy Louis to tell him all his secrets,
and to consult him in all his difficulties.

Chavigny, who up to this time had attached little
importance to the King's inclination for the new maid
of honour, looking upon it simply as a passing admiration for an attractive girl, too inexperienced to
take advantage of his favour, upon being questioned,
informed Richelieu that the King wrote to her daily,
and that she replied as often.   Richelieu at once
resolved on his course of action.   He would in future
see the correspondence himself.   Each letter was to

20

be skilfully unsealed by his secretary, Desmaret, and read, before it was delivered.

It was not possible for even the hard, stern Richelieu to peruse these letters unmoved. He had been once young and passionate himself. He could not but appreciate the delicacy and eloquence with which the King veiled his passion, and softened intense love into the semblance of friendship. Nor could he avoid feeling some admiration for the sweet and simple nature that breathed in every line written by the maid of honour. Both were evidently ignorant of the ardour of their mutual attachment. What was to be done? He must consult the King's confessor.

Father Caussin, a Jesuit, had been only nine months confessor to the King. He was learned, conscientious, and guileless. Richelieu had selected him for this important post in the belief that he would assume no political influence over his royal penitent. The General of the order had objected to his appointment on the same grounds. In person Caussin was tall and spare. His long black cassock hung about his thin figure in heavy folds. His face was pale and emaciated. Yet a kindly smile played about his mouth, and his black eyes beamed with benevolence. Such was the ecclesiastic who seated himself opposite to Richelieu.

"My father," said the Cardinal, saluting him stiffly, and leaning forward and laying his hands on some papers placed beside him on a table, as though they related to what he was about to say.—"I have summoned you on a very grave matter." Nothing could be more solemn than the Cardinal's voice and manner. The pleasant smile faded at once out of the confessor's face. He became as grave, if not as stern, as the Cardinal, leant his head upon his bony hand, and turned his eyes intently upon him. "Circumstances have come to my knowledge," continued Richelieu, "which, in my opinion, justify me in asking you a very searching question." Caussin moved uneasily, and in a somewhat troubled manner interrupted him.

"Your Eminence will not, I trust, desire to trench upon the privacy of my office,—for in that case I could not satisfy you."

Richelieu waved his hand impatiently, placed one knee over the other with great deliberation, and leant back in his chair. "My father, I am surprised at your insinuation. We are both Churchmen, and, I presume, understand our respective duties. The question that I would ask is one to which you may freely reply. Does it appear to you that his Majesty has of late shown indifference in his spiritual duties?" Caussin drew a long breath, and, though relieved, was evidently unwilling to answer.

"Pardon me, my father," again spoke the Cardinal, a slight tone of asperity perceptible in his mellow voice, "I ask you this question entirely in the interest of the holy order to which you belong. Many benefices have fallen vacant lately, and it is possible,—it is *possible*, I repeat, that I may advise his Majesty to fill up some of them from the ranks of the Company of Jesus." His half-closed eyes rested significantly on Father Caussin as he said these words.

Caussin listened unmoved. "There are, doubtless," said he, "many members of our order who would do honour to your selection, Cardinal. For myself, I want no preferment;—indeed, I should decline it." He spoke with the frankness of perfect sincerity.

Richelieu looked down, and worked the points of his fingers impatiently on the table. His hands were singularly white and shapely, with taper fingers. As a young man he had loved to display them; the habit had remained with him when he was thoughtful or annoyed. "Well, my father," said he, "your answer?"

Caussin eyed the Cardinal suspiciously,—"I am happy to reassure your Eminence; his Majesty is, as usual in the most pious sentiments."

"Hum!—that is strange, very strange; I fear that the benevolence of your nature, my father—" Caussin drew himself up, and a look as much approaching defiance as it was possible for him to assume passed into his pleasant face. Richelieu did not finish the offensive sentence. "It is strange," he went on to say, "for I have reason to *know*—I ask you for no information, reverend father—that his Majesty's feelings are engaged in a mundane passion which, if encouraged, may lead him from those precepts and exercises in which he has hitherto lived in obedience to the Church."

"To what passion do you allude?" asked Caussin cautiously.

"To the infatuation his Majesty evinces for the new maid of honour, Louise de Lafayette. The lady is self-willed and romantic. She may lead him into deadly sin."

Caussin started. "I apprehend nothing of the kind," replied he drily.

"True, my father, but that is a matter of opinion. I think differently. Absolution, after repentance," continued the Cardinal pompously, "may wash out even crime, but it is for us,—you, his Majesty's confessor, and I, his minister, both faithful servants of the Holy Father,"—Caussin looked hard at the Cardinal, who was by no means considered **orthodox** at Rome,—"it is for us to guard him from even the semblance of evil. I ha**ve sent for you,** my father, to assist me in placing **Louise** de **Lafayette** in a convent. It will **be** at least a measure of precaution. I shall require **all** your help, my father; will you give it me?" Richelieu, as he asked this important question, **narrowly** observed Caussin from under his drooping eyelids. The confessor was evidently embarrassed. His kindly countenance **was** troubled; and he was some time in answering.

"To dedicate a young and pure soul to God," he replied, at length, with evident hesitation, "is truly an acceptable work; but has your Eminence considered that the lady in question is of the most blameless life, **and** that by **her** example and influence his Ma-jesty **may be** kept **in** that path of obedience and **faith** which some other attachment might not insure?" **As** he asked **this question** Caussin leaned forwards to-wards Richelieu, speaking earnestly.

"**Father** Caussin," said the Cardinal in his **hardest** manner, **and** motioning with his **hand** as though commanding special attention, "we **must** look in this matter beyond his Majesty's feelings. I **have** good reason for alarm. A crisis is impending," and he turned again to the **papers** lying on the table with a significant air. "**If** Louise de Lafayette has any **vo**cation, let her **be** advised to encourage it. Consider in what manner you can best bend the King's will to comply. You tell me the lady is a good Catholic; I rejoice to hear it. She comes of a family of heretics. She may be sincere, though I much doubt it. At all events, she must be removed; simply as a matter of precaution, my father, I repeat, she must be removed. Let me beg you to consult the General of your order upon this matter immediately. Understand me, I am advising this simply as a matter of precaution, nothing more." All this time Caussin had listened intently to the Cardinal. The troubled look on his face had deepened into one of infinite sadness. His brow was knit, but there were doubt and hesitation in his manner.

"I can only consent to assist your Eminence," he replied, in a low voice, after some moments of deep thought, "on the condition that the lady herself freely consents. I can permit no violence to be done to her inclinations, nor to the will of his Majesty. If the lady is ready to offer up herself to the Church through my means, it will doubtless redound to the credit of our order; but she shall not be forced."

"Certainly not, certainly not," interposed Richelieu, in a much more affable tone. "I do not know why your reverence should start such a supposition."

"I will consult our General, Cardinal," continued Caussin; "but I am bound to say that the influence the lady has hitherto exercised has been most legitimate, most orthodox, altogether in favour of our order, to which she is devoted, and of the Church. She is a most pious lady."

"All the more fit for the privilege I propose to bestow upon her," answered Richelieu, with unction; "she will be safe from temptation within the bosom

of the Church, a blessing we, my father,"—and Richelieu affected to heave a deep sigh, and cast up his
eyes to heaven, "we, who live in the world, cannot
attain. We act then in concert, my father," he added
quickly, in his usual manner, "we act for the good of
his Majesty's soul?"

Caussin bowed acquiescence, but mistrust and
perplexity were written upon every line of his honest
face, as he observed the evident satisfaction evinced
by the Cardinal at his compliance.

Richelieu rose: "We will force no one's inclination, my father," he said blandly, "but all possibility
of scandal must be removed. You must at once prepare his Majesty. It will be a good work, and will
greatly recommend you to your order." Caussin, with
a look of the deepest concern, bowed profoundly and
withdrew. When he was alone, the Cardinal re-seated
himself and fell into a deep muse. "Now," said he,
at length, speaking to himself, "her fate is sealed. I
will take care that her vocation shall be perfect. This
presumptuous girl shall soon come to rejoice, ay, rejoice, that she is permitted to take refuge in a convent. As for Caussin, he is a fool. I must remove
him immediately."

Richelieu, as he said of himself, never halted in
his resolves. Caussin was shortly sent off by a *lettre
de cachet* to Rennes, narrowly escaping an intimation
from the Cardinal to his Superior that it would be
well to exercise his devotion to the order as a mis-
sionary in Canada.

CHAPTER III.

A Noble Resolve.

THE Court had removed from the Louvre to Saint-Germain, always the favourite abode of the melancholy monarch.

Louis suffered tortures from the galling restraints his position entailed upon him in his intercourse with Mademoiselle de Lafayette. He rarely saw her alone. When he addressed her, he was conscious that every eye was fixed upon them. Their correspondence, carried on by means of Chavigny, was, he felt, full of danger. His only comforter in his manifold troubles was this same treacherous Chavigny. Prompted by the Cardinal, Chavigny urged the King, on every possible occasion, to make some arrangement with Mademoiselle de Lafayette to meet in private. "If she loves you," said this unworthy tool, "if you really possess her heart, she will long to meet your Majesty with greater freedom as much as you can do. It is for you to make some such proposal to her. Do it, Sire; do it without delay, or I assure you the lady will think you careless and indifferent." Thus spoke Chavigny. Louis listened, meditated on what he said, and was convinced. He gave himself up to the most entrancing day-dreams.

The season was summer. The weather was hot, and the tall windows of the great saloon were thrown open. The Court had gathered round the Queen, who was engaged in a lively conversation with Mademoiselle de Montpensier, the young daughter of the Duc d'Orléans. Seeing that her services were not required,

Louise de Lafayette, pensive and silent, stole away to the balcony outside the windows. She stood alone, lost in her own thoughts. With noiseless steps Louis approached her. He lent by her side over the balustrade, bending his eyes on the broad plains towards Paris.

"You are thoughtful, Sire," said Louise timidly. "Will you tell me your thoughts?"

"If I do," replied Louis, casting a fond glance upon her, "will you trust me with yours?"

A delicious tremor passed through her whole frame. She cast down her large grey eyes, and smiled. "Indeed I trust you, Sire," she murmured softly; "you know I do."

"But trust me more,— let our communion be more intimate. A brother's love is not more pure than mine," whispered the King; "but," and he hesitated and blushed, "I have never enjoyed the privilege of a brother." Louise raised her eyes inquiringly. The King was greatly confused. "A brother—" and he stopped. Then, seeing her earnest look of curiosity— "A brother," he repeated, "salutes his sister: I have never enjoyed that privilege, Louise." He was scarcely audible. "Let my self-denial, at least, secure me all your confidence."

"Oh, Sire, you have it, entire and unreserved; you know it. I might distrust myself, but you, Sire, never, never!"

"How happy you make me!" returned the King, and a sickly smile overspread his haggard face. "I understand—I appreciate your attachment to me; but oh, mademoiselle, how can my feeble words express mine to you?—how can I describe that which is without bounds—without limit? You can live without me. You can find solace in your own perfection, in the admiration of those around you—but I, I am nothing without you. I am a mere blank—a blot upon a luxurious Court—an offence to my superb wife. No one cares for my happiness—not even for my existence, but you. When I cannot approach you, I am overcome by despair. Oh, Louise, give yourself up to me, in pity—without fear, without restraint. Let me see you every day,—let me be encouraged by your words, led by your counsels, soothed by your pity, blessed by your sight. You say you do not doubt me. What then do you fear?"

The maid of honour looked at him with tearful eyes. His earnestness, his desolation, his entreaties, melted her heart. Her unconscious love made her pulses beat as quickly as his own.

"You know that I am devoted to you,—what more can I say?" she whispered softly.

"I have a favour to ask you," said Louis anxiously, —"a favour so great I hesitate to name it." He was greatly agitated. At this moment the passionate love he felt animated him with new life, and lent a charm to his countenance it had never borne before.

"A favour, Sire?—it is granted before you speak. How is it that you have concealed it from me?"

"Then I am satisfied,"—the King heaved a sigh of relief,—"what I ask depends entirely on you. You will grant it."

"Am I to promise?"

"Well, only give me your word; that is enough."

"Sire, I give you my word; from the bottom of

my heart, I give you my word. Tell me what it is
you desire." And she raised her face towards the King,
who contemplated her with silent rapture.

"Not now—not now," murmured he, in a faltering voice; "I dare not; it would require too long an
explanation,—we might be interrupted," and he turned
and glanced at the scene behind him,—at Anne of
Austria, blazing with diamonds, radiant with regal
beauty, her silvery laugh surmounting the hum of conversation. He saw the brilliant crowd that thronged
around her where she sat. Great princes, illustrious
ministers, historic nobles, chivalric soldiers, grave di-
plomatists, stately matrons, ministers of state, her ladies
in waiting, and the five other maids of honour, in the
glory of golden youth. He saw the dazzling lights,
the fluttering feathers, the gorgeous robes, the sparkling
jewels, standing out from the painted walls,—all the
glamour of a luxurious Court. Then he gazed at the
sweet face of the lonely girl whose loving eyes were
bent upon him awaiting his reply,—his soul sank
within him.

"Would to God I were not King of France," he
exclaimed abruptly, following the tenor of his thoughts.
Then, seeing her wonder at this sudden outburst, he
added, "The favour I ask of you shall be made known
to you in writing. This evening you shall receive a
letter from me; but,"—and he drew closer to her and
spoke almost fiercely,—"remember you have pledged
yourself to me—you cannot, you dare not withdraw
your word. If you do,"—and an agonized look came
into his face,—"you will drive me to madness."
Saying these words, he suddenly disappeared. She
was again left standing alone on the balcony.

Louise de Lafayette was startled, but not alarmed. The notion that the King was capable of making any indecorous proposition to her never for a moment occurred to her; at the same time she felt the utmost curiosity to know what this secret might be. She formed a thousand different conjectures, each further than the other from the truth. On entering her room at night, she found a letter from the King. She hastily tore it open, and read as follows:—

"I have long adored you, and you only. During the whole time that you have been at Court, I have been able but thrice to address you alone, and to chance only did I even then owe that inexpressible privilege. It is impossible for me to endure this restraint any longer. If you feel as I do, you will not desire it. I have therefore commanded that my hunting-lodge at Versailles should be arranged as much as possible in accordance with your taste. There is a garden laid out, filled with the flowers you love; there are secluded lawns; there is the boundless forest. Above all, there is freedom. Come then, my Louise, and share with me this rural retreat—come where we can meet, unrestrained by the formalities of my Court. Bring with you any friend you please. At Versailles I hope to spend part of every week in your company. My happiness will be perfect; you will find me the most grateful of men. You will have nothing to fear. Do you dread calumny? Who would dare to attack a lady as pure as yourself? May I not claim your consent when I rely on your promise to grant whatever I ask? I feel that you cannot deny me, for you have repeated a thousand times that you trust my principles. You cannot doubt my honour. To refuse

me would only be to insult me. Surely, Louise, you
would not do that! It would wound me to the very
soul. It would destroy every hope of my future life.
(Signed) "LOUIS."

When Mademoiselle de Lafayette read this artful
letter, which had been composed by Chavigny under
the direction of Richelieu, and copied out by the
King, she was utterly confounded. The fatal veil
which had so long concealed the truth fell from her
eyes. Even to a girl pure and simple as herself, all
further delusion was impossible. This letter and the
feelings that dictated it were not to be misunderstood.

"Merciful heavens!" cried she, clasping her hands,
"with what a tone of authority, with what assurance,
he proposes to dishonour me! This, then, is the
attachment I believed to be so pure! What! does he,
the husband of the Queen of France, suppose that I
would encourage a guilty passion? Wretch that I am!
Instead of helping him, I have led him into sin! I had
no right to engross his thoughts. He is already
estranged from his wife, and I have severed them still
further! O God! what will the Queen think of me?
How can I atone for this horrible sin? I must—I will
—reconcile them. Then God may forgive my involuntary crime!"

Again and again, with tears streaming down her
cheeks, she read and re-read the letter. She pressed
the paper to her lips. The next moment she dashed
it on the floor in an agony of remorse.

"Oh, how can I reply?" sobbed she. "What can
I say to temper the blow which must sever us? He
will be in despair—he will die. But my reputation,

my honour—his own—his duty to the Queen! No, I
will never consent to such degradation — my soul
revolts at the thought! How gladly would I sacrifice
my life for him, but I cannot commit a sin. I must
leave the palace, I must go—Whither?"

As she listened to the echo of her own words, an
unformed thought suddenly darted into her mind.
Go — yes, she would go where none could follow.
Youth, beauty, wealth, the sacrifice should be complete. She would prove, even in separation, how great
had been her love. "*There is no other way,*" she said,
speaking aloud, and an angelic smile lit up her face.
She cast herself upon her knees, and prayed in peace.
Her prayer finished, she took up her pen and replied
thus to the King:—

"Your Majesty desires that we should no longer
meet in the presence of witnesses. Before knowing
what was required of me, I promised to comply. I
will not withdraw my word; but I entreat of your
Majesty the liberty of myself selecting the place where
these private interviews are to be held. When I have
received your Majesty's assent, I will inform you where
this place is to be. In eight days' time I shall be
prepared to receive you. Your Majesty can then judge
of the extent of my confidence, and of the unbounded
devotion I feel towards you.

"LOUISE DE LAFAYETTE."

CHAPTER IV.

The Sacrifice.

NEXT morning, as soon as it was light, Louise sent for the King's confessor. She showed him the King's letter, and confided to him her resolution. Caussin listened in silence; but the kindly old man, priest though he was, could not restrain his tears — so touching was her innocence, so heartfelt her sorrow. He understood the simple goodness of her heart; he trembled at the sacrifice she was imposing on herself; but he could not combat her arguments. He promised, therefore, to assist in making the needful arrangements, and he pledged himself to support the King in the trial awaiting him.

The coach was in waiting which was to bear her to her future home. All at once she recollected she had still one final sacrifice to make. The letters of the King, which she always carried about her, were still intact within the silken cover in which she preserved them. She drew these letters from her bosom, and gazed on them in silent agony. Her eyes were blinded by tears. She dared not read them again, for she knew they would but increase her grief. As she held them in her hand, remorse at what she had done preponderated over every feeling. Thus to have enthralled a husband belonging to another — her sovereign and her mistress—came suddenly before her in its true light. She felt she had forgotten her duty. Once more she kissed the crumpled leaves over which her fingers had so often passed; she deluged them

with her tears.   Then she lit a taper and set fire to
the whole.

She sat immovable before the burning fragments;
her eyes fixed, her hands clasped.   As the flame rose,
glistened, and then melted away into light particles
of dust that the morning air, blowing in from the
open window, bore away fluttering in the breeze, she
seemed to look upon the death of her love.   "Alas!"
cried she, "now all is over."   Vows of eternal constancy, entreaties that would melt a heart of stone,
confidence beyond all limit, affection that enshrouded
her in folds of unutterable tenderness—gone,—vanished into air!   Such was the image of her life: a life
bright in promise, gay and dazzling, to smoulder
down into ashes, too fragile even to claim a resting-
place.

Louise de Lafayette wrote a few lines to the
Duchesse de Sennécy, praying her to convey her dutiful salutations to her Majesty, and to request her dis-
missal from the post of maid of honour, which, she
said, "she felt she had fulfilled so ill."   Then she addressed the following note to the King:—"I request
your Majesty to meet me this day week, at noon, in
the parlour of the Convent of the Daughters of Mary,
in the Faubourg Saint-Antoine."

When the King read these lines his heart sank
within him.   The austerity of the place, a rendezvous
in a convent of peculiar sanctity, where he knew Mademoiselle de Lafayette always resorted at the solemn
season of Lent and Passion Week, where he could
only converse with her between double bars, was not
the place of meeting of which he had fondly dreamed!
Yet his natural delicacy made him fully appreciate the

modesty of Louise and the gentle rebuke she administered to him for his too pressing solicitation in naming a place of meeting. At the convent, although they would certainly be alone, no scandal could possibly attach to the interview. More than this he never for an instant imagined. The habits of piety in which Mademoiselle de Lafayette lived, and her frequent retreats for religious purposes, raised in his mind no suspicion. He should see her, and see her alone, undisturbed, unwatched. On that thought he dwelt with rapture; time would, he hoped, do the rest.

Punctually, at noon, the King arrived at the Convent of the Daughters of Mary. He was received by the Abbess in person, and conducted into the parlour. Here she left him. A moment more, a curtain was withdrawn, and, behind double bars of iron, Louise de Lafayette stood before him. She wore the dark brown robes and corded girdle of the order, the long white veil of the noviciate falling round her lovely face. The King stood transfixed, his eyes riveted upon her.

"Forgive me, Sire," said she, in a voice full of sweetness, "forgive me for having dared to dispose of myself without your leave. But, Sire, a too fervent attachment had led us both into danger. I had forgotten my duty in the love I felt for you,—your Majesty forgot you were a husband. That letter, in which you proposed meeting me at Versailles, opened my eyes to the truth. God be thanked, there was yet time for repentance. This morning I have taken the white veil, and in a year I shall pronounce the final vows. My life will still be passed with you, Sire; but

3*

it will be a life of prayer." As she spoke she smiled sadly, and awaited his reply.

"Great God!" exclaimed Louis at length, when he could find words. "Is this a vision? Are you an angel already glorified?" He sank upon his knees before her.

"Rise, Sire," said she solemnly; "such a posture befits neither the dignity of your station nor the sacredness of mine. I am no angel, but still your tender friend; a friend who watches over you, who only lives to remind you of your duties. You will share my heart with the holy virgins among whom I live, the saints in heaven, and my God. Let not even the tomb divide us—live, Sire, such a life that we may be reunited among the spirits of the just."

"Oh, Louise!" exclaimed Louis, in a voice choked with emotion; "Louise, who alone fills my despairing, my solitary heart! at your feet I abjure all profane, all unholy thoughts. Speak—command me! my spirit follows you. But, alas!" and he rose to his feet and wrung his hands in bitterest anguish, "what is to become of me in the midst of my detestable Court? Suffer me to follow your example; let me too, within the walls of a cloister, seek that resignation and courage which make you so sublime."

"Good heavens, Sire!" exclaimed Louise de La-fayette, "what do I hear? You, a sovereign, a husband, bury yourself in a cloister! Our situations are utterly unlike. I, a solitary girl, have but withdrawn from a world to which you were my only tie. Your glory, the glory of France, your own welfare, and the welfare of the Queen, are to you sacred duties. And now, Sire, listen to me," and she approached close to the bars which divided them, and a look of the old melting tenderness passed for a moment over her beautiful face, "Sire, if ever I have been dear to you, listen. The sin for which I feel most poignant sorrow—the sin which years, nay, a life of expiation cannot wipe out—is—that I have by my selfish, my miserable attachment, alienated you from the Queen." Louis was about to interrupt her, but she signed to him to be silent. "I know, Sire, what you would say," she broke in hastily,—"that our attachment has in no way altered your relations towards her Majesty. True, it is so; but my influence over you ought to have been devoted to reunite you. It ought to have been my privilege to render both your Majesties happy as man and wife, to give heirs to France, to strengthen the Government. Alas, alas! I have sinned almost beyond forgiveness!" and for awhile she broke into passionate sobs, which all her self-command could not restrain. "Her Majesty, Sire, is a most noble lady, beautiful generous, loyal, courageous. For twenty years she, the greatest queen in Europe, has been neglected, almost scorned by you her husband. Under these trials her lofty spirit has not flinched—she has been true to you and to herself. Temptation, provocation, nay, insults have not shaken her virtue. Believe nothing against her, Sire—her soul is as lovely as her body. Sire, the Queen is childless, devote your whole life to her and to France; tend her, protect her, love her. Then, and then only, shall I be reconciled to God." As she spoke her sweet grey eyes turned towards heaven, her countenance was transfigured as in an ecstasy; no saint standing within a sculptured shrine could be more pure, more holy.

The King gazed at her awestruck. "Dispose of me as you will," murmured he; "command my life—but, remember that now I have lost you, happiness is gone from me for ever!"

"Adieu, Sire," said Mademoiselle de Lafayette. "The hour-glass warns me that **our** interview is over. Return in six months and tell me that I have been obeyed."

She drew the dark curtain across the bars, and the Abbess entered. Louis returned hastily to Saint-Germain.

CHAPTER V.

Monsieur le Grand.

IN the broad valley of the Loire, between Tours and Saumur, the train stops at the small station of Cinq-Mars. This station lies beside the Loire, which glides by in a current so broad and majestic, as to suggest a series of huge lakes, with banks bordered by sand and scrub, rather than a river. On either side of the Loire run ranges of low hills, their grassy surface gashed and scored by many a rent revealing the chalky soil beneath, their summits fringed with scanty underwood, and dotted with groups of gnarled and knotted oaks and ragged fir-trees, the rough roots clasping cairns of rock and blocks of limestone. In the dimples of these low hills lie snugly sheltered villas, each within its own garden and policy. These villas thicken as the small township of Cinq-Mars is approached,—a nest of bright little houses, gay streets, and tall chimneys telling of provincial commerce, all clustering beneath chalky cliffs which rise abruptly

behind, rent by many a dark fissure and blackened
watercourse. Aloft, on a grassy marge, where many
an old tree bends its scathed trunk to the prevailing
wind, among bushes and piled-up heaps of stones,
rise the ruins of a feudal castle. Two gate towers
support an arch, through which the blue sky peeps,
and some low, broken walls, without form and void,
skirt the summit of the cliff. This ruin, absolutely
pathetic in its desolate loneliness, is all that remains
of the ancestral castle of the Cöiffiers de Cinq-Mars,
Marquis d'Effiat. From this hearth and from these
shattered walls, now razed "*to the height of infamy*,"
sprung that handsome, shallow, ambitious coxcomb,
known as the Marquis de Cinq-Mars, who succeeded
Mademoiselle de Lafayette in the favour of Louis XIII.

Deprived of Louise de Lafayette, the King's spirits
languished. In spite of his partial reconciliation with
Anne of Austria, and the birth of a son, he was sullen
and gloomy, spoke to no one, and desired no one to
speak to him. When etiquette required his presence
in the Queen's apartments, he seated himself in a
corner, yawned, and fell asleep. The internal malady
of which he died had already undermined his always
feeble frame. His condition was altogether so critical,
that the Cardinal looked round for a companion to
solace his weariness. Henri de Cinq-Mars had lately
come up to Paris from Touraine. In years he was a
boy, under twenty. He was gentle, adroit, and amusing,
but weak, and the Cardinal believed he had found in
him the facile instrument he sought.

Cinq-Mars was presented to the King. Louis was
at once prepossessed by his handsome person and
distinguished manners. Cinq-Mars, accustomed from

infancy to field sports and country life, angling in
the deep currents of the Loire and the Indre, hunting
wild boars and deer in the dense forests of Azay and
of Chanteloup, or flying his gear-falcon from the
summits of his native downs, struck a sympathetic
chord in the sad King's heart. One honour after the
other was heaped upon him; finally he was made
Grand Seneschal of France and Master of the Horse.
From this time he dropped the patronymic of "Cinq-
Mars," and was known at Court as "Monsieur le
Grand," one of the greatest personages in France. For
a time all went smoothly. King and minister smiled
upon the petulant stripling, whose witty sallies and
boyish audacity were tempered by the highest breed-
ing. He was always present when the Cardinal conferred with the King, and from the first gave his
opinion with much more freedom than altogether
pleased the minister, who simply intended him for a
puppet, not for an adviser. When the Cardinal
remonstrated, Cinq-Mars shook his scented curls,
pulled his lace ruffles, talked of loyalty and gratitude
to the King, and of personal independence, in a
manner the Cardinal deemed highly unbecoming and
inconvenient. Monsieur le Grand cared little for what
the Cardinal thought, and did not take the trouble to
hide this opinion. He cared neither for the terrible
minister nor for the eccentric Louis, whom he often
treated, even in public, with contempt. It was the
old story. Confident in favour, arrogant in power, he
made enemies every day.

Monsieur le Grand, however, passed his time with
tolerable ease when relieved of the King's company,
specially in the house of Marion de l'Orme, Rue des

Tournelles. He was presented to her by Saint-Evré-
mond, and fell at once a victim to her wiles. Marion
was the Aspasia of the day, and the charm of her
entourage was delightful to him after the restraints of
a dull and formal Court. Here he met d'Ablancourt,
La Chambre, and Calprenéde, the popular writers of
the age. The Abbé de Gondi and Scarron came also,
and even the prudish Mademoiselle de Scudéri did
not disdain to be present at these *Noctes Ambrosianæ*.
Marion de l'Orme, then only thirty, was in the zenith
of her beauty. Her languishing dark eyes exercised
an absolute fascination over Cinq-Mars from the first
instant they met. Her affected reserve, the refinement
of her manners, the *entrain* of her society, free without license, captivated him. He believed her to be
virtuous, and desired to make her his wife. Marion
de l'Orme was to become *Madame la Grande!*

This was precisely what that astute lady had
angled for. Hence her reserve, her downcast eyes,
her affected indifference. She saw that she was dealing with a vain, ignorant boy, who, in her hands, was
helpless as an infant. Truly, he was madly in love
with her, but he was a minor, and under the guardian-
ship of the Dowager Marquise de Cinq-Mars, his
mother, who might possibly not view an alliance with
Mademoiselle Marion de l'Orme as an honour to the
ancestral tree of the Effiats de Cinq-Mars. The marriage must be secret. Early one morning they started
from the Rue des Tournelles in a coach, and never
stopped until they had reached the old castle among
the hills of Touraine, above the feudatory village of
Cinq-Mars. In the chapel of that now ruined pile
their faith was plighted. Marion promised love, Cinq-

Mars constancy. They were incapable of either. For eight days the old castle rang with the sounds of revelry. Cinq-Mars and Marion were as in a fairy palace; life was but a long enchantment. But at the end of that time Nemesis appeared in the shape of the Dowager Marchioness, to whose ears the report of these merry-makings came at Paris. Cinq-Mars replied to his mother that it was all a *passetemps*, and that Mademoiselle de l'Orme—well—was still Mademoiselle de l'Orme; that he loved the Principessa Maria di Gonzaga (to whom the handsome profligate had, indeed, paid his addresses before leaving Paris, the better to throw dust in the eyes of the world), and that he should shortly return to Paris and his duty with his Majesty.

The mediæval chatelaine, however, was not to be deceived. She knew of the secret marriage, and nothing could exceed her rage. That Marion de l'Orme should sit on the feudal dais upon the seigneurial throne—that she should wear her jewelled coronet, should eat out of her silver dish, and inhabit her apartments—the thing was atrocious, scandalous, impossible. She flew to the Cardinal, with whom she had some friendship, and informed him of what had occurred. The Cardinal, who had formerly favoured Marion de l'Orme with more than his regard, was as much incensed as herself. That his protégé, Cinq-Mars, should supplant him, made him, old as he was, furiously jealous. That Cinq-Mars should dare to abandon the splendid position he himself had assigned him, leave the morbid Louis a prey to any adventurous scoundrel whose adroit flattery or affected sympathy might in a few hours render him arbiter of the Court and master of the kingdom, was, to Richelieu's thinking, an unpardonable crime. The artful prelate immediately took his measures. A royal ordinance was speedily framed, making all marriages contracted by persons under age, and without the consent of guardians, null and void!

Cinq-Mars returned to Court indignant, insolent, defiant; swearing vengeance against the meddling Cardinal, and ready to enter into any scheme for his destruction. Mademoiselle Marion de l'Orme re-opened her salon in the Rue des Tournelles.

As for Louis, from whom the knowledge of this little escapade had been carefully concealed, he received back the truant with greater favour than ever. Cinq-Mars, confident in the King's attachment, and looking on him as too feeble to combat his own audacious projects, spoke words which Louis had not heard since the beloved voice of Louise de Lafayette had uttered them. "He ought to rid himself of the Cardinal, and rule for himself," said Monsieur Le Grand; "if not by fair, then by foul means." "*Let Richelieu die*," cried Cinq-Mars, "as he has made others die—the best blood in France: Montmorenci, Chalais, Saint-Preuil, Marillac, and so many others." It is certain that the King listened to these proposals favourably. He actually consented to conspire against himself and the State which he governed. Louis was too stupid to realise the absurdity of his position. He permitted Cinq-Mars to coquet with the Spanish Government, in order to insure the support of Spanish troops to be sent from the Netherlands to defend Sedan against the Cardinal and his own army in case of failure. But Richelieu, now fully alive to the

dangerous ascendancy of Cinq-Mars,—for he had spies
everywhere, specially the soft-spoken Chavigny, who was
always about the King,—openly taxed his Sovereign
with treachery in a message borne to him by the
Marquis de Mortémart. Louis was dumb-foundered
and terrified. He wrote a letter that very same day,
addressed to the Chancellor Séguier, apologising for
his seeming infidelity to his minister. "He did not
deny," said he, "that Monsieur le Grand desired to
compass the Cardinal's death," but, with incredible
meanness, he added, "that he had never listened to
him." Monsieur le Grand, whose weak head was by
this time completely turned, fully believing himself
invincible, openly discussed what he should do when
he was himself prime minister. Suspecting Louis of
being too weak to be his only supporter, he turned to
Gaston, Duc d'Orléans. Monsieur, whose life, like
that of his brother's, singularly repeats itself, bethink-
ing himself of early times and of a certain moonlight
meeting on the terrace of Saint-Germain, at once
addressed himself to the Queen. But she had already
suffered too much to allow herself again to be drawn
into danger. When Monsieur detailed the plot, and
asked her significantly, "What news she had lately
had from her brother, the King of Spain?" she answered that she had had no news, and instantly
changed the conversation. This did not at all cool
Monsieur's ardour, such as it was. Three times he
had been banished from France for treason, and
three times he had returned, as ready as ever, with or
without the Queen, to conspire, to betray, and to be
again banished. So the traitor prince and the vain-
glorious favourite, both intensely hating Richelieu,

laid their heads together to destroy him by means of Spain. To them was joined the Marquis de Thou, one of the *jeunesse dorée* of the Court, along with Fontrailles, secretary to Monsieur. The great Cardinal, sitting in the Palais Royal like a huge spider in his web, ready to pounce upon his prey as soon as it had reached the precise spot where he intended to seize it, was familiar with every detail. Monsieur was to **receive** four hundred thousand crowns in order to raise levies in France; he was also to declare **war** against France in concert with Spain.

The Cardinal was to be assassinated or imprisoned for life; Gaston was to be proclaimed regent for his nephew Louis XIV. It was the old story, only, now an heir was born to the throne, Monsieur did not dare to claim the first place. Fontrailles, a creature of his own, he allowed to be sent into Spain. The treaty was signed at Madrid by Fontrailles, on the part of Monsieur and Cinq-Mars, and by the King of Spain on his own part. This done, Fontrailles flew back to France, with the precious document stitched in his clothes. Scarcely was the ink dry, before Richelieu was provided with a copy.

The Court was at Narbonne, on the Mediterranean, whither Cinq-Mars had led the King, in order to be near the Spanish frontier. Richelieu was at this time greatly indisposed, and in partial disgrace. He hung about the Rhone, sometimes at Tarascon, near Avignon, sometimes at Valence, conveniently near to be informed by Chavigny of everything that happened. Chavigny, deep in Louis's confidence, pendulated between the King and the minister. At the fitting moment, Chavigny requested a formal audience. It was the afternoon of the same day that Fontrailles had returned to Narbonne, the treaty with Spain still stitched in his clothes. Contrary to custom, when Chavigny knocked at the King's door, Louis requested Monsieur le Grand to retire. This alone ought to have aroused his suspicions. While Chavigny talked with the King, Cinq-Mars, ashamed of letting the Court see his exclusion from the room, lolled in the ante-room reading a story. Fontrailles found him there.

"How now, Monsieur le Grand," said he, "do you allow his most Christian Majesty to give an audience at which you are not present? You are getting him into bad habits."

"It is only Chavigny," replied Cinq-Mars, not taking his eyes off his book; "he can have nothing particular to say, for he is here every day. I am weary of the King's company. I have been with him all day, and I want to finish this story, which is much more interesting than his stupid talk." And Cinq-Mars threw himself back in his easy-chair, and resumed his reading.

"Ah, Monsieur le Grand," said Fontrailles, smiling at him curiously, "fortune favours you. You are a beautiful man. Look **at** me, with my hump" (Fontrailles was deformed); "I use my eyes; I am going to-night **to** meet Monsieur, before I leave Narbonne. I have brought him that little present from Madrid you know of. I have it safe here in my pocket," and Fontrailles tapped his side and grinned. "Come with me, Monsieur le Grand," said he, coaxingly, and he tried to take his hand, but Cinq-Mars repulsed him. "Come with me; believe me, the air of Narbonne is heavy at this time of year. I am not sure that it is not deadly, very deadly, indeed—especially for you, Monsieur le Marquis.

A little change will do your health good. I am going. Come with me where we can breathe;" and Fontrailles laughed a short dry laugh, and looked out of the window upon the blue expanse of ocean, whose waves beat against the yellow shores of the Mediterranean.

"I pray you, Fontrailles, do not trouble me," said Cinq-Mars, looking up over his book and yawning. "I really must have some time to myself, or I shall die. Besides, I want to see his Majesty when Chavigny goes; he is staying longer than usual, I think."

"Yes, Monsieur le Grand, too long for a man coming from the Cardinal, methinks."

Fontrailles still stood watching Cinq-Mars. His deep-set eyes were fixed upon him intently, as Cinq-Mars, with perfect indifference, went on reading his story. Fontrailles passed his hand thoughtfully over his brow two or three times. A look of pity came into his face as he contemplated Cinq-Mars, still reading. He was so young, so fresh, so magnificent; his golden locks long and abundant; his pleasant face faultless in feature; his delicate hands; his perfumed clothes,—all so perfect! Should he try to save him? A tear gathered in the eye of the hardened conspirator.

"Monsieur le Grand," said he softly, stepping up nearer to Cinq-Mars and placing his hand on his red and silver shoulder-knot—"Monsieur le Grand, I say——"

"What, Fontrailles, are you not gone yet? *Ma foi!* I thought you were far on your road to Monsieur——"

"No, Monsieur le Grand; no, I am not gone yet."

Cinq-Mars put down his book, sat upright, and looked at him.

"What the devil do you want with me, Fontrailles?

I will meet you and Monsieur le Duc to-morrow. For to-night, peace."

"Have you no suspicion of what Chavigny is saying to the King all this time, Marquis?" asked Fontrailles with an ominous grin.

"None, my friend; but I shall hear it all before his *coucher*. His most gracious Majesty is incapable of lying down to rest before telling me every syllable," and Cinq-Mars snapped his finger and thumb contemptuously towards the door of the room within which Louis was closeted with Chavigny.

"Are you quite sure of the King, Monsieur le Grand?" asked Fontrailles significantly, still leaning over Cinq-Mars and pressing his hand upon his shoulder-knot. "It is needful for you to be quite sure of him. His Majesty is apt to be weak and treacherous."

Cinq-Mars nodded his head; then, as if something had suddenly struck him, he rose, and in his turn began to gaze curiously at Fontrailles, whose manner and countenance were strangely expressive of some unspoken fear.

"You are very tall, Monsieur le Grand," said Fontrailles abruptly, speaking low, with his hand placed over his eyes, the better to contemplate Cinq-Mars, now drawn up to his full height, and staring at him with wonder; "you are very tall," he repeated, "and I am such a little man. You are very handsome, too —the handsomest gentleman in all France—and •very gracious to me also—very kind and gracious."

Fontrailles spoke thoughtfully, as a man who turned some important matter over in his mind.

"Have you come here only to tell me this, Fontrailles?" answered Cinq-Mars, laughing, and again he yawned, passed his jewelled fingers through his clustering locks, and again took up the book which he had laid down on a table beside him, and reseated himself. Fontrailles, however, had never taken his eyes off him. His gaze had deepened into an expression of deep sorrow, although he spoke jestingly. Whatever train of thought occupied him, it had not been broken by what Cinq-Mars had just said.

"You are very tall," he again repeated, as if speaking to himself, in a peculiar voice; "so tall, indeed, that you could do without your head, Monsieur le Grand, and yet be taller than I am. Perhaps this makes you careless. I am short, and I could not afford to lose my head—so—I am going to leave Narbonne instantly. The air here is as deadly to my constitution as it is to yours. Marquis, pray do believe me. Will you come with me—the tall man with the little one?—both needing a change. Will you come?"

Cinq-Mars did not heed him a whit. Fontrailles laid his hand heavily on the thick shock of Monsieur le Grand's golden curls.

"No, *mille diables*, no!" roared Cinq-Mars in a rage, shaking him off; "I will not go. Why should I go? For God's sake leave me. I am just at the catastrophe of my story, and you keep on tormenting me like a gadfly."

"Excuse me, Monsieur le Grand," replied Fontrailles submissively, "I did but advise you for your good. I desire your company for the sake of that comely head of yours; but, as I said, you are tall, and I am short, which makes a great difference. It is a long journey across the mountains of France into the Low Countries," added he, sighing. "That will be my road—a long and weary road. It might fatigue your excellency. I am going, Monsieur le Marquis. I am gone—Adieu!"

Cinq-Mars did not look up, and Fontrailles, turning upon him a last look full of pity, disappeared.

CHAPTER VI.

Death on the Scaffold.

WHEN Chavigny left the King, Cinq-Mars entered the royal chamber. Louis was silent, absorbed, and melancholy—would answer no questions, and abruptly dismissed the favourite on the plea that he was fatigued and needed rest.

Monsieur le Grand was naturally surprised at the change. The significant words of Fontrailles recurred to him; too late he repented his careless indifference to the friendly warning. But after all, if the King failed him, there was Monsieur and there was the treaty. What had he, Cinq-Mars, to fear when the King's brother had so deeply compromised himself? The Cardinal, too, was ill—very ill; he might die. Still, as he turned to his own suite of apartments his mind misgave him. The King had not told him one word of his interview with Chavigny; and although Chavigny would have denied it upon oath on the consecrated wafer, Cinq-Mars knew he was the Cardinal's creature and his go-between with the King.

When Cinq-Mars reached his rooms he found a letter from his friend, De Thou. "Fly," said this letter—"fly instantly. I have certain intelligence that the Cardinal is acquainted with every particular of the treaty signed at Madrid. For myself I have nothing to fear; but you have incurred the deadly hatred of Richelieu."

Thereupon Cinq-Mars, hurriedly disguised himself in a Spanish cloak, with a Sombrero hat slouched over his face, stole out of the prefecture where the King was staying, and made his way as fast as he could run to the city gates. They were closed. Then, fully aroused to the urgency of his position, the strange words of Fontrailles ringing in his ears, he sought out the abode of a humble friend, whom he had recommended to serve the Court with mules for the journeying to the south from Paris—a man of Touraine, whom he had known from his boyhood. He roused him from sleep—for the night had now closed in— and acquainted him with his danger. The faithful muleteer did his best. He hid him under some loose hay with the mules in the stable. It was in vain. Cinq-Mars had been seen and tracked from the prefecture to the muleteer's house, and the scented exquisite —whose word a few hours before ruled the destiny of France—was dragged out headlong from the hay, his fine clothes torn and soiled, his face scratched and bleeding, amid the hooting of the populace and the jeers of his enemies.

De Thou, his friend, was arrested on the same day, not as guilty of conspiring, but simply as being cognizant of the existence of the treaty of Madrid, which Fontrailles had carefully carried off into the Netherlands stitched in his clothes, a copy of which lay with the Cardinal.

Monsieur Duc d'Orléans was also, for the fourth time, arrested and imprisoned.

The effect of that copy of the treaty which Cha-

4*

vigny had shown to the King, while Cinq-Mars read his story, was instantaneous. Louis became greatly alarmed. He understood that Richelieu knew all, and therefore must be fully aware that he had himself encouraged and approved a plot to kill him. The same day that Cinq-Mars was conducted a prisoner to the Castle of Montpellier, Louis insisted upon going himself to Tarascon, to make a personal apology to Richelieu. He was already so weakened by the disease of which he died, that he was forced to be carried in a chair into the Cardinal's lodgings. They were together many hours. What passed no one knew, but it is certain that the "*amiable criminal*," as Cinq-Mars is called by contemporary authors, was the scapegoat sacrificed to the offended dignity of the Cardinal; that Monsieur, the King's only brother, was to be tried for treason; and that Richelieu should be restored to the King's confidence. In his eagerness to propitiate his offended minister, Louis actually proposed to take his two sons from the custody of the Queen and place them with the Cardinal, in order to guarantee his personal safety. This abject proposition was declined by Richelieu, who was unwilling to provoke the Queen's active hostility at so critical a moment.

Richelieu had conquered, but he was dying. Though his body was broken by disease, his mind was vigorous as ever; in revenge and hatred, in courage and fortitude, his spirit was still lusty. In his enormous thirst of blood, none had ever excited him like the airy Marquis de Cinq-Mars,—a creature of his own, whom he had raised to the dizzy height of supreme power, to become his rival in love and in power. The great minister felt he had made a mistake: it angered him.

He had not patience to think that he should have been taken in by a butterfly, whose painted wings he had decorated with his own hands. He, the all-potent Cardinal, the ruler of France, circumvented by a boy! He swore a big oath that not only should Cinq-Mars die, but that death should be made doubly bitter to him.

Richelieu was now at Valence on the Rhone. How was he to reach Lyons, where the trial was to take place? The distance is considerable. His limbs were cramped and useless, his body racked by horrible pain. But go he would; if he died upon the road he would go. So he ordered a room of wooden planks to be constructed, gilt and painted like a coach, and lined with crimson damask. This room contained a bed, a table, and a chair. Within reclined the Cardinal. Too ill to bear the motion of a carriage, he was borne on the heads of twenty of his body-guard by land. Houses, walls, and gateways, were knocked down to make way for him. By water he was conveyed in a towing boat pulled up the Rhone against the current by horses to Lyons. Attached to this boat was another, in which the prisoners Cinq-Mars and De Thou were carried. So Richelieu passed onwards, with all the pomp of a Roman pro-consul conducting barbarian princes first to adorn his triumph, then to die! As for Monsieur, he had already made his peace with his brother and Richelieu. He turned King's evidence, and betrayed everybody. Fontrailles, who alone could have convicted him, was safe across the frontier. "Talk not to me of my brother," even the besotted Louis exclaimed, when he heard that Monsieur was again at liberty; "Gaston ever was, and ever will be, a traitor."

The only crime which even the ingenuity of Richelieu could prove against Cinq-Mars was that he had
joined with Monsieur in a treaty with Spain. Now
the original transcript of this treaty was lost, Fontrailles
having carried it with him into the Netherlands, stitched
in his pocket. If Monsieur the Duc d'Orléans, therefore, had declined to speak, Cinq-Mars and his friend
De Thou must have been acquitted. But Monsieur,
on the contrary, loudly demanded to be interrogated
on his own complicity and on the complicity of Cinq-
Mars. The Cardinal had already showed what was in
his mind, by giving orders, as soon as he was lifted
out of his portable chamber, on arriving at Lyons, and
before the trial had begun, "for the executioner to
hold himself in readiness."

The trial was on the 12th of September, 1642. It
began at seven o'clock in the morning, at the Hôtel
de Ville. The Chancellor Séguier, a personal enemy
of Monsieur le Grand, who had affronted him in the
days of his greatness, was the president, and Monsieur
Duc d'Orléans the principal witness. Monsieur's evidence was given with touching candour. He was so
careful to tell all the truth, so skilful in bringing out
all those facts which were calculated to place Cinq-
Mars in the most odious light, that the charges were
easily proved to the satisfaction of the judges. The
trial was over in a few hours. Then the two young
men were summoned before the judges in the council-
chamber to hear their sentence. It was read out to
them by Monsieur de Palleruc, a member of the criminal court of Lyons. According to this sentence they
were both to be beheaded; Cinq-Mars was to be tortured. He listened with calmness, De Thou with

resignation. They both shook hands with their judges.
"I am prepared to die," said Cinq-Mars to Séguier,
the Chancellor, "but I must say the idea of torture is
horrible and degrading. It is a most extraordinary
sentence for a man of my rank and of my age. I
thought the laws did not permit it. Indeed, I do not
fear death, gentlemen," continued the poor lad, turning to the judges, "but I confess my weakness,—I
dread torture. At least, I beseech you, let me have
a confessor."

His request was complied with, and Father Malavette, a Jesuit, was brought into the council-chamber.
As soon as he saw him Cinq-Mars ran forward and
embraced him. "My father, they are going to torture
me," he cried; "I can scarcely bring myself to bear
it! What is your opinion?"

"That you must submit to the hand of God, Monseigneur. Nothing happens but by his permission."

Cinq-Mars bowed his handsome head, covered with
the sunny curls, and was silent. From the council-
chamber he was led by Monsieur de Lanbardemont,
an officer of the court, to the torture-room. Here he
remained about half an hour, and suffered torture,
both ordinary and extraordinary. His supple limbs
and delicate skin were horribly lacerated. He was
unable to walk when he came out, and was supported
by the officials. "Let me now think of my soul," he
said faintly; "send my confessor to me, and permit me
to be alone with him." This wish was granted, and
an hour passed, during which he confessed and received
absolution. Then he said to Father Malavette, "I have
not eaten for twenty-four hours, my father, and I am
very weak. I fear if I do not take something I may

swoon upon the scaffold, though indeed, I assure you,
I do not fear to die." A little wine and bread were
brought to him, of which he partook. "Ah! my father,"
said the poor boy of twenty-two, "what a world it is!
Everybody I know has forsaken me. How strange it
is! I thought I had many friends, but I see no one
cares for me now but poor De Thou, whom I alone
have brought to **this** pass."

"Alas! my son, you are young, or you would not
wonder at this," answered **Father** Malavette sorrowfully; "'put not your faith in princes.' What says Ovid
too, who, like you, enjoyed the favour of Augustus,
and was then cruelly punished?

" 'Donec eris felix , multos numerabis amicos.' "

"But, my father, when I was the favourite of his
Majesty, I tried to serve my friends in every way I
possibly could, yet now I am alone."

"No matter," said the priest, shaking his head,
"your service to them only made them your enemies."

"Alack, I fear it is so," replied Cinq-Mars, sighing
deeply. Then he asked for paper, and wrote to his
mother. He prayed her to pay all his debts, and again
expressed his utter astonishment at the conduct of his
friends. At three o'clock in the afternoon both he
and De Thou were carried in a hired coach into the
Place des Terraux, lying over against the banks of the
river Soane, in the outskirts of the city. Here the
scaffold was erected. Every house in the Place was
covered by temporary balustrades and balconies; the
roofs also were crowded with spectators. Thousands
had come together to see the favourite die.

Cinq-Mars with difficulty mounted the ladder lead-

ing to the scaffold, with the help of Father Malavette.
Then, still holding him by the hand to steady his
wounded limbs, he raised his plumed hat from off his
head, and, with a graceful air, saluted the multitude.
He turned to every side, and passed round to each
face of the platform, so that all might see him and
receive his salutation. He wore a court suit of fine
Holland broad cloth, trimmed with gold lace; his
black hat ornamented with red feathers was turned
back in the Spanish style. He had high-heeled shoes
with diamond buckles, and green silk stockings, and
he carried a large scarlet mantle, to cover his body
after decapitation, neatly folded on one arm. His fair
young face was perfectly serene, and his clustering
curls, slightly powdered, were scented and tended as
carefully as heretofore. Having bowed to the crowd,
he replaced his hat on his head, and, with his hand
resting on his right side, he turned round to look
about him. Behind were two blocks, covered with red
cloth. Beside them stood the executioner. He was
only a city porter—the regular official being ill—a
coarse and brutal fellow, with a bloated face, wearing
the dress of a labourer. When he came up to Cinq-
Mars with scissors to cut off his hair, M. le Grand put
him away with a motion of disgust. He begged Father
Malavette to do him this office, and to keep his hair
for his mother. While the long ringlets which fell
over his shoulders were being cut off, Cinq-Mars turned
towards the executioner, who had not yet taken the
axe out of a dirty bag which lay beside him, and asked
him haughtily, "What he was about?" and "Why he
did not begin?" The rude fellow making a wry face
in reply, Cinq-Mars frowned, and addressed himself to

Father Malavette. "My father," said he, "assist me in my prayers, then I shall be ready."

After he had prayed very devoutly, and kissed the crucifix repeatedly, he rose from his knees, and again in a firm voice repeated, "I am ready, begin!" Then he added, "My God have mercy upon me, and pardon my sins." He threw away his hat, unloosed the lace ruff from about his throat, put back his hair from his face, and laid his head on the block. Several blows descended ere his head was severed from the body; the executioner being unready and new to his office. When the head fell it gave a bound, turned itself a little on one side, and the lips palpitated visibly, the eyes being wide open. The body was covered with the scarlet mantle borne by Cinq-Mars on his arm for that purpose, and carried away to be buried.

The King, informed by the Cardinal of the precise day and hour when Cinq-Mars would suffer death, —for every detail had been virtually arranged before Richelieu left Valence in his wooden chamber,—took out his watch at the appointed time, and, with the most perfect unconcern, remarked to Chavigny, "At this moment Monsieur le Grand is making an ugly face at Lyons."

Then Richelieu ordered that the feudal castle of Cinq-Mars, in the valley of the Loire, should be blown up, and the towers razed "to the height of infamy."

CHAPTER VII.

The End of the Cardinal.

WHEN the Louvre was a walled and turreted stronghold, with moat and drawbridge, bastion and tower, lying on grassy banks beside the river Seine, then unbordered by quays and untraversed by stone bridges, an ancient castle, strongly fortified, stood in the open country, hard by, without the city walls. In the time of Charles VI., the mad king, husband of the notorious Isabeau de Bavière, this castle belonged to Bernard Comte d'Armagnac, Constable of France, the ally of the English against his own sovereign, and a leader in those terrible civil wars that desolated France throughout the space of two reigns. Hither the English and the Burgundians often repaired, to meditate some murderous *coup de main* upon the capital, to mass their bloodthirsty troops for secret expeditions, or to seek a safe retreat when the fortune of war was adverse. As time went by this castle grew grey with age; the rebel nobles to whom it belonged were laid in their graves; no one cared to inhabit a gloomy fortress, torn and battered by war and sacked by marauders. The wind howled through the desolate chambers, owls hooted from the rents in its turrets, and noisome reptiles crawled in the rank weeds which choked up its courts. It came to be a gruesome place, lying among barren fields, where the ruffians and desperadoes of the city resorted to plan a murder or to hide from justice. This God-forgotten ruin and the foot-trodden fields about it were purchased at last by

wealthy nobles, who loved the fresh country breezes
beyond the new streets which now arose on this side
of the river. The materials of the old castle served
to furnish walls for the palaces of the Rambouillets
and the Mercœurs, historic names in every age of the
national annals. Here they kept their state, until
Cardinal Richelieu, either by fair means or foul, it
mattered little to him, bought and destroyed their
spacious mansions, pulled down all that remained of
the castle walls, filled up the ditches, levelled the
earth, and, on the ill-omened spot, raised the sumptuous pile known as the Palais Cardinal, near, yet
removed from, the residence of the sovereign at
the Louvre. The principal buildings ran round
an immense central square, or courtyard, planted
symmetrically with trees and adorned with fountains and statues. From this central square four
other smaller courts opened out towards each point
of the compass. There was a chapel splendidly decorated, and, to balance that, two theatres, one sufficiently spacious to hold three thousand spectators,
painted on panel by Philippe de Champagne. There
were ball-rooms furnished with a luxury unknown before; boudoirs—or rather bowers—miracles of taste
and elegance; galleries filled with pictures and works
of art, and countless suites of rooms, in which every
decoration and adornment then practised were displayed. Over the grand entrance in the Rue Saint-
Honoré appeared, carved in marble, the arms of Richelieu, surmounted by a cardinal's hat and the inscrip-
tion "Palais Cardinal." Spacious gardens extended at
the rear.

Still the Cardinal, like Wolsey at Hampton Court,

added wall to wall of the already overgrown palace, and bought up street after street within the city to extend the gardens, until even the subservient Louis showed some tokens of displeasure. Then, and not till then, did the Cardinal cease building. At his death he presented his palace to the sovereign; and from that day to this the Palais Cardinal, now Palais Royal, has become an appanage of the State.

Before us stands the Palais Cardinal—solitary, in the midst of lonely gardens, sheltered by waving groves. The greensward is divided by straight walks, bordered by clipped lime-trees, rounded at intervals into niches for statues and trophies; balustraded terraces border deep canals, and fountains bubble up under formal groups of yew or cypress. The palace casts deep shadows on the grass. It is very still. High walls encircle the enclosure. The very birds are mute. Not the bay of a hound is heard. Moss gathers on the paths and among the tangled shrubberies, and no flowers catch the radiance of the sunshine. Within is the great, the terrible Cardinal. The ground is sacred to the despot of France, the ruler of the monarch, the glance of whose eye is death or fortune. Journeying direct from Lyons in his chamber on wheels—after the execution of Cinq-Mars—to Fontainebleau, where he rested, he is come here to die. Yonder he lies on a bed of state, hung with embroidered velvet in a painted chamber, the walls covered with rare pictures and choicest tapestry, the windows looking towards the garden. The moment approaches when he will have to answer for his merciless exercise of absolute power over king and people, to that Heavenly Master whose priest and servant he pro-

fesses to be. How will he justify his bitter hatred,
his arrogant oppression of the great princes and
nobles of France? How will he meet the avenging
ghosts of the chivalrous Montmorenci, the poetic Chalais, the gallant Cinq-Mars, the witty Saint-Preuil, the
enthusiastic Urbain Grandier, in the unknown country
whither he is fast hastening? Who tried to seduce,
then to ruin, the Queen, Anne of Austria, and send
her back, divorced and disgraced, into Spain? Who
turned the feeble Louis into a servile agent of his
ambition, and exercised over his weak mind a tyranny
as shameful to himself as degrading to the sovereign?
True, Richelieu may plead reasons of State, a rebellious
nobility, traitorous princes, and an imbecile king; but
the isolation of the throne, begun under his rule, was
both barbarous and impolitic, as after ages showed.
True he possessed rare genius, and his life was in-
dustriously devoted to what he called *"the glory of
France;"* but it was a mean and selfish glory, to attain which he had waded through the noblest blood
of the land.

Look at him now—he has just received extreme
unction. A hypocrite to the last, he folds his hands
on his breast and exclaims—"This is my God; as in
his visible presence, I declare I have sacrificed myself
to France." When he is asked by the officiating priest
—"If he forgives his enemies?"—he replies, "I have
no enemies but those of the State." Now the hand of
death is visibly **upon** him. In a loose robe of purple
silk, he lies supported **by** pillows of fine lace. He is
hardly recognisable, **so** great have been his sufferings,
so complete is his weakness; his bloodless lips pant
for breath, his hollow eyes wander on vacancy, his

thin fingers work convulsively on the sheets, as though striving against the approach of invisible foes.

But, before he departs, a signal honour is reserved for him. Behold, the rich velvet curtains, heavy with golden embroideries, are held aside by pages who carry plumed hats in their hands, and Louis XIII. enters hastily. He is bareheaded, and is accompanied by the princes of the blood and the great ministers of State. Louis is so shrunken and attenuated, so white and large-eyed, that in any other presence he might have been deemed a dying man himself. As he advances to the *ruelle* that encloses the bed, he composes his thin lips and pinched face into a decent expression of condolence. How can he but *affect* to deplore the death of a minister whose fierce passions overshadowed his whole life like a moral upas-tree? Nevertheless the fitting phrases are spoken, and he embraces the ghastly form stretched out before him with a semblance of affection. The expiring Cardinal presses the hand of his master, and makes a sign that he would speak. Louis bows down his head to catch the feeble voice, which says—"Sire, I thank you for this honour; I have spent my whole life in your service. I leave you able ministers; trust them, Sire; but,—" and he stops and struggles fearfully for breath,— "but, beware of your Court. It is your *petit coucher* who are dangerous. Your favourites have troubled me more than all your enemies." Then the Cardinal sinks back fainting on his pillows.

Louis withdraws with affected concern; but, ere he reaches the spacious ante-room, lined with the Cardinal's retainers in magnificent liveries, he bursts into an inhuman laugh—"There goes a great politician to his death," he says to Chavigny, who is beside him, and he points with his thumb towards the Cardinal's chamber; "a wonderful genius. Now he is gone I shall be free—I shall reign." He chuckles with delight at the idea of being at last rid of the Cardinal; and a grim smile spreads itself over his ashen face.

It is a ghastly joke, as cruel as it is selfish. As if Louis's life were bound up in the existence of his great minister—he is himself a corpse within a year!

CHAPTER VIII.
The Queen-Regent.

LOUIS XIV. was four years and a half old when his father died at Saint-Germain, aged forty-two. Tardy in everything, Louis XIII. was six weeks in dying. The state christening of his son was celebrated during his illness. When asked his name, the little lad replied, "I am Louis XIV."

"Not yet, my son, not yet," murmured the dying King, "but shortly, if so it please God."

Anne of Austria, named Regent by her husband's will, rules in her son's name. A splendid Court assembles round her, at the Louvre, at Saint-Germain, and at Fontainebleau. Her exiled favourites are there to do her homage. The Duchesse de Chevreuse, after a long sojourn in Spain, England, and Flanders,— for she loves travel and the adventures of the road, either masked, or disguised as a page, a priest, or a cavalier,—is reinstated in her Majesty's favour. In Spain the Duchess's vanity was gratified by enslaving a royal lover—the King of Spain, brother of Anne of Austria; in England she diverted herself with foment-

ing personal quarrels between Charles I. and Henrietta
Maria; in Flanders—a dull country—she found little
to amuse her.

Mademoiselle de Hautefort (soon to become **Duchesse** and Maréchale de Schomberg) returns in obedience to the Queen's command, who wrote to her
even while the King was alive, "Come, dearest friend,
come quickly. **I am all** impatience to embrace you!"

The **Duchesse de** Sennécy arrives from the provinces, and the Chevalier de Jars from England. The
latter had been imprisoned in the Bastille, and threatened with torture by Richelieu, to force him to betray
the Queen's correspondence with Spain at the time of
the Val de Grâce conspiracy. He had been liberated,
however, but while the Cardinal lived had remained
in England.

These, among many other faithful attendants, resume their places at the *petit* **coucher,** in the *grand
cercle,* and at the morning *lever.*

Then there are the princes and princesses of the
blood-royal:—Monsieur the Duc d'Orléans—no longer
breathing vows of love in the moonlight, but a veteran
intriguer—living on the road to Spain, which always
meant rebellion, together with his daughter, *La Grande
Mademoiselle,* a comely girl, the greatest heiress in
Europe; Cæsar, Duc de Vendôme, son of Gabrielle
and Henry IV., with his Duchess and his sons, the
Ducs de Mercœur and De Beaufort; Condé, the un-
crowned head of the great house of Bourbon—more
ill-favoured and avaricious than ever—his jealous temper now excited against the bastards of the house of
Vendôme, with his wife, Charlotte de Montmorenci,
sobered down into a dignified matron, devoted to her

eldest son, the Duc d'Enghien, and to her daughter, the Duchesse de Longueville, the brightest ornament of the Court; the Duc de la Rochefoucauld and his son, the Prince de Marsillac, the author of "Les Maximes," to become a shadow on the path of the last-named Duchess, who is to die in a convent; the great House of La Tour d'Auvergne, Viscomtes de Turenne and Ducs de Bouillon, from which springs Henri de Turenne, the rival of young Condé; Séguier, Duc de Villemer, generously forgiven for the part he took against the Queen as Chancellor, at the Val de Grâce; and, last of all, Henry, Duc de Guise—by-and-by to astonish Europe by his daring escapade at Naples, where, but for Masaniello, he might have been crowned King, with the Queen's beautiful maid of honour, Mademoiselle de Pons, at his side.

There is also about the Court a young man named Giulio Mazarin, born in Rome of a Sicilian family, late secretary to Cardinal Richelieu. He has passed many years in Spain, and can converse fluently in that language with her Majesty whenever she deigns to address him. He has a pale, inexpressive face, with large black eyes, *à fleur de tête*, generally bent on the ground. His manners are modest, though insinuating; his address is gentle, his voice musical. Like all Italians, he is artistic; a *conoscente* in music, a collector of pictures, china, and antiquities. So unobtrusive and accomplished a gentleman cannot fail to please, especially as he is only a deacon, and, with a dispense, free to marry. The Queen, who often converses with him in her native tongue, appreciates his merits. Her minister, the Bishop of Beauvais, leaves the Court. He finds that his presence is useless, as the Queen acts entirely under the advice of this young Italian, whom she also selects as guardian to the young King, who, poor simple boy, looks on Mazarin as a father.

The Regency begins auspiciously. Fifteen days after the death of Louis XIII. the decisive victory of Rocroy was gained over the Spaniards by the Duc d'Enghien, a youthful general of twenty-two. Paris was exultant. The roads were strewed with wreaths and flowers; tapestry and banners hung from every window, fountains of choicest wines flowed at the corners of the streets, and amid the booming of cannon, the blare of trumpets, the crash of warlike instruments, and the frantic shouts of an entire population, the Queen, and her little four-year old son, ride in a gold coach to hear a *Te Deum* at Notre-Dame.

Her Majesty's authority is much increased by this victory. Mazarin, under favour of the Queen, gradually acquires more and more power. He presides at the council; he administers the finances—for which he came to be called "*the plunderer;*" he tramples on the parliament and bullies the young King. The princes of the blood and all the young nobles are excluded from offices of state or places in the household. Every one begins to tremble before the once modest young Italian, and to recall with dismay the eighteen years of Richelieu's autocracy.

But Mazarin has a rival in Henri de Gondi, afterwards Cardinal de Retz, now coadjutor to his uncle, the Archbishop of Paris. No greater contrast can be conceived than between the subtle, shuffling Italian, patient as he is false, and Gondi, bold, liberal, independent, generous even to his enemies, incapable of

envy or deceit, grasping each turn of fortune with the
ready adaptiveness of genius, and swaying the passions of men by his fiery eloquence; a daring statesman, a resolute reformer, one of whom Cromwell had
said—"that he, De Retz, was the only man in Europe
who despised him."

Gondi considered himself sacrificed to the Church
—for which he had no vocation—and did his utmost,
by the libertinism of his early life, to render his ordi-
nation impossible; but in vain. Although he had ab-
ducted his own cousin, and been the hero of number-
less scandals, the Archbishopric of Paris was considered
a sinecure in the family of Gondi, and Archbishop
and Cardinal he must be in spite of his inclination
and of his excesses. In politics he was a republican,
formed on the pattern of Cato and of Brutus, whose
lives he had studied at the Sorbonne. He loved to
be compared to Cicero and to Cataline, and to believe
himself called on to revolutionize France after the
fashion of a factious conspirator of old Rome. He
longed to be anything belligerent, agitative—tribune,
general, or demagogue. "Ancient Rome," he said,
"honoured crime, therefore crime was to be honoured."
"Rather let me be the leader of a great party than an
emperor!" exclaimed he, in the climax of one of his
thrilling perorations. The mild precepts of the gospel
were clearly little to his taste. He had mistaken not
only his vocation but his century. He should have
lived in the Middle Ages; and as an ecclesiastical
prince-militant led armies into battle, conquered terri-
tories, and made laws to subject peoples. Yet under-
lying the wild enthusiasm of his language, and the
reckless energy of his actions, there was a kindly, al-

most gentle temper that imparted to his character a
certain incompleteness which accounts for the falling
off of his later years. Grand, noble as was De Retz,
Mazarin ultimately beat him and remained master of
the situation.

Under the guidance of Gondi (De Retz) the parliament, paralyzed for a time, soon learns its power,
and gives unmistakable tokens of insubordination
by opposing every edict and tax proposed by the
Government. Some of the most fractious of "these
impertinent bourgeois," as Condé called them, were
arrested and exhibited in chains—like captives in a
Roman triumph—at Notre-Dame on the occasion of a
second *Te Deum* sung for a second great victory gained
by young Condé. Mazarin, by this act, overtaxed the
endurance of the citizens. In one night two hundred
barricades rise in the streets of Paris. The Queen-
Regent can see them from her windows. This ebullition of popular fury appears to Gondi as the realisa-
tion of his youthful dreams. The moment has come
to make him a tribune of the people. He has loyally
warned the Regent of the impending peril. The Queen
considered his words mere bravado, and treated him
personally with suspicion and contempt. Gondi was
warned that Mazarin had decided on his exile. His
generous nature was outraged: "To-morrow," he said,
"before noon, I will be master of Paris." Noon did
see him master of Paris; but, loose as was his estimate
of the sacredness of his office, he was still Archbishop-
Coadjutor; he could not personally lead the rabble,
or publicly instigate the citizens to rebellion. A man
of straw must represent him, and do what he dared
not—harangue at the crosses and corners of the streets,

head the popular assemblies, and generally excite the passions of the turbulent Parisians to fever heat. This man of straw was found in the Duc de Beaufort, grandson of Henri Quatre, through Gabrielle d'Estrées, —a dandy, a swaggerer, but a warrior.

Now the Duc de Beaufort, hot-headed and giddy, without either judgment or principles, cares little for either Cardinal, Coadjutor, or Queen,—is utterly indifferent as to who may rule or who may serve, provided always his own claims, as prince of the blood, to the most lucrative posts are admitted. But he does care very much for an affront offered to the Duchesse de Montbazon, of whom he is desperately enamoured.

The Duchesse de Montbazon, step-mother of the Duchesse de Chevreuse, and lady in waiting to the Queen, finds late one evening, on returning to her hôtel, two love-letters dropped on the floor of her private closet. One is from a gentleman, the other is from a lady; both are unsigned. She of course at once decides that the handwriting of the one is that of the lady she most hates, that of the other, the lover of that same lady, whom she hates even more, if possible, than the lady herself. Now the lady whom she hates most is the Duchesse de Longueville, younger, more attractive, and more powerful than herself. The gentleman she selects is the Count de Coligni, who had deserted her for the sake of the Duchess. The next morning, at the Queen's lever, Madame de Montbazon shows these two love-letters to every one, and being the mistress of a caustic tongue, makes some diverting remarks on their contents. Her words are repeated to the Duchesse de Longueville; she denies the fact altogether. Her mother, the Princesse de

Condé, Charlotte de Montmorenci, broadly hints to
Anne of Austria that the Prince de Condé, the greatest general France had ever possessed since the days
of the Constable de Bourbon, will join the malcontent
parliament, nay, may even lead Spain into France, if
her Majesty does not instantly cause the Duchesse de
Montbazon to retract all she has said of his sister.
Such is patriotism under the Regency! The Queen,
overwhelmed by the clamour of the two duchesses,
invokes the help of Cardinal Mazarin. The Cardinal,
in his Italian-French, soothes and persuades both,
muttering many classic oaths of *Cospetto* and *Corpo di
Bacco* under his breath. He goes to and fro between
the ladies, flatters both, and proposes terms of apology. Every suggestion is objected to; an hour is
spent over each word. Such a negotiation is far more
difficult than the government of France. All conclusion seeming impossible, the Queen at last speaks with
authority. She says that "if Madame de Montbazon
will not retract she shall lose her place at Court."

So Spain is not at this time to invade France under
the command of Condé, and the Duchesse de Longueville is to receive an apology.

The apology is to be made at the Hôtel de Condé.
The Duchesse de Longueville—a superb blonde, with
melting blue eyes, golden brown hair, transparent complexion, and a dazzling neck and shoulders, a coronet
of orient pearls and a red feather on her head, a
chaplet of the same jewels clasping her throat, wearing a robe of blue tissue, bordered and worked with
pearls—stands in the great saloon of her father's ancestral palace. Her feet rest on a dais of cloth of
gold and silver; the dais is covered by a canopy

spangled with stars. The walls of the saloon are covered with bright frescoes of birds, fruit, and flowers, panelled into golden frames. Four great chandeliers of crystal and silver are placed on pedestals at each corner of the room, lighting up a glittering crowd of princes and princesses of the blood who stand beside the Duchess on the estrade. The greatest nobles of France are present. The doors are flung open, and the Duchesse de Montbazon, a dainty brunette, brilliant, audacious, enticing, who, although forty, is still in the zenith of her charms, flashes into the room in full court costume, her sacque (or train) of amber satin brocaded with gold reaching many yards behind her. The colour on her cheeks is heightened either by rouge or passion; her eyes glitter, and her whole bearing is of one who would say, "I *must* do this, but I defy you." She knows that all the gentlemen take part with her, if the ladies side with her enemy. She walks straight up to the dais on which the Duchesse de Longueville, *née* Princesse de Condé, stands, stops, looks her full in the face, then leisurely and with the utmost unconcern casts her eyes round on the company, smiles sweetly to the Duc de Beaufort, and bows to those princes and nobles who are her champions, particularly to the Ducs d'Orléans and De Guise. Then she unfolds her painted fan, and with insolent unconcern reads what follows from a slip of pink paper attached to one of the jewelled sticks.

"Madame, I come here to assure your highness that I am quite innocent of any intention of injuring you. Had it not been so I would humbly beg your pardon, and willingly submit to any punishment her Majesty might see fit to impose on me. I entreat you therefore to believe that I **have** never failed in 'the esteem which your virtues command, nor in the respect due to your high rank."

The Duchesse de Longueville's **soft** blue eyes, usually incapable of any other expression but tenderness or supplication, look absolutely wicked, so defiant is the bearing of Madame de Montbazon. She advances to the edge of the estrade, draws herself up with an imperious air, and casting a haughty glance at her rival, who, crimson in the face, is fanning herself **violently** and ogling the Duc de Beaufort, reading **also from her** fan, pronounces the following **words,** dictated by Cardinal Mazarin:—

"Madame, I am willing to believe **that you took** no part in the calumny which has been circulated **to** my prejudice. I make this acknowledgment **in** deference to the commands of the Queen."

Thus ends the quarrel; but not the consequences. The whole Court and city is in an uproar. The citizens **are** deeply interested, and to a man take part with the *chère amie* of Beaufort against the Duchesse de Longueville, and against Condé and Mazarin.

Condé is not sure if he will not after all lead the Spaniards against France. The Duchesse de Montbazon feeds the flame for her private ends. She lays all the **blame of** her humiliation on Cardinal Mazarin, which exasperates Beaufort to madness. She incites Henri, Duc de Guise, another of her adorers—the wildest, bravest, and most dissolute of princes—to challenge the Comte de Coligni, whom she had designated as the writer of one of the love-letters. A duel is fought **in** the Place Royale. The Duchesse de Montbazon watches the while out of a window of the palace of the Duc de Rohan, her cousin. Coligni is killed. He falls, it is said, into the arms of the Duchesse de Longueville, who is present on the Place, disguised as a page.

The Duc de Beaufort, whose turbulent folly fore-shadows the *grand seigneur* of later reigns and almost excuses the great Revolution, refuses to receive a royal herald, sent to him by the Queen, turns his back upon her Majesty at her lever, and threatens the life of the Cardinal. The Duchesse de Montbazon is banished.

CHAPTER IX.

The Duc de Beaufort.

THE Duc de Beaufort is summoned to a private audience at the Louvre. On his way up the grand staircase entering from the inner quadrangle he meets his mother, the Duchesse de Vendôme, and his sister, the Duchesse de Nemours, who, their attendance on the Queen over, are descending.

"Good God! Francis," cries his mother, raising her hands with a gesture of horror, "I thought you were safe at Rambouillet. *You* within the Louvre at this moment? You must be mad!" And she throws her-self upon him and tries to bar his further passage.

"Oh, my brother!" exclaims his sister Nemours, in the same breath, throwing her arms around his neck; "in the name of the Holy Virgin, do not tempt your fate. Fly, dear Francis—fly, while you can—our coach is waiting below—come with us instantly." And Ma-dame de Nemours takes him by the arm, and tries to draw him downwards.

Beaufort plants himself firmly on the stair. His

first impulse is to push them both forcibly aside, and to proceed; his next to curse their folly in the spicy *argot* of the *halles*. He does neither; but stands open-mouthed, his fierce eyes demanding an explanation he does not condescend to ask. The explanation is soon forthcoming.

"My son," cries his mother, bursting into tears, and seizing on his hand to detain him, as he makes a motion as if to evade them, "listen to me, I implore you. Your sister and I have been in waiting on the Queen many hours to-day. She is terribly incensed against you. People have been coming all day with tales to her here, at the Louvre. Crowds have filled her audience chamber."

"*Mille Diables!* What do you mean, mother?" bursts out Beaufort, shaking himself free from both ladies. "You call me mad, if any one be mad it is yourselves. I am here, summoned by the Queen herself, to a private audience. *Ventre de ma vie!*"—Beaufort much affects some of the favourite oaths of his grandfather, Henri Quatre—"what are her Majesty's humours to me?"

"Oh, Francis," sobs the Duchesse de Nemours, "what have you done? You have threatened the life of Cardinal Mazarin. The Queen knows it. She has sent for you to secure your person. She can have no other motive. Nothing can exceed her indignation. She said, in my hearing, that you had personally insulted her; that your party, the *Importants*, was the curse of her reign; and that the Duchesse de Montbazon corrupted the princes of the blood by her intrigues. In the name of heaven, do not venture near her Majesty if you value your liberty, or even your life!"

The Duchesse de Vendôme wrings her hands while her daughter is speaking.

"For my sake, quit Paris, my dear son. If you remain, not even Gondi can save you. Come with us instantly, and cross the frontier while you can."

Her words are broken; she trembles at her son's manifest danger; Beaufort looks at her, shakes his head, and bursts into a loud laugh.

"You are a couple of lunatics, both of you"—and again he laughs—"I shall not leave Paris; I will not even hide myself. Calm yourself, mother"—and he kisses her on the cheek—"her Majesty has summoned me to a private audience. I shall obey her. She is no traitress. I have been guilty of rudeness towards her. I go to wipe out the remembrance of it. I am rough, but not brutal, specially to the Queen. Besides, *they dare not arrest me.*" *

Saying which, he pushes his mother and sister, who still endeavour to stop him, on one side, and bounds up the stairs.

It is evening. Anne of Austria is alone in a spacious withdrawing room, from which her private writing-closet opens. Four lofty windows turn towards the river—one is open. She sits beside it, gazing at the dazzling tints of the summer sunset that lace the western heavens with bars of fire. In front rise the double towers of Notre-Dame. The fretted spire of the Sainte-Chapelle glistens against a bank of heavy clouds that are rapidly welling up from the south. These clouds deepen with the twilight. The lustre of a stormy sunset soon fades out. The sun disappears, and darker and denser clouds

---

* These words, spoken by the Duc de Beaufort, are the same as those of the Balafré, at Blois, before his assassination by Henry III.

gather and thicken, and obscure the light. Low thunder
rumbles in the distance, and a few heavy raindrops
descend. Long shadows fall across the floor, the corners
of the room grow dark, and only a few bright gleams,
lingering low on the horizon, rest on the Queen's face
and figure.

Anne of Austria has now passed into middle life;
her form is full, her movements heavy. The glorious
eyes are still lustrous, but no longer flash with the fire
of youth. Her hair, though still abundant, has lost its
glossy brightness. Her dress is rich, her bearing cold
and stately. She affects a distant, almost a haughty
manner, and is severe in exacting the most rigid
etiquette from all who approach her, save alone the
Cardinal. He comes and goes as he lists, smiling and
obsequious, but no longer humble or subservient as of
yore. Indeed, at times he treats her Majesty with absolute familiarity, to the utter dismay of the Duchesse
de Chevreuse and Mademoiselle de Hautefort. When
not engaged with Mazarin in state affairs, or in giving
audiences, the Queen passes her time in her oratory.
Not only is she devout herself, but exacts at all events
the same outward show of piety from her ladies.

Twilight has deepened into gloom, ere the Duc de
Beaufort enters. He stands in shadow, and as he
glances at the Queen, he inwardly apostrophises his
mother and sister as a couple of fools and gossips, for
imagining him to be in any danger of her displeasure.
His boisterous bearing—for he affects the manners of
the lowest of the populace, the better to sway them,
and by so doing to embarrass the minister—is visibly
softened. He remembers with pain the insults of which
he has been guilty in turning his back on the Queen,

when they last met, and in refusing to receive her
herald. He is both repentant and flattered at her summons. His obeisance to her is unusually low, and
some tokens of emotion betray themselves on his dissipated though handsome countenance.

"Good evening, cousin," **says** Anne of Austria, as
he enters, a gracious smile upon her face, and with
that queenly grace natural to her, she presents her
still beautiful hand to him, which he kisses kneeling.
"Where have you been these four days past? You are
a stranger at the Louvre."

Her voice is sweet, her look is gentle. It is impossible that what Beaufort has heard can be true.

"Madame," he answers, bowing, "had I not been
absent from Paris, I should not have failed to present
my duty to your Majesty. But I am only just returned
from a hunting-party at Rambouillet, whither I went
with my brother-in-law, Nemours. Until I came back
I did not know that you had asked for me. What can
I do for your Majesty's service? I am always at your
command."

"Ah, cousin, you **are always** at my command, I
know," answers the Queen, repeating his words, and
she **gives a** little laugh. Beaufort winces at the covert
rebuke. He feels that her meaning must be ironical,
yet she speaks caressingly, and the same gracious smile
still plays about her mouth.

"You once called me the most honourable man
in France, Madame; I am proud to remember it."
Beaufort speaks roughly, and in a loud voice; the momentary polish is passing away with the momentary
emotion. "I am what I ever was. I do not change.
I wish I could say the same of your Majesty. Madame,

you have greatly altered," and he looks at her straight in the face. Anne of Austria shifts her position, so as to sit in shadow, then she replies:—

"I have no *special* purpose in summoning you, cousin, save for the satisfaction your presence here gives me." Again Beaufort feels the covert stab, and observes that she studiously avoids noticing his remarks on her altered conduct towards him.

"You and I," adds the Queen, in a voice strangely monotonous, "are indeed old friends and comrades as well as cousins."

"You have not a truer friend in all France than I am," answers the Duke vehemently, and he advances a step or two towards the window, near which the Queen sits, raises his hand to emphasise his words, and lets it fall so heavily on a table near as to make the whole room echo. The Queen still smiles graciously.

"Yes, Madame, I am no courtier; I hate Courts; but before you made that Italian *facchino* your favourite you relied on Beaufort." As he pronounced the Cardinal's name his face hardens and his hands clench themselves; an almost imperceptible shudder passes over the Queen. Then he continues:—

"Was it not to Beaufort that you entrusted the sacred person of his Majesty and your own safety after the death of your husband, before the Regency was settled?"

Anne of Austria bows her head in silence. She is evidently determined not to take offence. If any one else had dared to mention the Cardinal to her in such language she would have ordered him to the Bastille.

Had the Duke been less giddy this knowledge ought to have curbed him, especially after the warning he had received; but his thoughts are now passing into a different channel, and he heeds it not.

"Yes, cousin, I have known you long, and closely," is the Queen's cautious rejoinder. "You have been at Rambouillet, Prince," she continues; "have you had good sport? The canals there are, I am told, full of fat carp. Do you love fishing?"

The Duke stares at her without replying. The Queen, who appears to desire to continue the conversation, yet to avoid all discussion, still speaks—

"My son will grow up to be a keen sportsman, I hope. The royal forests must be better guarded. Did you and the Duc de Nemours find any deer at Rambouillet?"

Spite of the Queen's unusual loquacity, there is something in her manner which irritates the excitable Duke. He cannot altogether convince himself that she is not mocking him. He had come certainly repentant, but his fiery temper now overmasters him at the bare suspicion.

"Did your Majesty send for me to put such questions as these?" cries he roughly. "If so, I would rather have stayed at Rambouillet."

"Truly, Duke," replies the Queen evasively, colouring at his bluntness, "it is difficult to content you. I have already said that I summoned you for no special purpose, save that we might converse together"—and she stops suddenly, and hesitates—"as cousins, and *as friends.*"

This last word is spoken slowly and with manifest effort. Her voice, which has a strange ring in it, is drowned by a clap of thunder, still distant, and a flash of lightning illuminates the room for an instant, and rests upon the long fair hair and frowning countenance of Beaufort. Her words are bland, but her bearing is distant and constrained. Even the unobservant Beaufort is struck by this anomaly; but he attributes it to some vestige of displeasure at his late conduct.

"I trust, Madame, you will always treat me with the confidence proper to both these titles," he replies stiffly.

Her words appease, but do not satisfy him. Even while speaking, the Queen has turned her head towards the door of her writing-closet, and listens. The wind roars without, and the waters of the Seine dash themselves against the low walls that border the Quay, but no sound within is audible. Anne of Austria resumes the conversation as though talking against time. But Beaufort, naturally unobservant, is now too much excited to notice this. He has forgotten all that his mother and sister had said. Not the slightest suspicion crosses his mind.

"It is a boisterous evening," continues the Queen, looking out of the window—a faint flash of lightning plays round her darkly robed figure—"but the storm is still distant. By-the-bye, my cousin, am I to congratulate you on being appointed beadle of Saint-Nicholas des Champs?" asks the Queen, still smiling. "The bourgeoisie must be greatly flattered by your condescension."

"That is a matter of opinion," answers Beaufort. "I glory in belonging to the people. I would rather be called *Roi des Halles* than King of France."

The Queen says no more, again she listens. She

seems more and more embarrassed, and the conversation languishes. The Duke begins to be conscious that something is amiss. He even goes the length of secretly wishing that the interview were over. A heaviness oppresses him; it is stiflingly hot, and the thunder sounds nearer. The image of his mother weeping bitterly rises up, unbidden, before him. Can there be any truth in her warning?

"Yes," continues Beaufort after an awkward pause, "Yes, I may be too much of a *Frondeur* to please you, Madame, and for my own safety also." Again the Queen turns her head, and listens anxiously. "A *Frondeur* against a government headed by an *alien* — not a *Frondeur* against you, my cousin — never against *you*. To *you* I am ever loyal. You know this." His voice grows thick. He is much moved. "You, my cousin, can never forget my long exile after the death of Cinq-Mars at Lyons for your sake. Surely you cannot forget?"

Anne moves uneasily; she taps her small foot on the floor impatiently. Her eyes are bent outwards upon the approaching storm, which draws each instant nearer. The heavens are now like a wall of blackness, save where the lightning glitters for a moment. Yet she neither calls for lights, nor closes the window.

"Next to the Duchesse de Chevreuse," Beaufort continues, "Richelieu hated me, because I was devoted soul and body to you, and he knew it. Ah, my cousin, had the Duchess and I, your two friends, spoken, where would you have been now? Not on the throne, certainly. I carried your secret safely into England with me — I would have carried it to the grave — and you are Regent of France."

Whatever the Queen may feel, she carefully conceals it. A stony expression spreads itself over her face, and the smile on her lip becomes almost a grimace, her mouth is so tightly set.

"If I am grown rough and coarse," he continues, "like the rabble among whom I live—if I offend you by my frankness, remember Beaufort was faithful to you in adversity—most true and faithful."

The tears come into his eyes as he speaks; he brushes them off with his sleeve. The Queen is not at all moved by this appeal. A third time she turns her head as if listening for some expected sound—then, hearing nothing, her eyelids drop, and she plays with her fan.

"These are difficult times, my cousin," she says at last, speaking slowly. "Much depends on the princes of the blood. I reckon on you, Duke, as a firm pillar of the State," and she touches him with her fan.

Beaufort starts. "Would I were such a pillar!" he exclaims with warmth. "Take Gondi as your minister, my cousin. Send Mazarin back to the Roman gutter from whence he sprung. You would have no more trouble with the parliament. I warrant you they would obey you like lambs, my cousin. Banish Mazarin, and I will lead you and the young King in triumph throughout France. Not a *Frondeur* would be left in the land. If there were, I would shoot him with my own hand. Answer me, Madame; will you try?"

Beaufort stretches out his hand as he speaks to clasp that of the Queen. Anne neither stirs, neither looks up, nor touches his hand. To speak is evidently difficult to her. Surely she must be expecting some one, for she again turns her head towards the writing-closet and listens. A sharp clap of thunder rattles through the room; when it is past her eyes rest upon the Duke, who is eagerly awaiting her reply. The set smile is still on her lips; she is about to answer him, when a distinct sound of footsteps is heard within in her writing-closet. A page enters, and announces Cardinal Mazarin's arrival to consult her Majesty on urgent state business. Beaufort's face darkens. Ere the page has ceased speaking, the long-gathering storm bursts forth with fury. A tremendous peal of thunder shakes the palace, and big drops of rain are driven through the window. The Queen rises hastily and signs to the page to close the sash. She is evidently greatly relieved. "I regret this interruption, Prince," she says, speaking rapidly, "but it is unavoidable. I must not keep the Cardinal waiting. I cannot, however, consider your audience as over. Will your highness favour me by remaining in the apartments of the ladies of honour until I am free?" and, not waiting for his reply, she hastily passes into her closet. Deluges of rain fall, flash after flash lights up the heavens, and peals of thunder rapidly succeed each other.

The Duc de Beaufort finds the Duchesse de Chevreuse and Mademoiselle de Hautefort sitting together in one of the apartments of the suite allotted to the ladies in waiting. As he enters they both rise hurriedly, and contemplate him in mute astonishment.

"Why, Duke," cries the Duchess, "is it possible? You here? You in the Louvre?"

"And why not, madame? What do these chatter-

ing women mean?" he mutters to himself. "One would
think I were a monster."

"What! have you not heard, that you are accused
of a plot to assassinate the Cardinal?"

"The Queen knows the particulars," broke in
Mademoiselle de Hautefort. "She told me so at her
lever this morning."

"Perhaps you will kindly inform me what these
particulars are, madame?" replies Beaufort savagely.

"Why, Duke, you must be out of your senses!"

"Not that I know of, madame; pray let me hear
of what I am accused."

"Why, that in order to take the Cardinal's life
you had stationed soldiers in ambush along the road
to Longchamps, to fire on him, as he passed in his
coach on his way to dine with the President Maison."

"The simple-hearted Cardinal! Imagine, your
highness," cries the Duchess, "Signor Giulio, after
having said his prayers, trotting along demurely in
his red coach, a perfect angel—wanting only wings
to fly away from a wicked world, innocent of so much
as an evil thought! We know you are a *Frondeur*,
Duke, but you are also a barbarian to desire the
life of such a saint," and the Duchess laughs her
merry laugh.

"Perhaps, madame," says Beaufort, turning towards Mademoiselle de Hautefort, "you will have the
goodness to proceed in the relation of my supposed
crime?"

"I have neither the wit nor the high spirits of her
Grace of Lorraine," replies she, "to jest. I assure
you, Duke, it is a very grave matter. You are in the
utmost danger. The Cardinal has made her Majesty

believe that his life was only saved by the accidental arrival of the Duc d'Orléans—who was going to dine at the same party—on horseback, and who, as a violent shower of rain came on, dismounted and got into the Cardinal's coach. His presence saved the Cardinal, the guard could not fire upon his Royal Highness. You may imagine the agitation of her Majesty."

"Capital, capital!" exclaims the Duchess, clapping her hands, and still laughing; "admirably done. I never gave your highness credit for so much invention. What a pity the Duc d'Orléans did not start a little sooner," adds she, in a lower voice, "or that it rained! Signor Giulio would have been in heaven by this time."

The Duc de Beaufort sees that Mademoiselle de Hautefort looks both concerned and vexed at this levity. He had left his mother and sister as he entered in tears. Was it possible all this might be true?

"I beseech you, Duke, to leave the Louvre while you can," says Mademoiselle de Hautefort, very earnestly.

"But I am waiting here, madame, at the express command of her Majesty, until Mazarin, with whom she is now engaged in the council-chamber, retires."

"Are they alone?" asks the Duchess.

"Yes, madame."

"Then, Duke, I do advise you at once to escape while you can. If her Majesty told you to remain, and she is now closeted with Mazarin, the sooner you pass the gates of Paris the better; unless your highness particularly desire to air the best set of rooms in the Bastille; and even they are dull," she adds, with that invincible desire to **laugh** and make others laugh, at once her charm and her defect.

Careless as is the Duc de Beaufort, his confidence is shaken. He had taken up his velvet **cap to depart, when a knock is** heard at the door.

"Come in," cries the Duchess.

It was Guitaut, Captain of the Queen's Guards. **He** walks up **to the** Duke, and lays his hand on his shoulder: "I command your highness to follow me, in the name of the King and of the Queen-Regent."

Even the Duchess becomes serious.

Beaufort eyes Guitaut for some time in silence. "This is very strange, Guitaut. There must be some mistake. I am here by her Majesty's commands, awaiting a further audience."

"I know nothing of that, **your highness.** My instructions are precise. You are **under arrest.**"

Beaufort unbuckles his sword. He presents it to Guitaut. Then he turns to the Duchess and Mademoiselle de Hautefort, whose countenances express the concern they both feel. "You are witness, ladies, that I, a prince of the blood, am arrested when, in obedience to her Majesty's commands, I am awaiting the honour of a further audience. *Pardieu*, that sneaking varlet, Mazarin, shall pay for this. The Coadjutor will revenge me. Lead on, Guitaut. Where is it to be? The Bastille?"

"I have **orders to** conduct your **highness** to the Castle of Vincennes," replies Guitaut, bowing.

"To Vincennes! And by the Queen's order! *Ventre de ma vie!* she is a traitress after all!"

CHAPTER X.

Midnight Visitors.

THE Queen could no longer appear in the streets
without insult. The mob laughed in her face, and
called her *Madame Anne*. They saluted Mazarin with
howls, as her *Bon ami;* some said *Amant*. The words
sound much alike when shouted by a mob, and are
not indeed always different in point of fact. Gondi,
in the parliament, uttered thrilling words about *la
belle France* going to perdition between a Spanish
regent and an Italian minister. No president was
found to rebuke him. Indeed, when he demanded
that the law respecting aliens holding offices of state,
passed against Concini (Maréchal d'Ancre) in the
regency of Marie de Medici, should be amended to
suit the present crisis, his words were received with
such a fury of applause that the roof was very nearly
brought down about his head. Yet if any single
member of that noisy parliament had been asked what
national misfortune he dreaded, what unpunished
crime, what neglect, or what personal hardship he
desired to redress, he would have found it difficult to
answer. It was the fashion for every one to be dis-
contented and to rebel. If citizens, to call themselves
Frondeurs; if nobles, *Importants*. To object to everything; to harass the Government, refuse to pay taxes
and subsidies; and to threaten to call in Spain on the
most trivial pretences. And this because two duchesses
had quarrelled, and certain hungry princes had lost
the sinecures they craved for. Thus began the civil

war of the Fronde, which lasted during the whole of the minority of Louis XIV.

Mazarin, when he heard that the parliament, lashed on by Gondi, the Coadjutor, seriously proposed to revive an obsolete law, which would connect his name with that of Concini, who had been shot down like a dog within the precincts of the Louvre, was alarmed. Not being a soldier like Richelieu, nor a patriot like De Retz, but only a soft-spoken Italian, with a slight frame,—no unnecessary bones or muscles,—long thin hands, and a sallow, womanish face, he applied to the all-powerful Condé for help. Condé effected a compromise with Gondi. So no more was heard of the obnoxious law at that particular time. But the parliament had, like a young lion, tasted blood in the way of power, liked it, and was not to be appeased. Spite of Condé, seditious edicts and offensive measures, all suggested by the Coadjutor, continued to be passed; and Mazarin shut himself up within four walls, fearing for his very life.

It is night and very dark; only a few ill-trimmed lamps placed on pulleys across the street, and under the signs of the various shops, at long distances from each other, cast a dim and flickering light. The unpaved streets are muddy and full of holes; a mob is collecting in the darkness between the Louvre, the Church of Saint-Germain l'Auxerrois, and the garden of the Palais Royal. It thickens every moment; group after group of men and some women emerge from the gloom. They pour down from Saint-Jacques and from Saint-Antoine, from the quays and the heart of the old Roman city about Notre-Dame and the Hôtel Dieu. They gather from all quarters. Before an hour has passed, a

dense multitude, many thousands in number, are packed
together.   Those who stand under the dim lamps have
a dogged, resolute look.   All eyes are directed towards
the Palais Royal, separated by a high wall from the
street. The huge building rises up a gaunt **mass** before
them. Not a light is to be seen at any of the windows;
not a sentinel is visible, they are withdrawn within
the postern.   Threats and oaths and ribald jests pass
from mouth to mouth loudly and without fear; savage
cries and shouts of laughter ring along the silent
streets.   Anne of Austria, with her two sons, **is** within
the palace.   She is quite aware what **is** passing without. From an upper window, in a darkened room, she
watches the citizens pressing closer and closer to the
gates.   From amid the tumult, groans and imprecations
are now audible; the words reach her ears.   "Where is
the little King?" cries one.   "We will see him!" shrieks
another.   "You fool! he is not here," answers a third,
a smith, as black as his forge, from the slums of Saint-
Antoine.   "Why not? where should he be but at
home?" another voice **asks.** "We will force the gates,
and find him!" roars a stumpy man, with stentorian
voice, shaking his fist, and struggling **to** the front.
"Find him! where will you find him? he **is** in Spain,"
shouts one at his elbow. "Curses on the Italian priest!"
howl many voices in horrible chorus.   This cry excites
the entire multitude **to** frenzy; it is taken up from
all parts, and **a** volley of groans and curses for a time
drowns all else.   The crowd surges to and fro, like
breakers on a rocky shore. Each moment it approaches
nearer **the** palace.   **A** tall spare man, an emissary of
De Retz, who all along has taken an active part in
inciting the people, seizes on the moment as propitious,

and calls out in a loud voice, "Death to Mazarin!"
Thousands re-echo, "Death to Mazarin!" With hideous
gesticulations they throw their arms aloft; caps fly into
the air; innumerable hands are clapped in savage
applause. "Death to Mazarin!" passes down the lines
of the long streets. It is heard at the crossways, and
at every side alley and opening, dying away in the far
distance into indistinct murmurs.

The Queen hears this death-cry standing at the
darkened window, and trembles. Again the maddened
people shout, "Death to Mazarin!" and again, "Death!"
is echoed from afar. "He has spirited away our little
Louis into Spain to kill him!" "He has murdered the
Regent!" yells out the tall, spare man, forcing his way
hither and thither. "Death to the traitor!" "To the
gallows with all foreigners!" is the murderous response
of the mob.

Fresh cries now arise, led by the tall, spare man
with the powerful voice. "Vive Gondi, our noble
bishop! We will have Gondi! the Queen shall choose
Gondi, our Coadjutor!" "Come forth and answer to
us, Dame Anne!" shrieks a shrill woman's voice, very
near the palace, during a momentary lull. "Come
forth, or we will break in and shoot you! Where is
our *Roi des Halles?* Where is Beaufort? Come out
to us, and speak like an honest woman! Let Beaufort
free!—Give up your lover, Mazarin!" bellows a fat
beldame from the Halles. "Give up the *bon ami,* and
we will roast him at the Grève, and dance round the
bonfire!" and hideous peals of laughter, yells, hisses,
and imprecations rise out of the night. Then, growing
impatient, the whole mass, with one accord, vociferate,
"We will see the King! where is the King? Show us

the little King, or we will set fire to the palace. The
King! the King!"

A tremendous rush is made from behind; those
in front fall down, screaming that they are killed; others
trample upon their bodies. The gates are forced; the
foremost find themselves within the court. Pushed on
by the press from behind, they now stand under the
colonnade, then beneath the portico, on past the
Queen's Guards, who, commanded only to defend, not
to attack, stand back, drawn swords in their hands,
darkly eyeing the rioters. The lofty portals of the
Palais Royal are wide open; there are lights within the
ample hall. Beyond is the grand staircase, with gilded
banisters. Finding no obstacle, the rioters mount the
stairs. On the first landing a woman stands, immovable. It is the Queen. She is alone. She is pale,
but betrays no fear. The rude intruders draw back,
amazed at the vision of majesty and loveliness before
them. Anne of Austria beckons to them to advance.
She places her finger on her lip, commanding silence.
The rabble, before so noisy, are instantly hushed as
by a charm. Signing to the foremost to follow her,
she leads the way, through sumptuous chambers and
vaulted galleries, to the King's sleeping-room. She
approaches his little bed of gilt lattice-work, and gently
drawing aside the lace curtains, displays Louis XIV.
in the sound and tranquil sleep of childhood. The
citizen *Frondeurs* are satisfied. The mothers bless his
baby face and rich auburn curls. The men contemplate
the Queen with awe. She stands beside the bed, surveying them with royal unconcern. When they have
stared their full at the little King and at her, those
who have already entered turn back. No others dare

approach. Ashamed and silent, they retreat across the halls and through sculptured galleries in a very different spirit to that in which they came.

* * * * * *

Anne of Austria grows more and more devout. She spends long hours in her oratory, prostrate before an image of the Magdalene. She often retires to the Val de Grâce, where she has built a splendid church, as a thank-offering for the birth of her sons. For days together she wears closely fitting serge dresses, buttoned up to the throat, like a lay nun. She fasts, and chastises herself with a severity proper alike to a sinner or a saint.

Yet there are whispers, and confidences, and anecdotes touching her intimacy with Cardinal Mazarin, not quite in accordance with such excessive austerity.

It is a *liaison* too public for intrigue, uneasy enough for marriage!

The constant reproaches she addresses to her ladies in waiting for their lack of devotion, tends rather to enrage than to edify these pretty sinners. Mademoiselle de Pons, with a smile and a toss of the head, draws Mademoiselle de la Mothe into a corner, and repeats some hard words the Queen has spoken to her. Mademoiselle de Hautefort, of a quick, impulsive temperament, is continually either in a passion or in tears. The Duchesse de Chevreuse is unusually grave, and more silent than she ever was before. The Duchesse de Noailles, lady of the bed-chamber, her attendance at the Palais Royal over, orders her coach and, in company with the Duchesse de Sennécy, returns home to her hôtel in the Place Royale, in a very bad humour. Here a party of ladies, "her nineteen bosom friends," are awaiting her arrival. They are all eager for gossip, and all pledged to a vow of eternal secrecy, a promise they will keep as long as the retailer of the scandal is speaking. Coffee has been handed round in delicate cups of Oriental porcelain. Bonbons and cakes, served on trays of gold *repoussé*, have been discussed; the ladies lean back in their chairs, to listen with greater ease. Then the Duchesse de Noailles, addressing herself particularly to Madame de Sennécy and a certain Comtesse de Lude, remarkable for a thin pinched face and a very red nose, begins.

CHAPTER XI.

The two Duchesses.

"MESDAMES, you have asked me to give you some details of what is passing in the palace. I will do so; but do not imagine, for Heaven's sake, that I wish to spread evil reports or to act *la scandaleuse*. Far from it; as long as I remain in the Queen's service, whatever her conduct may be towards me, I shall bear it. I shall not dream of revenge."

"Oh, dear no, not in the least," the ladies murmur; "nothing can be more proper."

"But, really, when I see such an affectation of devotion, that serge gown, and no ornaments except on state receptions; such severity, too, towards every one who dresses like the rest of the world—she told me the other day my dress was too *décolleté*—can you conceive?—it is more than human nature can bear. It sets me remembering certain stories well known to everybody within the palace, when her Majesty wore low dresses too, and was not *quite* such a *dévote* as she pretends to be now."

The assembled ladies assent silently. The Duchesse de Noailles, who is excited and has spoken quickly, having stopped to take breath, the Duchesse de Sennécy seizes the moment to break in—

"You may do as you please, dear Duchess, but for my part I am indignant with her Majesty. She has no gratitude. I might have ruined her years ago, when my cousin, Louise de Lafayette, could turn the late King Louis XIII. round her finger; one word from her, and the Queen would have been exiled! I am indignant, I repeat—I am actually not allowed to choose my own confessor! Her Majesty insists that I should select a Jesuit—a protégé of Mazarin—a man, as I believe, not to be trusted. And the reason she gives is, 'that it is for the good of my soul!' I can take care of my own soul, I suppose. I always confess twice a year. What is it to her Majesty if I do not confess at all?"

All the ladies murmur acquiescence, and the red-nosed Countess, Madame de Lude, says, "It is an impertinence."

"Every one must see," continues Madame de Sennécy, speaking rapidly, for she observes that Madame de Noailles is eager to proceed, "the power Mazarin exercises over her. In her youth Richelieu loved her: now it is Mazarin. She is born to ensnare the Sacred College—perhaps his Holiness himself, if he crossed the Apennines——"

"Oh, Duchess," exclaim several voices, "how shocking!" and some ladies hold up their fans before their faces.

"Gently, madame," says Madame de Noailles, interrupting; "I detest calumny. I only speak of the
past—that cannot hurt her Majesty."

"I speak of the present," cries Madame de Sennécy with irritation. "There is quite enough to talk
about in the present, without recalling the past. The
partiality of the Queen positively injures Mazarin. I
believe that this is the principal reason of the great
animosity against him among the citizens of Paris,
who call themselves *Frondeurs*."

"But, my *très chère*," answers Madame de Noailles,
—the Mrs. Candour of that day, who, although quite
as spiteful as her friend, had more discretion, and
dreaded the mischief that might arise by-and-by if the
·tongues of all the assembled ladies were let loose,—
"but, my *très chère*, it is believed that her Majesty is
privately married to Mazarin; the Cardinal has never
taken priest's orders; the Queen is a widow. Madame
de Motteville is of this opinion; *enfin*, I believe it myself: else that sneaking, honey-mouthed Italian, whom
we all knew as 'Signor Giulio,' secretary to the great
Richelieu, would never dare to be so unkind to the
King and the little Duke, or so arrogant to her Majesty."

"*Ciel!* how contemptuously Mazarin answers the
Queen sometimes—how meekly she bears it!" exclaims
Madame de Sennécy. "Beringhen tells me that he
will not allow the King and his brother proper
body-linen, and that the sheets of their beds are in
holes."

"*Ah, Dieu!* what a shame," cry the ladies—"the
King of France!"—and the red-nosed Countess declares, "That the parliament ought to know it."

This idea alarms Madame de Noailles extremely. She does not want to lose her place at Court, yet it is sweet to her to hear the Queen abused, who had so sternly forbade her to appear again before her in such low dresses.

"Well, Mazarin is bad enough, mesdames," cries Madame de Sennécy (not to be quelled by the frowns and signs of her senior); "he is bad enough—the blood-sucker—as that dear handsome Duc de Beaufort calls him; but, for my part, I can tolerate him much better than those nieces of his, who come up one by one from Rome—Mancini and Martinozzi, or whatever he calls them—with their bold Italian looks and big eyes, devouring every man they see. How intolerable they are!"

"They are quite improper," puts in the red-nosed Countess, "and very ugly."

Some of the ladies say they do not think so. Others declare that they are sallow, bony, and ill-shaped. Madame de Sennécy ends the discussion by declaring that one is deformed, and that the other limps; a statement utterly untrue, but which is received as gospel. Madame de Noailles declares that she is sure the Queen would never allow such creatures to be about the Court if she could help it. It is most dangerous for his Sacred Majesty to be educated with them. He might become attached to Olympia for instance, the eldest unmarried one.

A shudder passes through the assembled ladies at such a monstrous supposition. The red-nosed Countess opines that the princes of the blood should have such hussies imprisoned in the Bastille, and fed on bread and water.

"Ah, ladies," cries Madame de Noailles, in her shrill voice, "how little you know of the intrigues of a Court! Mazarin fully intends to marry his saucy niece, Olympia, to the King. The Queen cannot help it; she is in his power; she is his **wife**."

"It is to be hoped so," mutters Madame de Sennécy; and the red-nosed Countess shakes her head, and by this significant gesture endorses her doubt of the fact.

"I wish you would listen to me," says the Duchesse de Noailles peevishly. "I was alluding to some curious old stories connected with the Queen; but, perhaps, ladies you **know** them **already**," and she looks inquiringly around.

"Very imperfectly," lisps a thin demoiselle of uncertain age, who had been disappointed of the situation of maid of honour. And the red-nosed Countess settles herself in her chair, drinks another cup of coffee, and begs Madame de Noailles to proceed. Madame de Sennécy also joins in the same request. Another lady, a hanger-on of the Duchesse de Noailles, who had not yet spoken, **says**, "It is well known that Madame la Duchesse **relates** everything **in** such a piquante manner." Thus encouraged, the Duchess begins:—

"I desire to speak of the past. The past cannot injure her Majesty. I am without prejudice, and incapable of malice." The Duchesse de Sennécy laughs behind her fan. "I have listened to all Madame de Sennécy has said with deep concern;" and she crosses her hands, and looks up at the ceiling with mock solemnity. "I am lady of the bed-chamber to the Queen—a position involving certain duties, certain reserves. God forbid I should forget them!" Madame de Sennécy stares at her with amazement, wondering what is coming next. "Her Majesty was so cautious formerly—so cautious, I say—nothing more—it is not likely she should commit herself now. I do not therefore agree with Madame de Sennécy in her opinion that she is privately married to Mazarin."

"Then she ought to be," the red-nosed Countess says sententiously.

"Remember she had Madame de Chevreuse to help her formerly," thrusts in Madame de Sennécy sharply.

"With your permission, ladies, I will begin my narrative. But if you interrupt me, I cannot do so," and Madame de Noailles draws herself up with an offended air. "A thousand pardons!" every one exclaims. Not a sound is heard. The Duchess, somewhat pacified, surveys her audience. "I presume, ladies, we all adore the miracle wrought in the person of his present Majesty for the continuance of the royal line; I say, in the person of our present Majesty, Louis XIV., a miracle which was brought about by the intercession of that saint, your cousin, Mademoiselle Louise de Lafayette;" she turns towards Madame de Sennécy, who bows. "It was Mademoiselle de Lafayette who persuaded the King to visit the Queen at the Louvre. A miracle—eh, my dear friends?" and a malicious smile plays about her mouth, and she casts up her eyes and pauses; "a wonderful miracle after twenty-two years of sterility, and the King, too, almost in his grave!"

"Quite so," replies the Duchesse de Sennécy; "incredible!" All the ladies laugh. The red-nosed

Countess declares she never had believed it; which was exactly what Madame de Noailles intended, though she would not have said so for the world!

"Well, after this truly miraculous event, and when their Majesties were as much alienated as ever—for the Queen never forgave the insult the King put upon her at the Val de Grâce, in summoning her before the council, and making the Chancellor search her papers—their Majesties being, I repeat, as much alienated as ever, the Beau Buckingham came to Court.* But, mesdames, this is a long story; you will be fatigued."

"No, no—not in the least," answer all the ladies speaking at once. "Go on Duchess, pray go on; tell us about the Beau Buckingham. Did he not let pearls fall from his dress, and when they were picked up refuse to take them back?" asks the Duchesse de Sennécy.

"Exactly," replies Madame de Noailles. "Buckingham was a grand seigneur."

"Pray go on, madame."

"Well, mesdames, an embassy came from Charles I. of England—poor man, he had his head cut off afterwards—how perfidious those English are!—to ask the hand of our Princess Henrietta Maria—daughter of Marie de Medici and Henry IV.—in marriage. The Beau Buckingham was the ambassador chosen, and such a one was never seen before; so magnificent, so handsome, so liberal. His dress, his manners, his cortége, all were perfect. He seemed like a prince out of a fairy tale, just arrived from the moon, who

---

* George Villiers, Duke of Buckingham, favourite of James I., and of his son, Charles I., assassinated by Felton, 1628.

spoke nothing but diamonds and rubies, and at whose feet flowers sprung up. All the ladies lost their hearts to him, the husbands shut themselves up in a rage, and the lovers hanged themselves in sheer despair!

"He soon saw how matters stood with the poor Queen. She dared scarcely open her mouth, and looked so terrified in the presence of her husband and Cardinal Richelieu, that what with her beauty and her evident sufferings, she might have touched a heart of stone. Now the Beau Buckingham was far from having a heart of stone where the ladies were concerned. So, *le voilà amoureux*, the Beau Buckingham! Indeed, from the first moment he came to Court he saw only the Queen. To her all his looks, all his attentions, were directed,—and such looks, such devotion! *Bon Dieu*, how well I remember him in a justaucorps of white satin embroidered with gold, leaning against a pillar gazing at the Queen, who evidently was aware of his glances. His long beautiful hair streamed over his shoulders in rich chestnut curls, his noble face beamed with expression; in one hand was a cavalier's hat covered with snowy plumes, the other was placed on his heart.

"The Queen was sensible to his homage. Poor Queen! she really was very ill used; it must have been delightful to be loved at last. Indeed, it was quite evident to me, as well as to the whole Court, that Buckingham's feeling was returned. Sometimes she gazed also, nor did her looks want fire. But, mesdames, I hope you do not misunderstand me," and the Duchess glanced deprecatingly round the circle; "I assure you I am not censorious; I am only relating_facts, undoubted facts, which happened long

ago—in order to convince you all that Madame de
Sennécy is mistaken, and that even when young her
Majesty was eminently cautious. She is so still. Be-
lieve me, she is not married to Mazarin."

"Pray proceed, dear Duchess," cries Madame de
Sennécy; "never mind Mazarin; your story is most
interesting."

"We want to hear the *dénouement,*" say all the
ladies, and the red-nosed Countess opines that "it is
easy to understand what that will be."

"Her Majesty used to delight in dancing. Now
she often danced with Buckingham. This was only
etiquette, as he represented Charles I. of England at
the Court of France. Her Majesty was always very
cautious, I assure you, very cautious. Buckingham
did all he could to retard the negotiation of marriage,
and Richelieu, who knew the Queen well and had
watched her closely, having, I suppose, discovered her
secret, did everything, on the contrary, to hasten his
departure.

"There was a story about some diamonds—an
aigrette, I believe. I never quite understood it, ladies,
but of course Madame de Chevreuse did—some diamonds that the King had given to the Queen, and
which she gave to Buckingham, who was imprudent
enough to wear them in public. This nearly caused
her ruin, for she was surrounded by enemies and
spies. The Cardinal got wind of it, and informed
the King, and his Majesty called on the Queen to
wear these diamonds on a certain day, and but for
the exertions of certain musketeers of the Queen's
Guard, by name Athos, Porthos, and Aramis, who
journeyed night and day to fetch them from England

—at least, so goes the tale—Anne of Austria would have been imprisoned, or perhaps beheaded, *à la mode Anglaise*, particularly as the Cardinal preferred that mode of execution. You remember that charming Monsieur le Grand, who had his head cut off?" says Madame de Noailles, appealing to the red-nosed Countess.

"Ah! I should think so, the husband of Marion de l'Orme, the Marquis de Cinq-Mars, a sad profligate and coxcomb, who richly deserved his fate."

"At last Buckingham was to go," continues the Duchess; "he could spin out his time no longer. All the Court accompanied him to Amiens. Madame de Chevreuse was with the Queen, who did all she could to conceal her grief, for, believe me, she is very cautious. Ah! her Majesty knows what it is to be in love though, spite of caution and serge gown, and her *petit air dévot*. She ought to be more charitable, and let her ladies dress as they please, eh, mesdames?" and the Duchess looks round, and sees every eye fixed eagerly upon her; the red-nosed Countess, with a visible sneer on her face, and Madame de Sennécy, full of gratified spite, smiling sarcastically. "Madame de Chevreuse did, ladies, hint to me, that the long evening spent at Amiens was not passed—hum!—well not passed *all* in public. For a single moment her Majesty did, extraordinary to say, forget her usual caution, and you know, ladies, a moment may do much."

All the ladies laugh behind their fans, and the red-nosed Countess gives it as her decided opinion "that the Queen is not married to Mazarin," for which the Duchesse de Sennécy warmly applauds her excellent judgment, and adds, "she had always said so."

"There was a fête at Amiens," continues Madame de Noailles, her eyes sparkling with malice, "a shady garden, and a moon not too bright—a lover's moon, we will say—revealing much, not all. It is certain that by the management of Madame de Chevreuse, the Queen and Buckingham had a charming little *àpart* during the fête, in a grove at the end of the gardens, near the city walls. There was a cry, and Putange, who was in waiting, but—instructed by Madame de Chevreuse—standing apart, though within call, hearing the Queen's voice, rushed forward and found her nearly fainting, and Buckingham on his knees before her."

"*Bagatelle!*" breaks in Madame de Sennécy, "what a romantic story!"

"Certain it is, Buckingham sailed from France that same night. Madame de Chevreuse had too much on her own hands (*en fait d'amour*) to know more than what Putange told her. Buckingham sailed, the Queen returned ill to Paris, and was nursed by the Duchesse de Chevreuse. Some say that Buckingham returned again privately. At all events, the Queen, as long as Richelieu and Louis XIII. lived, led a miserable life. Mesdames," and the Duchesse de Noailles gives a triumphant glance round the circle, "I have proved, I think, that her Majesty is seldom incautious," and the Duchess smiles a bitter smile, and again looks round for approval and acquiescence.

Just as the ladies had all risen with great animation to give their various opinions and to thank the

Duchess, the rattle of a heavy coach is heard below. In a few moments the door is flung open, and Madame la Duchesse de Chevreuse is announced.

CHAPTER XII.
"Put not thy Trust in Princes."

MADAME DE NOAILLES rises to receive the Duchesse de Chevreuse, and kisses her with effusion, but is startled at the sight of her blanched face and despondent air. She is plainly dressed in a dark travelling costume, bows to the Duchesse de Sennécy and to the other ladies, and sinks down on a couch.

"Good heavens! what is the matter?" asks Madame de Noailles, with intense curiosity, taking her by the hand; "you are strangely altered since I left the palace a few hours since."

The Duchesse de Chevreuse glances at the circle of ladies, the "nineteen bosom friends," whose eyes are riveted upon her as if to read her thoughts. The red-nosed Countess in particular has advanced close to her, in order not to lose a syllable; her mouth is wide open, to assist her ears in listening.

"I have come on private business of some importance to myself, dear Duchess," says Madame de Chevreuse, speaking under her breath. "I did not know that you received this evening. It is unfortunate."

Madame de Noailles, who is dying to hear what she has to say, looks at her guests with an unmistakable expression. The Duchesse de Sennécy rises at once.

"Allow me to wish you good evening, my dear

friend," says she, and departs. The red-nosed Countess
is forced to rise and follow her example, how much
against her will it is plain to see; the other ladies
retire with her.

Madame de Noailles and the Duchesse de Chevreuse are now alone. Madame de Chevreuse heaves
a profound sigh; a tear rolls down her cheek, out of
which the dimples are faded. Her thin lips are
white, and she shivers.

"Tell me, Duchess, what misfortune has happened?" asks Madame de Noailles, taking her hand.

"A misfortune, yes, for I love her—I love her
dearly. I have devoted my life to serve her; without
me she would not now be Regent of France."

Madame de Chevreuse speaks in broken sentences;
her looks are wild; her mind seems to wander; her
large prominent eyes are fixed on vacancy.

"Duchess, for God's sake rouse yourself. What
has happened? Is it the Queen?" And Madame de
Noailles wrings the hand of her friend to rouse her.

"Yes—it is the Queen," replies Madame de
Chevreuse slowly, becoming more conscious, and
gazing at her. "Her Majesty has dismissed me. I
am on my way to Tours—exiled."

"Gracious heaven!" exclaims Madame de Noailles;
"what ingratitude!"

"Duchess, I thank you for your sympathy; but, I
beseech you, say not one word against my beloved
mistress. When I entered this room it seemed to me
that sorrow had made me mad—my brain was on
fire. I am better now, and calmer. My royal mistress may live to want me, as she has so often done
before. She may recall me. At Court—in exile—

absent or present, I am her humble and devoted slave."

"She will want no one as long as she has Mazarin," says the Duchess, with a sneer.

"So I fear," returns Madame de Chevreuse.

"But what has happened since I left the palace?" again eagerly asks Madame de Noailles.

"I will tell you. I have never been the same to her Majesty since the old days, when I was banished, after the Val de Grâce, by Richelieu. She received me well after I returned, when she was Regent; but I have loved her too devotedly not to feel the difference. While, on my side, the long years that I had spent flying over Europe to escape the machinations of the Cardinal, had only made me more devoted to her, the Queen—who formerly trusted me with every thought—had grown serious, reserved, and ascetic. I am pious enough myself,"—and a gleam of fun passes into her weary face, and causes her eyes to sparkle,—"I never eat meat in Lent, and always confess at Easter. But her Majesty has become a bigot. She was always reproving me, too, for those little *agaceries* (vanities she called them) which no one lives without. 'My age,' she said, 'forbade them.' Now I only own to forty, Duchess; that is not an age to go into a convent, and to think of nothing but my soul. Why should I not enjoy myself a little yet?" And her large eyes find their way to a mirror opposite, and dwell on it with evident complacency.

"But the Queen reproaches everybody," returns Madame de Noailles. "Conceive—she reprimanded me for wearing a dress too *décolleté*."

Madame de Chevreuse smiles faintly; for it was

indeed true that the older Madame de Noailles grew, the lower her dresses were cut.

"People who hated me made the Queen believe," continues Madame de Chevreuse, "that I wanted to govern her—to use her patronage. If it were so, I should have done it long ago. It was the Princesse de Condé who told the Queen so; she hates me. When I assured her Majesty that it was false, she seemed to believe me. Then came the affair of Madame de Montbazon and the letters found in her room, one of which she said was written by the Duchesse de Longueville, the daughter of my enemy, the Princesse de Condé. How could I help what my stepmother said? —she is a spoilt beauty, and very injudicious—but her Majesty blamed me, nevertheless. I implored her to forgive my stepmother; and for this purpose, I offered her Majesty yesterday a collation in those fine gardens, kept by Regnard, beyond the chestnut avenue of the Tuileries—you know these gardens, Duchess?"

"I do," replies Madame de Noailles.

"Her Majesty had often wished to go there. I asked my stepmother to be present, in the full belief that the Queen's kind heart would relent when she saw her, and that she would restore her to favour. Alas! I was mistaken. I do not know the Queen now, she is so changed. She came accompanied by the Princesse de Condé. No sooner had she set eyes on Madame de Montbazon, who was conversing with me, than the Queen gave me a furious glance, called the Princesse de Condé to her side, and bid her command the attendance of her pages; then, without another word, her Majesty turned her back on me, entered her coach, and departed." ·

"Heavens!" exclaims Madame de Noailles, turning up her eyes, "no one is safe, unless they are allies of Cardinal Mazarin."

"An hour afterwards," — and the Duchesse de Chevreuse raises her handkerchief to her eyes,—"I received an order to quit Paris for Tours. Alas, I have not deserved it!"

"It is the Cardinal," cries Madame de Noailles. "He will drive out all her old friends; they are inconvenient——"

While she speaks the door opens, and Mademoiselle de Hautefort enters the saloon, unannounced. She is bathed in tears: her eyes are swollen with excessive weeping; she cannot repress her sobs. The two ladies rise, and endeavour to soothe her; but her passionate sorrow is not to be appeased. For some time she cannot utter a word. Madame de Chevreuse hung over her affectionately.

"Dearest friend," she says, kissing her, "I guess what has happened. You are exiled; so am I. Come with me into Touraine; let us comfort each other until better days."

"Oh, speak not to me of better days," sobs Mademoiselle de Hautefort. "They can never come to me. My dear, dear mistress, you have broken my heart!" and she bursts into a fresh passion of tears.

The Duchesse de Chevreuse sits down beside her and chafes her hand. Madame de Noailles, who sees in the departure of these two ladies a chance of greater promotion and increased confidence for herself, forms her countenance into an expression of concern she does not in the least feel.

"My dear friend," says Madame de Chevreuse, endeavouring to calm the agony of grief which shook the whole frame of Mademoiselle de Hautefort, "let us share our sorrow."

"The Queen must think herself rich in friends, to cast away such devoted servants," observes Madame de Noailles sententiously, contemplating the group through her eye-glass. "Do speak, Mademoiselle de Hautefort."

She had gradually become more collected, and her violent sobs had ceased; but now and then her bosom heaves, as bitter recollections of the past float through her mind.

. "Speak," whispers the Duchesse de Chevreuse in her softest voice, "it will relieve you. In what manner did our royal mistress dismiss you?"

"Late last evening," answers Mademoiselle de Hautefort, in a tremulous voice, stopping every now and then to sigh, and to wipe the tears that streamed from her eyes, "Mademoiselle de Motteville and I were assisting the Queen at her coucher. As is our habit we were conversing familiarly with her. The Queen was undressed, and just preparing to get into bed. She had only her last prayer to say, for she lives on prayer, like a true saint." Madame de Noailles draws down the corners of her mouth and scarcely endeavours to hide her derision. Even the Duchesse de Chevreuse smiles. "Mademoiselle de Motteville and her sister the Comtesse de Jars, and Mademoiselle de Beaumont, had just left the ante-room from whence they had been speaking with the Queen. I was on my knees before her taking off her shoes. All at once I remembered that a gentleman, who attends upon the ladies in waiting, called Nédo, a Breton—you knew him, Duchess?" Madame de Chevreuse answered that she did. "Had asked me to obtain a better appointment for him." Mademoiselle de Hautefort pauses. The scene seems to rise before her, and a fresh fit of violent sobbing prevents her from speaking. "Alas!" she exclaims at last, "why—why did I presume to trouble her Majesty for such a trifle? A stranger to me too! I have lost what was dearer to me than life —herself. She refused me," continues Mademoiselle de Hautefort, "I was nettled. Oh, Duchess," says she, turning to Madame de Chevreuse, "how often have you borne my hasty temper! How I reproach myself now! That temper has ruined—undone me!"

"What would Monsieur le Maréchal de Schomberg say if he heard you?" asks Madame de Noailles slily.

"Do not name him to me," cries Mademoiselle de Hautefort impatiently. "Schomberg is nothing to me in comparison with the Queen. Had I remained with her, I could never, never have married!"

"Well, you will now," and the Duchess laughs. "But what happened? Do go on."

"Alas! I lost my temper. I was irritated at her Majesty refusing me so small a favour. I told her she had forgotten the claims of her old friends, who had suffered so much in her service."

"That was wrong, ungenerous," interposes Madame de Chevreuse. "A favour ceases to be a favour, if it be made a subject of reproach; besides——"

"Ah! I know it too well!" and Mademoiselle de

Hautefort almost groans with anguish; "and it is that which breaks my heart; it is my own fault. The Queen, in one moment, became more excited than I had ever seen her. Her face turned crimson, she threw herself on her bed, commanded me to close the curtains, and to retire. I disobeyed her. I could not help it. I cast myself on the ground within the *ruelle* of her bed. I clasped my hands. I told her I called God to witness of my love, my devotion to her. I implored her to recall the past, to remember his Majesty Louis XIII."

"Ah! you were very wrong," exclaims Madame de Chevreuse; "most impolitic, most undutiful. You have a good heart, mademoiselle, but you are too impulsive."

"It is true," answers Mademoiselle de Hautefort humbly. "Her Majesty grew more and more displeased, she said that she must have me know she would allow **no** one about her who did not **love** and respect her; then she went **on to** say that **I** had made observations upon her valued servant, Cardinal Mazarin, which were very displeasing to **her**. I replied too hastily that it **was my** care for her honour that had made me do so; that **reports were circulating** injurious to her, and that I longed to see the departure of **a** minister whose presence compromised her."

"What imprudence!" cries Madame de Chevreuse, lifting up her hands. "How could you dare to say this?"

"It is quite true, however," rejoins Madame de Noailles, "and it was the part of **a true** friend to tell her."

"Would to God I had been silent!" continues Ma-

demoiselle de Hautefort; "no sooner were the words
out of my mouth than the Queen sternly ordered me
to extinguish the lights and to withdraw. I rose from
my knees more dead than alive and departed. When
I awoke this morning I received an order commanding
me not to approach within forty miles of the Court.
Oh it is dreadful!"

"Come with me into Touraine, my carriage waits
below. We will stop at your lodgings in order to
give your people time to pack. Come, dear friend,
we have lived side by side among the splendours of a
court, we have suffered persecution for the same mistress, we love her devotedly, spite of all injuries. Let
us now comfort each other in exile."

Mademoiselle de Hautefort casts herself into the
arms of the Duchess.

"You will not keep her long," observes Madame
de Noailles with a smile, "we shall soon see her back
at Court, as Madame la Maréchale de Schomberg,
more blooming than ever."

"No, no," sobs Mademoiselle de Hautefort.
"Never!"

"Adieu, madame," says the Duchesse de Chevreuse,
saluting Madame de Noailles, and taking Mademoiselle
de Hautefort by the hand. "Excuse our abrupt departure, but the sooner we quit Paris the better. My
friend and I would desire in all things to obey her
Majesty's pleasure. Let us hope to meet in happier
days. *Ma chère*," adds she more gaily, addressing the
maid of honour, "we shall not die of *ennui* at my
château."

Mademoiselle de Hautefort only replies with sobs.
The idea of departing overcame her.

"Some gentlemen of our acquaintance will attend us."

"How like the Duchess! She cannot exist without lovers," mutters Madame de Noailles, to herself. Meanwhile she attended the two ladies to the head of the staircase, with great apparent affection kissing them on both cheeks. She watched their departure from a window and waved her hand to them, affecting to weep.

"What a relief they are gone!" she exclaims, taking out her watch. "*Ma foi*, how long they have stayed! It is time for me to dress for the Queen's circle. Now they are gone, there is no one in my way at Court. I am sure of favour—perhaps of confidence. Her Majesty must unbosom herself to some one; why not to me? In half an hour I must be at the palace," and she rang and ordered her coach.

The Duchesse de Chevreuse was never again called to the side of Anne of Austria. Her hatred of Cardinal Mazarin forbade it. She became one of the principal leaders of that "Ladies' Battle," the Fronde.

Nor was Mademoiselle de Hautefort ever forgiven her bluntness on the Queen's very equivocal behaviour. As Maréchale de Schomberg, however, she re-appeared at Court, but found Anne of Austria lost to her for ever.

The Duchesse de Noailles wore dresses cut in accordance with her Majesty's taste. Although she never became the Queen's confidante, for many years she held a high station at Court.

CHAPTER XIII.

Charles Stuart.

LOUISE DE MONTPENSIER—only daughter of Gaston, Duc d'Orléans, second son of Henry IV. and of Marie de Bourbon-Montpensier—was, as has been said, the greatest heiress in Europe. Her girlhood was passed with Anne of Austria. When Louis XIV. was born the Queen called her *ma fille*. When Mademoiselle romped with the boy-king, she addressed him as *mon mari*.

In spite of the long nose of the Bourbons, *la Grande Mademoiselle*, as she was called, was fairly good looking. She was tall and shapely, with regular features, a good skin, finely cut blue eyes, pencilled eyebrows, a large, though well-formed mouth, and good teeth. Flowing ringlets of light hair framed her face and fell over her rounded shoulders. She had, moreover, an unmistakable air of command.

Her character may be best described in negatives. She was not a heroine, although circumstances made her appear one. She understood politics, but had little capacity for a ruler. She had no fortitude, although possessing a certain elevation of character that lifted her above commonplace. She was selfish and cold-hearted, yet capable of warm attachments. She was ostentatious in the use of her great wealth, but not charitable. She was blinded by conceit, yet was not wanting in shrewdness and judgment. She was haughty, yet loved to condescend to the populace. She was excessively ridiculous, yet affected extreme dignity. Whatever advantages she possessed were but

too well known to herself. Of her faults—and they
were many—she was entirely ignorant. Placed between two parties, the Queen and the Fronde, she was
courted by both, and grew headstrong and ambitious
in consequence. Although she ardently desired to
marry her cousin Louis XIV., she went out of her
way to offend, nay, even to outrage him. Yet unconscious of all her follies, to the day of her death she
firmly believed she was by wealth, position, and genius
raised upon a pedestal which all Europe contemplated
with admiring curiosity. Every crowned bachelor
within the civilised world, according to her, sought
her hand in marriage.

After the defeat at Worcester, Charles Stuart
escaped to the Continent. His mother had already
fled to France. Poor Henrietta Maria (wrinkled, and
prematurely old, with tear-furrowed cheeks, and dull,
hollow eyes, her fragrant curls, so often painted by
Vandyke, grown grey, her royal carriage bowed by
the weight of adversity) lived with her young daughter
Henrietta, afterwards Duchesse d'Orléans, sister-in-law
of Louis XIV., at the Louvre, in right of her birth as
Fille de France. For a time this Queen of Shadows,
the relict of a defunct monarchy, bore the splendour
of her former state. But one by one her ladies in
waiting, grooms of the chamber, maids of honour,
footmen, chamberlains, and pages disappeared. At
last she grew too poor even to procure sufficient fuel
to keep out the winter cold. Though living in a
palace, she was glad, with the young princess her
daughter, to lie in bed for the sake of warmth.

Mademoiselle patronised this afflicted relative, and
frequently visited her. But she does not appear to

have ministered to her necessities. Henrietta was
resigned, even humble to the exalted princess, her
niece; and dwelt often on the personal charms of her
eldest son, Charles Stuart.

She painted him with a brush dipped in the
roseate colours of a mother's fancy. He was, she
said, brave, gallant, handsome, witty, accomplished.
He had splendid black hair, a rich complexion, as of
one much exposed to battles and an adventurous life,
and the bearing of a Paladin. He would be certain
to crush his enemies, and sit upon his father's throne,
she told her niece. But the wily heiress, while she
listened to the eager gossip of the broken-hearted
Queen, was pre-occupied by a matrimonial intrigue
carried on by a certain Abbé de la Rivière, to make
her Empress of Germany.

"I perfectly understood my aunt's drift," she says;
"but I liked the Emperor better."

When Charles Stuart, having escaped almost by a
miracle from England, arrived at Fontainebleau, where
the Court was staying, he was presented to Mademoiselle by his mother. Charles saluted her as a cousin
and a friend, saluted her in dumb show, however, for
he could speak no French. The exiled Queen, therefore (already grasping in anticipation the revenues of
the principalities, dukedoms, forests, and castles of
her wealthy niece), set herself to act interpreter.

Charles Stuart had a melting eye and a manly
presence. He dallied with his cousin, sat beside her
when she played, led her to her coach, held the flambeau while she adjusted her dress, was again found at
her door—having run on in front—to assist her to
descend, and generally ogled, languished, gazed, and

sighed, to the very utmost of his power. But a dumb
lover is dull, and love-making by proxy never answers.
La Grande Mademoiselle, already in imagination invested with the diadem of an Empress, did not fancy
a prince who was only an exile, and who could not
even plead his own cause. She looked on him as a
bore—indeed, worse than a bore, an object of pity.

The Queen of England tried hard to melt her
heart. She even coaxed her; with her own hands she
decked her soft hair with jewels for her Majesty's
ballet. She flattered her into a belief that she was
as beautiful as Venus. She declared that Charles
Stuart's heart was breaking, that his health suffered,
that he would die. No mother ever served a son
better than did this poor distracted lady. But there
was her son, with his swarthy, hard face, as strong
and hale as an oak sapling, his wanton black eye
wandering over the belles of the French Court,—a
living contradiction to all she said! At last, Charles
Stuart, who cared less for the well-filled purse and
boundless dominions of his cousin than his mother,
who knew what it was to be pinched with cold and
hunger, grew impatient, and insisted on an answer.
He sent Lord St. Germains to Mademoiselle to say
that he was so passionately in love with her, he could
no longer bear suspense. Mademoiselle replied with
the discretion of a maiden, and the judgment of an
heiress, conscious that she was dealing with a royal
fortune-hunter—

"The Prince of Wales did her great honour, but
as she understood that he required much pecuniary
assistance to recover the Crown of England, his birth-
right, she feared she might find herself overwhelmed

with expenses incompatible with the wants of a person of her exalted rank. That she must, in consequence, make sacrifices and adopt resolutions difficult to contemplate. That she might risk the loss of her entire possessions on the chance of Charles's re-conquering his kingdom; and that, having been educated in splendour as one of the greatest princesses in the world, the prospect alarmed her."

Yet there must have been some charm about the hard-featured, stalwart youth that attracted her; she would not say, "No." In order to throw down a bait, she hinted that she desired him to change his religion.

"Impossible, madame," was the reply of Lord St. Germains. "A king of England cannot change his religion. He would exclude himself for ever from the throne!"

Again, however, Charles was permitted to approach her, and to make a last attempt. She relished a little mild flirtation with an exiled King, although she vastly preferred marriage with an Emperor. Nevertheless, she curled her hair in honour of the occasion, a thing not usual with her.

"Ah, look at her!" said the Queen-Regent, when she appeared in the evening: "it is easy to see she is expecting a lover. See!—how she is decked out!"

Mademoiselle blushed, but was too discreet to commit herself by a single word.

When Charles Stuart entered the Queen's saloon he looked provokingly well. His mother, nervously alive to every trifle, felt this. A man with such a constitution was not adapted to play the part of a despairing lover. When questioned by the Queen about his

affairs in England, he replied that he knew nothing.
Mademoiselle instantly formed a bad opinion of him.
She turned to her lady in waiting, Madame de Fiesque,
and whispered —

"He is too much of a Bourbon for me. Quite
engrossed by trifles" (*the race has not changed*). "He
can talk about dogs and horses and the chase to her
Majesty, but he has nothing to say about the revolution in England."

Later in the evening, at the royal table, Mademoiselle was shocked at Charles's coarse appetite. He
despised orlotans and Italian pastry, and threw himself
upon a joint **of beef.** Not satisfied with that, he ended
by a shoulder of mutton. "A despairing lover ought
not to have such a monstrous appetite, or he should
satisfy the cravings of hunger beforehand," thought
Mademoiselle. He stared fixedly at her, with his big
black eyes shaded by heavy eyebrows, while he was
shovelling huge pieces of meat down his throat, but
he never spoke. Truly this was not a fashion of
pushing his suit with a fastidious princess who desired
to be an empress!

Mademoiselle yawned, looked at him under her
eyelids, shrugged her shapely shoulders, and called
her lady in waiting **to** her side to amuse her. Thus
passed the precious moments which were to decide
the momentous question—would she, or would she
not?

At length, having gorged in a prodigious manner,
Charles Stuart rose. He made Mademoiselle a formal
bow, and opened his mouth to speak for the first time.
"I hope," he said, in very bad French, "my Lord
St. Germains has explained to your Highness the

sentiments with which you have inspired me. I am, madame, your very humble servant."

Mademoiselle rose to her feet, made him a formal curtsey, and replied, "Sir, I am your very humble servant."

So **ended** this wooing; but poor Henrietta Maria, figuratively rending her clothes and sprinkling ashes on her **head** at such a conclusion, could not let Mademoiselle **off** without one Parthian shot. "I see," said she, "**my son is** too **poor** and **too** unfortunate for you, my niece. It is quite possible, however, that a king of eighteen may be better worth having than an elderly emperor with four children." This little ebullition of spite is pardonable in an unfortunate Queen whose heart was broken. Let it not lie heavy on her **memory!**

Meanwhile, the struggle between the Queen-Regent and her ministers on one side, and the parliament and Gondi on the other, had become **more** and more envenomed. At length the Queen-Regent, under advice of Mazarin, resolved by a *coup d'état* to restore the royal authority.

It is Twelfth-night. Anne of Austria is spending the evening in her closet, watching the King and his brother, **the Duc** d'Anjou—both dressed in character —struggle **on the** floor over the remains of the cake from which they had dug the "bean" and the "ring." Louis XIV. is a handsome boy, docile yet spirited; Philip of Anjou is puny, peevish, and cowardly.

Anne of Austria leans against the back of a chair, and watches the two boys. Her ladies watch her. There is a strange rumour that her Majesty is to leave Paris that very night. To look into her placid face, such an idea seems absurd. By-and-by, Mazarin and some of the princes of the blood come in to ask her pleasure for the morrow. They do not remain, as there is a supper at the Maréchal de Grammont's in honour of the day. When they are gone, the Queen turns to Madame de la Trémouille.

"I shall go to-morrow to the Val de Grâce. Give orders that everything may be ready for me. Call Beringhen; it is time for his Majesty and the Duke to go to bed."

The King at once comes forward to bid his mother good night. The Duke begins to cry.

"What is it, my son?" says the Queen.

"I want, Madame, to go with you to the Val de Grâce to-morrow—do let me!" and he kneels and kisses her hand.

"If I go, my son, I promise to take you. Now, good night, Philip," and she raises him in her arms, and kisses him; "do not keep his Majesty waiting."

She retires early. Those ladies who do not sleep at the Palais Royal leave, and the gates are closed.

At three o'clock in the morning, Mademoiselle de Montpensier, at the Palace of the Luxembourg, is awakened by a violent knocking. She rouses her women, and orders them to see who is there. It is a messenger from the Queen.

"Let him enter," says Mademoiselle, speaking from her bed. It is well to say that Mademoiselle was entirely concealed by heavy curtains, and that the bed stood in a deep alcove.

"The Captain of the Queen's Guard awaits your highness's pleasure," calls out Monsieur de Comminges, from the door.

"What has brought you here at this time of night, Comminges?" asks Mademoiselle from her bed.

"Your highness, the Court is leaving Paris secretly. Her Majesty commands your attendance. Here is a letter which will explain the Queen's wishes."

"Monsieur de Comminges," replies Mademoiselle —who at that time had not conceived the possibility of being one of the *à la mode* leaders of the Fronde, and pointing the guns of the Bastille against her cousin, the King—putting the letter under her pillow, "the commands of her Majesty are sufficient for me. I need no letter to enforce them. Retire, Monsieur le Capitaine, into the ante-room. I will rise instantly, and accompany you. But tell me, Monsieur de Comminges"—calling after him—"where are we to go to?"

"To Saint-Germain en Laye, your highness."

In a short time Mademoiselle is ready. Without waiting for her women, or what she calls her "equipage" (which she desired to have sent after her), she goes out into the night accompanied by Monsieur de Comminges, whose coach waits without. It was pitch dark, but with the help of a flambeau they traverse the unpaved and ill-lit streets, and reach the garden entrance of the Palais Royal without accident. There they find another coach drawn up under some trees. Within sits Anne of Austria; the two princes are each in a corner—Louis XIV. very sleepy and cross, the Duc d'Anjou crying. Mademoiselle is instantly transferred into the royal coach.

"Are you frightened, my cousin?" asks the Queen, speaking out of the darkness to Mademoiselle.

"Not in the least, Madame," is her reply. "I will

follow your Majesty anywhere," and she takes her place
opposite to her in the coach.

It is a long and weary drive to Saint-Germain.
When they arrive it is breakfast-time. But the Queen
commands every creature, including her children, into
the chapel to hear mass. As soon as they had time
to look round, they find the palace (a dreary, gaunt
edifice at all times) cold and wretched beyond de-
scription in a dark January morning. The rooms are
entirely empty—Mazarin having made no provision
for the Queen's arrival, out of fear, perhaps, that her
flight might become known. There are neither beds,
furniture, nor linen. There is not a servant or attendant
of any kind but such as have accompanied them. When
it is night the Queen lies down to rest on a little camp
bedstead. The King and his brother fare no better.
Mademoiselle is accommodated with a straw mattress
in a magnificent saloon on the third floor. There
were plenty of mirrors and much gilding, and the
windows were lofty, and commanded an extensive view,
but there is not a single pane of glass in one of them!
No one has a change of linen. What was worn by
night was washed by day. The Queen laughs at
everything. She says—"It is an escapade which will
at most last three days; when the citizens find that the
Court has left the Palais Royal they will speedily come
to their senses."

CHAPTER XIV.

The Ladies' War.

WHEN the citizens of Paris find that the Court had left the Palais Royal, instead of coming to their senses, they were furious. The Coadjutor, who had broken with the Regent, ruled supreme. He skilfully availed himself of the crisis, and caused the parliament to pass the act against aliens. This measure outlawed Mazarin as an enemy of the King and of the State, a conspirator, a perjurer, and a thief; confiscated his possessions, and enjoined all faithful subjects to shoot him without trial.

Civil war breaks out. The troops of the Queen-Regent were but feebly attacked. It was the *hearts* of her generals that were vigorously assailed by the lady commandants of the Fronde, whose artillery was blandishments and enticements.

Every soul in Paris armed himself, and took the field in whatever costume he usually wore. The nobles led the way in feathered hats, satin doublets, silk stockings, and high-heeled boots. No one knew what they were fighting for. The cry was, "*Vive la Fronde!*" "*Mort à Mazarin!*"

The Duchesse de Longueville, supported by her brother, the great Condé, took possession of the executive government at the Hôtel de Ville. She was quickly joined by the Duchesses de Chevreuse and De Montbazon. The Duc de Beaufort was set at liberty. But as it was quite a "Ladies' War," he acted only as subordinate. The Duchesses distributed all the military posts and honours among themselves—they created

themselves generals, lieutenants, and colonels, like so
many Bellonas. War was waged on quite new principles: Maréchal d'Hocquincourt, defending Peronne
for the Queen-Regent, assured the Duchesse de Montbazon, who invested it for the Fronde, "That Peronne
was at the service of the fairest of the fair."

Not so *la Grande Mademoiselle*. She ranged herself
on the popular side against the Court, and commanded
at the Bastille. She fought in good earnest, and pointed
the well-loaded guns of that fortress against her King
and cousin, who, with his army, lay encamped without
the walls of Paris. Louis retreated precipitately to
Saint-Denis.

We are in the Hôtel de Ville, within the apartment
of one of the very prettiest aides-de-camp attached to
the Duchesse de Longueville. This fair lady, Mademoiselle de Rosny, has just finished a most elaborate
toilette, and having arranged the innumerable little
curls (then so much in vogue) round her face, and
fastened the proper quantity of ribbon in her dark
locks, takes a last fond look in the glass, and then
seats herself in the happiest possible state of expectation.
Now there is a certain all-conquering beau—Monsieur
d'Aumale by name—who has more than half achieved
the conquest of her heart; and she has a kind of presentiment that the morning will not pass without a
visit from this pearl of cavaliers. Nor is she mistaken:
a soft knock at her door announces the approach of
some one. How her heart beats! It must be M. d'Aumale!
So she says, "*Entrez!*" in a trembling voice, and
d'Aumale stands before her.

"Mademoiselle de Rosny," he exclaims, "I am in

the utmost haste, I am come to beg you to be present at the most singular spectacle you ever beheld."

"What may it be?" replies she, rather chagrined that instead of a tender love-scene, such as she anticipated, M. d'Aumale seems so preoccupied.

"It is a review, mademoiselle, ordered by the council; but, ha! ha! such a review! *Morbleu*, you will never guess of whom—the oddest idea! It is no other than a review of priests, monks, and seminarists, all sword in hand, and ready to charge the enemy. It is the strangest idea of defence that ever was conceived; but as we have lady-generals, and the grande Mademoiselle for commander in chief, we are now to have an army of priests for them to lead to battle. These tonsured recruits are actually now all assembling on the bridge near Notre-Dame. You must be quick."

"Was ever anything so ridiculous!" and Mademoiselle de Rosny laughs. "But I shall be terrified at their awkwardness; they will be sure to fire too low and hit us."

"Oh, but you must come. I will be your guard; I pledge myself that you shall return uninjured," and d'Aumale gives the lady a tender glance. "Besides, to reassure you, I believe that these monk-warriors are not even to be trusted with matches; the arquebuses and cannon are as empty and as innocent as when in the arsenal; so there is nothing to fear. If you will come, I will conduct you in my new coach—the very model of elegance—I will answer for it there is not such another in all Paris."

"That will be delightful!" cries the lady. "I do admire those new coaches so much, if it were not for this abominable war, I suppose they would become universal. Well, Monsieur d'Aumale, I am ready! let us see these monks; it will be a good story with which to entertain Madame la Duchesse de Longueville this evening at her reception. How the Duc de Beaufort will laugh!"

In high glee Mademoiselle de Rosny departed, accompanied by her admirer, her pleasure not a little heightened by the idea of appearing in a coach, then by no means common in Paris, and reserved generally for royalty, or for grand occasions, or state processions —heavy lumbering vehicles, such as figure in the old prints of that period, with a sloping roof like a house, and drawn by Flemish horses of huge dimensions. On arriving near the bridge, they stop under the shadow of the cathedral, and there behold the most extraordinary spectacle. All the young monks in Paris are crowded near Notre-Dame, with the exception of the Benedictines and some other orders, who refused to take any part in this mummery. At least fifteen hundred ecclesiastics, drawn up in excellent order, are executing the various manœuvres of march, halt, right-about face, &c., with tolerable precision. The greater number have fastened up their black robes, and invested their lower limbs with most uncanonical garments. The reverend fathers, with their hoods hanging over their shoulders, are booted and spurred, many wear helmets and cuirasses, and all carry such halberts, lances, swords, and bucklers as they had been able to lay hands on. Others grasp a crucifix in one hand, and in the other a pistol, a scythe, an old dagger or a knife, with which each intends to perform prodigies of valour against the enemies of the Fronde. As they advance and retreat on the dusty soil in lines and columns, they present the appearance of an immense flight of crows hovering over a field of newly cut wheat.

To this martial array is added the clamour of drums, trumpets, and warlike instruments, accompanied with no end of benedictions, *Oremus*, and chanted psalms. At the head of the troops is a bishop, meta- morphosed into a commander. He moves very slowly, by reason of his corpulence and the weight of the armour he wears, and looks like a dilapidated St. George, minus the dragon. Then come Carthusians, Begging Friars, Capuchins, and Seminarists, each different order led by their abbot or prior. They all advance gravely with the orthodox goose-step. Cries of "Down with the Regent!" "Death to Mazarin!" "*A bas* the Italian beggar!" "Long live the Union!" "*Vive la Duchesse!*" "*Vive la Fronde!*" add to the clamour of the martial music and the psalms. Made- moiselle de Rosny is fain to hold both her ears, not- withstanding all the sweet things her companion is whispering. The mob of Paris *en masse* is assembled to witness this extraordinary review, and to rejoice in the unexpected aid contributed by the Church in the general emergency. Nor is M. d'Aumale's the only coach on the Quai Notre-Dame that day; many other possessors of such vehicles have been attracted by the scene. The Legate is among the number. The crowd is immense, the applause enthusiastic.

"*Ciel!*" calls out Mademoiselle de Rosny, on a sudden. "Look—Oh look! Monsieur d'Aumale, you have deceived me, I am sure. They are going to fire!"

"No, no," replies d'Aumale, "believe me, you are

mistaken. 'Give the monk his rosary, the soldier his sword,' says the motto. *Messieurs les moines* will not venture to burn their hands in attempting to handle firearms."

"But I tell you," cries the **lady,** "they are going to fire! Good heavens, the guns are all turned this way! Oh, d'Aumale, we shall be murdered. Help! help! I implore you!" And she catches hold of him, and begins to scream after the most approved fashion preparatory **to a** fit of hysterics.

D'Aumale looks out **of** the window. "In the name of heaven, beware—beware!" he shouts to the priests. But in **the confusion his** voice is inaudible. The ecclesiastical artillerymen, awkward and inexperienced, have already lighted the matches, and the cannon, which were loaded, explode right and left in the crowd. A fearful cry arises from the Legate's coach.

"Thank Heaven, d'Aumale, we have escaped,— this time at least," gasps Mademoiselle de Rosny in a low voice, for she is **now** calmed by excessive fear.

"Yes, but I fancy some one else has been seriously wounded. I **will** alight **and** see," says d'Aumale, unfastening the **door.**

A dense crowd surrounds the coach belonging to **the** Legate. The secretary of his eminence had been **shot** dead by a bullet through the chest, the Legate's confessor is wounded in the head, and his two valets also much injured. Never was there such confusion. M. d'Aumale hastens back to secure the safe retreat of the fair De Rosny. They are soon disengaged from the crowd, and rolling back over the muddy ground to the Hôtel de Ville. Here we must bid them farewell, assuming that mademoiselle soon secured the possession of the much-admired coach by a speedy marriage with its handsome owner.

CHAPTER XV.

Mazarin Played Out.

THE marriage bells peal merrily for the august espousals of Louis XIV. with the Infanta Maria Theresa, daughter of the King of Spain. The troubles of the Fronde are over. Gondi, the Coadjutor, now Cardinal de Retz, is imprisoned. Cardinal Mazarin has cemented a peace between France and Spain. He has triumphed.

Mazarin left Paris with a great retinue of coaches, litters, and mules, attended by bishops, secretaries, lawyers, and priests, to meet the Spanish ambassador, Don Luis da Haro, on the frontier, there to arrange the preliminaries of the treaty and the marriage. Don Luis had already arrived, attended with equal splendour. A whole month was lost in the all-important question of precedence. Should Mazarin call on Da Haro, or Da Haro "drop in" on Mazarin? This momentous point was never settled. Mazarin, the wily Italian—*Il Signor Faquino*, as the Prince de Condé calls him — took to his bed, hoping that the anxiety felt for his health by Da Haro would induce him to pocket his Castilian dignity and make the first advance. But Da Haro was not to be caught, and obstinately shut himself up, eat, drank, and made merry with the most dogged patience, and the most entire want of sympathy. So it ended in this wise—no visit was made at all. The great plenipotentiaries met, quite unofficially, on

9*

the Island of Pheasants, in the middle of the River
Bidassoa, dividing France and Spain. There the real
business was very soon dispatched. In process of
time, the King and the Infanta were married.

The Infanta was very small, fair, and plump.
There was an utter absence of expression in her freshly
complexioned face; her eyes were large and gentle,
but said absolutely nothing of any soul within. Her
mouth was large, her teeth were irregular. Her dress
horrified the French ladies. It was unanimously voted
tawdry, ill-made, and unbecoming. As for the ladies
in attendance on her, it was not possible to find words
to paint their grotesqueness. They were black-skinned,
scraggy, and awkward. They had hideous lace, and
wore enormous farthingales. One of them, the "governess of the Infanta," is gibbeted in the pages of
history as "a monster." She unhappily wore what
are designated as *"barrels"* under her dress. Such
was the first effect of *crinoline* on the ladies of the
French nation.

The Duchesse de Noailles was appointed lady of the
bed chamber to the new Queen. She was recommended
to this office by the Queen-dowager, Anne of Austria,
her aunt.

Cardinal Mazarin has now reached the summit of
power. He has imprisoned his rival Cardinal De
Retz, and has tranquillised a great nation. He has
even received the solemn thanks of the once turbulent
parliament. He has equalled, if not exceeded, the renown of Richelieu. After the sounding of those marriage bells he returns to Paris, to repose upon his
laurels. See him! the artistic egotist, who all his life,
has fed on the choicest grapes from his neighbour's

vine, and sipped the most fragrant honey from flowers not his own. See him within his magnificent palace, the outward and visible evidence of the enormous wealth which he no longer fears to display. Louis XIV. looks on him as a father. Anne of Austria trembles when he frowns. All France is subservient to his rule. The walls of his chamber are lined with artistic plunder:—pictures set in gorgeous frames of Florentine carving; statues, mirrors, and glittering chandeliers; tables and consoles, bearing ornaments of inestimable value, in marble, bronze, porcelain, pottery, enamel, and gems. Richest hangings of tapestry, and brocaded satin and velvet, more costly than the gold which surrounds them, shade the intrusive sunshine, and tone all down to that delicious half light so dear to the artistic sense. Everything has been arranged by the hand of a master; and there he sits, this master, dying. The seeds of disease, sown on the frontier where he was detained by Da Haro, have developed into a mortal malady.

He has just risen from his bed. He reposes in a chair on wheels, in which he is rolled from frescoed gallery to marble vestibule; from corridors of pictures to precious libraries; from dainty retiring-rooms to painted pavilions, from guard-room to saloon—those superb saloons where he received the Court.

He even penetrates to the stables, and surveys his priceless stud; he ventures into the magnificent gardens which surround his palace, to feast his eyes on all his vast possessions. Returning again, greatly fatigued, to the picture-gallery, he bids his attendants pause. He rests, absorbed in thought, under a Holy Family, by

Raphael, a work beyond price, now in the Louvre. Here he desires his attendants to leave him. His secretary, who is never beyond call, he commands to wait his pleasure in the ante-room, behind the thick silken hangings that veil the door. Inadvertently this door is left ajar, and the secretary, curious to know what his master is doing, looks through a chink in the curtain, and watches him. The Cardinal, when he has glanced round carefully—to be sure he is alone—lays hold of a crutch placed ready to his hand, and with the utmost difficulty struggles to his feet, for they are swollen, and almost useless from gout. After many efforts he disengages himself from the chair, and reaches the ground, then, balancing himself upon the crutch and any object near at hand, he moves a few steps, stopping for lack of breath. (The secretary doubts if he should not rush in before he falls, so uncertain and tottering are Mazarin's movements; but he forbears, fearful of angering the Cardinal, whom suffering has made irritable.)

Mazarin sighs deeply as he limps on from picture to picture, and surveys his favourite works.

"I feel better," he says, speaking aloud. "If I could only get my breath, I should recover. *Diamine!* I shall—I will recover. I cannot leave my pictures—such a collection,"—and he turns round with difficulty, and surveys the galleries—"not yet complete—to pass into other hands. No, no—it cannot be; I **feel** stronger already. I—alone in my gallery—without those spies always about me to see my weakness—I can breathe." And he draws a long breath. The long breath ends in a groan. "That divine Raffaello!" and again he sighs, and turns to the gem of his collection, a Nativity. "Raffaello is my religion. *Credo in Raffaello!* What *anima!* That exquisite Virgin! and the Christ nestling in her arms! I wonder who sat for that virgin? She must have been a perfect creature! I salute her *di cuore.* That picture came to me from the King of Spain—a bribe. Who cares? I never refuse a present. The King knows my taste. He sent me word there were many more to come if I concluded a peace. I did conclude a peace; I took that picture and others; but, *Sangue di Dio,* I was faithful to France. Ah, ha! I was too sharp for him—a dull king! That *torso* there, dug up at Portici—what stalwart limbs! what grand proportions! How finely the shadows fall upon the thigh from that passing cloud. Ahi! my foot!" (and he shakes on his crutches so violently, the secretary's head and shoulders are inside the room, only the Cardinal does not see him). "I am better now," falters Mazarin, "much better;" then, taking a few steps onwards, he pauses before a Titian. "Venus, my Goddess!—*Laus Veneri.* Oh, the warmth of the flesh tints, the turn of that head and neck— divine! I gave a great price for that picture; but, *Cospetto!* it was not my own money," and he laughs feebly. "It will sell for double! That Paolo Veronese **and** that Tintoretto yonder came from the sale of Charles I. of England, after his execution—those English ruffians! What supple forms, what classic features! —like my native Romans in the Imperial city, where the very beggars think themselves equal to kings; and **so** they are, *per Dio.* Glorious Italy! *Ah, cielo!*" and he creeps on to a favourite landscape by Caracci, lit, as it were, by the living sunshine of the south. "Ah, that sun—I feel it—wonderful! wonderful!—a gem of the eclectic school of Bologna, given to me by the Archbishop. Poor man, he was not, like me, satisfied with art—ha, ha!"—his laugh ends in a severe fit of coughing. "He liked nature. He could not stand inquiry.—I helped him. Oh, my foot!" (And he totters so helplessly, that the secretary, watching him with curious eyes, again nearly rushes in; for if Mazarin dies his salary ceases.) Recovering, however, he steadies himself against the pedestal of a marble group just arrived from Rome, "Leda and the Swan." He drags himself with difficulty into the recess where it is placed, shifting his position, in order to catch the precise light in which to view the rounded limbs of the figure. "What grace, what *abandon*, in that female form!—a trifle *leste* for the gallery of a prelate—presented, too, by a lady—a woman of taste, above prejudices. No one has seen it. I must invite the Court—the Queen-mother will be scandalised. Ha, ha! the Queen-mother!" and he feebly winks and laughs; his laugh brings on another fit of convulsive coughing. (The secretary is on the threshold.) "I must not die before I have disposed of my pictures," Marazin mutters, breathing again; "I cannot bear to die!—now, too, that I have triumphed over all my enemies." The Cardinal sighs heavily, shakes his head, and casts a longing glance round the painted walls. He tries to move onwards; but his strength fails him, suddenly his hands are cramped, the crutch falls on the floor, he groans, sinks into a chair, and faintly calls for assistance.

The secretary is with him in an instant, and summons the attendants. Weary, and utterly exhausted, they lay him on his bed, where he weeps and groans, as much from anguish of mind as from bodily pain. He feels that nothing can amuse or delight him more, neither singing men nor singing women, the wonders of art, or the flattery of Courts. From henceforth to him the world must evermore be mute; the flowers in the gardens he has created shall no longer fling their scented blossoms at his feet; to him the birds are dumb in the groves he has planted, the fruits cease to be luscious, and the sun is already darkened by the shadow of death. His face turns of an ashy hue, and he feebly calls for his physician.

One of the many attendants that hover about his bed, (each one hoping to be remembered in that will of his, of which all Paris has heard,) flies to fetch him. He appears in the person of Guénaud, the Court doctor of that day.

Mazarin has revived a little. **He is** propped up on pillows, to relieve his breathing, **which, by** reason of the oppression on his chest, is laboured and difficult. At the sight of Guénaud he trembles; his teeth chatter. He has summoned the leech, and now he dares **not hear** what he has to say. Mazarin, with his sensuous Italian temperament, clings wildly to life. He shrinks from the dark horrors of the grave—he, who **adores** sunshine, warmth, open air, and beauty.

"Well, Guénaud, well. You are in haste to come to me."

"Your eminence sent for me," replies the physician gravely, bowing to the ground; **then he** contemplates the Cardinal with that all-seeing eye for obvious symptoms and for remote details, that makes the glance of a doctor so awful to the sick.

"I—I am better, Guénaud—much better, *now;* I

had fatigued myself among my pictures. But I did
much, Guénaud—I did *too* much. I even crawled to
my stables—to my garden; I am gaining strength.
To-morrow——"

Mazarin stops; a severe fit of coughing almost
suffocates him. Again the ashy hue—grey as the shadows of departing day when the sun has set—over-
casts his features. Guénaud does not reply, but still
contemplates his patient attentively. The Cardinal
looks up; a hectic colour flushes his cheeks.

"Come," says he, "speak; be honest with me. I am
better?" Guénaud bows.

"I trust so," replies he.

"*Sangue di Dio!*"—and the Cardinal grows crimson, and clenches his thin fingers with nervous agony
—"speak. Your silence agitates me. What have you
to tell me? How long have I to live? Shall I recover?"

Guénaud shakes his head. Mazarin's face again
becomes of a sudden deadly pale. He leans back on his
pillows, and sniffs a strong essence in a filigree bottle
lying by his side. "Guénaud," says he, "I dread death,
but I am no coward. I am prepared for the worst."

"I rejoice to hear it," answers the physician solemnly,
feeling his pulse. "You will have need of all your
fortitude."

"Is it so? Well, then, let me hear my fate?"

"Your eminence cannot live long. Nothing can
save you."

A strange look of determination comes into the
Cardinal's eyes as Guénaud speaks. Mazarin was, as
he said, no coward; but the flesh was weaker than the
spirit, and shrank from suffering and disease. Now

that he has heard the truth, he bears it better than would appear possible in one so slight, nervous, and attenuated.

"I cannot flatter your eminence," continues Guénaud, "your disease is incurable; but I admit that remedies may prolong your life, though they cannot preserve it. Remedies, **ably** administered, can do much, even in fatal cases."

"I respect your frankness, doctor," says the Cardinal calmly. "Speak out; how long can I last?"

"Your eminence may hope to live for two months, perhaps, by following the rules I shall prescribe."

"Well, well—two months! Ah, it is a short time," —and a nervous spasm passes over his face, and his hands twitch with a convulsive spasm. "I do not die of old age; I have sacrificed my life to France and to the King. I never got over that negotiation at the Pyrenees. Well, well—so be it. At least, I know my fate. This interval must be consecrated to the care of my soul. Two months! I shall do my best. All my brother prelates will assist me——"

"To live, your eminence?"

"No, no, Guénaud,"—and the shadow of a smile passes over his thin white lips,—"no, no, not to live, but to **die**; to die for the sake of the abbeys, bishoprics, and **canonries my** death will leave vacant. In two months one may have a world of indulgences; that is something. The Holy Father will rejoice at having my patronage; he is sure to give me a helping hand; and plenty of indulgences. I stand well with the Pope, Guénaud. But—but my pictures, my statues—a collection I have been making all my life, at such a vast expense. Who knows, Guénaud? you may be mistaken," he added, brightening up, his mercurial nature rushing back into its accustomed channel at the recollection of what had been the passion of his life. "Who knows, I may get better!" and his eye turns sharply upon the physician, with a sparkle of its accustomed fire; "eh, Guénaud—who knows?" Guénaud bows, but is silent. "You may be mistaken. *Non importa*, I must think of my soul. It is indeed a great trial—a sore trial—a man of my age, too, with so many years to live! and such a collection! You know my collection, Guénaud?"

"Yes, your eminence," answers he, bowing.

"The finest in Europe," sighs Mazarin, "and not yet finished; fresh works coming in daily. A great trial—but I must think of my soul. Go now, Guénaud; come again to-morrow. Perhaps—who knows? —you may see some change, some improvement—who knows?"

Guénaud shakes his head silently, and withdraws.

Meanwhile the Queen-mother, Anne of Austria, informed of Mazarin's desperate condition, hastens to visit him. She is attended by her gossiping ladies, eager to catch every word, and with nods and winks, and sighs of affected sympathy—to comment on her sorrowful expression.

Her Majesty is pale and sad; tears gather in her eyes as she advances towards the bed on which Mazarin lies, and she asks with a timid yet tender voice after his health. He replies that he is very ill, and repeats to her what Guénaud had told him. If I were to add that he displayed to the Queen and her ladies one of his bare legs, to afford ocular demonstration of his reduced condition, I fear I should be accused of imitating the *mauvaise langue* of Madame de Noailles. But he really did so, to the great grief of Anne of Austria, and to the utter discomfiture and horror of her less sympathizing ladies in waiting, who rapidly retreat into the recesses of the windows, or behind the draperies of the apartment, to escape so unpleasant a spectacle.

"Look!" exclaims Mazarin, thrusting forward his leg—"look, Madame, at the deplorable condition to which I am reduced by my incessant anxiety for the welfare of France! And to leave my pictures too,— my statues. Ah, Madame, it is a bitter trial!"

Soon after this extraordinary interview, and when all the world believed Mazarin to be dead or dying, the cunning Italian, determined once more to dupe the whole Court, and deceitful in his death as he had been in his life, gave orders that his convalescence should be announced. He caused himself to be painted white and red, dressed in his Cardinal's purple robes, and placed in a sedan chair with all the glasses down. Thus he was wheeled along the broad terraces of his garden, taking care to be well observed by the vast crowd collected by the news of his recovery. For a moment he presented the appearance of health and vigour. But the effort he had forced himself to make, in order to enact this ghastly comedy, was too much for his remaining strength. He swooned in his sedan chair, and was brought back and placed on his bed, never to rise again. Thus died as he had lived, Cardinal Mazarin, a dissembler and a hypocrite; but a great minister. Not cruel or bloodthirsty, like Richelieu, though equally unscrupulous, Mazarin gained the end he had in view by patience, cunning, and intrigue.

At his death he left France, already exhausted by the
wars of the Fronde, completely subdued; and in such
a state of abject submission to the throne, as paved the
way to the extravagance and oppression of Louis XIV.'s
reign.

CHAPTER XVI.

Louise de la Vallière.

THE young King Louis XIV. was active, vigorous,
and graceful. He excelled in outward accomplishments, in riding, dancing, and fencing; but intellectually
he was both idle and ignorant. His education had
been purposely neglected by Cardinal Mazarin; and
he was so fully aware of it, that he carefully avoided
displaying his ignorance by a too facile or rapid address. Even in youth he was grave and ceremonious;
in later years he became pompous and overbearing.
On the other hand, the refinement of his mother's
nature was reproduced in the son of her love. He
was brought up by her side in a circle as elegant and
refined as the Hôtel de Rambouillet in its palmiest
days. He never forgot the lesson he then learnt, that
the outward proprieties of life must be studiously observed, whatever freedoms may be permitted in private.
He desired all his life to be considered pious, just,
and moral. He failed in each, for his passions were
strong and his temper was imperious. The vicissitudes of his early life during the civil wars of the
Fronde, when he was often obliged to fly at a moment's
notice from place to place, gave him, however, a power
of assuming calmness and dignity under all circum-

stances, which he could never have acquired in less eventful times.

Above all sovereigns Louis understood the art of reigning, of appearing to be a great king when he was really but a shallow, vain, irresolute man, extraordinarily accessible to flattery. Yet that a son of Louis XIII. should say with truth, "*L'état c'est moi*," and dare to drive out the national Parliament solemnly assembled in the legislative chamber, *whip in hand*, is one of the most striking anomalies in history.

In person Louis resembled his father. He was dark, broad shouldered, and rather short, with regular features and a prominent nose. But he had all the fire of his mother's Spanish eyes, and withal the grandest manners and the most royal presence ever seen. From a boy he was an ardent admirer of the fair. All his life he continued to be secretly ruled by female influence. Indeed, his long reign may be divided into three periods, corresponding with the characteristics of the three women who successively possessed all the love he could spare from himself. He was gentle, humane, and domestic with La Vallière; arrogant, heartless, and warlike with De Montespan; selfish, bigoted, and cruel, with De Maintenon.

His boyish philandering with the handsome nieces of Cardinal Mazarin has been already noticed. What subtle plans developed themselves in the brain of that unscrupulous schemer never can be known; but he could not have arranged matters better to place one of his nieces on the throne of France. Nor to his Italian notions would this have been extraordinary. Mazarin would have argued that a Mancini was as

well born as a Medici, whose arms were a pill, and
that Martinozzi was as ancient a name as Bourbon.

Anne of Austria looked on with displeasure.
Mazarin wore an imperturbable front, a sphinx-look,
ready to answer either way, as circumstances might
prompt. By the time that Maria Mancini came from
Rome, Louis's passions were thoroughly roused. The
young lion had tasted blood, and found it pleasant to
his palate. Maria was far less beautiful than her
sisters,—indeed, that bitter-tongued chronicler, Bussy
Rabutin, calls her "ugly, fat, and short, with the air
of a *soubrette;*" but she had the temper of an angel,
and seemed to the boyish Louis a soft, plaintive,
clinging creature, who appealed to his pity. In reality
she had a force of character ten times greater than
his own, and the courage of a heroine.

In Maria Mancini, Mazarin made his great move
in the matrimonial game. Louis gave signs of a serious
attachment. Anne of Austria set a watch upon him.
It was needful. Louis had a temperament of fire,
Maria was born under an Italian sky. Nothwithstand-
ing the watch set Louis found opportunity to promise
marriage to Maria. He repeated this promise with
protestations and oaths, but, cautious even in his youth,
he did not, like his grandfather Henry IV., commit it
to writing.

Mazarin, informed by his niece of what had passed,
opined that the time to speak had come. He ventured
to sound the Queen-mother. He spoke of the charms
of genuine attachment, the happiness of domestic life
on a throne; he hinted at the Queen's own unhappy
career, sacrificed as she had been to a political alliance.
He enlarged on the antiquity of the Latin races,

specially those of Rome and Sicily, "all of them," he said, "once reigning houses, and poverty," he added, "did not make blue blood **red**."

The Queen, however subservient to the Cardinal on all other matters, flared out—"If ever my son condescends to marry your niece," cried she, "I will disown him. I will place myself, with his brother, Philip of Orleans, at the head of the nation, and fight against him and you, Cardinal Mazarin."

The Cardinal **had many** consolations; he was fain to yield. Maria was **sent to** a convent. Poor Maria—to go **to** Brouage **instead** of sitting on a throne! It was very hard. Lou**is was** in despair. When they met to say adieu, he wept.

"What, Sire!" she exclaimed; "you love me—you weep—and **we** part?" and she turned her liquid eyes upon him with a look **of** passionate entreaty.

Perhaps the tears in the King's eyes blinded him, or he did not hear her; **at all** events, he heeded neither **her** look nor her inuendo, **and she** went.

Then those marriage bells **so**unded from over the frontier of which **we have** spoken. The King espoused the Infanta of Spain, **and** Maria Mancini became La Principessa Colonna, and lived at Naples.

*   *   *   *   *   *

The Court is at Saint-Germain. Louis XIV. was born there, **and until** Versailles and Marly were built, he made it **his principal** residence. In one of the principal saloons, on **the** first floor, lying midway between the turreted angles of the façade, looking over the plain towards Paris, Louis XIII. had ended his miserable existence, his private band playing a "De Profundis," of his own composition, during his death throes.

His morbid nature—reproduced in his descendant,
Louis XV., who said he loved "the scent of newly
made graves"—made him await the approach of death
with a sort of grim curiosity. **As** he lay on his bed,
opposite the windows, his dim eyes resting on the wide
expanse outstretched below, he called Laporte to him.
He was so near his end that he articulated with difficulty. "Remember, my good Laporte," he gasped,
"**that** place, below there where the road turns under
that rise,"—and he raised his shrunken finger, and
pointed to **a** particular spot, on the road **to** Saint-
Denis, along which his funeral procession must pass
to reach the tombs of his ancestors—"that place there.
It has been newly gravelled, Laporte. It is rough, and
will shake me. Let the driver go gently over the
loose stones. Be sure to tell him I said so."

This was not like his son, Louis XIV., who came
to detest Saint-Germain because this very Cathedral
of Saint-Denis, where he must be buried, was visible
on **the** horizon line. Such an object did not suit a
monarch who desired to be thought immortal.

The Court is at Saint-Germain. It is a cool, delicious evening, after a day of unusual heat. The
summer evenings are always charming at Saint-Germain, by **reason of** the bowery freshness of the adjacent forest, from which cool breezes come rippling
through the air, and fan the heated atmosphere. **The**
sombre château **is** now a mass of deep shadow, **save**
where the setting sun lights up some detail of its
outline—an arched window, a rich cornice, a pillared
portico, or a pointed tower, which stand out against
the western sky with fugitive brightness. The parterre
blazes with summer flowers, the perfume of which

creeps upwards in the rising dews of evening. The formal gravel walks are bordered by statues and orange-trees; the splashing of many fountains stirs the air. A flock of peacocks strut on the greensward, their long tails catching the last rays of the sunset. The summer birds make delicate music among the shrubberies; and the giant elms, in the outer park, divided from the garden by an open **iron** railing, bow their rounded heads to the breeze.

When **the sun has** set, a merry party, consisting of four of the maids of honour, leave the château by a side door. They run swiftly along the terrace,—frightening the peacocks, who drop their tails and fly screeching into the trees,—and ensconce themselves in a trellised arbour, garlanded with honeysuckles and roses, hid in a thicket of flowering shrubs skirting one side of the parterre. **Once** there, their tongues are let loose like so many cherry-clappers.

It was so nearly dark that the maids of honour did not notice the King as they scudded along the garden, who, attended by the mischief-loving Comte de Lauzun, had also stolen out to enjoy the evening. Louis watched them **as** they ran, and then, hearing their voices in such eager talk, was seized with an intense desire to know who they were, and what they were saying. He dare not speak, for they would hear him, and perhaps recognise his voice. Signing to **his** confidant Lauzun to follow him, he softly **approached** the arbour in which the four girls are hid.

He finds that they are all talking about a fancy ball given the night before by Madame Henriette, Duchesse d'Orléans, his brother's wife; and particularly about a ballet **in** which he himself had danced.

The King and Lauzun, favoured by the increasing darkness of the night, and well entrenched behind the shrubs, lose not a syllable.

The question is, which dancer was the handsomest and the most graceful? Each pretty lady has, of course, her own predilection. One declares for the Marquis d'Alençon, another will not hear of any comparison with M. de Vardes, a third stoutly maintains that the Comte de Guiche was by far the handsomest man there and everywhere else (an opinion which, *par parenthèse*, Madame herself takes every opportunity of showing she endorses, displaying, moreover, this opinion somewhat too openly, notwithstanding her designs on the heart of the King himself, whom she fancies, and others declare, is, or has been, her admirer). The fourth damsel is silent. Called upon to give her opinion, she speaks. In the sweetest and gentlest of voices she thus expresses herself:—

"I cannot imagine how any one could have been even noticed when the King was present. He is quite fascinating."

"Ah, then, mademoiselle, you declare for the King. What will Madame say to you?"

"No, it is not the King nor the crown he wears that I declare for; it is not his rank that makes him so charming: on the contrary, to me it is rather a defect. If he were not the King I should positively dread him. His position is my best safeguard. However——" And La Vallière drops her head on her bosom and falls into a deep reverie.

On hearing these words the King is strangely affected, he whispers to Lauzun not to mention their adventure; they retire silently as they came, and reenter the château. The King is in a dilemma. If he could only discover who this fair damsel is who prefers him to all others with such naïveté—who admires **him** for himself alone, and not for his rank—a preference as flattering as it is rarely the lot of a monarch to discover! All he knows is that it must be one of the maids of honour attached to the service of Madame Henriette, his sister-in-law, and he cannot sleep all night, he is so haunted with the melting tones of her voice, and so anxious to discover to whom it belongs.

In the morning, as soon as etiquette allowed of his appearing, Louis hurries off to the toilette of **Madame,** whom he finds seated before a mirror of the rarest Dresden china, looped up with lace and rib-**bons,** her face and shoulders covered with her long brown hair.

"Your Majesty honours me with an early visit," says she, colouring with pleasure as he enters. "What plans have you arranged for the hunt to-day? When **are** we to **start?**"

Louis, with his usual politeness—shown, be it recorded to his credit, towards any woman, whatever might be her degree—gallantly replies that it is for her to command and for him to obey. But there the conversation drops, and the Duchess observes that he is absent and preoccupied. This both chagrins and disappoints her. Piqued at his want of *empressement*, she turns from him abruptly and begins conversing with the Comte de Guiche, who with ill-disguised uneasiness had stood aloof watching her warm reception of his Majesty.

Henriette, the royal daughter of the Stuarts and the Bourbons, without being positively handsome, has

the air of a great princess. The freshness of her
complexion is, however, all that is English about her.
Her forehead, high and broad, but too much developed
for beauty, gives a certain grandeur to her expression;
her eyes are sparkling, but placed too near together.
Still her face is intelligent and lively. She is tall, slim,
and very graceful. Around her long neck, on which
her small head is admirably set, is bound a single
string of fine orient pearls, and a mantle and train of
turquoise *faille* fall back from a flounced petticoat of
yellow satin.

While Madame Henriette talks with the Comte
de Guiche, Louis is at liberty to use his eyes as he
chooses, and he hastily surveys the group of lovely
girls that stand behind the Princess's chair. One
placed a little apart from the rest rivets his attention.
Her pale and somewhat melancholy countenance im-
parts an indescribable air of languor to her appearance,
and the graceful *tournure* of her head and neck are
admirable.

"Can this be she?" he asks himself. He hopes
—he fears (he was young then, Louis, and not the
blasé débauché he afterwards became)—he actually
trembles with emotion, suspense, and impatience.
But determined to ascertain the truth, and regardless
of the furious glances cast at him by Madame,—who
evidently neither likes nor understands his wandering
looks, directed evidently to her ladies, and his total
want of *empressement* towards herself,—he approaches
the fair group and begins conversing with them,
certain that if that same soft voice is heard that had
never ceased to echo in his ears, he shall at once
recognise it. He speaks to Mademoiselle de Saint-

Aignan, but his eyes are fixed on the **pale** face of La Vallière, for she it was whom he so much admired. La Vallière casts down her eyes and blushes.

The King advances towards her and addresses her. He awaits her reply with indescribable anxiety. She trembles, grows still more pale, then blushes crimson, and finally answers in a voice tremulous with timidity; but it was *the* voice! He has found her. This, **then, is** the unknown, and she loves him; her **own lips** confessed it. Delightful! He leaves the apartments of Madame abruptly in speechless ecstasy.

From that day he sees, he lives only for La Vallière. Ever in the apartments of his sister-in-**law,** it was evident even to her that he did not come **to** seek her, and her rage knew no bounds. She had hitherto had ample reason to believe that the attachment the King felt for her somewhat exceeded that of a brother. With the spiteful penetration of a jealous woman, she now discovers how often the eyes **of** Louis are fixed with admiration **on** the timid, **downcast** La Vallière. She is not, therefore, long in guessing the object of his preference, and the cause **of** his frequent visits to her apartments. From this moment she hates poor Louise, and determines, if possible, to ruin her.

The King on his part, unconscious of the storm he was raising about La Vallière, is enchanted not only with herself, but with all he hears of her character. She is beloved by every one; her goodness, sweetness, and sincerity are universally acknowledged, **and** the account of her various good qualities tend **to** **enhance** her merit.

When the Court returns to Saint-Germain (now,

can one fancy romance within those dingy walls?—
but so it was), Louis is desperately, head and ears
over, in love. A party of pleasure is arranged to
take place in the forest under a tent formed of
boughs, tapestry, and flowers. The ladies invited to
this sylvan retreat are habited as shepherdesses and
peasants. They form charming groups, like Sèvres
china. On their arrival the most delicious music is
heard from the recesses of the leafy woods, which as
it plays at intervals, now here, now there, among the
trees, is the signal for the appearance of various
groups of satyrs, fauns, and dryads, who after dancing grotesque figure-dances, and singing verses in
honour of the King, disappear, to be quickly replaced
by another troupe. These present flowers, and also
sing and dance as no dryads or fauns had ever
dreamed of in classic bowers, but in a style quite
peculiar to the age and taste of *le Grand Monarque*,
who liked even nature itself to appear as artificial and
formal as he was himself. This agreeable fête has
lasted all day, and the company is about to return,
when, conceive the alarm—a violent storm comes on,
thunder rolls, the sky is suddenly overcast, and a
heavy rain, enough to drench the whole Court to the
skin, descends with remorseless violence. How every
one scudds hither and thither! The thickest trees are
eagerly seized on as a slight protection against the
storm. Others hide themselves in the bushes, some
penetrate deeper into the cover of the copse wood.
Spite of the rain, and the destruction of the dresses,
the ladies come to vote it rather an agreeable incident
on the whole, when they find their favourite cavaliers
beside them, placed, perchance, somewhat nearer than

would have been *comme il faut* in the Court circle.
For although the ladies might really at first have been
a little terrified, the gentlemen are certainly not likely
to be troubled with any nervousness on account of a
thunderstorm, and preserve sufficient *sang-froid* each
to select his lady-love in order to protect her from
the weather. Thus it chanced that Madame Henriette
finds herself under the care of the Comte de Guiche;
the fair Mancini, once beloved by the King, now
Comtesse de Soissons, is under the protection of her
dear De Vardes; and Mademoiselle d'Orléans—*la
Grande Mademoiselle*—is completely happy, and forgets
the thunder, rain, and, more wonderful still, her own
dignity, at finding herself escorted by Lauzun!

The King, nowise behind his courtiers in gallantry, at once offers his escort and his arm to support La Vallière, who, naturally timid, is really
frightened, and clings to him with a helplessness that
enchants him. All the world knows she is a little
lame, a defect which was said in her to be almost a
grace. Now she does not perhaps regret that this in-
firmity prevents her running as quickly as the rest, and
thus prolonging the precious moments passed alone
with the King. Louis places her under a tree, where
they are both protected from the rain and are
shrouded by the thick boughs which hang low and
fringe the grass.

The King seizes on this happy opportunity to declare his passion, and to whisper to La Vallière the
love she has inspired ever since that evening, when
he had overheard her. Poor Louise! She had never
dared to imagine that her love was returned, and she
well-nigh faints as the King proceeds. Her heart

beats so violently it is almost audible. She is
actually on the point of rushing from under the tree,
when the King lays hold of her hand, and retains
her.

"What!" cries he, "do you fear me more than the
storm? What have I done to frighten you? you whom
I love, whom I adore! Why do you hate me? Speak,
I implore you, Louise."

"Oh, Sire! do not say hate. I revere you—I love
you—as my King, but——"

"Sweet girl, I breathe again. But why **only**
love me as your Sovereign—I, who cherish your
every look, who seek only to be your servant—your
slave?"

Saying **this,** Louis falls on his knees upon the
grass; he seizes her hands, which he covers with
kisses; he swears he will never rise until she has promised to love him, and to pardon the terror his declaration has caused her.

Mademoiselle de la Vallière cannot control her
emotion. She implores him to **rise.**

"You are my King," she says, "the husband of
the Queen. My royal master, I am your faithful subject. Can I say more?"

"Yes, dearest, promise me your love. Give me
your heart; that is the possession I desire," murmurs
Louis.

Pressed by the King to grant him some mark of
her favour, La Vallière becomes so confused she cannot reply. Louis grows more and more pressing, in-
terpreting her emotion as favourable to his suit. In
the midst of the tenderest entreaties the thunder again
bursts forth, and poor Louise, overcome at once by

fear, love, and remorse, swoons away. The King naturally receives the precious burden in his arms. He seeks hastily to rejoin the other fugitives and his attendants, in order to obtain assistance. Ever **and anon** he stops in the openings of the forest to gaze at her, as she lies **calm** and lovely in repose, her long eyelashes sweeping her delicate cheeks, her half-closed lips revealing the prettiest, and whitest teeth. I leave my readers to imagine if Louis did not imprint a few kisses **on** the fainting beauty he bears so carefully in his arms, and if now and then he did·not press her closer to his breast. If in this he *did* take advantage of the situation chance had afforded him, he must **be** forgiven; he **was** young, and he was deeply in love.

Words cannot describe the surprise felt by La Vallière on recovering to find herself alone, borne along in the King's arms, in the midst of a lonely forest. History does not, however, record that she died of terror, or that she even screamed. The respectful behaviour of the King doubtless reassured her.

The moment she opens her sweet blue eyes he stops, places her on the ground, and supports her. He assures her that being then near the edge of the forest, **and not far** distant from the château, they are sure to **meet** some of his attendants. Louise blushes, then grows pale, then blushes again, as the recollection of all the King had said to her while under the shade of the greenwood gradually returns to her remembrance. She reads the confirmation of it in his eyes. Those eyes are **fixed** on her with passionate ardour. Disengaging herself from his arms, she thanks him, in **a** faltering voice, for his care a thousand times—for his condescension. She is so sorry. It was so foolish to faint; but the thunder—his Majesty's goodness to her——. Here she pauses abruptly; her conscience tells her she ought at once to reject his suit; her lips cannot form the words.

While she is speaking, a group of horsemen are visible in the distance, at the end of one of those long woodland glades which divide the forest. On hearing the voice of the King, who calls to them, they gallop rápidly towards him. The King and La Vallière reach the château shortly after the other ladies, none of whom, as it appeared, had been in . haste to return.

From this moment La Vallière's fate is sealed. Long she had loved and admired the King in secret; but until she learnt how warmly he returned this feeling she was scarcely aware how completely he had enthralled her. The ecstasy this certainty gave her first fully revealed to her the real danger of her situation. Poor Louise! Is it wonderful that, as the scene of this first and passionate declaration, she should love the old Château of Saint-Germain more than any other spot in the world?—that when suffering, the air restored her? when unhappy (and she lived to be so unhappy), the sight of the forest, of the terrace, revived her by tender reminiscences of the past?

When the secret of Louis's attachment to La Vallière transpired (which, after the scene in the forest was very speedily), nothing could exceed the indignation of the whole circle, who each conceived that they had some especial cause of complaint.

Louis's old love, the Comtesse de Soissons (Mancini), with the thirst for practical revenge, bred in her hot Italian blood, held council with De Vardes and De Guiche, how to crush her, whom she styled "the common enemy." A letter was planned and written by the **Countess** in Spanish, addressed to **the Queen, purporting to** come from the King of **Spain.** This letter detailed every particular of her husband's *liaison* with La Vallière. The bad spelling **and** foreign **idioms, however,** betrayed it to be a forgery.

The letter was **placed** on the Queen's bed by the Comtesse de Soissons herself. Instead of falling **into** the Queen's hands, as was intended, it was found by De Molena, Maria Theresa's Spanish nurse. She carried it straight to the King. He traced it to Madame de Soissons. She was banished.

Madame Henriette d'Orléans was more noisy and abusive than any one. Her **vanity** was **hurt.** Her feelings were outraged at the **notion** that **the** King, heretofore her admirer, should **forsake** her openly for one of **her** own women! It was **too** insulting.

"What!" cried she **in her rage,** "prefer an ugly, limping *fillette* to *me*, the daughter of a king? I **am** as superior in beauty **to** that little minx as I am in birth! *Dieu! qu'il manque de goût et de délicatesse!*" Without even taking leave of Louis she shut herself up **at** Saint-Cloud, where she made the very walls ring with her **complaints.**

The poor, quiet little Queen, **the only** really injured person, wept and mourned in **private.** She was far too much afraid of that living Jupiter Tonans, her husband, to venture on any personal reproaches. She consoled herself by soundly abusing La Vallière in epithets much **more** expressive than polite.

In this abuse she was joined by Anne of Austria, who, in her present austere frame of mind, was the last person in France to spare La Vallière.

An explanation was decidedly needful.

CHAPTER XVII.

The Convent of Chaillot.

MADEMOISELLE DE LA VALLIÈRE is summoned to the presence of the Queen-mother. She is sitting in the Grey Chamber, next to her oratory. Louise is aware that Anne of Austria never gives audiences in the Grey Chamber except on the most serious occasions. The Queen-mother wears a dark dress, in cut and shape like the robe of a nun; her grey hair is gathered into a head-dress of white lace, and she carries a rosary at her side. She looks old and sad; her stately form is bent, her face is thin, her features are drawn, and wrinkles obscure her once brilliant eyes.

The Duchesse d'Orléans is seated by her side. Louise enters. She dares not advance beyond the door. Standing there she makes deep obeisances to the Queen-mother and to Madame Henriette. She blushes scarlet, then turns pale. Her head drops on her bosom; as she stands before them she feels more dead than alive.

"I see you are there, Mademoiselle de la Vallière," says the Queen, frowning. "I wish to speak to you in the presence of your late mistress, Madame Henriette de France, my daughter-in-law. You are aware why we have sent for you?"

"No, Madame," answers the maid of honour faintly, "but I humbly await your orders."

"What affected humility!" exclaims Madame Henriette with a sneer. "You act uncommonly well, *petite*."

"All the better if she be humble, my daughter," rejoins the Queen-mother, speaking of La Vallière as if she were not present—"all the better. It is some step towards repentance that she is conscious of her crime. It will save us the trouble of insisting on it. Pray to God, mademoiselle, to pardon you; you have no hope but in heaven." And she casts a stern glance at her.

The tears gather in La Vallière's soft blue eyes. They course each other down her pallid cheeks, and fall, spotting her pale blue dress. Her head, covered with a profusion of short fair curls, is still bent down. She looks like a delicate flower bowed before a cruel tempest.

"What are you going to do with those fine diamond bracelets the King presented to you the other day out of the Queen's lottery?" asks Madame Henriette tauntingly, interrupting the Queen.

Anne of Austria makes a sign to her to be silent. Poor Louise for an instant turns her eyes imploringly upon her. Madame grows pale with spite as she remembers those superb diamond bracelets that the King drew as a prize from the lottery,—which she had fully expected he would present to herself,—were given by him to La Vallière. She is so wroth she cannot leave Louise alone; again she attacks her. "Your vanity is insufferable, mademoiselle. Do you imagine, *petite sotte*, that any one cares for *you?*

Mademoiselle de Pons is the belle of the Court. His Majesty **says** so."

At this malicious stab Louise shudders.

"My daughter," interposes the Queen-mother, "do not agitate yourself. I understand your annoyance at having introduced such a person as Mademoiselle de la Vallière at Court. Let *me* address her. She is unworthy of your notice. You understand, of course, mademoiselle, that you are dismissed," she says, turning towards her and speaking imperiously.

"But, your Majesty——" and La Vallière's streaming eyes are again lifted upwards for an instant—"what, oh what have I done?"

"Ask yourself, mademoiselle. Unless there are to be two queens of France, you must go. You cannot wish me, the mother of his Majesty, to enter into details on a subject so painful to my feelings."

"No, I should think not," breaks in Madame Henriette, "unless you have no sense of decency. A little unworthy chit like you to dare to trouble royal princesses; you are as impertinent as you are disreputable."

At these cruel words La Vallière staggers backwards, and **almost** falls. Then she again turns her swollen eyes towards the royal ladies with absolute terror.

Ah, heaven! she thinks, if the King did but know her agony, her sufferings! Ah, if he were but here to speak for her! But not a word passes her lips.

Madame Henriette's eyes fix themselves on her with a look of triumph. She becomes absolutely radiant at the sight of the humiliation of her whom she calls "her rival."

"You know our pleasure, mademoiselle," says Anne of Austria, rising from her arm-chair. "You will return from whence you came—Touraine, I believe. You will be conducted by Madame de Choisy; but, indeed, you need no escort; you have nothing to fear *now*," and the Queen-mother casts a look of withering contempt on the wretched **girl** more offensive even than her bitter words.

Louise shrinks backwards. She would fain escape.

"**Do not** forget, mademoiselle, before you go, to thank Madame Henriette de France for all her goodness to you," says the Queen, arresting her with a motion — "goodness, indeed, you have so ill **requited**."

"No, no!" cries Madame; "I want no thanks. I only want to be rid of her. Let her go, my mother; I ask no more."

The two Princesses rise together. They both deliberately turn their backs upon La Vallière, and leave the room. For some moments she stands as if **turned into** stone. Then **she** gives a wild scream, raises her small **hands**, clutches **the** delicate curls that hang about her face, and rushes from "the Grey Chamber."

"Dishonoured — banished! Ah, God! what will become **of** me?" she cries distractedly when she has locked herself in her own room. "Ah! what will my mother say when she knows all? Holy Virgin, I am lost!"

She paces up and down the floor—she sobs, she moans. Everything about her reminds her of the **King.** She handles the presents he has given her; she takes out his letters; she kisses them; she presses them to her bosom. She tries to collect her thoughts, but the murmur of the night wind, sweeping over the trees in the adjacent forest and whistling round the angles of the palace, catches her ear. To her excited imagination it wails lamentations over her. As she listens she seems to hear her mother's voice reproaching her. Now as the **blast rises** higher and higher it is her father, who curses **her** in the tempest that sweeps by. Trembling in every limb she rises and dashes the glittering baubles she still holds **in her** hands to the ground. Her head reels, her reason totters. Fresh sobs and fresh torrents of tears come to her **relief.** Suddenly the same idea, in the same place, rushes into **her** mind as **had** struck Louise de Lafayette, yet under widely different circumstances. Louise de Lafayette, a creature so pure, so angelic as to start back dismayed from the faintest whisper of a too ardent love—she, Louise de la Vallière, held up to public contumely, dismissed the Court! She must fly; she must never be heard of more. She can never return home. A convent must hide her. "God alone and the blessed saints are left to **me!" she cries;** "wretch that I am, let me seek them where they may be found."

As soon as the grey morning comes creeping into her room, lighting up her white face and crushed figure, as she leans back in the chair where she has sat immovable all the live-long night, she rises, and puts together a little bundle of necessaries. She covers herself with a cloak, and softly opening the door, makes her way down the nearest flight of stairs. No **one** sees her, for the day is only dawning. She glides swiftly out of the palace, passes the gate, where the sentinel is sleeping at his post, and finds herself in the street of the little town of Saint-Germain. Her heart beats so quickly, and her steps are so rapid, that she is soon obliged to stop for want of breath. Not knowing where to go, she leans against the corner of a house. She strains her eyes up and down the street in every direction, but sees no one of whom she can ask her way. At last, at the bottom of the *grande rue*, a country-woman appears, carrying a basket on her arm. She is on her way to market. Louise flies towards her. The woman stares at her. La Vallière's lips move, but she has no breath to speak.

"God speed you, pretty lady. Where are you going so early?" asks the peasant.

"*Ma bonne,*" at last answers La Vallière, when she has recovered her breath, "can you tell me the way to Chaillot? I want to go to the convent."

Now, Chaillot was a convent founded by Henrietta Maria, Queen of England, situated between Saint-Germain and Paris, no vestige of which now remains.

"Surely, *belle dame*, I can tell you. Come with me, I am going that way," and the woman stares at her again. "Why are you out so early? Are you from the palace?"

"No, no!" gasps La Vallière, terrified to death lest the woman's suspicions should be aroused, and that she would refuse to let her follow her. "I am not from the palace. Ask me nothing. I can only tell you that a great misfortune has happened to me, and that I am going to consult the Superior of Saint-Marie, at Chaillot, who is my friend."

The peasant asks no more questions, and La Vallière, who clings to her side, arrives in due time under the walls of Chaillot.

"There, mademoiselle, is the Church of the Sisters of Sainte-Marie. God speed you."

Louise rings the bell, and asks the portress to be permitted to speak with the Superior.

"She is in retreat, madame, and cannot be disturbed," the portress replies.

"In the name of God, my sister, tell her that a person in great affliction craves her help."

The portress does not immediately answer, but leads her into a hall within, at one end of which is the latticed *grille* which divides the professed nuns from the lay sisters.

An hour passes, and no one appears. La Vallière, fatigued by the unaccustomed exercise, almost distracted, gazes wistfully at the bare walls that surround her. This then is to be the living tomb of her youth, her love. This grim refuge or the grave. She turns to the strong door, bound with iron bars, by which she entered, and shudders. She watches the handle; no one comes, not a sound breaks the silence. It seems to her that God and man have alike forsaken her—a creature so vile, so unworthy. Her repentance has come too late. Heaven's mercy-gates are closed! A wild, unreasoning terror seizes her—her brain beats as with iron hammers—she grows cold and faint—a mist gathers before her eyes—a deadly sickness creeps over her—she falls senseless on the stone floor.

When she opens her eyes, she is lying upon a clean bed, shaded by snowy curtains, in a little white-washed cell; two dark-robed Carmelite sisters are bending over her.

It was not long before the King heard that La Vallière had fled. Not daring to make too public inquiries, he sent for the superintendent of police, La Regnie.

"Find Mademoiselle de la Vallière," he says, "dead or alive; find her instantly—instantly, I say, or I dismiss you from my service."

This was not difficult; the trembling steps of the fugitive were soon traced. La Regnie returns, and informs his royal master that La Vallière is within the Convent of Chaillot. Louis does not lose a moment in following her. He appears at the convent gate, accompanied by his confidant, Lauzun. He demands admittance. Some of the older nuns, scandalized at the idea of a man entering the cloister, refuse to unlock the gate; but the Mother-Superior, wiser in her generation, herself descends, and key in hand undoes the fastenings, and welcomes his Majesty with the utmost deference.

Meanwhile, La Vallière, somewhat recovered from her swoon, sits alone beside a narrow window which overlooks the convent garden. She feels dull and oppressed; her eyes are dazed; her head is heavy.

The perfect silence around her, the homely little cell looking into a peaceful garden, full of herbs and vegetables for the service of the convent, in one corner a grove of cypress-trees, which overtops the high walls that encircle it, is all new and strange to her. She seems to have passed into another world. She remembers but indistinctly all that has happened; she has almost forgotten how she came there. A pensive melancholy paralyzes her senses. She is very weak and helpless; her brain is still confused. It is all very strange. She cannot collect her thoughts; but over all the mists of memory, plain and distinct, rise a face and form dear to her beyond life.

Suddenly a sound of approaching footsteps awakens the echoes of the long corridor leading to the cell. As well as steps there is a confused hum of many persons talking. At first she listens vaguely; then, as the sounds grow nearer, she springs to her feet. A sound has struck upon her ear—a sound sweeter than music. It is the King's voice! The door is flung open, and Louis—his handsome face flushed with excitement, his eyes beaming with tenderness—stands before her.

"Come," he says softly, whispering into her ear, and pressing her cold hand within both his own, "come, my beloved, you have nothing in common with this dreary place. I am here to carry you away. Fear no one; I will protect you—I will glory in protecting you. Rise, my Louise, and follow me."

The Carmelite sisters stand peeping in at the door. The Superior alone has followed his Majesty into the cell. Some moments pass before Louise commands her voice to speak; at last, in a scarcely audible whisper, and trembling all over, she says—

"Sire——," then, not daring to meet the King's impassioned glance, she pauses; "Sire," she repeats, "I did not come here of my own accord. I was obliged to leave. My remaining at Saint-Germain offended her Majesty and other great personages"—she stops again, overcome by the recollection of the scene with the Queen and the Duchesse d'Orléans—

"personages, Sire, whom I dare not—I *could* not offend." Her **soft face is** suffused with a blush of anguish; she hangs down her head. "I was **sent** away, Sire; it was not my wish to go—indeed it was not my wish!" she adds, in a voice **so low and** tremulous that Louis could not have **heard** what **she** said had he not bent down his ear close **to her white lips.**

"'Then you shall return, dearest, **for** mine. I am **master,** and my wish is law. I care nothing **for** 'august personages;' they shall learn to obey me—the sooner **the better.**"

"But, Sire, I cannot be the cause of strife. The Queen-mother and Madame have dismissed me; and they were right," she added in a very faint voice. "I dare not offend them by my **presence, after——**" she stops, and can say no more.

"Think of the future, Louise, **not of the** past; it is gone," and Louis takes her **trembling hands** in his. "A future lies before **you full of joy. Leave** the Queen-mother to me, Louise. Come—come with me," **and with gentle violence he** tries to raise **her** from her chair. "Follow me, and fear nothing."

"Oh, Sire," whispers Louise, the colour again leaving her cheeks, "do not tempt **me** from my **vocation.**"

"Do not talk to me of your vocation," returns Louis roughly; "what is your vocation to me? Can you part from me so lightly?" he adds, more gently.

"Alas, Sire, I dare not return **to Co**urt; every look would condemn me!"

"**Condemn** you! Believe me, I will place you so

high that no one shall dare to condemn you. Am I
not the master?"

"Oh, suffer me to lay my sins upon the altar! Do
not seek to prevent it," sighs La Vallière, clasping her
hands. "But, remember, Sire, oh, remember, that in
my heart you can have no rival but heaven." She
speaks with passion, but she dares not look up at him;
had she done so, she would have quailed before the
expression of his eyes;—they devour her.

All this is said very low, in order not to be overheard by the Superior, who, although she has retired
as far as the doorway, is still present.

"Louise, you do not love me. You have never
loved me," whispers Louis, and he turns away. He is
deeply offended; her resistance to his commands en-
rages him.

"Ah, heaven!" La Vallière sighs, and turns her
blue eyes, swimming with tears, towards him, "would
to God it were so!" She speaks in so subdued a tone
—she is so crushed, so fragile—that the King's compassion is suddenly excited; he looks steadfastly into
her face; he trembles lest she may die under this trial.
Again he takes her hand, raises her from her chair,
and draws her towards the door.

"If you love me, Louise, follow me. I cannot live
without you!" he adds almost fiercely. "Fear nothing.
Her Majesty shall receive you. The Queen-mother
and Madame"—at their names La Vallière quivers all
over—"shall offend you no more. Leave this horrible
cell, my Louise. Come, and let me enshrine you in
a temple worthy of your beauty, your goodness, and
of my love," he adds, in a fervid whisper, which makes
her heart throb with rapture. "Come!"

Louise returns to Saint-Germain. She is created Duchesse de la Vallière, and is appointed Lady of the Bedchamber to Queen Maria Theresa.

CHAPTER XVIII.

Fouquet, Superintendent of Finance.

NICHOLAS FOUQUET, Marquis de **Belle-Isle** and Vicomte de Mélun et Vaux,* held the post of Superintendent of Finance under the Regency of Anne of Austria. He was continued in this important office after the accession of Louis XIV. Fouquet was insinuating, specious, hypocritical, and sensual; a munificent patron to those about him, and an adorer of the beautiful in art and nature. He was, moreover, one of those courtly financiers so constantly met with before the Revolution, who, however the country starved, always found funds "for the service of his Majesty."

In course of time, Louis grew alarmed at Fouquet's reckless expenditure; his personal magnificence was boundless, but there was not a *sous* of state money in reserve. Colbert was consulted by the King. Colbert was jealous of Fouquet's position; he examined his accounts, and found them incorrect. The King courteously pointed out the errors to Fouquet, who persisted in the perfect accuracy of his figures. Louis, convinced of the Superintendent's dishonesty, resolved to dismiss him on the first opportunity.

But this falsification of accounts was his least cause of offence to his Sovereign. Fouquet had pre-

---

* Vaux-Praslin, near Mélun, is still a superb château. It was sold by the son of the Superintendent to the Maréchal de Villars, who, in his turn, sold it to the Duc de Praslin.

sumed to imitate the Olympian tastes of the *Grand Monarque.* If Louis was a god, his Superintendent was at least a demi-god, and claimed a demi-god's privilege of "loving the daughters of men." Unfortunately, too, he dared to raise his eyes to those particular idols worshipped by the King. His disgrace was therefore certain. Some indistinct rumours of the danger that threatened him reached his ears. He was moved, but not alarmed. He racked his fertile brain how best to recover favour, and he determined to give so magnificent a fête in honour of the King at his country-seat, Vaux, near Mélun, as should remove all suspicion of his loyalty. Such were the customs of the age. Having for years systematically robbed the State, Fouquet was to reinstate himself in favour by a still more public theft!

Before Versailles arose on the sand-hills lying between Saint-Cyr and the wooded uplands of Saint-Cloud, Vaux was the most splendid palace in France. The architect was Le Vau, celebrated by Boileau. The *corps de logis* was surmounted by a dome supported by sixteen marble arches, resting on pillars; two immense pavilions formed the wings. The gardens, designed by Le Nôtre, were decorated with statues, and balustraded terraces bordering canals, and water-works, in the Italian fashion—"surprises," as they were called. All was formal and symmetrical; the very plants and shrubs were only permitted to grow to order. Nature was banished to the distant woods, which spread in verdant folds about the rising ground behind the château, and decked the greensward of the park, ere it reached the waters of the Seine flowing below.

The fête was fixed for the 17th of August. It was

a splendid day; the sky was unclouded, and the golden sunshine lighted up the deepest recesses of the forest, when Louis started in the morning from Fontainebleau, where the Court was then staying. He was escorted by d'Artagnan and a **regiment of musketeers.**

There was a goodly company; the King **drove La** Vallière and the Comtesse de Guiche in his *calèche;* the Queen-mother came in her coach; other ladies were **in** litters. The Queen, who was in an interesting **state** of health, stayed at home. Fouquet stood ready, at the grand entrance of his palace. He received the King kneeling, and presented to him the golden keys of Vaux. Louis touched them with his . fingers, raised Fouquet from the ground, and **in** a few gracious words assured him of his favour **and** protection; with what truth we shall **see.** The same ceremony was repeated by Madame Fouquet to the Queen-mother, with a like result.

On entering the vestibule, **even** the Gallic **Jupiter** was **am**azed **at** the magnificence of all he saw. The suite of rooms were arranged in allegorical order, each **named** after a god or goddess; the ceilings and walls painted to represent their attributes and the events **of** their **lives.** The **sun and** moon, the planets and fixed stars, also formed an important feature in the decorations. The seasons added their attributes, and together with the winds lent themselves gracefully to the necessities of the general arrangements. His Majesty was invited to repose in the billiard-room, dedicated to Hercules, who by a happy invention prefigured himself. From the billiard-room he entered the grand **saloon,** where the sun, in gorgeous colours of saffron, crimson, and scarlet, covered the entire ceiling. Louis smiled a smile of gratification; the sun was his acknowledged emblem. Was it possible, he thought, that Fouquet might be forgiven? The Superintendent advanced. He bowed to the ground, and asked leave to explain the legend.

"The sun—the centre of the universe, the creator of light, heat, and life—is your Majesty. Deprived of your gracious presence, we sink into darkness and death. That star beside the sun is myself, Sire, receiving light from your Majesty's benignant rays."

Louis frowned, and bit his lip. It seemed to him that the star was dangerously near the sun; it displeased him. He changed his mind, and now decided that that too assertative star must be extinguished.

From the saloon, Louis passed into a retiring-room, dedicated to the Muses and the Virtues, all with open mouths, grouped round a figure of Fidelity, whose praises they sang.

"Who is represented by Fidelity?" asked Louis, turning to the Duc de Saint-Aignan, in attendance on him.

"I have just been told that Fidelity represents Fouquet himself, your Majesty."

"What on earth can Fidelity have to do with a Superintendent of Finance?" muttered Louis, shrugging his shoulders. "And that female figure conducting Fidelity—who is that?"

"Prudence, I am told," replied Saint-Aignan. "Prudence; and the one on the other side is Reason."

"Prudence, Reason, and Fidelity guiding Fouquet. *Ma foi*, it is not bad," and an ironical smile passed over the monarch's face. "But we have not done with the paintings yet. Who are the others?"

"That figure, Sire, in a golden-coloured robe, is Clio, I am told, the Muse of History. With one hand she assists Fidelity into heaven, with the other she records the annals of his life."

"The annals of *his* life," muttered the King (for Fouquet stood near at hand, to be summoned by his Sovereign when wanted). "It will be well for him if history does not record his signal disgrace. He may prove another Phaeton, this M. Fouquet, and fall from .the stars into eternal darkness. Jupiter still grasps his thunders. Let us leave this room—it stifles me," said Louis aloud. "What is the meaning of the device of the serpents I see everywhere?" again inquired Louis of the Duke.

"The serpents represent Colbert, the rival of Fouquet, Sire. Fidelity, Reason, and Discretion crush these serpents as you see."

"Really, these allegories are charming, M. Fouquet," said Louis, with a covert sneer, turning towards his host, and speaking in a loud voice, "but allegories are not always truthful." Fouquet bowed to the ground, and turned very pale.

After having examined the interior of the château, and partaken of a sumptuous refection, the King was invited to pass into the garden to see the illuminations.

There the whole horizon was aglow. On three broad terraces, of the purest white marble, which extended along the entire façade of the building, rows of golden candelabra bore myriads of wax lights.

Rows of gigantic orange-trees, in full blossom, shone
with orbs of variegated light, that glittered on the
dark surface of the polished leaves. Below, in a vast
square, fashioned into a sunken parterre of flowers,
arranged in various patterns, cunningly concealed
lamps of every hue were hidden among the leaves,
their innumerable flamelets forming a carpet of living
fire. Jets of flame leaped from tree to tree. Beyond
the parterre, the broad canal banks blazed and palpitated with fiery heat. The waters, of a ruddy hue,
now reflecting the gorgeous scene, now riven into *jets
d'eau* and fountains which blaze upwards for an instant, throwing up clouds of rockets that sport like
comets among the stars, to fall back in cascades of
golden sparks. Beyond, in the woods, each noble
forest-tree, in minutest detail of every branch and twig,
stood out in relief against what appeared a vault of
fire. Long vistas led far away among stalwart oaks
and feathery limes, growing out of a sea of flames.
All around there was nothing but fire—dazzling, overwhelming fire. Now it turned to green, then by some
magic touch it changed to blue, then flashed into
crimson; while *feux de joie* and cannon roared from
concealed batteries, and shook the very air. Behind,
the architectural lines of the château were marked by
clusters of golden lamps. Every room shone brighter
than at noon, and the central dome, with its graceful
colonnade, blazed like a volcano. On the terrace, in
front of the château, military bands clashed with
joyous symphonies. When these ceased, soft music
sounded from out the fiery woods, from violins and
flutes, swelling in the cadences of some tender melody.
The crowd below, changing with the metamorphose of

the lights, formed a fitting fore-ground to this burning perspective.   It was a scene of artificial life after Lancret, backed by a conflagration.   Brocaded trains swept along the fine gravel of the walks.   Wreaths of diamonds sparkled on voluminous wigs, which fell in heavy curls over neck and shoulders.   Long white feathers, and finest Brussels lace, fringed and decked turned-up hats of velvet.   Glittering officers were side by side with comely pages, brighter than butterflies. Gold embroideries shone on delicately coloured velvets, satins, and watered-silks; priceless jewels glittered on knee and shoe, on neck and arm, on waist and **dra-pery**; torsades on hats, and sword-hilts flashed and multiplied the fiery marvels of the night.   Even *le Grand Monarque*, as he paused upon the terrace to observe the scene, deigned to express his admiration and surprise.   But his praise was scant, his words cold, he spoke morosely, and his brows were knit.

The more he investigated the magnificence of Vaux, the more he believed the accusations of Colbert. Fouquet heard the praise; **he did** not observe the frown.   He was radiant.   **Louis** looked round, anxious to escape from the glare and the crowd.   He longed to retire into some shady grove with La Vallière.   She was very beautiful that evening.   Louis reproached himself for ever having caused her pain.   She wore a dress of white stuff, worked with golden leaves; a blue ribbon, tied in a knot in front, encircled her small waist.   Her light hair, untouched by powder, and sown with flowers and pearls, fell over her shoulders; two enormous emeralds hung in her ears.   Her arms were uncovered, but to conceal their thinness, she wore **above** the elbow a broad circlet of gold set with

opals. Her gloves were of fine Brussels lace, showing
the rosy skin beneath. Her graceful yet dignified
manners, her tender blue eyes, breathing nothing but
love and gentleness, her look of patient goodness,
were never more charming than when seen among the
painted and powdered belles of that intriguing Court.
It was impossible for Louis to have a word with her
in private. Every feminine eye was bent upon him.
All the ladies—young, old, fair and dark—pressed
round him as he moved among the alleys and terraces of the illuminated garden. He was the rose
that attracted alike the butterflies and the grubs—
the sunshine and the shadow. Like royalty of all
ages, Louis soon grew weary of this espionage, and
called for the Duc de Saint-Aignan. He was no-
where to be found. At last, after having walked up
and down the three terraces, admired the great cascade
and the grotto, afterwards to be repeated at Saint-
Cloud, he sought out the Queen-mother. She was
seated on the terrace, surveying the illumination at a
distance. Louis leaned over the marble balustrade
near her.

"This is magnificent, my mother," said he; "so
magnificent that I believe every word Colbert has told
me. Colbert showed me peculations on paper; I see
them here with my own eyes. Think of the millions
he must have spent! Look at my palace of Saint-
Germain—dilapidated, dismal; Fontainebleau still unfinished. It is shameful! Fouquet is a mushroom,
who has nourished himself out of my revenues. I can
crush him—I *will* crush him—destroy him!" and the
King stamped his foot savagely on a pavement of
coloured marbles.

"My son, do not speak so loudly," replied the Queen.

At·this moment Saint-Aignan appeared ascending the steps from below.

"Where have you been, Duke?" asked Louis sharply.

. "A thousand pardons, your Majesty. They searched for me in the wrong place. You will not, however, have reason to regret my absence," and he gave the King a look full of meaning, and signed to him to move farther off from all possibility of listeners. "Sire," continued he, "I have made a discovery."

"A discovery! Where? What have you found?" and Louis drew closer to him.

"Sire, I fear you have a rival," and Saint-Aignan glanced significantly at the Duchesse de la Vallière, who sat on a settee behind, not far from the Queen-mother.

"A rival! Ridiculous! You have been asleep and dreaming, Duke."

· "No, Sire; on the faith of a peer of France, no. Your Majesty has a rival, I repeat."

"What do I care for rivals! I have her heart," and Louis glanced tenderly at La Vallière.

"But is your Majesty so certain?"

"Certain? Ask me if I live!" exclaimed Louis with warmth. "But tell me what you mean. Speak, Duke, and speak quickly, for we may be interrupted."

"Well, Sire, some fairy, who I suppose watches over your interests, told me to wander over the château and examine the more private chambers. No one was by. Every one was in the garden with your Majesty to see the illuminations. At the end of a long gallery, in a distant part of the house, I came upon a boudoir—such a bijou of a room!—evidently belonging to Fouquet. On the walls hung the portraits of some of the fairest ladies of the Court. It is a hall of beauty, Sire."

"Go on," said **Louis** impatiently; "I understand."

"Among these beauties, Sire, was—well—there was the lady you honour with your special attentions— Madame la Duchesse"—and Saint-Aignan stopped, and **again** indicated La Vallière, who, unconscious of what was going on, sat near, her delicate cheek resting **on her** hand.

"You need **mention** no names, Saint-Aignan. I tell you, I understand," replied the King with evident irritation. "And pray what does it matter if you did find the portrait of that lady there? I see nothing in **it** at all remarkable. No hall of beauty would be complete without her likeness. Who **were** the other portraits?"

"Ah, Sire, that is precisely the point I am coming to. They were all portraits of **ladies** who are or have been the acknowledged mistresses of Fouquet. If Madame la Duchesse de——"

"**I beg** you again not to mention any names, Duke," broke **in the** King haughtily, a storm gathering on his brow.

"If that lady, Sire, had not resembled the others, why should she have been there?"

To this somewhat daring question Louis did not vouchsafe a reply. His countenance darkened into an expression of silent rage. His eyes glittered as he passed **his** hand over them. When he spoke there was doubt, anxiety, **as** well as anger in his voice and manner. "I am astonished, I confess," said he, speaking very deliberately. "I am quite at a loss to explain it. Her portrait is there, you say. It may be, Saint-Aignan. I cannot doubt your word, but—it is impossible that——" He paused, and his eyes rested on her guileless face.

"Sire, it is not for me to differ from your Majesty," rejoined Saint-Aignan, fearful lest he had injured self in the King's opinion by his over-frankness; "your superior **intellect** and far-seeing judgment will unfold to you mysteries impervious to my grosser comprehension; but I repeat, in the boudoir of M. Fouq**uet** I saw the portrait of Madame La Duchesse—I beg your Majesty's pardon—placed among those of ladies whose relations with him **are** more than equivocal."

"I will speak to the lady myself. She is ignorant of this, I venture my life," said Louis, his eyes again fixing themselves wistfully upon La Vallière. "In the meantime, Duke, I thank you for **your zeal** in my service. Now, remember, until **our return** to Fontainebleau *silence*—absolute **silence**—or I shall never **forgive** you." Louis placed his finger on his lip—Saint-Aignan, glad to end so perilous an interview, bowed, and immediately fell back among the crowd of courtiers who hovered about the King.

Louis's blood boiled within him. He had controlled himself in the presence of Saint-Aignan, but it was with the greatest difficulty he could any longer restrain his passion. He longed then and there to call in the musketeers, and arrest Fouquet on the spot. D'Artagnan and his followers were at hand; it would have been the work of an instant. At a loss what to do, and feeling the necessity for some expression of

the violent rage he felt, he approached his mother,
Anne of Austria, who was leaning back in her chair,
absorbed in a deep reverie. She was only present at
that dazzling fête in body — her mind was far away.
To her the pomps and vanities of the world were become a mockery and a toil; she longed for the seclu-
sion of the cloister.

"It is all over," whispered the King, and his voice
grated huskily in her ear; "Fouquet will be arrested
to-night."

"What has he done?" asked Anne of Austria.

"I have excellent reasons, my mother; besides,
Fouquet may escape to Belle Isle — here I have him,
I hold him!" and Louis, in his heat, shook his fist in
his mother's face.

"You are strangely moved, Louis. I do not know
your reasons, but I advise you, for the sake of your
own dignity, to choose a more suitable moment than
during a fête at which you are present in his own
house."

"Every time is good to catch a traitor."

"Yes; but, my son, there is such a thing as decorum. The Superintendent has given you a superb
fête, which you have accepted. You are under his
roof; you cannot arrest him while you are his guest.
It is out of the question."

"But, my mother, I have reasons of state."

"Then they must wait. What would the Court —
what would France — say to such an act? Take care,
my son, that those who may never know your justification do not condemn your act. Even *you* are not
above public opinion."

Louis did not reply, but the Queen-mother perceived that her words had convinced him.

The Court returned to Fontainebleau in the same order as it came.

A *lettre de cachet*, dated the day after the fête, consigned Fouquet to the fortress of Pignerol. Louise de la Vallière was enabled to soothe his Majesty's suspicions, with regard to the portrait, by assuring him that if his indignation had been aroused, her feelings had been **much more** grossly outraged.

CHAPTER XIX.

Death and Poison.

"ANNE, daughter of Philip III., King of Spain, and Margaret of Austria, his wife, married to Louis XIII., King of France, surnamed the Just, mother of Louis XIV., surnamed Dieudonné, and of Philip of France, Duc d'Orléans, born September, 1601, died January, 1666."

These words stood **at the** head of a will which was signed *"approved*, Louis." **Anne** of Austria has stood before us, from her fifteenth year until now; first, the golden-haired girl, next the persecuted wife, **then the** stately regent, finally the devoted and conscientious mother. **And** now her time has come; she is dying **at the Louvre.** Her malady is a cancer in the breast, long concealed, now aggravated by the ignorance of quacks. Latterly it has become an open wound, the seat of intense suffering. Her daintily nurtured body and sensitive skin, which could not bear the touch of any but the finest and softest linen, the delicate habits **of** her daily life, her extreme refinement of mind **and** person (not common in those days even among

princes), have come to this: "God punishes me in that
body which I have too carefully tended," she said. But
the Queen's mind had long been weaned from the
world, her once lofty spirit schooled to the uses of adversity, and she bears her protracted sufferings with admirable meekness and resignation. Her face shrunken,
drawn, and ashen, her frame bowed with intense pain
rather than the weight of years, have lost all trace of
their singular beauty; but the hands and arms are
still white, plump and shapely. To the last, her son
Louis XIV. reverently kisses those taper fingers that
had fondly entwined themselves among his clustering
curls from boy to man. As long as that silvery voice
could make itself heard, it was as a peacemaker and
as a friend. When Maria Theresa, her niece, complained to her of the King's too apparent *liaison* with
La Vallière, the dying Queen stroked her cheek, and
comforted her, praying her to pardon the fire of youthful blood, and to remember that Louis, if erring, both
loved and respected her. She reminded her, "that she
(Maria Theresa) had at least a much happier lot than
her own." Overcome by suffering during the long
watches of the night, when she could not sleep, she
weeps; as the tears roll down her wrinkled cheeks,
Mademoiselle de Beauvais wipes them away with her
handkerchief.

"I do not really weep, *ma bonne*," said the dying
Queen; "these tears that I shed are forced from me
by intense anguish; you know I never cry." The Archbishop d'Auch, seeing her condition, told her plainly
that the doctor despaired of her life.

"I thank God," she answered. "Do not lament,"
added she, turning to her ladies, whose sobs caught

her ear; "we must all die. I am still among you; when I am gone, then grieve for me, not yet."

Her son, Philippe d'Orléans, sat constantly beside her bed. While he was present she never allowed herself to utter a complaint, but when he left her, she turned to Madame de Motteville and said, "I suffer horribly. There is no single part of my whole body that is not rent with pain." Then raising her eyes to heaven she exclaimed, "Praised be God, it is his will, his will **be** done—I submit to it with all my heart; yes, with all my heart." Yet in this condition she took the liveliest interest in all that concerned her sons and the King of Spain, and caused every letter to be read aloud to her coming from Madrid. Two nights before her death she bade good night to her children with a haste unusual with her. It was because she did not wish them to witness sufferings she could no longer conceal. As soon as they were gone she desired that the litany of the Passion should be chanted throughout the weary hours of the night. Now and then her groans interrupted the solemn office. When her women strove to mitigate her agony, she pushed them away, saying,

"My vile body is given up to the justice of God. I care not what becomes of it."

In the morning the King, of whom she was ever devotedly fond, and who warmly returned her love, remained many hours with her. That afternoon she grew worse. During the night her son Monsieur hid himself in the curtains of her bed, not to leave her, as she had earnestly desired he would do. The next morning, it was deemed advisable to administer extreme unction. The King and Queen, Monsieur d'Or-

léans, Madame his wife, and Mademoiselle de Montpensier were present. They went out to meet the
Lord's body and to bear it to her. After she had
communicated, a heavenly expression spread over her
countenance, her eyes shone with unnatural brilliancy,
and the colour returned to her cheeks.

"Observe my dear mother," whispered the King,
who was standing at the foot of her bed, to Mademoiselle de Beauvais, "I never saw her look more
beautiful." Then she called her children round her,
and solemnly blessed them. These four, her two sons
and their wives, knelt by her bedside. They kissed
her hands and shed tears of a common grief. The
curtains were then closed, that the Queen might take
a little rest. When they were undrawn, the film of
death had gathered on her eyes.

        *   *   *   *   *   *

Beautiful Saint-Cloud, enfolded in softly undu-
lating hills, its sheeny lawns and majestic avenues
descending to the Seine, whose clear waters dance
and ripple below in the soft spring light;—Saint-Cloud,
with its dimpling uplands and lofty summits, on whose
topmost verge stands what was once a Roman watch-
tower, looking towards Lutetia, the ancient Paris, now
a Grecian temple called the Lanterne de Diogène;—
Saint-Cloud, dense, leafy, forest-like; yonder a deep
glen, in which the morning shadows lie; above, grassy
meads of finest greensward, where the primrose and
the cowslip, the anemone and the foxglove blossom
under scattered groups of noble trees, gay with every
shade of green; oaks yellow with new leaves; delicate
beech and the soft foliage of the tufted elm; all rising
out of a sea of paler-tinted copsewood. Midway on

the hill-side, the ground suddenly falls; and the woods
melt into sculptured terraces, on which the spray of
many fountains catch and reflect the morning sun.
These terraces are again broken by a magnificent cascade, which dashes downwards, to be presently in-
gulfed by the overhanging trees, before it falls into
the river.

It is early summer. The air is full of perfume.
The scent of new-made hay and the odour of dew-
laden flowers are wafted from the terraces towards the
palace, lying in the lowest lap of the hills, shut in by
hanging gardens, its pillared portico basking in the
sunshine.

From the days of Gondi, the Italian banker, the
friend of Zametti, who was more than suspected of
poisoning la belle Gabrielle—for both Gondi and
Zametti had country houses there—Saint-Cloud was
a fair and pleasant place. Hither came Catherine de
Medici to give great fêtes and banquets, and to visit
such of her countrymen as lived near the palace, all
of them skilful Italian Jews, dealing largely in money,
with which they were ready to supply the royal coffers
—on exorbitant interest, be it well understood—who
received her with oriental magnificence, and dressed
out height, the terrace, and garden with silken flags
and embroidered banners, in the Italian style, to do
her honour. Within the palace of Saint-Cloud was
struck down Henry III., the last of Catherine's sons,
the last prince of the royal house of Valois, by the
hand of Jacques Clément, the Dominican. Here Henri
Quatre was proclaimed king, and here, in due process
of time, came to live the Duc d'Orléans, brother of
Louis XIV.—Philippe d'Orléans, once a peevish child,

is now a soft, effeminate gentleman. In person he is the *replica* of the King, only in fainter colours; a water-colour sketch of an original design in oils. He lives among his favourites, whom the world stigmatizes as gamblers and scoundrels, especially the Chevalier de Lorraine, who governs Monsieur despotically.

All the world (except her husband) adores the brilliant Henriette, Duchesse d'Orléans, his wife and cousin-german, who, with her mother, Henrietta Maria, suffered so much at the Louvre from poverty, that they lay in bed for warmth. Now, her brother, Charles II., sits on the throne of England, and she loves not to have the days of her adversity recalled. Henriette d'Orléans is not an absolute beauty. Like her mother, her features are irregular, and her mouth large, but her fresh English colouring tells well among the olive-complexioned ladies of the Court. She is tall, and eminently graceful. Her sunny smile, her ready wit, her joyous manners, win every heart she cares to gain. But, as we have seen, she can be both haughty and cruel. Once she had hoped to marry her elder cousin, the King; but the Mancini girls stepped in, and she was forced to content herself with his younger brother, Philip, whom she despises and dislikes.

Now matters have grown worse than ever between the spouses, for the Duke of Monmouth—illegitimate son of Charles II. by Lucy Waters—has come to Court, and does not conceal his admiration for his English relative, nor observe those precise rules of etiquette needful at the French Court. What makes matters worse is, that Madame, exasperated by her husband, is defiant, and publicly encourages his attentions. Monsieur, weak-headed and irritable, complains to

everybody. He says he shall leave the Court, unless
Madame conducts herself better. Madame rejoins that
he only persecutes her because she happens to be aunt
to the Duke of Monmouth. To spite Monsieur, she
uses her influence with the King, and Monsieur's
favourite, the Chevalier de Lorraine,—who whispers
these tales about her into her husband's ear,—is packed
off; exiled to the sea-girt fortress of the Château d'If,
near Marseilles. This aggravates Monsieur, who treats
Madame worse than ever. They have fresh quarrels
every day, during one of which Monsieur calls Madame a "*vaurienne*." Even when they ride together
in the King's coach, Monsieur must insult and taunt
his wife. "He believes in astrology," he says, "and as
his horoscope foretells he shall be the husband of
many wives, and Madame looks ill, he hopes he shall
soon have a change." At this rude speech Madame
weeps, but says nothing. All this is very bad, and
creates such a scandal that Louis interferes; he ex-
postulates with his brother.

The King, to give Madame a little respite, appointed
her at this time his ambassadress into England, to
treat with her brother, Charles II. In her suite she
carried the beautiful Bretonne, Louise de la Querouaille,
who became afterwards so well known in this country
as the Duchess of Portsmouth.

After a time Madame returns from England, blooming in health and joyous in spirits. She cannot bring
herself even to affect common concern for the death
of her mother,—poor broken-down Henrietta Maria,—
who has just died from taking an overdose of opium.
Monsieur refuses to meet his wife at Amiens, a public
slight which nettled her exceedingly, especially as the

Chevalier de Lorraine has returned from banishment, and is again at Saint-Cloud.

Madame is now twenty-six, and as strong and healthy as any young woman can be. Very early on a certain morning, in the first days of June, a page rides out of the park gates of Saint-Cloud in furious haste. He bears a message of life and death to the King, who is at Saint-Germain. He spurs his steed along the paved roads which lead from palace to palace, along the heights. The word he carries is—*that Madame is dying*. Never did messenger of evil cause such consternation. The King flies to Saint-Cloud; he loved the sweet princess. He is followed by the Queen, accompanied by *la Grande Mademoiselle*. When the royal coach draws up under the grand portico, Valtot, the Court doctor, is there to receive them. He says the illness of Madame is nothing but a violent attack of colic, and is of no consequence whatever. But this attack of colic had seized Madame so suddenly she could not bear to be carried to her own bed, but lay on a little couch in a recess of one of the reception-rooms. A very serious attack of colic, truly. When Maria Theresa enters, she finds Madame in convulsions; her long hair streaming over her face and pillow, her limbs cramped, her body contorted, her nightgown unfastened to relieve her breathing, her arms bare and hanging out of the sleeves, her face bearing every appearance of approaching death.

"You see what a state I am in," she whispers to the Queen between the paroxysms. "Save me, oh save me—my sufferings are horrible!"

The Queen kisses her hand. Every one was affected. The King leans over her with the utmost affection.

"Surely," cries the King to Valtot, "you will not let her die without help?"

Except the royal party no one seems to care about her. Monsieur is quite indifferent. He laughs and talks in the very room where she is lying.

The end came soon. In a few hours, Madame died in horrible agony. Her corpse immediately turned black.

*   *   *   *   *   *

Louis XIV. is in his private closet at Saint-Germain. He is in his robe de chambre, and he has been weeping; three extraordinary events for the King, not to hold his usual lever, to wear his robe de chambre, and to weep.

A dreadful rumour has just reached him—the words *poison* and *murder* have passed from mouth to mouth about the Court. At last he has heard them. What!—his beloved sister-in-law, she who but two days before had danced with him in a ballet, dressed as Aurora; she—the pride of his Court, the cynosure of all eyes—poisoned! Oh, horrible! By whom was this poison given? By his brother? Impossible. By one of his disgraceful favourites whom Madame hated? The Chevalier de Lorraine, perhaps? Was he the murderer? The King cannot brook suspense or delay. He sends privately for Morel, the *maître d'hôtel* of his brother. Morel comes trembling; he guesses the reason of the summons.

"Morel," says the King in an unsteady voice, "I have sent for you to tell me the truth. Now, on pain of instant death, answer me. Who murdered my sister-in-law? Presume not to equivocate or to deceive me. Did the Duchess die by poison?"

"She did, your Majesty."

Louis shudders. "By whose order was it administered?"

"By the order of the Chevalier de Lorraine," answers Morel. "Poison was put into a cup of chicorée-water, the Duchess's usual beverage, by the **hands** of the Marquis d'Effiat. Before God, your Majesty, I am innocent of all save the knowledge of this crime."

Louis, seeing that Morel is about to cast himself **on** his knees before him, by a stern gesture forbade **it.** He then motions him to proceed.

"The Duchess, Sire, complained of thirst; soon after a cup of chicorée-water—the cup of porcelain, which her Highness always used—was presented; she drank its contents to the last drop. Soon after she was seized with convulsions. Your Majesty knows the rest."

There is a pause. "Tell me," asks Louis, speaking with a great effort, "tell me, had my brother—had the Duc d'Orléans any part in this crime?"

"I believe not, Sire," answers Morel, shaking from head to foot, for the King's looks are not reassuring. "They dared not trust him; he would have betrayed them. But it was believed that the death of Madame would not be——"

"Answer as I desire you, sir. Answer the questions I address to you, nothing more," interrupts the King, scowling at him, at the same time greatly relieved by hearing that his brother was not an accomplice. "I have heard what I want to know. I am satisfied. I will spare your life, wretched man," and he turns from Morel with disgust, "because you have spoken the truth; but you must leave France for ever.

Remember, the honour of princes is in your hand, and that wherever you fly, their vengeance can pursue you. Therefore, be silent, if you value your life."

The King dared investigate no farther; too foul a picture of his brother's life would have been revealed to public curiosity. The death of this charming, though frivolous princess, remained unavenged, her murderers unpunished, and she was soon forgotten in the dissipation of a Court where the Sovereign set an example of the most heartless egotism.

As for Monsieur, nothing daunted by the suspicions attached to his name, and although believed by many to have been a direct accomplice in Henriette's death, he determined to bring home a fresh wife to Saint-Cloud and the Palais Royal. This he did in the person of a German princess (ever the refuge of unfortunate royalty in search of wives), a formidable she-dragon rather, by name Charlotte de Bavière, a lady certainly well able to defend herself in case of need. What a contrast to the feminine, fascinating Henriette! Charlotte's autobiography remains to us, a lasting evidence of her coarseness of mind and of body. This is the opening page:—

"I am naturally rather melancholy. When anything annoys me, I have always an inflammation in my left side, as if I had a dropsy. Lying in bed is not at all my habit. As soon as I wake I must get up. I seldom take breakfast. If I do, I only eat bread and butter. I neither like chocolate, coffee, nor tea. Foreign drugs are my horror. I am entirely German in my habits, and relish nothing in the way of food but the *cuisine* of my own country. I can only eat soup made with milk, beer, or wine. As to *bouillon*, I detest it. If I eat any dish that contains it, I am ill directly, my body swells, and I am fearfully sick. Nothing but sausages and ham restore the tone of my stomach. I always wanted to be a boy," this extraordinary "Princess" continues, "and having heard that Marie Germain became one by continually jumping, I used to take such fearful leaps, that it is a miracle I did not break my neck a thousand times."

This **was** the mother of the Regent Orléans.

Charlotte de Bavière was walking one **evening** alone in **the** dusk through the almost interminable suite of rooms which encircled the four garden fronts of the Palais Royal. Many of these rooms had been constantly inhabited by her predecessor, Madame Henriette. It was stormy weather, and the gathering clouds were rapidly darkening what little daylight was left. The wind moaned among the branches of the trees without; it whistled through the rooms within, swaying the rich curtains to and fro. **The** shutters were not yet closed. The Duchess wandered on from room to room until she reached a remote apartment on the ground-floor, which had been much frequented by Madame Henriette—a garden pavilion opening by large windows and a flight of steps to a parterre. At this window Charlotte stood watching the clouds passing over the moon which had just risen, as they were drifted rapidly onwards, driven by the wind. How long she remained there she could never tell. All at once a slight sound behind her, like the rustling of drapery along the floor, caught her ear. She turned, and saw advancing from the door towards the spot where **she** stood a white figure, wearing the form of the late Duchess, her predecessor, Henrietta of England.

She knew her instantly from her portraits. What passed between these two—the dead and the living wife—never was told. Charlotte, all her life long, insisted on the perfect truth of this story, but would say nothing more. In time it came to be understood that some awful secret connected with the Orleans family, only to be known to the **head** of the house, was revealed by the phantom.

CHAPTER XX.

At Versailles.

THE Duchesse Louise de la Vallière, after her return from Chaillot, lived much at the Hôtel Biron, a residence at Versailles presented to her by the King. Her two children, the Comte de Vermandois and Mademoiselle de Blois, were with her. The Hôtel Biron, a sumptuous abode, situated between "court and garden," lay in a hollow close to the yet unfinished Palace of Versailles, on the same side as the reservoir. Adjoining were the royal gardens, already planned and partially completed by Le Nôtre. These gardens, with the formal groves and symmetrical thickets which enclose them, sloped downwards from the grand terrace of the southern front, and overshadowed the hôtel, giving it a sequestered, not to say, melancholy aspect. On the other side a wooded park stretched away in the direction of what was in time to become the site of the two Trianons. The new Palace of Versailles was as yet covered with scaffolding; innumerable workmen laboured night and day on the north and south wings. The *corps de logis*, of brick and stone, was alone completed, and though greatly

enlarged and beautified, still retained those suites of
small rooms—*les petits appartements*—portions of the
original hunting-lodge which was so often visited by
Louis XIII. in his hunting expeditions.

La Vallière lived a life of extreme retirement. She
rarely appeared at Court, except upon occasions of
state, and received only such visits as etiquette rendered necessary. Save the King, her confessor, and a
few intimate friends, she avoided every one. The
splendour of the retreat assigned her by the King
pained and humiliated her. She was but too conscious
that in permitting herself to be dowered and ennobled
by him, she was exposing herself to the charge of
ambition, arrogance, and avarice—she, who only
loved the man, and who shrank abashed from the
sovereign!

The very letters patent by which Louis created her
Duchesse de la Vallière infinitely wounded her. It
was intolerable to her to be publicly addressed as "his
singularly and entirely beloved Louise Françoise de la
Vallière, possessed of His Majesty's special and particular affection." Vainly had she endeavoured to
combat his resolution thus to distinguish her; vainly
had she entreated him to allow her to sink into ob-
livion, forgotten by all save himself. Louis had
declared, and with truth, that after her flight to
Chaillot and her return to Saint-Germain, all mystery
was impossible. He could not bear, he told her, to
see her continually suffering affronts and mortifica-
tions in his own Court, to which her sensitive nature
specially exposed her, and from which even he could
not screen her.

Vainly did he invoke all his authority as a sovereign, all his devotion as a man, to raise the object of his love beyond the reach of calumny. Vainly did he surround her with all that the luxury of kings, the treasures of the state, and the refinements of love could devise to reconcile her to her position. He could not stifle her conscience. Louise could not bring herself to leave him, but she sank under the consciousness of her sin.

When, by a formal declaration of the parliament, her children were legitimatized and created princes of the blood royal, she was in absolute despair. Again she conjured the King never more to let her name be heard. But, selfish even to her, Louis commanded that she should appear in the Queen's circle, and receive the congratulations of the Court. A prey to anxiety and remorse, silent, yearning, solitary, her health gave way. Her lovely figure lost its roundness, her violet eyes their lustre. She grew dull, oppressed, and tearful, and her lameness increased.

The Comtesse du Roule, formerly maid of honour to Madame Henriette d'Orléans at the same time as La Vallière, was one of the few friends she still received.

They had not met for some time when Madame du Roule called on her. Madame du Roule found Louise seated alone in a pavilion overlooking the palace of Versailles. She was so lost in thought she did not hear her friend's footsteps. When she rose to receive her she looked more delicate and dejected than usual.

"Dear Louise," said the Comtesse after having saluted her, "how I grieve to see you so unhappy. Can nothing be done to console you? Remember you are ruining your looks. Do you imagine that his Ma-

jesty will care for you when you have made yourself
wrinkled and ugly?"

"Alas, Celestine, I cannot help it! I ought not to
be here," and Louise kissed her tenderly, and placed
her on a seat beside her. "This magnificent hôtel,
these royal servants, my luxurious life—daily remind
me of my degradation. While I was unknown and
poor, lost among the crowd of a great Court, I was
my own mistress. My heart was my own to bestow.
Now"—and she placed her hand on her heart as if
she suffered—"a price seems put upon me. I cannot
bear it! Ah, why did I leave Chaillot?" and her head,
covered with light baby curls, sank upon her bosom;
and she heaved a deep sigh.

"But, Louise, if you love the King," said the Comtesse, laying her hand gently on that of La Vallière,
"you must accept the inevitable position, else some
one less scrupulous and more mercenary than yourself
will certainly take it."

"Ah, Celestine, that fear is ever present to me. It
is agony to me; it keeps me here. Do not imagine
that I misunderstand my position. I suffer because it
is too painfully evident. Yet I love the King too
much to resign him. Love! ah, more—I worship
him!" and she raised her head, and an inner light
shone from her soft, grey eyes, that made them glow
with passion. "Is he not my master—my sovereign!"
she continued; "am I not bound to obey him? Could
I exist without him? Who else but Louis could have
brought me back from Chaillot? Who else could
have torn me from the altar to which my heart still
clings? Celestine, I know I shall return to that convent."—The Comtesse smiled incredulously.—"But,"

continued La Vallière, "when I see my faded face in
the glass, and I know I am faded and changed"—
Madame du Roule shook her head deprecatingly—"I
tremble—oh, I tremble lest I should lose him! I know
I ought to rejoice at his loss," added she in a broken
voice; "yet I cannot—I cannot!" and the tears streamed
from her eyes, and she covered her face with her
hands.

"Have you perceived any difference in the behaviour of his Majesty of late?" asked Madame du
Roule, when La Vallière became more composed.

"Oh, what a question, Celestine! Such an idea
never crossed my mind—changed now, at this time—
could it be possible? When I spoke of losing him, I
meant in the course of years—long, long years.
Surely he would not change now?" An agonized expression came into her face as she spoke, and she
turned appealingly towards her friend for reassurance
against what presented itself to her as some horrible
dream.

"I only **ask you this question for** your good, dear
Louise," answered the Comtesse soothingly, imprinting
a kiss on her pallid cheek.—La Vallière threw **her
arms** round her neck, and made no reply.—"I see you
are incapable of judging for yourself. If I ask a pain-
ful question, it is to spare you, not to wound you.
Answer me honestly, Louise—is **his** Majesty changed?"

A shudder passed over the slender frame of La
Vallière. For a time she could not bring herself to
reply; then hesitatingly she answered: "I have fancied
—but, oh heavens! may it be only a fancy—that his
Majesty finds his visits to me more dull than formerly.
I am so ¦depressed myself, that must be the reason,"

and she bent her eyes upon her friend, hoping that she would assent; but Madame du Roule only listened with grave attention. "He has sat," continued Louise, evidently forcing herself to a painful confession, "he has sat for half an hour at a time quite silent, a thing unusual with him. He has remarked, too, repeatedly, on my altered looks; he has often regretted my low spirits. He is most considerate, most tender; but"— and she faltered more than ever—"I fear that I depress him; and I have tried—" here her voice dropped, and her eyes fixed themselves upon a medallion portrait of Louis that hung round her neck by a chain of gold. She contemplated it earnestly.

"That is just what I feared, Louise," and the Comtesse laid her hand softly on her shoulder to rouse her from the deep reverie into which she had fallen; "that is precisely what I feared. If you cease to amuse the King, others will; he will leave you."

"Holy Virgin!" cried Louise, starting from her chair and clasping her hands; "do not say so; such an idea is death to me!"

"Louise, be calm; reseat yourself, and listen to me. You rarely go to Court; but you well know that his Majesty is surrounded from morning till night with crowds of most fascinating, most unscrupulous women. They follow him like his shadow; he cannot shake them off—even if he would. The poor Queen, who is as stupid as an owl, sits in a corner, sighs and sulks, or plays at cards, and loses thousands to pass away the time. But she says nothing, and has no influence whatever over her husband. By-the-way, she is very jealous of you, Louise, and calls you 'the lady with the diamond ear-rings.'"

La Vallière blushed, then sighed; and again her dreamy eyes sought the medallion portrait of the King, which she still held within the palm of her hand.

"Rouse yourself, Louise; believe me there is need," urged the Comtesse. "When the King visits you next, throw off these gloomy vapours; or, if you cannot, invite some friend to be present and assist you in entertaining him."

The tears gathered in La Vallière's eyes, and slowly coursed each other down her cheeks.

"Alas! has it come to this, then? Do you indeed, Celestine, counsel me to call on another to do that which was once my privilege? How he once loved my company! how he praised my gentleness and my timidity, which charmed him inexpressibly, he said, after the boldness of the ladies of the Court."

"All this is folly," said Madame du Roule impatiently. "The King is robust, happy, and fond of pleasure. He delights in the society of women. You must, Louise, either return to Chaillot, as you say you desire to do (excuse my frankness, dear, it is for your good), or you must change. His Majesty is neither a penitent, nor ill, nor sad. Do you know any one you can invite here when he comes?"

"No," replied La Vallière with a look of infinite distress upon her plaintive face. "No one I could trust. Besides, the King might resent it as a liberty. It is a matter needing the nicest judgment."

"The person, whoever she is," said Madame du Roule, "must be sincerely attached to you, polished, agreeable, and sympathetic. She must be good-looking, and not too old either; for the King loves youth and beauty. There is the new lady-in-waiting, the

Marquise de Montespan. You have seen her. She is a mere girl, just come to Court, and belongs to no clique. She is as witty as a Mortémart ought to be, and gloriously handsome. Such eyes, dear Louise, such colour! and there is plenty of fun, not to say malice, about her. I would not have her for an enemy! When she was presented to the Queen, there was the most extraordinary sensation at Court—people stood on chairs to look at her."

"But, dear Celestine, what a hag I shall look beside this fresh young beauty?" cried La Vallière in alarm.

"You need have no fear of that. The King is perhaps the only man in the whole circle who does not admire her. You would be quite safe to invite her. She is full of badinage, positively a child in her love of amusement; her lively sallies will help to pass the time. She desires, too, greatly to be presented to you, and has already conceived a romantic friendship for you."

"Ah, Celestine, are you sure that this girl, this Mortémart—they are a dangerous family—seeks me for myself alone? Are you sure that she has no deeper motive for all these professions? I confess I have my misgivings."

"You are quite mistaken, Louise. She is a naïve creature, clever indeed, but guileless. You could not make a better choice. Take my advice, ask his Majesty's permission to invite the Marquise next time he comes. Believe me, he is perfectly indifferent to her. He will be grateful to you for the attention; he will be amused. You will find him return to his first ardour, he will be as devoted as at first. You will recover your spirits; you will return to Court" (La Vallière shook her head sadly), "and all will be well!"

CHAPTER XXI.

Madame de Montespan.

ATHANASE DE MORTÉMART, Marquise de Montespan, the most beautiful woman of her age, was, at this time, twenty-two years old. She was fair, but not so fair as La Vallière. Her features were faultless, and there was an aureole of youth and freshness about her that made her irresistible. She affected to be careless, impulsive, even infantine; but she was in reality profoundly false, and could be insolent, cruel, and domineering; a syren or a fury, as suited her humour or her purpose. There was no mercy in those voluptuous eyes that entranced while they deceived; no truth in those coral lips that smiled only to betray.

No sooner was she informed that the Duchesse de la Vallière would receive her, than she flew to the Hôtel Biron. Louise was astounded at her extraordinary beauty.

"How much I thank you, Marquise, for your goodness in sparing a few hours from the gaieties of the Court to visit a poor recluse like me."

"On the contrary, Madame la Duchesse, it is I who am grateful;" and the Marquise kissed her on both cheeks. "Ever since I came to Court, I have longed to become acquainted with you. No words can express the love and respect I entertain for you."

"Alas! madame, I fear that you cannot know me. I deserve no respect," replied La Vallière sadly. "If you can love me, I shall be satisfied."

"Love you, dear Duchess! I will devote my life to you, if you will permit me such an honour," cried Madame de Montespan, her eyes flashing with eagerness. "Will you allow me to look on you as an old friend?"

"I shall consider it a privilege," replied La Vallière.

"I have so often talked about you with the Comtesse du Roule, that I feel already as though we were long acquainted," continued Madame de Montespan; and she seized La Vallière's small hand and pressed it. La Vallière returned her caress more quietly. "Dear Duchess," exclaimed De Montespan impulsively, "I am so young, so inexperienced."

"And so beautiful," added La Vallière, smiling.

"Well, I am told so, madame. Your counsel will be invaluable to me. I am yet but a novice at Court."

"I will be a mother to you," replied Louise meekly. But, in her inmost heart, she asked herself, "Am I indeed so old, so changed, that she can accept this offer from me? It seems but yesterday I was as young and as light-hearted as herself!"

"I know little of the Court now," replied La Vallière, speaking in a very subdued voice. "What I do know, can be of little service to you. Heaven guard you from my experiences!" and a deep sigh escaped her.

"Oh, Madame la Duchesse, wherever you are, *there* is the Court. Your modesty only adds to your merit. We all know *you* are the dispenser of all favour, all power — that your word is law." This was spoken rapidly by the Marquise, who all the while kept her eyes on the Duchess to study the effect of her flattery.

"God forbid," replied La Vallière coldly; and a look of displeasure contracted her brow for an instant. "I possess no power of that kind, madame. I would never permit myself to exercise any such influence over his Majesty, I assure you."

The crafty Marquise saw she had made a mistake, and instantly set about repairing it. She sighed, affected an air of deep concern, and cast down her magnificent eyes. Then she timidly stretched out her hand to clasp that of La Vallière.

"Will you teach me your patience, your resignation? Will you teach me to bear sorrow?"

"Gracious heavens! what can a creature so young and brilliant know of sorrow?"

"Much. Alas! too much!" The beautiful Marquise raised her handkerchief to her eyes. "Monsieur de Montespan never loved me. It was a marriage arranged by my sister, Madame de Thiange. She sacrificed me to family arrangements; he to his love of play—he is a desperate gambler. Worse still, he is a libertine." She paused, and tried to blush. "Can I, dare I hope, Madame la Duchesse, to find a friend in you? Nay more—a protectress? May I be permitted to ask your counsel?"

"Reckon on me," cried La Vallière, who was deeply interested by this artful appeal. Madame de Montespan cared no more for her husband than he did for her. "Come to me whenever you need advice, whenever you want sympathy or protection. Come to me freely —at all hours, at all times—this house is yours."

"But, Madame la Duchesse, his Majesty may perhaps object to my presence here. I do not think he

likes me. He has scarcely once addressed me during
the few times I have been at Court."

"Ah, I will arrange that," answered La Vallière, her
face all aglow with excitement. "I will manage that
you shall be here when he comes. To see you, dear
Marquise, as I do now, must be to esteem and respect
you. His Majesty's heart is so excellent, all his ideas
so great, so noble! You shall help me to entertain
him; you have such charming spirits, such a sunny
smile."

Madame de Montespan gave a little start. She
could with difficulty conceal the delight this speech
gave her, La Vallière had so completely fallen into the
trap she had laid. Again she kissed her thin white
hand, and pressed the long delicate fingers that lay so
confidingly in her own.

"What an honour!" she exclaimed. "How happy
I shall be to serve you in the smallest way, in return
for all your goodness!"

"To serve *me!*" repeated La Vallière, gazing at
her vacantly. "Not to serve me—that is impossible.
Ah, no one can serve *me*. My life is a long remorse.
I love—with my whole soul I love. That love is a
crime. I can neither leave the King, nor can I bear
to remain. God's image rises up within me to shut
out his dear form from my eyes. Alas, alas!—I prefer
him to God." La Vallière melted into tears. She
sank back on her chair, lost to all else but the agony
of her own feelings.

Madame de Montespan observed her with a look
of sarcastic scrutiny. No shade of pity tempered her
bold stare. Her eyes were hard as steel, her full lips
were compressed.

"How I admire your devotion to his Majesty," she said, in the most insinuating voice. "It is extraordinary." Her kind words singularly belied her cruel expression, but Louise, blinded by her tears, did not observe this. "What astonishes me is that, feeling as you do, you can endure to remain here—so close to the palace, almost living in the Court, so long. In such magnificence too," — and she gave a spiteful glance round the superbly decorated saloon. "You must have extraordinary self-command," she added artfully, "immense self-denial. I suppose you see his Majesty often, Madame la Duchesse?" she asked this question with well-affected indifference, fixing her eyes steadily on poor La Vallière, who still lay back in her chair weeping. "He is always at Versailles. It must be a great trial, and with your religious convictions too." As she spoke she carefully noted the effect each word produced upon La Vallière.

"Alas!" replied her victim, her cheeks now suffused with a burning blush, "I see him almost daily. Those hours are all that render life endurable."

"Do you really mean this, dear Duchess?" returned Madame de Montespan, feigning extreme surprise. "I should have imagined that the refinement of your nature would have rendered the indulgence of a guilty passion impossible."

"Ah! I see you despise me," groaned poor La Vallière, overcome by shame. "I cannot wonder. Young and pure as you are, I must be to you an object of horror."

"Oh, Madame la Duchesse, what a word! On the contrary, I admire the sacrifice you make."

"Alas!" interrupted La Vallière, "it is no sacrifice.

I cannot tear myself from him because—because—"
she stopped for a moment, then added hastily, "I fear
to give him pain. It seems to me I ought to bear
anything rather than hurt one whose love has raised
me so near himself. I have not the courage to wound
him—perhaps to embitter his whole life. No,—although
conscience, duty, religion command it, I have not the
courage." La Vallière turned aside and hid her face.

Madame de Montespan fell into a deep muse.
Again an expression of cruel determination passed
over her fair young face, and she gave La Vallière
a glance in which malice, anger, and contempt, were
mingled. La Vallière, absorbed in her own sorrow,
did not perceive it.

"How I grieve for you, dear friend," Madame de
Montespan continued, speaking in her sweetest voice.
"How I respect your scruples. Are you sure," added
she, carefully noting the effect of her words, "that the
King would *really* suffer from your absence as keenly
as you imagine?"

"I have never dared broach the subject," answered
La Vallière, looking up. "My remorse I cannot hide.
He knows I suffer, he sees I am ill. But I would not
for worlds openly acknowledge that I wish to forsake
him."

"Yet, dear Duchess, this struggle will kill you.
What a balm to your sensitive feelings the solitude of
a convent would be! Among those holy sisters, in a
life of prayer, you would find new life."

"I know it—I know!" cried La Vallière passionately; "but how to leave him—how to go?"

"Perhaps, Duchess, I may assist you," and Madame
de Montespan bent, with well simulated interest, over

the slight form beside her, and gazed inquiringly into the trusting eyes that were turned so imploringly upon her. "I might be able to place this dilemma before his Majesty as your friend, dear Duchess. A third party is often able to assist in a matter so delicate. If his Majesty would indeed suffer as poignantly as you imagine, your departure is out of the question. I could at least learn this from himself in your interest."

Louise sprang to her feet, she threw her soft arms round Madame de Montespan, and nestled her pale face on her bosom.

"At last I have found a real friend," she cried; "at last I have found one who understands me. But," and she looked up quickly into the other's face, with a confidence that was most touching, "you will say nothing to his Majesty. Not a word. Be here when he next comes. (I will ask his permission.) You will then be able to judge for yourself—to counsel me. I would rather suffer torture, I would rather die, than give him a moment's pain—remember that," and La Vallière put out her little hand and pressed that of Madame de Montespan, whose face was wreathed with smiles.

"Do you think that his Majesty will consent to my presence here?" asked Madame de Montespan, carefully concealing her feelings of exultation, for she foresaw what the reply must be.

"I will make him," cried La Vallière. "I will teach you exactly how to please him—what to say —never to contradict him—to watch the turn of his eye, as I do. The ice once broken, your tact, your winning manners, will make all easy."

Madame de Montespan acquiesced. She strove to appear careless, but she knew that her fate was on the balance. If she met the King there, she was resolved her rival should not long trouble her.

"Then you will tell me what I ought to do," continued La Vallière. "I shall be for ever grateful to you—you will reconcile me to myself!"

*   *   *   *   *

When next the King visited La Vallière, Madame de Montespan was present. She was as plainly dressed as was consistent with etiquette. At first she said little, sat apart, and only spoke when the King addressed her. But afterwards, gradually feeling her way, she threw in the most adroit flattery, agreed with all he said, yet appeared to defer in everything to La Vallière. Sometimes she amused him by her follies, and brought with her a team of mice she had tamed and harnessed to a little car of filigree, to run upon a table; sometimes she astonished both La Vallière and the King by her acute observation, her daring remarks and pungent satire. The King's visits to the Hôtel Biron became longer and more frequent. If Madame de Montespan was not there he asked for her, and expressed regret at her absence. The Comtesse du Roule inquired anxiously of La Vallière if Madame de Montespan was useful to her. Reports had reached her which made her uneasy. It was said that this beautiful young friend, whom she had so unwittingly introduced to La Vallière, had designs of her own upon the King; and that she openly boasted that she would speedily supplant the Duchess.

Madame du Roule had also heard that Monsieur de Montespan had appeared at the Queen's circle

dressed entirely in black, and that on being asked by
the King for what relative he wore such deep mourning,
had replied—

"For my wife, Sire."

La Vallière laughed at this story, and would not
listen to a syllable against her new friend.

CHAPTER XXII.

Broken-hearted.

IT was evening. The day had been intensely hot.
Now, stormy clouds scud across the western skies, and
the sun sets in a yellow haze, which lights up the surrounding woods. Groups of stately elms that tuft the
park cast deep shadows upon the grass; their huge
branches sway to and fro in the rising wind, which
moans among the thickets of laurels and lilacs separat-
ing the grounds of the Hôtel Biron from the royal
gardens of Versailles.

Louise La Vallière sat alone in a gorgeous boudoir
lined with mirrors and gilding. She was engaged on
some embroidery. As she stooped over the frame on
which her work was strained, her countenance bore
that resigned and plaintive expression habitual to it.
She was still graceful and pretty, and her simple attire
gave her the appearance of a girl.

As the failing light warned her that night was
approaching, she put aside her work, seated herself
beside an alcoved window which opened upon a terrace, and listened to the wind, each moment growing
more boisterous among the neighbouring forests that
topped the hills towards Saint-Cloud.

Suddenly the door opened, and Madame de Montespan appeared. After saluting La Vallière, she seated herself in an easy-chair opposite to her. Her bearing was greatly changed. No longer subservient and flattering, she was now confident, familiar, and domineering. Her eyes wandered round the room with a defiant expression. The very tone of her voice showed how much she assumed upon the consciousness of favour. She was more beautiful than ever; many jewels adorned her neck and hair which she had never worn before.

"Louise," said she, with an air which, if intended to be gracious, was only patronising, "I can only stay for an instant. How dismal you look! what is the matter?"

Louise shook her head despondingly. "Nothing more than usual."

"The Queen is just arrived from Saint-Germain; I am in attendance. I escaped for a few minutes, accompanied by the Comte de Lauzun. We came through the gardens and the thicket by the private alley. You must not ask me to stay; her Majesty may inquire for me. Lauzun is waiting outside on the terrace by the new fountain."

"Will he not come in?" asked La Vallière.

"No, he is in attendance on his Majesty, who is engaged at this moment with the architect. He may call for him at any moment."

"Do you think I shall see his Majesty this evening?" asked La Vallière timidly, looking up and meeting the haughty stare of the Marquise.

"I imagine not. It is late, and his Majesty has said nothing of such an intention."

"Yet he is so near," murmured Louise sadly.

"Monsieur de Lauzun tells me that the flotilla of

boats is ordered for this evening. There is to be a
water party on the canal; the shores are to be illuminated. I trust it will not rain."

"How I envy you—not the water party, but that
you will see the King," and La Vallière's eyes glistened.

"Adieu, adieu, *ma belle!* I can't keep Lauzun
waiting," and Madame de Montespan rose and left
the boudoir as hastily as she had entered it.

Louise had also risen to attend her to the door.
She did not reseat herself, but stood gazing wistfully
after her. She anxiously bent her ear to catch every
sound. Louis was close at hand; he might still come.
A thrill of joy shot through her at the thought. Once
the sound of footsteps was audible, and a flush of
delight overspread her face. The sound died away,
and again the night wind, sighing without, alone broke
the silence. Her heart sank within her. She rebuked
herself, but in vain; spite of remorse, spite of self-
conflicts, Louis was dearer to her than life.

It was rapidly growing dusk; only a little light still
lingered in the room. A feeling of utter loneliness, a
foreboding of coming misfortune, suddenly overcame
her. The shadows of approaching night seemed to
strike into her very soul. She started at her own
footstep as she crossed the parquet floor towards a
taper which stood upon a marble table, covered with
costly trifles given to her by the King. She stretched
out her hand to light it. When she had done so,
something sparkled on the floor close to the chair on
which Madame de Montespan had been seated. Louise
stooped **down** to see what it was. She at once recognised some golden tablets which she had often

noticed in the hands of Madame de Montespan. The diamonds, set in the rich gold chasing, and the initials, had caught the light. The snap was open. It was so dark that La Vallière held it close to the taper in order to close the spring. In doing so the tablets fell open—her eyes fixed themselves on the pages. An expression of horror came into them as she gazed. Could it be, or was she dreaming? All the blood in her body rushed to her heart. She put down the light which she had held, and, with the tablets in her hand, sat down to collect her senses, for her head was dizzy. Could it be? Yes; it was the handwriting of the King. How well she knew it—each stroke, every little turn of the pen, how she had studied it! As she passed page after page through her quivering fingers, each bore the same well-known characters. She tried to read; a film gathered over her eyes. Yet she must read on. She pressed her hand upon her brow; her brain seemed on fire. At length a desperate resolution gave her power—she read. There were verses of passionate fondness, signed "Louis." The first dated three months back; the last only yesterday.

She would have wept, but the thears froze ere they reached her eyes. With a great effort she collected her scattered senses and began to think. Madame de Montespan must have dropped these tablets on purpose. She saw it all. They fell from her hand upon the floor. Lying there she gazed at them in silence. Then she glanced round the room. It was now quite dark; the burning taper only served to deepen the gloom—Louise knew she was alone in the world; the King loved another.

With the composure of despair she took up a pen

to address him before she fled, for fly she intuitively felt she must. She was not capable of reflection, but it came to her quite naturally as the only thing that remained for her to do, to fly; and where could she go but to Chaillot, to the dear sisterhood?

"You have ceased to love me," she wrote; "the proofs are in my hand, written by yourself. The last time we met you told me how dear I was to you; let me never hear your beloved voice speak another language. I do not reproach you; you have treated me as I deserved. But I still love you as when we first met among the woods of Fontainebleau. If ever you waste a thought upon me, remember that death alone can quench that love."

Alas for the weakness of human nature! La Vallière, once within the walls of Chaillot, shut herself into the same cell she had before occupied, and repented that she had come. "I ought to have seen the King, and to have questioned him myself. Madame de Montespan may have purposely deceived me. That she must be false I know too well. Who can tell if it is not all a device to rob me of Louis? I may myself be but a tool in her hands. If I had seen him all might have been explained. He is my master; I had no right to leave him. Oh! I wish I had not come!"

Thus she reasoned. Her soul was not yet wholly given to God. Further trials await her. Breathlessly she waited for what might happen; the creak of a door made her heart beat; every footstep made her tremble.

At the end of some hours the door opened and the Prince de Condé was announced.

"What, alone! Once he would have come himself," she murmured.

Composing herself as best she could, she rose to meet him. The Prince placed in her hands a letter from the King; he desired her to return immediately to Versailles with the bearer.

La Vallière meekly bowed her head and obeyed.

No sooner had La Vallière returned to the Hôtel Biron than the King arrived. He was ruddy with health; his eyes flashed with the vigour of manhood. His bearing was proud, yet dignified. On his head was a hat trimmed with point lace and jewels, from which hung a fringe of white ostrich feathers, which mixing with the dark curls of his peruke, covered his shoulders.

"Let us live our old life again," said he, uncovering, and taking her hands in his. "I hate explanations. Believe me, your presence here, *under all circumstances*," and he accentuated these words, "is necessary to my happiness."

"But, Sire, Madame de Montespan?"

Louis became crimson; a momentary frown knit his dark eyebrows.

"I desire you to receive her as heretofore," he replied hurriedly. "Louise, it is a sacrifice you must make for my sake. You will not refuse. It will endear you to me more than ever."

As he spoke he looked at her tenderly.

"Sire, I cannot," she replied firmly, casting her eyes on the ground.

"How! You dare to refuse me? Louise, I command you." The King drew himself up; he laid his hand heavily on her shoulder. Then, seeing how wasted and frail she was, and how her slight form quivered under his touch, he added in a softened tone, "Louise, I entreat you."

A deep blush suffused her cheeks. Some moments passed before she could command her voice. "Sire," she replied at last, and her white lips trembled, "Sire, I can never again live the old life,—but I will obey you."

The King was about to rush forward to embrace her. She stopped him by a gesture gentle yet determined. He fell back.

"Sire, you love another. Hitherto I have quieted my conscience by the conviction that I was needful to you. Now I know it is not so. Take back these tablets, Sire. Can you deny these verses, written by your own hand but a few days since?"

Louis stood before her, silenced, confounded. Her composure astonished him. Before him was La Vallière—hitherto his slave, now so determined! Her hand rested on a table for support. She was deadly pale, and carefully avoided his gaze. He was deeply moved.

"Do I not offer you enough?" said he.

"No, Louis, it is not enough. I will obey you; I will receive Madame de——" Her voice dropped, and the hated name was inaudible. "Nay, I will do more; I will again appear at Court if you command it, but all hope, all joy, is dead within me."

She uttered these words deliberately. It was despair that gave her courage.

Then she raised her eyes, and rested them for the first time on him, with an agonized expression. "I must have your undivided love as heretofore, or——" and she paused. "I know that my words are sinful," she added. "I have fled from you; now I am returned for a little space."

Louis looked perplexed. "But, Louise, believe **me**, that you are still inexpressibly dear to me; my heart has wandered, it is true, but **you yet** possess **my** affection, my esteem."

"**It** is **not** enough," repeated La Vallière in a low voice, "it is not enough. You are turned from **me**, you have joined in deceiving me; I am supplanted."

The tears sprang involuntarily into the King's eyes as he stood with folded arms contemplating her. He did not dare approach her. How strange it seemed that one so meek and gentle could be so firm. Never before had her lips uttered anything to him but words of tenderness.

Once more she spoke.

"As long as you desire it, Sire, I will remain. It is a penance I shall offer up to God, to remain and to see you love another." She turned her large grey eyes up to heaven as **she spoke**. "**When** you give me permission, I shall **become a** Carmelite."

"I will **never** permit it!" cried Louis, stamping his foot upon the **floor**. A scowl passed over his face, he was angry, offended, at her obstinacy; his imperious will could not brook contradiction. "You have never loved me!" he exclaimed.

"Sire!" cried La Vallière. "Not loved you!"

"No; you have always preferred your religious scruples to me. You have tormented me with your remorse. You know nothing of the intoxication of passion. *You* ought to have gloried in my love, as others do," he muttered, in a low voice, turning from her.

"Sire," cried La Vallière, stung to the quick by his injustice, "I am at this moment forcing my conscience to obey you and to remain."

"You are too weak, too feeble, for a great passion," continued the King hurriedly. "Others can feel it, however."

"I have never sold myself for ambition, Sire, as others do. I never desired anything of you but your-self, and I have lost you."

Louis, crimson with passion, did not reply. He strode up and down the room in moody silence. La Vallière for a time was also silent. Her eyes followed him. His face was hard, and no glance told her that he even pitied her. It was too much. The strain upon her gentle nature gave way. The pent-up tears rushed to her eyes, she burst into heart-rending sobs and sank upon a seat. The King watched her, but he spoke not a word. His look was stern and set. For a while her tears flowed fast, and her bosom heaved wildly. Then she rose to her feet, and approached him. "All is over!" she said, in a voice almost inarticulate with sobs. "Never—never—will I trouble your Majesty more. Your will shall be now as ever my law. Eternal silence shall cover my justly merited sufferings. I have nothing more to say. Permit me to retire." She turned and left the room; her heart was broken.

Bossuet was her director. To him she applied for counsel. She told him that her very soul yearned for a convent. Bossuet questioned her,—her passionate remorse, her penitence, her courage, her resignation touched him deeply. She seemed to be purified from

all earthly stain. Bossuet advised her to take six
months to **consider** her vocation, during which time
she was to speak to no one of **her** project. La Vallière bowed her head and obeyed. At the termina-
tion of the time, she publicly declared her intention
of becoming a Carmelite. The King received this
announcement with some show of feeling. He sent
Lauzun to her, and offered to make her abbess of the
richest convent in France. He entreated her not to
expose her feeble health to the austerities of so severe
an order. La Vallière replied that her resolution was
unalterable. Before leaving the Hôtel Biron she asked
for a private audience of the Queen. It was granted.
With a veil over her face, and dressed in the dark
robes of the order which she was about to enter, a
hempen cord round her waist, to which hung a rosary
and cross, she entered the Queen's private apartments
at Versailles. Maria Theresa was alone. La Vallière
raised her veil, her face was moist with tears, she
tottered forward with difficulty and sank upon her
knees.

"My royal mistress," said she, in a faint voice,
"I come to crave your pardon. Oh, Madame, do
not, I implore you, repulse me. Alas! if I have
sinned I have suffered. Suffered—oh, so bitterly, so
long! In a few hours I shall be forgotten within a
convent."

The Queen, a woman of the most kindly and
womanly feelings, was deeply affected.

"Ah, Madame la Duchesse," said she, "I have
learnt to know how much I owe you. My life was
much happier when you were at Court. I beg you to

believe I shall be glad to have you again about my person."

"Your Majesty honours me beyond expression," answered La Vallière, curtseying to the earth.

"Does the King know of your departure, Madame la Duchesse?"

"He will know it after I have acquainted your Majesty."

"Surely he will not consent?" asked the Queen.

La Vallière shook her head—"My mind is made up, Madame. If I live for one year, I shall be a professed Carmelite."

"I am sorry," replied Maria Theresa simply, "very sorry. If my good wishes can serve you, Madame la Duchesse, you have them most sincerely. Should you, however, carry out your intention, allow me to present you with the black veil. It is a public mark of respect I would willingly pay you."

La Vallière was so overcome she could not at once reply, then kissing the Queen's hand which she held out to her, she said, "Your Majesty's goodness makes me hope that, as you have deigned to pardon me, I may still, by a life of penitence, reconcile myself with God. I most humbly thank you."

This interview over, she returned to Versailles. She distributed her possessions as though she were already dead. She assembled her servants in her oratory and earnestly craved their forgiveness for all that she had said or done amiss. She exhorted them to be devout, to keep the fasts of the Church, and to serve God. She was thus occupied until past midnight. Towards morning she called her coach, and bid her people drive her quickly towards Chaillot.

As she passed along she gazed eagerly on the blooming country for the last time. It was the month of
June. The orchards were laden with the promise of
coming fruit; the newly mown grass, sparkling with
morning dew, made the meadows glisten, the birds
carolled in the hedge-rows, and the hills, embowered
in forest, rose green against the azure sky. Louise
was still young; it was her last look on that world
which had once been so pleasant to her.

At six o'clock in the morning she arrived at the
convent. The Superior, accompanied by all the nuns,
apprised of her arrival, was in waiting to receive her.

"My mother," said La Vallière, kneeling at her
feet, "I have used my liberty so ill, that I am come
to give it up into your hands."

Her long and beautiful hair was cut off before
she entered the convent as a novice. A year afterwards she made her profession. The Queen and the
whole Court were present—all save the King and
Madame de Montespan. Bossuet preached his celebrated sermon. Then the Queen Maria Theresa
descended from the tribune, where she had been
seated in company with *La Grande Mademoiselle*, and
invested her with the black veil. She kissed her
tenderly on the forehead as she did so.

La Vallière, now Sister Louise de la Miséricorde,
made an exemplary nun. She wore horse-hair next
her skin, walked barefoot along the stone pavement
of the convent, and fasted rigorously. She died at
sixty-six, wasted to a skeleton by her austerities. Her
end was peace.

CHAPTER XXIII.

M. de Lauzun and "Mademoiselle."

ON the line of rail to Orleans, two and a half leagues from Paris, is the station and village of Choisy le Roi. Of the enchanting abode once erected here, on the verge of grassy lawns bordering the Seine, nothing has been left by the revolution but a fragment of wall, built into a porcelain manufactory.

Choisy Mademoiselle, afterwards to be called by Louis XV. *Choisy le Roi*, was built by Mademoiselle de Montpensier, daughter of Gaston, Duc d'Orléans, under the advice of Le Nôtre. It was to serve as a summer retreat from the gloomy splendours of the Luxembourg; a *folie* where she might spend the summer heats, try her English horses, train her hounds, row on the river, tend her aviaries, and watch her flowers. Here, freed from all scrutiny, she could be imperious or devout, childish or solemn, vain or humble, as suited her fickle humour; here she could lay traps to catch obstinate emperors who refused to wed, fast upon the most delicate morsels, *bouder* the Court when neglected by her Jupiter-cousin the King, and cultivate such remains of beauty as still lingered on her oval face and almond-shaped blue eyes.

At Choisy all was formal, to suit the taste of its mistress. The *corps de logis*, a pavilion in one story, a mass of lofty windows, was flanked on either side by conservatories and orangeries which masked the offices. Within, the entire south front was occupied by a gallery, with frescoed ceiling and cornice; the walls covered with crimson satin, on which hung the family portraits of *La Grande Mademoiselle*. Each name was written under each portrait, so that all persons looking on them might read the lofty lineage of this grand-daughter of Henry the Great. At one extremity of the gallery was a chapel, at the other a writing-cabinet. Here, the victories and conquests of Louis XIV., painted in miniature, by Van der Meulen, were arranged. These miniatures also were inscribed with names and dates. A likeness of his Majesty on horseback, when a youth, hung over the chimney-piece. Beyond the writing-cabinet was a billiard-room, as well as a suite of private apartments devoted to the use of the Princess herself. Without, broad terraces were balanced by flights of steps, statues, vases, and trophies; *jets d'eau* rose out of marble basins, and precisely arranged flowers and orange-trees adorned the walks. There was a park of a hundred acres, with woods on either hand, trimmed to an exact resemblance of each other. Choisy, like its mistress, was in perpetual *costume de Cour;* nothing but the river, towards which the gardens sloped, was as nature had made it. Not even *La Grande Mademoiselle* could prevent the soft summer breezes from rippling its silvery current, the sun from playing vagrant pranks upon its wavelets, or the water-lilies from growing in wild profusion under the shadow of its tree-shrouded bays.

Besides Choisy, Mademoiselle possessed the Palace of the Luxembourg, before-mentioned, the Castles of Eu, d'Aumale, De Thiers, Dombes, Chatellerault, and Saint-Fargeau, each surrounded by such vast estates, that no one except the well-known *Marquis de Carrabas* ever had the like.

Mademoiselle, although firmly convinced that the world was, in great measure, created for her particular enjoyment, was wonderfully exercised in her mind at the difficulty she experienced in securing that much-coveted game (for which she had hunted all her life), an emperor, or even a king. She, however, appeased her wounded vanity by the conviction that she must be considered too masculine in understanding to consort with any living sovereign. Whatever happened, this royal lady never by any possibility could blame herself.

About this time, a Gascon gentleman of the Caumont family, whose name has been already casually mentioned, began to make much noise at Court. He was Captain of the Royal Guards, whose service was the special care of his Majesty's person, and Field-Marshal, also Governor of Berry. Loaded with honours, he had dropped the undistinguished patronymic of Peguillem altogether, and was known as the Comte de Lauzun. The King, whose understanding was, as a matter of course, superior to every one, had said when he was first presented to him at the Comtesse de Soisson's, that "Lauzun possessed more wit and penetration than any man in France." This opinion was accepted as law. That Lauzun was, by reason of his Gascon blood, cunning, heartless, and mercenary, as well as audacious, insinuating, and brave, is only saying that he was what all Gascons (going up to Court to make their fortunes) were. But that he was above the ordinary hungry adventurer, the sequel will show. Holding Court trumps in his hand, he knew how to play them well. He was a little man, slight and well formed, with a dull, fair complexion, reddish hair, keen penetrating grey eyes, and a most insolent bearing. No one could call him handsome, no one could deny that he could be morose, vindictive, and cruel. He spoke sharp, hard words, affected a certain soldierly swagger, and was capable of being alike cringing and impertinent.

Mademoiselle was no longer young. The unsuccessful chase after an emperor had occupied a large portion of her life. She lived at Court, and was necessarily thrown much into the company of Lauzun, who affected an indifference towards her, a rough and ready manner that piqued her vanity. So she came gradually (no crowned head appearing in the matrimonial horizon, only relays of dukes and insignificant princes) to find Lauzun fascinating and original. The pleasures of the Court palled upon her; she became pensive, even sentimental, and often retired to bowery Choisy to meditate on the chances and changes of life.

Finally she came to the conclusion that marriage alone would restore her spirits. But marriage without an emperor? It was a great come down, certainly. Yet there are no laws but the laws of passion in the kingdom of love. Mademoiselle reasoned that her sublimity was so exalted she could raise any man to her own level. In a word, she discovered that all earthly bliss depended on her marriage with Monsieur de Lauzun.

Now Mademoiselle was, as we have seen, a very determined, even masculine, lady. She had pointed the guns of the Bastille against her cousin the King; she had all but led an army into the battle-field. Having come to a determination, she proceeded in-

continently to carry it out. But she encountered un-
contemplated difficulties. The crafty Lauzun, who
read her like a book, became suddenly respectful and
silent. As she approached, he receded. Mademoiselle
was extremely embarrassed, and more violently in love
than ever. This was precisely what Lauzun intended.

We are in the Queen's apartments at the Louvre,
within a stately retiring-room. The walls are covered
with white brocade, on which is a gold pattern.
They are panelled by gilt scroll work. On the carved
ceiling, which is supported by pilasters, is painted
Apollo ushering in the day. The furniture is of
green damask; colossal chandeliers of crystal and gilt
bronze are reflected in mirrors placed at either end.
Over the mantelpiece, which is carved and richly gilt,
hangs a portrait of the King.

Mademoiselle, attended by her lady of honour,
enters about the time of the Queen's lever. She finds
Lauzun in a corner talking with the Comtesse de
Guiche. He takes no notice of her, though she gives
a slight cough to attract his attention. She does not
like it. Besides not saluting her, which he ought to
have done, he seems quite to have thrown off his
usual *insouciance*, and to find the conversation of the
Comtesse de Guiche much too interesting. Mademoiselle retires into the recess of a window, and watches
him.

Lauzun continues talking with unaccustomed eagerness. He still takes no notice whatever of Mademoiselle; her royal highness has therefore to wait—yes,
actually to wait; a thing she has never done in her
life before to an inferior—until he has done talking.

But when he does approach her, he advances with

such a noble air, he is in her eyes so handsome, that "To me," she says in her memoirs, "he seemed the very master of the world." Not only does she forgive him, but her whole heart goes out to meet him, and her pulses throb violently—so violently, indeed, she is obliged to wait for a moment ere she can address him.

Lauzun makes her a ceremonious bow, places his hand on his embroidered waistcoat and point-lace *jabot*, at the place where, if he had one, his heart would have been, casts down his eyes, and awaits her pleasure.

Now, it must be specially borne in mind that Mademoiselle, much against her will, may be now called "*an old maid*," which condition may reasonably excuse her ardour.

"I flatter myself, Count," she says—blushing at her own backwardness, yet infinitely gratified at the same time by Lauzun's attitude of respectful attention—"I flatter myself you take some interest in me." She looks up, expecting some outburst of protestation at the studied humility of her language. Lauzun, his hand still resting somewhere in the region of where his heart ought to be, bows again, but does not reply. "You are a faithful friend, I know, Monsieur de Lauzun," continues Mademoiselle, confused at his perfect composure, and evolving in her own mind the impossibility of saying all that she desires if he continues silent. "You are, too, a man of the world—" she hesitates. Still Lauzun is mute. "Even his Majesty has the highest respect for your judgment." Again she pauses, flushes crimson, not only on her cheeks, but over her well-formed neck and snowy shoulders. Lauzun **makes** a slight inclination, but otherwise maintains the **same** attitude. Mademoiselle's voice, ordinarily rather shrill and loud, is low and persuasive. She looks at him inquiringly, and stretches out both her hands as if to claim his special attention to what she **is** about to **say**. Lauzun **appears** not to observe her anxiety, **and** fixes his eyes **on the** ground. "**Will you favour me** with your advice, Monsieur de Lauzun? **I shall esteem it** a great kindness." Her tone is almost one of supplication.

"**I** am deeply sensible of the honour your highness does me," replies Lauzun, disengaging his hand from his waistcoat, and again bowing, this time very stiffly. "On what subject **may I** venture **to** advise your royal highness?"

Mademoiselle is conscious she has something very extraordinary to say. She hoped that, seeing her evident perplexity, Lauzun would have helped her. Not a bit. She must trust entirely **to** herself. Her pride comes **to** her help. She remembers who she is, draws herself up, steadies her voice, and takes a few steps nearer to where he is standing.

"**It** is a very delicate subject, Monsieur de Lauzun; **nothing** but **my confidence** in your honour and your **discretion would otherwise** induce me to broach it. But——" **and she falters.**

Lauzun does not stir, only with the slightest perceptible motion he **raises** his eyebrows, which Mademoiselle perceives, and, fearing that **he** is impatient, speaks quickly.

"Do you know—can you tell me——" here she **pauses;** then observing that he makes **a** hasty gesture, **she** forces herself to proceed—"you, Monsieur de

Lauzun, who are the confidant of the King, can you tell me whom he purposes me to marry?"

Having said thus much she is so overcome she would like to sink into a chair. There is none at hand; besides, she dare not leave Lauzun, so eager is she for his reply.

He raises his head and fixes his deep-set eyes upon her with a bold, cold gaze.

"I assure you, madame, I am absolutely ignorant of his Majesty's pleasure in this matter. I am persuaded, however, from what I know of the elevation of his sentiments on all subjects, that he would desire you solely to follow your own inclination." A malicious twinkle comes into his eye, and he smiles almost as it seems in mockery.

Mademoiselle becomes more and more discomposed. Never had an interview been so difficult to manage. "Surely," she thinks, "Lauzun is not laughing at me!" Yet she is too much in love to drop a conversation which she is determined shall lead to an explanation of his feelings towards herself. All this Lauzun is aware of; he rejoices in intensifying her perplexity.

"Monsieur de Lauzun," she says timidly, playing with one of the soft curls that falls upon her neck, "I hoped you could have told me. I earnestly desire your acquiescence in the choice I am about to make. You must necessarily be interested in it."

An appealing look comes into her face; but she tries in vain to catch Lauzun's eye. "At my age," and she sighs profoundly, "persons rarely marry contrary to their inclinations. Every crowned head in Europe has solicited my hand. Until lately, however, my heart was free." She sighs again, and gazes implor-

ingly at him. He must understand her, she tells herself, but as his looks are bent on the ground she cannot tell. Lauzun inclines his head, and seems to await
her further communications.

"I have seen no one to please me until lately,"
she goes on to say; "I love my country, Monsieur de
Lauzun; I think I could only be happy with a countryman—one—" (something rises in her throat, and
stops her utterance; she clears her voice)—"one whom
I know well—whom I esteem—whose person and
manners are agreeable to me; one with a high place
at Court, and who possesses the esteem of my cousin,
the King." All this is spoken significantly and with
marked emphasis.

A delicious glow runs through her frame. Breathlessly she awaits his reply.

"Your highness speaks with admirable sense," answers Lauzun with great deliberation. "How many illustrious persons about the Court would be honoured
by knowing your gracious sentiments. Permit me,
madame, to make them public."

"Not for the world, Monsieur de Lauzun," exclaims
Mademoiselle hurriedly. "I am speaking to you strictly
in confidence." Her countenance has fallen, and she
has turned very white. Lauzun watches her under his
eyelids, and enjoys her sufferings.

"Why should one so happy as your highness
marry at all?" he adds, seeing that she does not
speak.

"I am happy, certainly, if riches and royal birth
can confer happiness," she replies thoughtfully; "but
there are drawbacks, Monsieur de Lauzun. I wish to
confer my wealth upon a worthy individual."

("Myself, for instance," says Lauzun to himself; "I shall be delighted to spend it; indeed, I intend to do so.")

"Many people," continues Mademoiselle, "at this very moment wish me dead in order to inherit it," and a sigh escapes her. "I am very lonely, Monsieur de Lauzun, very lonely." Her face assumes a melting expression, such as he had never seen on it before. What could she say to make him understand her? Thinking of this she sighs again very audibly. Lauzun knits his brows and affects to be lost in thought.

"That is a most serious consideration, your highness. I admit it had not before occurred to me. Permit me time to consider of it before I tender any further advice."

A thousand hopes rush into Mademoiselle's mind. "He understands me," she tells herself, "but my exalted position alarms him. He will propose to me when next we meet."

At this moment the Queen entered the withdrawing-room.

CHAPTER XXIV.

A Fair Suitor.

THE following evening at her Majesty's circle Lauzun approaches Mademoiselle. A smile is on his face, and his manner is less formal. Mademoiselle seats herself apart in a recess, and signs to him to place himself beside her. "Now, now, he will speak," she repeats to herself.

"Are you prepared, M. de Lauzun, to give me your opinion on my approaching marriage?" The tone of her voice is low and sweet; her hand falls near his; he draws a little back.

"Believe me, madame, each word you have uttered is graven on my heart. I have founded many *châteaux d'Espagne* on them."

Mademoiselle is enchanted. "This is the moment," thinks she. She grows hot and cold by turns, and with difficulty conceals her delight.

"Pray speak to me with frankness, Count. I want to discuss with you the most important event of my life—my marriage."

"I am deeply gratified at being appointed president of your council, madame." Lauzun's manner suddenly changes. He is all at once disagreeable, stiff, and supercilious. He settles his ruffles over his hands, and pulls at his moustache. "Allow me to say, however, that no one in the world could enter into this delicate matter with more profound respect for you than myself."

Mademoiselle is strangely baffled; spite of herself the conversation is drifting away, she knows not whither. She cannot decide if Lauzun is gratified or offended at her advances—a strange dilemma for a love-sick princess worth many millions!

"Pray, Count, let us resume our discussion of your own opinion on the matter in question. Do you advise me to marry?"

"Your merit, madame, is so great, I know no one worthy of you." He speaks with the utmost indifference. "Why resign your present brilliant position?" he adds.

"Is he mocking me?" she thinks, "or is he bashful?" As this doubt presents itself, Mademoiselle's

heart sinks within her. "What can I say to make him
understand me?" she murmurs. When she next speaks
a slight asperity is apparent in her tone. She is not
used to be trifled with; she cannot brook it even from
Lauzun. She rises impatiently.

"I beg you will remember, Monsieur de Lauzun,
that I consider no sacrifice too great to ensure me the
husband I have described to you."

Lauzan feels that he may go too far; he instantly
assumes a look of intense humility.

"Such a man as you describe, madame, ought to
esteem himself supremely blest. He should love you
more than life!" He speaks with enthusiasm. Mademoiselle thrills with rapture; her cheeks mantle with
blushes. "At last the moment is come," she thinks.
She reseats herself and turns, with breathless impatience, towards Lauzun, who meets her ardent gaze.
Lauzun instantly checks himself; the cold look is again
on his face.

"Where will you find such a man?" he says.
"Will your highness permit me to search for one?"

"Monsieur de Lauzun, if you are in earnest you
need not search long," she replies significantly.
Could she then have caught his eye, all would have
been told.

"Pray inform me on whom your choice has fallen,
madame? We may both have fixed on the same
person."

Had she dared she would have openly named
himself, but he is suddenly grown so cold and distant, she is utterly discomfited. Lauzun crosses his
arms on his breast and falls into a muse.

"Have you ever, madame, contemplated the advantages of becoming a nun?" he asks abruptly. "Devotion is often the refuge of single women."

Mademoiselle is aghast. Her hands drop helplessly to her side, her head sinks on her bosom.

"Good heavens!" she thinks, "what evil fortune pursues me? Will no man ever understand I love him?"

"Upon the whole, madame, I advise you to remain as you are." Lauzun's voice is harsh, his sallow face is flushed. He is conscious of the difficulty of his position, with an ardent princess beside him, whose passion must be irritated to the utmost in order to induce her to overleap all obstacles. "It is too soon to yield," he thinks.

"I have the honour to tell you, Monsieur de Lauzun, I have selected marriage," rejoins Mademoiselle haughtily. She is fast losing her temper. Lauzun instantly assumes a deeply penitent air.

"For myself," he says meekly, "my only pleasure is in the service of his Majesty. I am fit for nothing else." As he speaks his dejected look sends a pang to her heart. "If I leave his Majesty, it will be——" he stops, Mademoiselle listens breathlessly—"it will be to enter a monastery. Nothing but my attachment to my royal master restrains me."

"Blessed Virgin!" ejaculates Mademoiselle, clasping her hands. "Who could have believed it?"

"I shall never marry," continues Lauzun. He hangs down his head, apparently overcome with despondency.

"How?—Why?" demands Mademoiselle eagerly. "For what reason?"

"Marriage has often been proposed to me, your highness, but there are insurmountable difficulties."

"Name them, I entreat you," she cries imperiously.

"My wife, madame, must be a paragon of virtue, or I should murder her. I dread the morals of the Court. Not the wealth of the Indies would tempt **me to** marry and to doubt. I would not unite myself to a princess of the blood, under such conditions."

"Noble **heart!**" exclaims Mademoiselle aside. "You can **very** easily find the virtuous lady you seek," she **adds** aloud, in a voice tremulous with suppressed passion. She turns towards Lauzun, and for a moment touches his hand which lies close to her own. "My choice is made," she adds resolutely. "I shall announce it to his Majesty to-morrow."

"For heaven's sake, forbear!" exclaims Lauzun, with real earnestness, starting to his feet; "you make me tremble. You must say nothing. It concerns my honour, madame," and he smote upon his breast. Mademoiselle turns her glowing eyes upon him. "My honour as your adviser, madame, I mean," adds Lauzun, correcting himself and speaking in an altered **tone.** But all his self-command could not wholly conceal the triumph he felt at having so successfully acted his part. "As your adviser, madame, I forbid you to speak to the King. The time is not yet come. (I hold her," he says to himself, "she is mine!")

At this moment a page enters and desires him to join **his** Majesty, who is walking up and down in the quadrangle with some gentlemen. Mademoiselle is as much at a loss as ever to make Lauzun understand her. Just as a crisis approaches, they are always interrupted. She longs to ask him why she should **not** tell the King? Once **or** twice she tried to do **so, but** Lauzun invariably turned the conversation into such **a** channel **as** effectually silenced Mademoiselle, **who** spite of her pride was easily abashed.

At last she hits **upon** an expedient.

"**I have the name** of **my** intended written on this slip **of paper, Monsieur de Lauzun,**" she says, and she offers **him a sealed note at their** next meeting.*

Lauzun draws back, stares **at** her, and frowns. "**I** do not **wish to** take the note, madame. I feel that it forebodes me misfortune, my heart beats so violently." Still he stretches out his hand and takes the paper which she offers.

This takes place in the morning, **at** the Queen's **lever.** Maria Theresa is **on** her way **to mass,** accompanied by Mademoiselle, **who is in a state of** indescribable perturbation. She **had** seen Lauzun open the **note,** and read the paper, on **which** is written the magic words, "*It is you.*"

This great princess, arrived **at** a mature age, and as proud as Lucifer, trembles like a leaf during mass, **and** requires all the restraints of etiquette to hide the **tumult** of her feelings. After mass the Queen goes to visit the Dauphin, who is ailing. Mademoiselle awaits her **return in a** gallery outside. Lauzun is there. He leans against the chimney-piece, lost in thought. A bright fire of logs is burning **on** the hearth. His countenance betrays nothing. **He** neither seeks nor avoids **her.** Mademoiselle rubs her hands, advances **to** the fire and shivers.

"**I am** paralyzed with cold," she says, in a soft

voice. She bends over the fire. Lauzun bows and
retires some steps to make room for her.

"I am more paralyzed than your highness," he
says stiffly, looking round to see that no one is near.
His face is inscrutable. "I have read the note you
did me the honour to place in my hands. I am not,
however, so foolish as to fall into such a snare; your
highness is amusing yourself at my expense. You
conceal the real name of your intended husband and
substitute mine. You do this to mortify me. You
are very cruel." He gives her a stealthy look. Mademoiselle staggers backwards; she supports herself
against a chair. She does not know whether to laugh
or cry. Then feeling that the moment so longed for
is come, she collects herself and speaks with dignity.

"I assure you, Monsieur de Lauzun, the name you
have read on that paper, is the name of the man I
mean to marry."

Lauzun shakes his head incredulously.

"Not only so, Monsieur de Lauzun, but I intend
immediately informing the King of my intention,
unless," adds she, in a tender voice, "you forbid me."
She would have liked to have gathered into one glance
all the love she felt for him. To have told him her
passionate admiration for his person, her respect for
his magnanimity in rejecting the splendid position she
offered him. She would have liked to do this; but,
in the face of such exalted independence, her womanly
delicacy takes alarm. She can neither look at him
nor utter a single word.

"Madame," says Lauzun at length, addressing her
with the utmost solemnity, "you have ill recompensed
the zeal I have shown for you. Henceforth, I can

approach you no more. Great as is my respect for your highness, I cannot permit myself to be exposed to ridicule. You are, madame, making me the butt of the whole Court."

Mademoiselle starts violently, then she places her hand upon his arm. "Lauzun," she says, and her voice sinks into a tone of the humblest entreaty, "I beseech you to understand me. My resolution may seem hasty, but your great qualities excuse it. I have made up my mind. I shall ask his Majesty's permission to marry you."

At last she has spoken! The woman has overcome the princess. Lauzun stands before her with downcast eyes—a victim, as it seems, to his own perfection. The time was now come that he must coquet no more. Placing his hand on his heart, he made her a deep obeisance.

"But, madame, I am only a Gascon gentleman. None but a sovereign is a fit consort for your highness."

"I will make you a prince, Count," rejoins she, with a tender look. "I will create you Duc de Montpensier. I have wealth and dignities; both are yours."

Her eyes sparkle, her cheeks burn. An air of mingled power, pride, love, and exultation overspreads her face. Her tall figure is raised to its full height; she clasps the hand of Lauzun; he raises it to his lips.

"Your highness overwhelms me," he whispers, with genuine feeling. For an instant, Lauzun—the cold, heartless Lauzun—felt her influence. Could he really love this exalted lady, who had thus honoured him? He looks fixedly into her face, now transfigured by the deep passions that stirred her inmost soul. Could

he love her? He, a penniless cadet, of an insignificant
name? Etiquette set at defiance, a princess at his feet,
enormous wealth, a royal dukedom in his grasp! Could
he love her?—For a moment a rush of wild thoughts
whirls through his brain. She worships him. He
could make her life a long enchantment. He was
about to kneel to her, to thank her, even to press her
in his arms. But he stops and steadies himself. No
—she is too old; wrinkles gather about her mouth,
her fair hair is partly grey, the bloom has long faded
from her cheeks, the fire of youth from her eye. What
is she but an old maid, inflamed by a furious passion
for a man greatly younger than herself? Should he,
the brilliant Lauzun, burn incense on the altar of such
an idol? Impossible. He would be the laughing-stock
of the Court! His lively imagination grasps the whole
situation in an instant. Lauzun's baser nature conquered. The momentary warmth fades out of his heart
for ever. He heaves a sigh of relief.

"Monsieur de Lauzun," says Mademoiselle, far too
much occupied with her own raptures to heed or to
understand what was passing in his mind, "you sigh.
Fear nothing; I will obtain his Majesty's permission
for our speedy marriage."

Would Louis XIV. consent to the marriage of his
cousin-german with a simple gentleman? Would
Madame de Montespan, with whom Lauzun had intrigued, fall into this arrangement, or would she use
her all-powerful influence against it? These are awful
questions. Lauzun's blood ran cold when he thinks
of it. Madame de Montespan is treacherous, and as
vindictive and clever as himself. Louvois, too, the
minister, is his enemy.

Mademoiselle, however, ignorant of these dangers, acted without a moment's hesitation. She wrote a long letter to the King, announcing her choice, and asking for his consent. Lauzun saw and approved the letter. It was then confided to Bontemps, who carried it to his Majesty.

Louis did not vouchsafe an immediate answer. He sent word to his cousin that she had better reflect well upon what she was about to do. But the countenance of the royal Jupiter beamed upon his favourite Lauzun with undiminished warmth, and he was most affectionate to his cousin. Both naturally drew favourable auguries. Mademoiselle was now steeped in the sweets of an acknowledged passion. Lauzun condescended to be gracious, spite of some little eccentricities such as not always approaching her, or even replying to her when she addressed him — eccentricities attributed by her to his great modesty and discretion. Still, the King had not given his consent.

One evening his Majesty played late at ecarté, so late indeed that it was two o'clock, and he was still at the table. Mademoiselle sat nodding on a brocaded fauteuil beside the Queen. She was determined to see every one out, and to speak to her royal cousin.

She longed so much to salute her lover Duc de Montpensier; to behold him raised to the Olympian circle that surrounded the family god. She longed for many things; life had of late become a delightful mystery to her. Each day unfolded some link in that delicious chain that bound her for ever to her adored Lauzun!

At last the Queen rose. As she passed by she whispered to Mademoiselle — "You must have some

very important business with the King to remain so
late. I can sit up no longer."

"Madame," she replied, rising, "it is a matter of
life and death to me. If I succeed it will be announced at the council to-morrow morning."

"Well, my cousin," said the poor Queen, who never
understood anything that was going on, and was
not intended to do so, "I wish you all success. Good
night."

By-and-by Louis left off playing. He rose, and
walked up to Mademoiselle. "What, cousin, you are
still here? You did not accompany her Majesty? Do
you know the time? It is two o'clock."

"Sire, I wish to speak a few words to you."

The King yawned, gave a glance towards the door,
then leant wearily against the wall. "Excuse me for
to-night, cousin," said he; "I am tired."

"I shall not be long," urged Mademoiselle; "but
do be seated, or I feel I cannot address you properly."

"No, I am very well thus. Speak, my cousin. I
am all attention."

This was an awful moment. Mademoiselle's heart
thumped audibly against her side. Her throat became
so parched no words would come.

"Sire," she began, and her voice failed her. The
King watched her; he had seen a good deal of women
by this time, and understood their ways. He knew
she was about to speak to him of Lauzun, and smiled.

"Take time, my cousin," said he graciously; "you
are agitated; take time."

"Sire," again began poor Mademoiselle—fortunately her voice now came to her, and she continued
—"I want to tell you that the resolution I had the

honour of submitting to your Majesty respecting the Comte de Lauzun is unshaken. I shall never be happy unless I am his wife."

"Yet, my cousin, you have hitherto been most severe on those princesses who have married beneath their rank—your step-sister, Madame de Guise, for example. Lauzun is certainly the most complete grand seigneur of my Court; but I still advise you to reflect well upon the step you are taking. I do not wish to constrain you."

Mademoiselle clasped her hands; her face beamed.

"I love and esteem you beyond measure, my cousin," added Louis, taking her hands in his. "I shall rejoice to have you always about my person. But be careful; Lauzun has many enemies. I do not forbid you; but remember, a sovereign is often forced to act against his will. This intended marriage is now little known; do not give time for all the world to discuss it. Let me warn you and Lauzun to be cautious; above all, lose no time, my cousin. Take my advice, lose no time."

"Oh, Sire!" exclaimed Mademoiselle in an ecstasy, "if you are with us, who can be against us?"

Louis embraced her, and they parted.

Any one less infatuated than Mademoiselle, less arrogant than Lauzun, would have understood the King's friendly caution, "*to lose no time.*" But they were both too intoxicated with their different feelings to heed the advice of the really well-meaning Louis. Lauzun lost his head completely. He accepted, day after day, the magnificent presents sent him by Mademoiselle. He ordered fresh equipages, horses, jewels and plate. He was created Duc de Montpensier. He shrank from the amorous ardour of the doting Princess, but he gloried in her munificence. Still unmarried, he revelled in it without a drawback! He was a mean, selfish fellow, Monsieur de Lauzun, like all men who marry heiresses they do not care for. The words of warning came again, and this time to his ear. "*Marry while you can*," was said to him. Mademoiselle, still enacting the masculine part, urged an early day, but she urged in vain.

CHAPTER XXV.

Under a Couch.

ABOUT this time Lauzun, soon to become cousin-german to the King, solicited the distinguished post of Grand Master of the Artillery. Already he commanded the Dragoons, and was captain of the hundred gentlemen pensioners who guarded the person of the Sovereign; but this was not enough. The King readily promised him the appointment; but time went on, and no warrant came. Lauzun grew uneasy—specially as each time he recalled the subject the King evidently evaded it. What did this mean? Who was his enemy? He spoke to the favourite, Madame de Montespan, although he was well aware he had given her good cause for hating him. Madame de Montespan, with the most winning smiles, promised him her assistance. Still no warrant came. Again Lauzun ventured to recall his promise to the King at his lever, while handing him his feathered hat and cane. Louis turned away his head, addressed the Duc de Roquelaure, and affected not to hear him. There was treachery somewhere! Lauzun shrewdly suspected Madame de Montespan.

He would know for certain that very day, and if it were so he would unmask her. He offered a heavy bribe to one of her confidential attendants, well known to him in the days of their *liaison*, and prevailed on her to introduce him into the saloon, where the King would visit Madame de Montespan before supper, that very afternoon. Louis, who told his mistress everything, and consulted her about all important appointments, would be sure to mention Lauzun's renewed application of that morning. At all events Lauzun would chance it. He knew the lady was from home, having seen her start, in company with the Queen and Mademoiselle de Montpensier, for a drive to Saint-Cloud. He had handed his betrothed into the royal coach. No sooner had they started than Lauzun was admitted into Madame de Montespan's apartments by her friendly attendant. She assisted him in his arrangements, and finally concealed him under a large couch covered with fine tapestry, on which Madame de Montespan usually sat. It was an undignified proceeding. He had to divest himself of his periwig and plumed hat, take off his richly embroidered satin coat, tuck up his shirt sleeves, and crouch upon his hands and knees on the dusty floor. But these are trifles to a man bent upon revenge!

Shortly before the hour of supper, which their Majesties eat in public, Lauzun recognized Madame de Montespan's voice within her boudoir. Then he heard steps approaching. He could swear to the King's solemn tread and the sound of his cane tapping on the floor.

Almost before he could settle himself in the best position for listening the King was announced. At the same moment Madame de Montespan entered from her boudoir on the other side of the saloon. He heard her advance to the door and receive the King. She kissed his hand; Louis saluted her on both cheeks, and led her to the couch under which Lauzun lay concealed.

"Your Majesty looks vexed this afternoon," said Madame de Montespan in a softly modulated voice. "What has happened?"

"I am exceedingly annoyed about that affair of Lauzun," replied Louis, seating himself in an arm-chair. "He has again applied to me about the Artillery this morning."

Madame de Montespan leant back indolently among the cushions, little dreaming who was crouching beneath so near her, and placed her feet upon an embroidered stool. A feather fan hung at her side, and as the weather was warm she took it up and moved it languidly to and fro, gazing absently at the King, who awaited her reply.

"Did you hear what I said, Athanaise? I am annoyed about Lauzun."

"I heard, Sire; but what can I say? You already know my opinion on that subject. Need I repeat it?"

This was said in a careless manner, as she sank back deeper among the cushions.

(Lauzun was all ears. "She has given her opinion then," he said to himself. "I think I can guess what it was.")

"I promised Lauzun the place, remember," continued the King. "He certainly merits it; but your friend Louvois will not hear of his appointment. He torments me every time I see him to give the Artillery to the Comte de Lude."

"I certainly advise you," returned the lady, glancing at herself in an opposite mirror and arranging the fringe of small curls that lay on her forehead, "to be guided by the advice of so experienced a minister as Louvois, rather than listen to such an empty-headed coxcomb as Lauzun."

("Ah, that is the opinion you have of me, is it?" muttered Lauzun. "Now I know you, you traitress!")

"But remember, Athanaise," said the King, taking out his snuff-box and applying the powder to his nose with great deliberation—"remember his attachment to me, his courage."

"His attachment to you, Sire!" and Madame de Montespan smiled ironically. "Do you believe in it?"

"Certainly. Then my word——"

"Bah! your word—that is nothing. Withdraw it."

("Ah! fiend," exclaimed Lauzun in a low voice, clenching his fists as well as his position allowed him; "this is the way you plead my cause, is it? Curses on you!")

"You need not fear for Lauzun," continued the lady blandly. "Mademoiselle will take care of his interests—the old fool!"

Madame de Montespan, in imitation of *La Grande Mademoiselle*, bridled, simpered, craned her neck, rounded her elbows, and stared superciliously under her eyelids. Louis laughed.

"Spare my poor cousin, Marquise. She is eminently ridiculous; but I love her sincerely. Her genuine affection for Lauzun touches me."

"For my part, Sire, I cannot understand how any woman can care for him. He is such a *petit maître*—ill-made, short, with a complexion like a lemon—altogether detestable. Not a man to my taste, certainly," added she contemptuously, at the same time casting a flattering glance at the King, as much as to say, in his presence no other man could possibly be thought of. The King understood the glance and the compliment, and smiled upon her.

"The ladies are not on your side, however," returned he. "They all adore Lauzun. But about this command of Artillery—to whom am I to give it?"

("Now I shall know all the depths of your treachery, Athanaise de Montespan!" said Lauzun half aloud to himself from under the couch.)

"Did any one speak?" asked the King quickly. "I thought I heard a voice."

(Lauzun bit his lips with vexation.)

"It must be my parrot, Sire," answered Madame de Montespan.—"In giving away so important a post you ought certainly to consult the welfare of France. All personal considerations should be sacrificed." De Montespan spoke pompously.

("*Sacré Dieu!*" murmured Lauzun. "She is a female Judas!")

"What can the welfare of France have to do with this appointment?" asked the King, smiling.

("That is what I want to know too," whispered Lauzun. "Speak, serpent!")

"No man in France is better adapted to fill this post than Lauzun," added Louis gravely.

"How?" cried Madame de Montespan, sitting upright, and speaking in a shrill voice and with much animation, as the King seemed to vacillate. "How, Sire? Can you forget that dissensions between Louvois offended, and Lauzun imperious, (and you know, Sire, his overbearing temper, and how audacious he can be), must be exceedingly prejudicial to the State?"

"Spoken like an oracle!" exclaimed the King, looking admiringly at her. "What a head you have for business, madame! You are as beautiful as Venus, and as wise as Minerva!"

"Your Majesty flatters me," replied the lady, casting an enamoured glance at him. "I only observe what is perfectly plain. I am sure your Majesty's penetration must have arrived at this conclusion already. Remember, Louvois may resign, if you affront him," continued she, fixing her bright eyes on Louis.

"Now, all the fates prevent it!" cried Louis with alarm. "I should be lost without Louvois."

"Then you must at once refuse Lauzun!" cried De Montespan with decision.

("By heaven, I will be revenged!" muttered Lauzun, stung with sudden rage at her perfidy, in a louder voice than he was aware of.)

"Now I am certain I heard some one speak!" exclaimed the King, frowning, and turning his ear towards the spot from which the sound came. He paused to listen. "Athanaise," said he, rising, and looking suspiciously at Madame de Montespan, "this is very strange. I demand an explanation." His Olympian brow was knit.

"Your Majesty is mistaken, you only heard my parrot in the ante-room. Surely you do not doubt me, Sire!" added she in a tearful voice, putting her handkerchief to her eyes. "Such an insult would kill me." Her bosom heaved. "Oh, Louis, you cannot love me if you entertain such unworthy suspicions." Sobs, real or false, here stifled her voice.

Meanwhile Louis rose hastily, and looked into the corners and behind all the cabinets, as if determined to make a thorough investigation of the whole room. This would have rendered Lauzun's position desperate. He positively shook with terror. Madame de Montespan still sobbed, her handkerchief pressed to her eyes.

The King took a few turns up and down the saloon, brandished his cane, and moved some chairs. The noise he made roused the parrot in the next room into a fury. It screeched so loud that for a time nothing else could be heard.

Finding no one, Louis, rather embarrassed, placed himself at a window. He looked back at the beautiful woman still weeping on the settee. "Come, no more tears, Athanaise," he said tenderly, approaching her with a penitent look and taking the handkerchief from her face. "Let this kiss seal my pardon. But the voice was really so distinct. I thought for a moment——" Madame de Montespan fixed her eyes reproachfully on him. "Well, no matter. Then you advise me to refuse Lauzun the post he desires?"

"Certainly," returned the lady with decision. She was now quite calm and alive to business.

A knock was heard at the door. Several gentlemen in waiting, attended by pages, entered and announced that supper was served and the Queen already at table.

"I must leave you, my angel," said the King, in a low voice, rising. "It is time you should prepare for the performance of Molière's play in the theatre arranged for to-night. Adieu, my adored Marquise. Forgive my want of courtesy," he whispered in her ear. "But the parrot's voice was so natural.—I will wipe off my fault in any manner you please."

"I ask for nothing, Sire," replied she in the same low tone, "but that you should refuse this place to Lauzun. Do this, and you are forgiven," and her eyes beamed on the King, who, after placing his hat, covered with a plume of snowy ostrich feathers, on his head, raised it, bowed to her, and kissed her hand. Then replacing his hat before he left the room with his attendants, he passed the outer entrance, where the *gardes du corps*, who never left him, presented arms.

Madame de Montespan passed into her closet.

When the saloon was empty, Lauzun, crimson in the face, foaming with rage, and much rumpled in appearance, emerged from his hiding-place. He hastily replaced his wig,—so hastily, indeed, that he put it on awry,—and dragged on his coat with such violence that he tore off the priceless Malines lace ruffles. Oath after oath fell from his lips as he dressed himself. "You shall pay for this, devil of a Marquise! *Morbleu*, I will make you wince!" he muttered—for he dared not speak louder until he had left the room. This he did, closing the doors with the utmost precaution behind him.

The suite of rooms assigned to Madame de Montespan led by a corridor to the landing of the grand marble staircase of the south wing. On the other side and across this landing were the state apartments, situated in the centre of the palace. To reach them Madame de Montespan must pass this corridor. Lauzun

placed himself behind the outer door, and awaited
her. After a long time she appeared. Her hair, just
touched with powder, was sown with diamonds. A
necklace of large single brilliants, linked together with
pearls, lay upon her neck. Her dress was of pink
satin, woven with gold; the low body fitting tightly,
displayed to the utmost advantage her exquisite form.
Her train of violet velvet, bordered by pearls and
passementerie of gold, swept the ground. She was a
miracle of loveliness. Lauzun made her a profound
obeisance. Taking the tips of her fingers within his
hand, he kissed them, and begged permission to be
allowed the honour of escorting her across the landing
to the state apartments. Madame de Montespan smiled;
his delicate attention flattered her vanity. Her anger
was appeased. The gay *sabreur* was returning to his
allegiance. Lauzun was now, too, a personage, as the
betrothed of Mademoiselle, and cousin to be of the
King. She almost repented she had urged the King
so strongly to refuse him the post of Grand Master of
the Artillery.

Lauzun, speaking in the softest and most insinuating voice, now asked her if she had condescended,
during her recent interview with the King, to remember
his humble suit to his Majesty, for which he had recommended himself to her all-powerful influence?

"This very afternoon I have done so," replied she
with the utmost effrontery. "Indeed, I have urged
your claims so strongly upon both his Majesty and
Louvois that I believe you will receive the appointment to-morrow."

"How kind you are!" answered Lauzun, affecting
to smile.

"Yes," returned the lady, "after all my eloquence, Monsieur le Comte, you must be successful," and she gave him one of those glances out of her serpent eyes, whose power she knew so well.

"Delightful!" rejoined Lauzun aloud. "I am quite satisfied." Then, placing his mouth close to her ear, while a Satanic look passed over his face, he hissed out, "Yes, I am satisfied, for now I have fairly unmasked you. You are the greatest liar in his Majesty's dominions!"

As he spoke her arm still lay confidingly on his. In a moment he had seized and crushed it violently. Madame de Montespan gave a piercing scream.

"Yes!" yelled Lauzun, planting himself before her —"yes, I can prove what I say. I have heard every word you said of me to the King. I was present— concealed."

"Ah!" shrieked Madame de Montespan, agonized with pain. She stopped, and leant against the wall for support. A look of real terror came into her face. She turned appealingly toward Lauzun, who stood before her glaring with passion, then, overcome by pain and fright, she staggered, and fainting, or affecting to faint, fell heavily upon the pavement. There Lauzun left her. Without calling for help, he strode rapidly down the grand staircase, and disappeared.

CHAPTER XXVI.
Signing the Marriage Contract.

A DAY is at length fixed. The contract between
Mademoiselle and Lauzun is to be signed at the
Luxembourg Palace. Mademoiselle arrays herself in
the white robe of an affianced bride. Lauzun is beside
her. He is ostentatiously humble; indeed, he had
never been thoroughly civil to her before.

As he enters the boudoir in her private suite of
apartments he salutes her with his grandest air, and
kisses her hand. Mademoiselle cannot take her eyes
off him. Her senile transports are ridiculous; Lauzun
feels that they are.

A table is placed in the centre of the room; at this
table sits Boucherat, notary to her royal highness.
He is dressed in the quaint, clerical robe, white bands,
and short wig that still distinguishes his profession in
France. The marriage contract, of portentous size,
lies open on the table before him. Boucherat, a tall,
spare man, with a singularly doleful expression of
countenance, looks discomposed, coughs several times,
then, finding that no one attends to him, looks up.
Mademoiselle is talking eagerly with Lauzun.

"Your royal highness,—" begins Boucherat, hesitating. "Will you permit me to address you, madame?" he adds in a louder tone, finding Mademoiselle pays no attention to him.

"What is it, my good Boucherat?" asks Mademoiselle, turning round at last towards him.

Boucherat rises to his feet. He bows, standing on
the tips of his toes, then folds his arms. He is purple

in the face, and appears to be suffering acutely, especially as, suddenly unfolding his arms, he rubs them violently together.

Lauzun laughs. Mademoiselle cannot altogether command her countenance.

"I have known your royal highness from a child," says Boucherat hurriedly, as though speaking between spasms of pain. "I have had the honour of serving your illustrious father, Gaston, Duc d'Orléans, as notary before your birth,—exalted lady." Here Boucherat stops, gasps as if going into a fit, wipes his forehead with his handkerchief, and adjusts his wig.

Lauzun roars with laughter, and Mademoiselle contemplates the notary with silent amazement.

"I have the honour to say,—great lady," continues Boucherat spasmodically, "that I have known you from a child. I have always obeyed you, blindly, as was my duty and my pleasure. I have obeyed you now, madame," and he utters a sound between a snort and a groan. "I have at your command drawn up these deeds, as you bade me. But," and he again stops, blows his nose violently, and makes a hideous grimace, "I cannot allow your highness to sign these deeds and contracts without presuming to ask you if you have fully considered their import." Here such a succession of twitches and spasmodic contortions passes over his countenance, that he is scarcely human.

"I have well considered what I am doing, Boucherat," replies Mademoiselle loftily, advancing to the table and taking a pen in her hand.

Lauzun, no longer laughing, stands contemplating Boucherat, with a savage expression.

"Your highness—permit me,"—pursues the notary,

not seeing him. "Is it to be an *entire* donation of the princedom of Dombes, the county of Eu, the dukedom of——"

"Yes, yes, Boucherat, an entire donation," replies Mademoiselle, interrupting him.

She dips the pen into the ink and prepares to sign.

"An *entire* donation, madame?" gasps Boucherat, rising noisily to his feet, then re-seating himself, and repeating this several times in his excitement. "Let me caution your highness——" Another snort and a succession of **loud** coughs silence him.

"This good man will certainly **have a** fit," says Mademoiselle half aloud. "What **can I** do with him? Do not agitate yourself, Boucherat," and she turns towards him. She well knows his great fidelity and attachment to herself. "Have no fear. I know what I am about. I shall never be more mistress of my fortune than when I give it to this gentleman."

She turns round and glances fondly at Lauzun, who is standing behind her. She starts back at the furious expression on his face. He looks diabolical. His eyes are fixed on Boucherat. The pen drops from her hand.

"Believe me, madame, I—I have reason for my caution;" and again all human expression passes from the face of the notary in a succession of the most violent winks.

"How, villain! **what** do you mean?" cries Lauzun, advancing. "I shall break my cane on your back **presently.**"

Boucherat rises, looks for a moment at Lauzun,

then at Mademoiselle, shakes his head, readjusts his wig, and reseats himself.

Mademoiselle had taken the pen—which Lauzun presents to her this time—again in her hand.

"Ah, your highness," groans Boucherat, "I have done my duty. God help and guard you!"

"Are these deeds as I commanded them, Boucherat?"

"Yes, madame; they are a donation, an *entire* donation, of the princedom of Dombes, the——"

"Be silent, scoundrel!" roars Lauzun, "or by heaven I will split your head open."

Boucherat shudders; his eyes seem to turn in his head; a look of horror is on his face.

Mademoiselle draws the parchment towards her.

"I sign here," she says, and she traces her name in a bold, firm hand, "Louise de Montpensier."

While she writes, Boucherat digs his hands into his wig, which, pushed to one side, discloses his bald head. Then with a piteous glance at his mistress, he flings his arms wildly into the air.

"Alas, alas! would I had died before this! the princedom of Dombes gone—the county of Eu gone! Oh, madame!"

"Be silent, madman!" roars Lauzun, "or, *pardieu,* I will throttle you."

* * * * *

The folding-doors leading into the state apartments are now thrown open. Mademoiselle appears, led by the Comte de Lauzun. These state apartments had been decorated by her grandmother, Marie de Medici, who had lived in this palace. The walls are ornamented with delicate arabesques, panelled with golden borders, and painted above in compartments. The vaulted ceilings are divided into various designs, executed by Rubens, illustrating the life of his royal mistress. Around hang the effigies of the Medici and the Bourbons, the common ancestors of Marie de Medici and her granddaughter.

Mademoiselle passes round the brilliant circle which forms itself about her, still holding Lauzun by the hand.

"Permit me," says she, in her stateliest manner, taking her position at the top of the throne-room under a canopy—"Permit me to present to you my future husband, the Duc de Montpensier. Let me beg all of you in future to address him by that title only."

The royal princes present and the great personages of the Court bow their acquiescence. The Maréchal de Bellefonds advances and salutes Mademoiselle.

"Permit me, madame," says he, addressing her, "to congratulate you in the name of your highness's devoted friends. I desire to thank you especially in the name of the nobility of France, whom I represent, for the honour you are conferring on our order by choosing from amongst us a consort to share your dignity. We esteem Monsieur de Lauzun one of the brightest ornaments of the Court; he is worthy of the proud station for which you have selected him."

"I thank you, Maréchal de Bellefonds, and I thank the nobility of France whom you so worthily represent. I thank you from my heart," and Mademoiselle curtseys with royal grace. "No one is so well acquainted as myself with the merit of Monsieur de Lauzun," and she glances proudly at her future husband. "I accept with pleasure the sympathy of his friends."

Lauzun bends, and kisses the hand of his affianced wife.

Then the Maréchal de Charost steps forth from a glittering crowd of officers. Charost is a captain in the royal body-guard.

"I must also thank your highness for the honour you confer on the army of France. My post is now without price; for what would a soldier not give, what sacrifices would he not make, to become the brother-in-arms of the husband of your highness?"

A laugh follows this hearty outburst of enthusiasm. It is scarcely audible, but Mademoiselle instantly suppresses it with a frown. Lauzun is a sacred object in her eyes, and she permits no jests, however flattering, to mix with his name. Turning towards the Maréchal de Charost, she replies with haughty courtesy—

"I thank you, Maréchal, and, in your person I thank the brave army of his Majesty, my cousin."

Before this august company separates it is announced that the marriage contract is to be at once submitted to the King, Queen, the Dauphin, the Duc d'Orléans, and the princes of the blood-royal.

The marriage is to take place next day at Charenton, at the villa of the Marquise de Créqui. The Archbishop of Rheims is to officiate.

CHAPTER XXVII.

Plot and Counterplot.

MEANWHILE, Madame de Montespan expatiated to all the Court on the impossibility of an alliance between Mademoiselle and the Comte de Lauzun. That Lauzun should be received as a prince of the blood would, according to her, for ever lessen that dignity so dear to the heart of the monarch.

Louvois, her creature—some said her lover—spoke more strongly. Not only France, he said, would be eternally disgraced, but his Majesty would be personally censured in every Court in Europe, for permitting one of his nearest relatives thus to demean herself. Monsieur, father of Mademoiselle, declared that such an alliance would be an affront to the memory of his daughter's illustrious grandfather, Henry the Great. Nobles and ministers, incited by Louvois, threw themselves at the King's feet. They implored him not to cloud his glorious reign by consenting to such a *mésalliance*. The poor weak Queen, worked upon by the artifices of the malicious De Montespan, who, as superintendent of her household, was constantly about her person, complained loudly of the insult about to be put upon her circle—she a royal daughter of Spain! All the princesses of the blood joined with her. The cabal was adroitly managed. It attacked the King's weak side. No man was ever such a slave to public opinion, or so scrupulously regardful of appearances, as Louis XIV. To him the *vox populi* was indeed "the voice of God."

About eight o'clock that evening, Mademoiselle

was summoned to the Louvre from the Luxembourg. "Was the King still at cards?" she asked the messenger.

"No; his Majesty was in the apartments of Madame de Montespan, but he desired to see her highness the instant she arrived."

As Mademoiselle drove into the quadrangle, a gentleman in waiting approached her coach, and begged her to enter by another door, leading directly into the private apartments. This mystery seemed to her excited imagination full of evil import. When she reached the King's cabinet, some one ran out by another door. It was Madame de Montespan. The King was sitting over the fire. His head rested on his hand. Mademoiselle stood before him trembling all over.

"My cousin," said the King at length, rising and offering her a seat beside his own, "what I have to tell you makes me wretched."

"Good God! Sire, what is it?" asked Mademoiselle in a hoarse voice. She had turned as white as the dress (that of an affianced bride) she wore. Her eyes were fixed upon the King in a wild stare.

"Calm yourself, my cousin," said Louis solemnly. "It is said by my ministers that I am sacrificing you, my relative, to the interests of my favourite Lauzun. I am also informed that Lauzun declares he does not love you—that it was you who offered yourself to him in marriage!"

Mademoiselle clasped her hands, then pressed them on her forehead. "Not love me?" she cried. "What a base lie! Lauzun tells me he adores me."

"Nevertheless, my cousin, such reports must have

some foundation," resumed the King, speaking with
great gravity. "They compromise me in my royal
person; they tarnish the glory of the Crown of France,
which I wear." His look and manner from grave had
become overbearing and pompous. It was quite evident
that whatever touched his own position he would ruthlessly sacrifice. "My cousin, I have to announce to
you that I cannot permit this marriage." He spoke
in a loud grating voice, raised his eyes to the ceiling,
stroked his chin with his hand, and seemed to swell
with self-consciousness.

A ringing scream was heard from Mademoiselle.
She lay back on her arm-chair motionless.

Having asserted his dignity, and conveyed in
proper terms to his cousin that neither her entreaties
nor her sufferings could for an instant be considered
when they encroached upon his royal state, Louis
relaxed his rigid attitude, condescended to turn his
eyes downwards upon poor Mademoiselle, and in a
voice kind, spite of his sublimity, added—

"I am very sorry for you, my cousin, very sorry.
You have good cause to complain of me; but my
duty as King of France is supreme. I cannot permit
you to espouse the Comte de Lauzun."

"Ah, Sire—" groaned Mademoiselle, in a voice so
choked by agitation it sounded strange in the King's
ears, and made him shudder; (for his selfish nature
instinctively caused him to shrink from every species
of suffering). She held out her hands supplicatingly
towards him, and vainly essayed several times to speak.
"Ah, Sire," she said at last in a voice scarcely audible,
"you cannot withdraw your word—the word of a
King. Consider," and she stopped and burst into an

agony of tears. "Consider, my cousin, no one can have anything to do with my marriage but myself."

No sooner had she uttered these words than Louis drew himself up; the long curls of the full-bottomed wig which covered his shoulders vibrated, and the diamond star he wore on his coat of peach-coloured satin glistened, so sudden had been his action. At the same time, such a stony look came into his hard face, as gave him the aspect of a statue.

"Excuse me, my cousin, my royal dignity, the splendour of my Court, the esteem of every crowned head in Europe are implicated. You seem to forget that you are born a *daughter of France*. But, madame, I remember it, and I shall shield my royal name from dishonour!"

Overcome as was Mademoiselle, she perceived the mistake she had made. Her brain reeled, her limbs quivered convulsively, but she staggered to her feet.

"Oh, Sire, hear me!" she cried. "Let me implore you," and she threw herself before him and clasped his knees, "do not, do not forbid me to marry my beloved Lauzun. No ordinary rule applies to him. Lauzun is good, great, heroic! Oh! who would become a royal position like Lauzun?"

Louis did not reply. Having sufficiently asserted his dignity, he no longer restrained his kindlier feelings. He put his arms round his cousin, and tried to raise her from the ground.

"No, no; let me kneel," cried she passionately, clinging to him, "until you have recalled those dreadful words. Sire, I have ever respected and loved you. I have lived beside you as a sister. Do not—oh! do not make my life desolate. For God's sake, let me spend it with the only man I ever loved! A man so made to love. Kill me! kill me! my cousin," and she wrung her hands convulsively; "but, if I am to live, let me live with Lauzun. I cannot—I will not give him up!"

Louis rose from the arm-chair on which he was seated. He knelt on the floor by her side. He again took her in his arms, and laying her head upon his breast, he soothed her like a child. Big tears rolled down his cheeks. He called her by every endearing name to comfort her. He did all, save consent to her marriage.

Mademoiselle was drowned in tears. Vainly did she, turning her swollen eyes upon the King, who soothed her so fondly, strain her ears to hear that one little word which was to dry them. She listened in vain; that word was never to be spoken. At last, faint with emotion, she signed to the King to raise her up, which he did, placing her on a chair. He kissed her burning forehead, and pressed her dry hands in his.

"My cousin," he said, "do not blame me. Rather blame yourself. Why did you not take my advice? I told you to lose no time. To marry at once. You should have done so. Why did you give me time to reflect—time for others to reflect? You ought to have obeyed me."

Mademoiselle dared not confess that it was Lauzun's fault she had not done so, but at this recollection a fresh burst of grief choked her utterance.

"Alas, Sire," she moaned at last, "when did you ever break your word before? Could I believe you would begin with me? To break your word, too, in such a manner!"

As Louis listened to her, he knit his brows, and looked gloomy and embarrassed.

"I am not my own master," he replied coldly, "in affairs touching my house and the honour of my race."

"Sire, if I do not marry Lauzun," groaned Mademoiselle, almost inaudibly, "I shall die. I never loved any other man. I ask my life of you, cousin. Do not take my life. You are sacrificing me to a court intrigue," she added faintly, catching at his hand, for she was fast losing heart; "but believe me, and let others know, that much as I love and respect your Majesty, and desire to obey you, I will never, never marry another man." Holding the King's hand, she kissed it, and gazed imploringly at him.

"Dear cousin, do not be so unhappy," he replied, at a loss what answer to make to such a home-thrust, which he knew to be so true. "Believe me, your obedience in this matter of Lauzun will make you doubly dear to me. You can command me in all other ways."

"Nothing—nothing can give life a value without Lauzun!" broke in Mademoiselle vehemently.

"My cousin," answered the King gravely, "I cannot permit you to be sacrificed. You are made a tool of. I cannot permit it. Now," he continued, rising,—and with difficulty suppressing a yawn—"you can have nothing more to say to me. I shall not alter my determination."

Mademoiselle wrung her hands, the King drew

her to him, and kissed her on the forehead. As he did so, a tear dropped upon her cheek.

"Oh, Sire!" cried Mademoiselle, "you pity me, and you have the heart to refuse me! You are the master of my fate. Have mercy on me! Do not give heed to others. Ah, Sire, you are destroying me!"

"Come to me to-morrow, my cousin," said Louis soothingly, much affected, but unshaken by her prayers. "Come and tell me you have forgiven me. Now, good night," and again he tenderly embraced her. Then he summoned his attendants to conduct her to her coach.

*   *   *   *   *   *

Lauzun had played deep for a great prize, and he had lost the game. He broke out into savage abuse, and called the King opprobrious names. Absolutely maddened by rage, he rushed to the palace. He was refused admittance. Yet he swore and cursed at the attendants until he forced them to let him pass. Then he strode up-stairs to the apartments of Madame de Montespan. Here he found the King seated by her side.

Louis rose, placed himself in front of the Marquise, and faced him with a look of the gravest displeasure.

"Sire," cried Lauzun, his face swollen with passion, "I am come to ask you what I have done that you should dishonour me?"

"Come, come, Lauzun," replied Louis, still standing before Madame de Montespan; "calm yourself."

Lauzun was too deep in the royal secrets to make an open breach with him either advisable or safe.

"No, Sire," roared Lauzun, emboldened by the

King's calmness; "permit me to say I will *not* calm myself. I will not permit this humiliation. There is my sword," and he drew it from its scabbard; "your Majesty has made me unworthy to wear it. Take it— take my life also."

Lauzun presented his sword. The King put it from him with an imperious gesture.

"Comte de Lauzun," said he with dignity, "I refuse to accept your sword. Let it still be drawn in my service. There is much to wound you in what has passed. I feel deeply for you. But my duty as King of France compels me to act as I have done."

This was a bold assertion in the presence of Madame de Montespan, who sat motionless behind the King, her cheeks blanched at the thought of what revelations Lauzun might make in his rage.

"I will make what recompense I can to you," continued the King. "You shall be raised, Comte de Lauzun, so high that you shall cease to remember this marriage you now so much desire."

"Sire, I will accept no gifts, no honours, from a monarch who has forfeited his word. Ay, Sire, I repeat it deliberately," seeing the King's glance of fury at his insolence, "forfeited his word. Here do I surrender this sword, which your Majesty conferred on me. Here do I break it, Sire, in your face as you have broken your word."

As he spoke, he bent his knee, snapped the blade in two, and violently dashed the fragments on the ground at the King's feet.

"And you, perfidious woman," he continued, addressing Madame de Montespan, "of whom I could reveal so much, whose treachery I have proved—you

who sit there unmoved—behold your handiwork! Do
I not know that it is you, who, for your own wicked
purposes, have influenced my royal master against me?"

Lauzun spoke so rapidly that all this had been
said before Louis could stop him.

"Comte de Lauzun," broke forth the King in a
voice unsteady with passion, "leave me—leave the
palace, I command you. Presume not to insult Madame de Montespan in my presence, or"—and he put
out his hand, grasped the gold-headed cane which lay
beside him, and strode up to where Lauzun stood,
crimson in the face—"or I shall chastise you as you
deserve!" and Louis brandished the stick in the air.

Then, as if thinking better of it, his uplifted arm
dropped to his side, he drew back some steps, flung
away the cane to the farthest corner of the room, and,
with a great effort, collected himself.

"Leave me!" he exclaimed, in a voice he strove
with difficulty to render calm. "Leave me instantly,
while I can still command myself. Go," and he extended his hand with authority, "go, until you learn
how to address your Sovereign."

Notwithstanding these altercations, Mademoiselle
de Montpensier did not leave the Court. She was
gracious to all who approached. She looked happy,
even radiant. Lauzun, also, after a short absence, resumed his service about the King's person. He was
sleek, prosperous, and more haughty than ever. All
this was very strange. That vindictive beauty, Madame
de Montespan, could not understand it. Her vengeance
after all had failed. The matter must be looked into.
Spies were immediately set. Every means of inquiry
the State could command was brought to bear on

Lauzun and the Princess. Their secret was soon discovered. *They were married!*

Madame de Montespan rushed to the King, and announced the tremendous fact. Lauzun was instantly arrested, and imprisoned at Pignerol. Mademoiselle, plunged in the depths of despair, left the Court for her Château of Eu, on the coast of Normandy.

CHAPTER XXVIII.
The Royal Governess.

It was the King's habit, when at Saint-Germain, to hear early mass in the chapel. On his return, he passed through the great gallery in which the Court was assembled, to make their morning salutations to him. There he also received the petitions of all who had sufficient interest to gain admittance. A woman, tall, finely formed, and of ample proportions, with a stealthy glance out of magnificent black eyes, a well-curved mouth, and a composed and dignified bearing, —quite a style to suit the royal taste,—with a black silk scarf edged with lace thrown over her head, and wearing a dress of common materials, but skilfully designed to set off her rounded figure to the best advantage, presented herself before him. In her hand she held a petition, at the top of which, in large letters, was written: "The Widow Scarron most humbly prays his Majesty to grant——"

Louis read no more; his eye was gratified by the petitioner, not by the petition, which he put into his pocket and forgot. But the lady appeared so often, standing in the same place in the gallery of Saint-

Germain, that his Majesty grew weary of her sight. At length he turned his back upon her.

Françoise d'Aubigné, of the Protestant family of that name, had married in her youth the poet Scarron —a dwarf, deformed and bedridden, a lover of loose company, and a writer of looser songs—for her bread. Scarron drew up the marriage contract without the assistance of a notary. The dower of Françoise was as follows. Four pounds a year, two large black eyes, a fine bust, well-shaped hands, and a great deal of *esprit*. Scarron covenanted to contribute the hump upon his back, plenty of brains, and a pension granted to him by the Queen-Regent, Anne of Austria, as *le malade de la Reine*. He regretted he could not offer either hands or feet, both being paralyzed. But he can assure his *fiancée* of a dower which she will gladly accept—*Immortality:* a prediction made in derision, which was strangely justified by events.

In the house of her husband, this enticing daughter of the d'Aubignés learned early "to be all things to all men." She copied her husband's ribald songs for him, she entertained his promiscuous circle of friends — the gross Villarceaux, Ninon de l'Enclos, Mademoiselle de Scuderi, a lady of the highest virtue, but who affected Bohemian society, and many others.

In process of time, Madame Scarron's youth, beauty, and talents opened to her the salon of the Maréchal d'Albret, where she made the acquaintance of Madame de Sevigné, and Madame de Chalais, to become the Princesse des Ursins. She also made a much more important acquaintance in Madame de Montespan.

When Scarron died, she found herself without a resource in the world. The King had disregarded her petition. By her friends' interest she obtained a place in the household of the Princesse de Nemours, affianced to the King of Portugal. Before quitting France, she called on all she knew. Among others, she visited Madame de Montespan. To her she related her ill-success at Saint-Germain.

"Why did you not **come** to me?" asked the **favourite**. "**I** would have protected you. I will even **now take charge of your** petition. I will see that his Majesty **reads it**."

"What!" cried Louis, when he saw the well-known name, "the Widow Scarron again? Why, I am deluged with her petitions. She is become a Court proverb, 'as importunate as the Widow Scarron.' What do you know of the Widow Scarron, Athanaise?"

The petition for the pension was nevertheless granted, and *la Veuve Scarron*, notwithstanding many scandalous reports of the past, was appointed governess to the illegitimate children born to the King and Madame de Montespan. Her devotion to her charges was extraordinary. The King, an attached father, was favourably impressed. He showed his approbation by a liberal allowance, out of which was purchased the château and estate of Maintenon, lying in a picturesque valley beside a river, sheltered by hills, in a woodland district between Versailles and Chatres. From this time the Widow Scarron was known as the Marquise de Maintenon, and became a devout Catholic. She had her own apartments at Court, and cut all her disreputable friends. She was constantly present when the King visited Madame de Montespan.

In the meantime, Mademoiselle de Montpensier returned to Court. Louis XIV. could not tolerate the absence of any of the princes and princesses of the blood-royal, stars of the first magnitude in that heaven where he blazed forth the centre of life and light. Louis had sent a message to her. Mademoiselle therefore dried her eyes, and appeared in her usual place in the circle. Surely, she thinks, the King will appreciate the sacrifice she is making in being present at festivities which, by recalling so vividly the image of Lauzun, drive her to despair!

A ballet is to take place at Versailles; the King is to dance. Mademoiselle forces herself to be present. She looks old, sad, and ill. She is preoccupied. Her thoughts are with Lauzun, in the mountain-bound fortress of Pignerol. There is but one person present in that vast company she cares about. With him she yearns to speak. It is d'Artagnan, Captain of the Musketeers, who accompanied Lauzun to Pignerol.

D'Artagnan, a Gascon, is a countryman of Lauzun. He perfectly understands the part he has to play with Mademoiselle; a part, indeed, he had carefully rehearsed with Lauzun while they were together. All the time the ballet lasts, d'Artagnan, in immediate attendance on the King, keeps his eyes fixed on Mademoiselle with a sorrowful expression. This agitates her extremely; she has the greatest difficulty in keeping her seat beside the Queen.

Supper is served in the Queen's apartment. Louis and Maria Theresa sit under a canopy of cloth of gold. Hundreds of wax lights blaze in gilded stands, and the King's twenty-four violins play. The Dauphin, Mademoiselle, and all the princes and princesses of

the blood present, are seated at the table. The ushers
and attendants admit the public to gaze at their Majesties. Every well-dressed person can enjoy this privilege, and the staircases and passages are filled with
crowds ascending and descending.

When the tedious ceremony is over, Mademoiselle
places herself near the door, and signs to d'Artagnan
to approach.

"Ah, Captain d'Artagnan, I saw you looking at me
all the time of the ballet," she says, with a sigh.

D'Artagnan, a bluff, soldierly fellow, but crafty
withal, and shrewd, a good friend and a bitter hater,
salutes her respectfully.

"D'Artagnan," continues Mademoiselle, moving ·
closer beside him, and dropping her voice into a
whisper, "you have something to tell me. I see it in
your face. You accompanied Monsieur de Lauzun to
Pignerol. Tell me everything you can remember."
Her manner is quick and hurried, her breath comes
fast.

"Your highness, I left the Comte de Lauzun in
good health."

"Thank God!" ejaculated Mademoiselle, clasping
her hands.

She feels so faint she is obliged to ask the Queen's
permission to open a window.

"Was he indisposed on his long journey?"

"No, madame; he was perfectly well. I never left
him. Even at night I slept in the same chamber. Such
were my instructions."

"Did he speak to you of me?" asked Mademoiselle
in a faltering voice, blushing deeply.

"Constantly, your highness. He spoke of you with

the utmost devotion. Next to the grief Monsieur de Lauzun felt at parting from your royal highness, I am persuaded he suffered most from the displeasure of his Majesty."

"Proceed, I entreat you," breaks in Mademoiselle eagerly. "Every word you say is inexpressibly precious to me. When did Lauzun first speak to you of me, and what did he say?"

"I must tell you," continues the artful d'Artagnan, watching her as a cat does a mouse—"I must tell your highness that before these unfortunate events I had avoided the Comte de Lauzun. I imagined he despised every one."

Mademoiselle shakes her head.

"Proper pride — a conscious superiority," she murmurs.

"Well, madame, when he was arrested on St. Catherine's day, at Saint-Germain, the Comte de Rochefort brought him into the guard-room, and consigned him to me. I started at once with him on his journey to Pignerol. From time to time he gazed at me, but did not utter a single word. When we passed your villa at Petit Bourg, he groaned, and tears gathered in his eyes."

"Poor Lauzun!" says Mademoiselle softly, lifting up her eyes.

"'That villa,' said the Count to me, 'belongs to Mademoiselle. Words cannot tell what I owe her. She is as good as she is great.'"

"Did Lauzun really say this?" asks Mademoiselle, with melting eyes.

"He did, madame," rejoins d'Artagnan with secret exultation at seeing how the bait is swallowed. "'I am unhappy, Captain d'Artagnan,' he went on to say, 'unhappy, but not guilty. I have served my King faithfully. I have worshipped Mademoiselle—not for her wealth, but for herself.'"

Mademoiselle puts her handkerchief to her eyes. She is convulsed with suppressed sobs.

"Yes, madame; this and much more was said to me by the Count. Indeed, his words were so touching that, soldier as I am, I wept, your highness—I actually wept."

"Excellent man," mutters Mademoiselle, stretching out her hand towards him. "I shall not forget your appreciation of so noble a gentleman."

D'Artagnan makes a profound obeisance.

("My promotion is now assured," he says to himself, "as well as poor Lauzun's pardon. Mademoiselle has great interest with his Majesty.")

D'Artagnan passes his hand across his eyes, as if to brush away tears, which he does not shed.

"I have seen much since I served his Majesty,"—he continues in broken sentences, simulating deep grief. "I am an observer of human nature;—but never—never did I know a man of such elevation of mind, with feelings so warm, so genuine, as Monsieur de Lauzun. The charms of his person, the dignity of his manners, his fortitude and patience in adversity, are more honourable to him than the splendour of his position as the first nobleman in France."

Mademoiselle, unable to contain her feelings, lays her hand upon d'Artagnan's hand, and presses it.

"Your penetration does you honour, Monsieur d'Artagnan. Yet so mean, so base is the envy of a Court, that it is whispered about, loud enough even for me in my exalted position to hear, that Lauzun cares only for my revenues—not for myself."

"Good God, what a slander!" cried d'Artagnan, with a face of well-simulated horror.

"Yes; but I do not believe it," hastily adds Mademoiselle.

"I can pledge my honour as a soldier, your highness, it is a lie," breaks in d'Artagnan, anxious for his friend's prospects.

"I know it—I know it," answers Mademoiselle with triumph.

"Ah, madame," continues d'Artagnan, shaking with suppressed laughter, "did I not fear to offend your delicacy, I could say more."

"Ah! did Lauzun speak often of me?" she asks, and a fire comes into her sunken eyes. "Tell me."

"He spoke of nothing else. Day and night your name was on his lips. My honour as a Gascon upon it."

"Repeat this to me," cries Mademoiselle with ecstasy.

"You little know, your highness, what tortures he suffers at being separated from you."

"Alas! Monsieur d'Artagnan, he cannot suffer more than I!" and Mademoiselle's sigh is almost a groan.

"Your highness has great influence over his Majesty. Is it possible that his imprisonment may be shortened?"

"Can you doubt that my whole life, my influence, my wealth, all I have, will be devoted to this object?" exclaims Mademoiselle.

("Good," thinks d'Artagnan; "I have served my

poor friend, and I hope myself, well. What an imbecile she is!")

At this moment there is a general move. The Queen, who has been playing cards, rises, and Mademoiselle is forced to accompany her.

Years pass; Lauzun still remains a prisoner at Pignerol.

Mademoiselle is at the Luxembourg. She is sitting in her closet writing, when a page enters, and announces Madame de Maintenon. This lady is now the recognised governess of the legitimatised children of the King, the bosom friend of their mother, the Marquise de Montespan. Already she is scheming to supplant her in the King's affections. Madame de Maintenon is singularly handsome. Her face is pale; her complexion marble-like; her eyes are large and lustrous, though somewhat fixed and stern. Her glossy, dark hair is raised high on her head, and a mantilla of lace is thrown over it. Her dress is of a sombre colour, but of the richest material. It rustles along the ground, as, with measured steps, she advances towards Mademoiselle. The latter is conscious of the stately bearing of the governess, who dares not, however, presume first to address her. Mademoiselle does not rise, but bends her head in acknowledgment of her salutation. She signs to Madame de Maintenon to be seated.

"You are come alone, madame," says the Princess. "I should have rejoiced to see your little charges—those dear children of whom I am so fond. Are they well?"

"I am happy to inform your highness they are in perfect health. The Duc de Maine looked lovely this morning when he went with me to mass in the royal chapel. I have come to bring you a little letter he has written to your highness," and the Marquise presents a note addressed in a schoolboy's hand. "Ever since he has corresponded with you, during his stay in Holland and at Barège, he finds such pleasure in writing to you, I do not like to forbid it."

"The dear child! I love him greatly," replies Mademoiselle, secretly wondering on what errand Madame de Maintenon has come.

"I have the honour to inform your royal highness," says the Marquise after a pause, fixing her black eyes keenly upon her, "my visit to you is official. I come from the King."

Mademoiselle falls back in her chair; a mist gathers before her eyes. "It must be about Lauzun she has come!" is her first thought.

"But before I proceed to the subject of my mission," continues Madame de Maintenon, speaking in a clear metallic voice, all the while contemplating Mademoiselle as if she were an object of minute study—"but before I proceed, allow me to offer to your highness the compliments of Madame de Montespan, who is hunting at Clagny with the King. She bids me pray you to think of everything to please his Majesty, in order that he may be inclined to grant what you have so much at heart."

Mademoiselle colours, and presses her hand to her heart, so violently does it throb.

"Madame de Montespan," continues the Marquise, "has the highest admiration for the constancy and the fortitude you have shown on a certain subject, madame. May I add my tribute of sympathy also?"

Mademoiselle smiles, and bows graciously. She is not ignorant of the growing power of the governess, and her high favour with the King.

"We who live at Court," adds the Marquise loftily, "know too well how often great princes forget those whom they once loved. Your highness is an illustrious exception. May I, madame, be permitted to address you on this delicate subject? It is the purpose of my visit."

"I entreat you to speak," cries Mademoiselle, greatly excited. "Tell me at once. I cannot bear suspense. Tell me, is his Majesty about to liberate Monsieur de Lauzun after so many years of imprisonment?"

"Well," replies Madame de Maintenon, with an air of immense importance, "you shall judge, Princess. His Majesty thinks that it is possible, under certain conditions——"

"Will he acknowledge Lauzun as my husband?"

"He will never sanction the marriage, your highness," answers the Marquise decidedly, avoiding Mademoiselle's eager gaze.

Here is a blow! Mademoiselle is absolutely stunned. Madame de Maintenon proceeds in the same monotonous tone:—

"His Majesty has considered the possibility of liberating Monsieur de Lauzun, but there are difficulties, not perhaps insurmountable, but which at present render his gracious intention impossible."

"Name them," cries Mademoiselle almost fiercely, suddenly sitting upright in her chair—"name them instantly." She has turned ashy pale; her hands, which she extends towards the other lady in her agitation, tremble. She is a pitiable object.

"Why, the fact is," and the wily governess hems once or twice, gives a slight cough, then clears her voice, "his Majesty does not choose that the **principality** of Dombes and the Château and estates of Eu, with which he is informed you have invested Monsieur de Lauzun, should go out of the royal family. This is the difficulty which at present weighs with the King. Madame de Montespan uses all her eloquence in your favour, **madame.**"

"I **am** obliged to her," answers Mademoiselle drily. "It was rumoured that she was the person who caused his Majesty **to** withdraw **his consent to my marriage.**"

This is dangerous ground, and Madame de Maintenon hastens to change the subject; she well knows how true are Mademoiselle's suspicions.

"I have nothing **to** do with the King's reasons," is her cautious rejoinder. "Doubtless they are excellent." Then she glances towards the door as if about to go. "Even with your royal highness I must be excused canvassing what these reasons are. I came simply to deliver a message with which **I was** entrusted, and to carry back to his Majesty your answer."

This speech, delivered with the most freezing coldness, almost **frightens** Mademoiselle into a fit. She is quite unable to argue with Madame de Maintenon, greatly her superior in intellect and in craft, specially now, when her excited feelings barely permit her to understand what is passing. She has sense, however, to make a sign to the Marquise, intimating her pleasure that she should not depart, **which** she is preparing to do.

"His Majesty observed," continues that lady, look-ing steadfastly out of the window, "that it seems strange these royal appanages should pass away into an undistinguished family, while those who are near and most dear to his Majesty are at this time abso-lutely portionless—the Duc de Maine, for instance."

"What!" exclaims Mademoiselle, "is it only by enriching the Duc de Maine that the Comte de Lauzun can be liberated?" As she puts this question her eyes flash, and her brow darkens. Then, seeing the stony gaze of the imperturbable Marquise fixed upon her, she composes herself, and awaits her reply with more calmness.

"I must again entreat your highness to remember," answers Madame de Maintenon, rising from her chair, and dropping her eyes on the ground with affected humility, "that I am here only as an ambassadress. I beg your highness to excuse aught I may have said to offend you. But, as I perceived a way of accommoda-tion open, I ventured to approach you as an am-bassadress—simply as an ambassadress." These last words are spoken with a kind of unctuous hypocrisy peculiar to herself. "Now, madame, if you permit, I will take my leave. My duties call me back to my beloved charges. I have been absent too long already."

Forthwith, every device was used to force Made-moiselle into compliance. The little Duc de Maine was represented as being fonder of her than of any other creature breathing—one of those singular attach-ments, in fact, that are sometimes observed in children, and are quite unaccountable. To favour this asser-tion, the worthy pupil of Madame de Maintenon was educated in a system of deceit. Every morning he addressed a little billet-doux to Mademoiselle, represented as the genuine effusion of a young and innocent heart, the same billet-doux having been indited by his governess overnight and copied by himself. Bouquets, presents, kisses, and caresses were lavished in the same manner. The child played his part so well that Mademoiselle actually believed at last in this simulated attachment. Madame de Montespan failed not, also, to pay the utmost court to Mademoiselle, and represented to her how earnestly she used her influence in order to induce the King to liberate Lauzun. After these manœuvres had been continued for some time, and the two *intrigantes* deemed that the mind of Mademoiselle was sufficiently prepared, Madame de Maintenon again set forth to pay another visit at the Luxembourg Palace.

This time she at once announced that the King had determined to liberate Lauzun. Mademoiselle, in transports of joy at the intelligence, so far forgot her dignity as to embrace the cunning messenger, and to load her with thanks.

After this ebullition had a little subsided, Madame de Maintenon gravely begged Mademoiselle not to thank *her*. She again acted merely as an ambassadress, she said. "But," she adds, "there is one person who does deserve her thanks; for nothing can exceed the earnestness with which he has urged her highness's petition. Nay, he has not feared to encounter the King's anger, so constant, so energetic have been his prayers. It is to him her gratitude is due."

"Who can have been this friend—this benefactor?" cried the Princess. "Tell me, I implore you, that I may load him with my gratitude."

"I can quite understand your feelings," returned Madame de Maintenon; "your wish to be informed of the name of this unknown benefactor is most **natural;** but to gratify you, I must break a promise— a most solemn promise—I have made *never* to reveal his name. He did not desire to be known; he wished **to** serve you **in secret."**

"Don't talk to me of secrecy, madame, **in such a** moment. **Tell me at** once to whom I am so deeply indebted."

"If I must speak," replied the inimitable **De** Maintenon (rejoicing at the success of her manœuvres), "it is the *Duc de Maine*, who prevailed on his father to grant the petition he knew would so delight his beloved friend and protectress. The affection he feels towards you is indeed something——"

"The darling child!" exclaimed Mademoiselle, "how I love him! **Is** it possible **he has done this** for me! How can I reward him?—what **can I** do to show **him** how grateful I am?"

This was precisely the point **to** which Madame de Maintenon had been labouring to bring the Princess. She now artfully observed that there was only one way of rewarding the *disinterested* attachment of the Duc de Maine in **a** manner worthy of Mademoiselle. "I feel **bound,** however," she continued, "to warn your highness that, after all that has been said, and the personal interest his Majesty feels in the success of these negotiations, he will be so incensed at any withdrawal on **your** part now, that your personal liberty—yes, madame," she repeated, seeing the Princess's look of terror, "your personal liberty will be in danger. You may be sent to the Bastille!"

The mention of such a possibility alarmed Mademoiselle beyond measure, and she anxiously inquired of Madame de Maintenon if she thought there was any chance of such a misfortune!

"Not if by your generosity you bind his Majesty, as it were, to fulfil the pledge he has now given," was the discreet reply.

Thus did Madame de Maintenon unfold her tactics, and work on the weak mind of the love-sick Princess. She saw that the point was already gained, and, fearing to destroy the favourable impression she had made, left Mademoiselle to ruminate on the approaching return of Lauzun, and all the happiness in store for her. Hastening back to Versailles, she communicated her success to the King and to Madame de Montespan, who were equally delighted at the triumph of their unworthy artifices.

CHAPTER XXIX.

Connubial Bliss.

The Duc de Maine was invested with the principality of Dombes and the county of Eu. The deeds were signed in Madame de Montespan's apartments at Versailles.

The sacrifice once made nothing could exceed the ecstasy of Mademoiselle. After a separation of many years, Lauzun would be restored to her arms! He was free—he would be with her in a few days! The exquisite certainty of bliss intoxicated her senses.

On her return to the Luxembourg she flew to her room, and took a hand mirror from her toilette. She gazed at herself in it attentively; she asked herself, as she has already done a hundred times before, "Can he still love me? Are my eyes bright? Are my cheeks rosy? Is my hair abundant as in the old days when Lauzun praised it?"

The examination satisfied her. Joy had effaced the wrinkles, and brought a passing bloom back to her face. She overlooked her grey locks, those she could powder. Her lips parted into a smile. While she was still looking at herself, and turning her head in various positions in order to catch the light, a page entered, and announced, "Monsieur de Baraille" (he was a friend of Lauzun). Baraille's sudden entrance startled her. She turned round abruptly, stumbled against a chair, and the mirror, an oval of rock crystal set in a gold frame, dropped from her hand.

"Ah! Monsieur de Baraille," she cried, looking at the fragments which strewed the floor, "why did you come in so suddenly? This is a dreadful omen."

*   *   *   *   *   *

Mademoiselle de Montpensier is at Choisy. The agitation of her mind is indescribable. She has the gravest reasons for displeasure. Lauzun is in France, but shows no desire to see her.

At last he makes his appearance. He is dressed in an old uniform, which he had worn before his imprisonment; it was now too short, and too small for him, and shabby and torn. His hair, of a reddish shade, has fallen off during his long imprisonment, and he wears a black wig with flowing curls, which covers his shoulders. He enters her cabinet, by the gallery, hung with the portraits of her ancestors. At sight of him Mademoiselle springs to her feet, and opens her arms to embrace him. Lauzun throws himself on the ground before her. She raises him, covers him with kisses, murmuring words of fond endearment into his ear.

For a few moments each, overcome by widely different feelings, remains speechless. Lauzun examines her curiously. This inspection does not seem satisfactory. He knits his brow, and slightly shrugs his shoulders. Altogether his manner is far from reassuring. He does not care to conceal his surprise at the change he sees in the royal lady beside him. She is now sixty, **her** face is pinched and lined by age; her form bent and attenuated. She has put powder on her grey hair, which is decked with ribbons, and rouge upon her shrivelled cheeks, in a vain effort to appear young. But even her blind infatuation can no longer deceive her. She is old and she knows it.

"I must ask your pardon," says Lauzun at last, **breaking an** awkward pause, **"for** having been so long on the road to Paris to join you. My health is very delicate, it is weakened by long confinement. I was ill at Amboise." (The truth being that he had been engaged in a violent flirtation with the wife of **the** governor, the Marquise d'Alluye. Mademoiselle **had** been informed of this.)

As Lauzun speaks, Mademoiselle raises her eyes, and looks him in the face. It was the same deep harmonious voice, full of subtle melody, that had once charmed her ear, like a cadence of sweet music. There were the same clear eyes, whose glance ruled her destiny. Those eyes that had haunted her day and night for so many years, through the mists of time and absence. There were the features whose every turn she had studied with unutterable tenderness; those lips which had parted to utter words on which hung her very life. There before her was her Lauzun,—the object of such longing desire, such tortured suspense; of such eager strivings, of such willing self-sacrifice. But oh, how changed!

Now the scales had fallen from her eyes. For the first time she saw him as he was. He was her Lauzun no longer. She felt that she was repugnant to him. An agony of grief welled up within her; she could have screamed for very bitterness of soul in the wild impulse of her despair. But at this supreme moment her pride came to her support. Should she let him mock the strivings of her tortured spirit? gauge the abyss of her misery with his cold steely eye? No; mortal as were the wounds his cruelty had inflicted, they should still be sacred. She would say nothing. As she looks at him (and, looking at him, gazes also through the long vista of years that his presence recalls) she composes her countenance to an unnatural calmness, and she replies to him, in a voice almost as careless as his own—

"It gives me infinite pain to hear you have been ill, but I rejoice to see you so perfectly restored. I never saw you looking better in my life."

A glare of anger passed into Lauzun's eyes, and he frowned. Again there was a long and awkward pause.

"You have laid out a great deal of money here at Choisy," he says with a sneer, his eyes wandering round. "I think you have been ill-advised to pur-

chase this place. It is a mere *guinguette*, lying in a
hole. What a useless building it is—so ill designed
too!" and he casts his eyes contemptuously down
the suite of rooms, the doors of which are open.

"Some people think it is not good enough for
me," answers Mademoiselle with forced calmness,
although her lips tremble in spite of herself.

"Have you paid for it, madame?" asks Lauzun
with the utmost impertinence.

"I have **paid** for it," replies the Princess.

Lauzun now rises, and strides up and down the
cabinet. He strolls into the adjoining gallery, eyeing
the precious ornaments with which the tables are
covered. He takes the most valuable articles in his
hands and carefully examines them, holding them up
against the light. Then he returns, stands opposite
Mademoiselle, and examines her features with a stare
of cynical scrutiny. She grows crimson under this insolent inspection, but says nothing.

"You would have done **much** better to have given
me the money you have squandered here. I have
suffered great misery."

"I have given you too much already, Monsieur de
Lauzun," replies Mademoiselle in an unsteady voice,
for his heartless greed smote her to the very soul.

"I fear you are horribly cheated," adds Lauzun,
not noticing her reply. Again he walks up and down
the room. "I could manage matters much better for
you. Will you make me your treasurer?"

He **speaks** eagerly, and there is a hungry gleam
in his eye that bodes ill for Mademoiselle's revenues.

"No, I will not," answers Mademoiselle firmly.
"If you **want** to know, I have paid for this place forty-

thousand livres. I sold **my string** of pearls to purchase it."

"Oh! you have sold your **string of** pearls without consulting me?" interrupts Lauzun with an offended air. "What waste! What folly!"

He stops in his pacing up and down **the** room, and fixes his eyes upon her in another **silent** scrutiny.

"I see you still wear coloured ribbons in your hair. Surely, **at** your age, this is ridiculous."

"The Queen does the same."

"**Are** you not older than the Queen?"

"I am old, Monsieur de Lauzun," replies Mademoiselle, stung to the quick, yet speaking with dignity; "but **persons of my** rank dress according to established etiquette. Have you nothing more to say **to** me, Lauzun?" she says in a low voice.

She can bear **no** more; her pride and **her** fortitude are rapidly forsaking her. She feels **she is** breaking down, spite of herself. She longs inexpressibly to fold Lauzun in her arms, to tell him all her love; to be-**seech** him to return it, even ever so little **a** return, for **that** vast treasure she **offers.** But she is withheld by absolute shame.

"I have made great sacrifices to restore you to liberty, **Lauzun," she** continues timidly, her voice almost **failing her,** and not daring to look up at him **for fear** of encountering his chilling gaze. "I have made many sacrifices. I understood that you approved **of them."** Lauzun does not answer. Mademoiselle speaks **humbly now, for** what is money, contempt, insult to her, **so** that he would love her, only a little? "I have also made arrangements with Colbert to pay **your debts."**

. "I am obliged to you," replies Lauzun, with a
sneer. "Let me tell you, however," and he advances
close to where she is sitting and fixes his eyes fiercely
upon her—"Let me tell you I would rather command
the Royal Dragoons and be back again at Court in
attendance on the King, than have all the money you
have, or ever can give me."

Mademoiselle turns very faint, and clasps her
hands. Her eyes close, as if she is going to swoon.
Lauzun contemplates her unmoved. He does not
offer her the smallest assistance.

"Good God!" she exclaims after a while, "how
much I am to be pitied! I have despoiled myself and
you are ungrateful."

"Louise," says Lauzun, feeling he has gone too
far, stooping and trying to kiss her hand, "spare me
hysterics. Let us talk business."

"We have talked nothing else," cries Mademoiselle,
her indignation rising at his heartless indifference.
"Not a word of affection has come from your lips,"
her voice grows thick and tears rush into her eyes.
Spite of herself, she is again rapidly giving way. It
was the old fight between heart and no heart, man
who feels nothing, woman who feels everything.

"I want my place at Court," says Lauzun abruptly.
"Will you use your influence to reinstate me? Else,
I would rather have remained in prison at Pignerol."
He speaks in a tone of the bitterest reproach.

"I will do what I can," Mademoiselle answers in
a husky voice.

"Do what you can!" retorts Lauzun, turning upon
her savagely, "do what you can! *Morbleu*, if you answer me like that, I will tell you the truth. You have

ruined me—you have destroyed my reputation—lost me my position. Louise d'Orléans, I wish I had never seen you!"

"It is false," returns Mademoiselle in a loud voice, her passion rising at his injustice; "it is false. I have not injured you—the King will tell you so himself." Lauzun is growing more **and more** defiant, almost threatening. **His** hand rests on the hilt of his sword. This is too much even for her to bear. "If you **have** nothing more to say, Monsieur de Lauzun, leave me." She speaks with the habit of command long years have given her.

"I will not go," cries he; "you have no right to **order** me. *Am I not your husband?*" Lauzun hisses out these last words, more like a venomous serpent than a man. He grasps the arm of Mademoiselle, who shrinks away from him. His whole bearing is wild and menacing. "You leave me without money, **you** who have lost me all I value in the world; you, who are old enough to be my mother!" Mademoiselle covers her face with her hands, she cowers before him. "Can you deny it? Instead of providing me with a proper residence and equipage when I came out of prison, I have not even a carriage of my own. I am in miserable lodgings with Rollinde, one of your people, **while** *you*—you live in a palace. I have no money to pay my debts."

"It is false," she replies, rising and facing him boldly. "I *have* paid your debts. If you have fresh ones they are gambling debts. Those I refuse to pay."

"But you shall!" roars Lauzun, stamping his foot and raising his hand as if to strike her. "I am your husband. I have a right to all you have."

"I will pay no more," shrieks Mademoiselle, now excited beyond fear. "Go to your friends, those ladies you love so well, Madame de Montespan and the others." She clenches her fist as the bitter pangs of jealousy shoot through her soul. "I will not pay such debts," she repeats; then she draws herself up, and faces him with a courage he has never seen in her before. It calms him instantly.

"Look at these diamond buttons you sent me. They are vile. You have such splendid jewels!" He lifts up his lace ruffles and displays a pair of solitaire diamonds of great beauty, which fasten his wristbands. He is as fawning and eager as a beggar.

"I will give you other diamonds," answers Mademoiselle with composure. "But what I do for you in future depends on your own conduct, Monsieur de Lauzun, or rather Duc de Montpensier, for such I have created you."

There was a depth of irony in thus addressing him by his title at this particular moment.

"Well, madame, as you please," answers Lauzun, contemptuously scanning her all over. "If I am not satisfied I shall go abroad and command foreign armies. I will go *anywhere* to rid myself of you. I hope never to see you again," and a look of undisguised hatred flashes from his eyes.

"You need not go far to rid yourself of me," cries Mademoiselle, incensed beyond bounds. "Leave me instantly, ungrateful man! You have sufficiently outraged me. In the presence too of my great ancestors," she adds, and with a stately action she extends her hand towards the portraits which hang around; "those ancestors, one of whose time-honoured titles I have given you. You might, I think, have chosen a more suitable spot for your insults," and she measures him from head to foot. Then with an imperious gesture she points to the door.

Still they met, Mademoiselle yet clung to Lauzun. In the month of September they are together at Choisy for a few days. Lauzun has enormous gambling debts and wants money, therefore he is come. On returning one evening from hunting he sees Mademoiselle seated under the shade of one of the fine old elms in the park, her favourite tree. She is in tears. It is nine o'clock at night, she has long awaited his return; now it is nearly dark. Lauzun gallops up to where she sits. He dismounts, gives his horse into the hands of a servant, and casts himself on the grass beside her. By so doing he splashes her dress with mud, but he offers no apology. He unfastens the heavy hunting boots he wears, and endeavours to draw them off, but he does not succeed. Then he turns suddenly round and thrusts them into her face.

"Here, Louise d'Orléans," he says, "make yourself useful; take off my boots." Mademoiselle betrays no emotion, she only rises and returns to the house.

They never met again. A brief record remained of her existence, graven on the tomb, where she lay, among "the daughters of France," unloved—unmourned; a sad example, that riches to a woman are too often a curse. The brief record is as follows:—

"Anne Marie Louise d'Orléans, eldest daughter of Gaston de France; Souveraine Princesse de Dombes, Princesse Dauphine d'Auvergne, Comtesse d'Eu, Duchessse de Montpensier; died 1693, aged sixty-six."

CHAPTER XXX.

Fall of De Montespan.

ABOUT this time Madame de Maintenon announced to the King that she had received a mission from heaven to convert him from the error of his ways. "I was brought to Court miraculously for this purpose; God willed it," she writes to her daughter. Singularly enough, this conviction of her mission coincided with the absence of Madame de Montespan at the baths of Bourbon.

Louis had come to view these temporary absences as a relief. He had grown somewhat weary of the once-adored Marquise. He inclined to think the society of Madame de Maintenon preferable. In her company the charms of friendship exceeded the delights of love. She was leading him up to heaven by an easy path strewn with flowers. Conscious as he was of his past sins, he yet liked the process of repentance.

The apartments of Madame de Maintenon at Versailles, on the same floor as his own, were well placed for constant intercourse. They no longer exist, but the situation is identified as having been near the south wing, contiguous to his own suite, which was separated from that of the Queen by the Salle de l'Œil de Bœuf, a corridor, and some smaller rooms.

The affection of her pupil, the Duc de Maine, and the esteem and approval of the Queen, strengthened Madame de Maintenon's position. Maria Theresa quite venerated the *ci-devant* Veuve Scarron.

Maria Theresa, who refused to doubt La Vallière's

purity, and who long defended the virtue of Madame de Montespan, was born to be a dupe. Her unsuspicious nature fell an easy prey to the duplicity of Madame de Maintenon, who would have imposed on a stronger-minded person than the guileless Queen. The King carefully intensified these good impressions. He confided to his consort the conviction of Madame de Maintenon that he would infallibly be "damned" if he did not cleave to herself alone, and live with her in love and unity. Such words from the lips of her august husband, whom she had all her life worshipped too entirely to have dared to appropriate to herself, won the Queen's whole heart. Never had she been so blessed. Her Olympian spouse spent hours beside her; his conduct was exemplary. Maria Theresa, overcome by the weight of her obligations to the wily *gouvernante*, treated her with the utmost distinction. She joined with the King in appointing her lady in waiting to the new Dauphine.

By-and-by Madame de Montespan, having finished her course of drinking and bathing at Bourbon, returned. That the waters had agreed with her was evident. Her eyes were more voluptuous, her aspect more enticing than ever. For a time the King's conviction of Madame de Maintenon's mission wavered; he forgot his salvation.

Madame de Maintenon, invested with the authority of a Christian prophetess, denounced his apostacy. Madame de Montespan was furious; quarrels ensued between herself and Madame de Maintenon, in which the choleric, frank-spoken sinner was overruled by the crafty saint. The King, called in as umpire, decided always in favour of the latter; she could clothe her wrongs in such eloquent language, she was so specious, so plausible, she continued to identify herself so entirely with his salvation, that he again became repentant. His coldness towards her rival increased. This rival, the governess of her children, insulted Madame la Marquise de Montespan. Her fury knew no bounds. She felt that her fall was approaching; that the ground on which she stood was undermined. She denounced her treacherous governess to the King; she declared that the Veuve Scarron had not been immaculate. She even caused a pamphlet to be printed in which names, places, dates, and details were given. She showed it to the King; Louis shook his head, and replied that she had herself defended her protégée so ably that he was unalterably convinced of her virtue. The Marquise de Montespan was bowed out of Versailles.

*   *   *   *   *   *

The influence of Madame de Maintenon changed the atmosphere of the Court. A holy calm succeeded to strife and agitation. Gallantry, gambling, intrigues, and women no longer formed the staple of general conversation. Religious discussions, theological disputes, and ecclesiastical gossip became the fashion. Anecdotes of the various Court confessors were discussed in the Œil de Bœuf with extraordinary eagerness. The priest of Versailles was a more important personage than a royal duke; Bossuet had more influence that Louvois; Père la Chaise overtopped the great Louis himself. The Court ladies became decided prudes, rolled their eyes sanctimoniously, wore lace kerchiefs, renounced rouge, and rarely smiled. No whisper of scandal profaned the royal circle. His

Majesty was subdued and serene, assiduous in the affairs of religion, and constant in his attendance on his comely directress.

On the 30th July, 1683, the Queen died. She expired in the arms of Madame de Maintenon. On her death-bed she gave her the nuptial ring which she had received from his Majesty. This gift was significant.

The concealed ambition of Madame de Maintenon, her greed of dominion, the insolence of the inferior about to revenge the wrongs suffered in her obscurity, a sense, too, of her own power, now roused her to grasp that exalted position which, even while the Queen lived, had tempted her imagination. Now began a system of coquetry, so refined, as to claim the distinction of a fine art. The lady is forty-five, and looks young and fresh for her age; her hair is still black and glossy; her forehead smooth, her skin exquisitely white; her figure lissom and upright, if ample. There is a hidden fire in her stealthy eyes; a grandeur in her bearing, that charms while it imposes. Not all the vicissitudes of her chequered career can wash out the blood of the d'Aubignés which flows in her veins. The old King is desperately in love with her. It is the first time in his life he has encountered any opposition to his will. There is a novelty in the sensation wonderfully enthralling. The conquest of a lady who can thus balk him acquires an enormous importance in his eyes. He has run the fortune of war both at home and abroad; he has carried fortresses by storm, assailed the walls of great cities; he has conquered in the open plain; but here is a female citadel that is impregnable. His attack and her defence are conducted in daily interviews, lasting six, and even ten hours. If he can win her, he feels too that his salvation is insured. A life of repentance passed with such an angel, is a foretaste of celestial bliss. There is something sublime in the woman who can reconcile earth- with heaven, and satisfy his longings in time and eternity.

*　　*　　*　　*　　*

Suddenly Madame de Maintenon announces her intention of leaving the Court for ever.

The King, who occupies his usual place in her saloon, sitting in an arm-chair placed between the door leading into the ante-chamber and the chimney-piece, listens with speechless dismay.

Madame de Maintenon, who sits opposite to him, on the other side of the chimney-piece, in a recess hung with red damask, a little table before her, stitches calmly at the tapestry she holds in her hand. She affects not to observe him, and continues speaking in a full firm voice. "My mission is accomplished, Sire. I have been permitted to be the humble instrument of leading your Majesty to higher and holier thoughts. Your peace with heaven is now made. I desire to retire, leaving my glorious work complete."

"What, madame! Do I hear aright? You propose to leave me?—me, a solitary man, to whom your society is indispensable?" There is a deep longing in the King's eye as it rests upon her, a tremulous solicitude in his manner that she observes with secret joy.

"Sire, I implore you to allow me to depart. I yearn for repose. I have remained at Court greatly against my will, solely for your advantage."

"Remain always," murmurs the King, contemplating her fondly; "my life — my happiness — my very being is bound up in you. Deprived of you, I may again fall into deadly sin. Do not forsake me."

These last words are spoken in a whisper, full of tenderness. He rises from his arm-chair and approaches her. Madame de Maintenon looks at him sharply; then moves her chair backwards. Louis stops midway and gazes at her timidly. He returns to his arm-chair, and sighs profoundly.

"Impossible, your Majesty," replies the Marquise stiffly, arranging the folds of her dress. "I repeat, my task is done. The Court is reformed, your salvation secure. But, while benefiting others, I have exposed myself to calumny. Sire, I am called your mistress. I am branded as the successor of Madame de Montespan."

"What villain has dared to assail your immaculate virtue? Tell me who he is, and there is no punishment he shall not suffer," and the King's face flashes scarlet. There is the old look of command upon his brow—the old decision in his manner.

"Sire," answers Madame de Maintenon quietly, "such passion is unnecessary. I am not worthy of it. I have already done all that is needful, let me go. I can serve you no longer."

"You are worthy, madame, of all that a man—that a monarch can lay at your feet," cries Louis with enthusiasm. A cynical smile plays upon her full-lipped mouth while the King speaks.

"I am at least worthy of respect, Sire. The suspicion of impurity is intolerable. I cannot bear it; I must go."

"You are too hurried, dearest madame," returns the King; "too impressionable. Whatever observations may be aroused by our intimacy, and my well-known attachment to you, they should not annoy you. Your character is an all-sufficient defence."

"Ah, Sire, this is not sufficient. I must fly from even the semblance of suspicion. You are a single man, I am a widow. I must leave Versailles. Your Majesty cannot wish me to remain, to become an object of contempt."

"Contempt? Impossible!" exclaims Louis abruptly. "No woman whom I, the King of France, have loved, has ever suffered contempt."

No sooner were these words out of his mouth, than the King had reason to repent having uttered them. The outraged prude burst into a flood of tears. After all, was her crafty scheming to be in vain? Would Louis not understand that as a wife—and a wife only —she would remain?

"Ah, Sire," sobs she, with genuine sorrow, "is this the return you make for my too great devotion to your Majesty's salvation? I, who have led you step by step towards that Deity, whose wrath your transgressions had so justly incensed? Is it for this I have rescued you from the flames of Purgatory—the fire of everlasting Hell?"

Louis turns ghastly pale; a nervous tremor seizes him. He dare not look Madame de Maintenon in the face, for her piercing black eyes glare upon him, and seem to scan his inmost soul. He dare not interrupt her; he must listen to all she has to say, so great is her empire over him.

She continues:—

"Am I sunk so low in your esteem that you mention me in the same breath with a Montespan, a Fontanges? Alas, I have soiled my good name to serve you, and is *this* then my recompense?"

As she speaks, in a hard resolute voice, her reproachful eyes rivet themselves upon Louis.

"Do you forget, Sire, that I am the woman whom your sainted Queen specially esteemed? On whose bosom she expired? To whom, as she drew her dying breath, she gave this ring?"

She takes from her finger the nuptial ring which Maria Theresa had given her. It was a single diamond of remarkable brilliancy. After contemplating it for an instant she drops it on the floor, midway between herself and Louis, then, with a stately gesture, she rises to depart.

The impress of many passions is visible on the countenance of the aged monarch. Love and pride are written there. Pride is on his broad forehead—in the carriage of his head—in his arched and bushy eyebrows—in his still erect form—in the action of his hands and arms, as they grasp the chair on which he sits upright. Pride, intense, inflexible pride. But his dark eyes glow with passion. Those eyes devour Madame de Maintenon, as she stands erect before him, her eyes turned towards heaven, the ring at her feet. His mouth, around which deep wrinkles gather, works —as did his father's—with a nervous spasm; but the parted lips seem to pant for the beloved object before him. At length he raises himself slowly from his chair —stoops—picks up the nuptial ring of his first wife —kisses it, and places it on the finger of Madame de Maintenon.

"*Mon amie*," he says, with solemnity, "do not leave me. As your husband I will defend you."

Even in the reign of Louis XIV. public opinion made itself heard. Placards appeared upon the walls of Paris to this effect:—

"LOST—The Royal Sceptre. The finder will be well rewarded."

The next day was announced, in the same place:—

"The Sceptre found—Discovered on the toilette of a hypocrite.
"The Scales of Justice, also lost, found hidden in the sleeve of a Jesuit."

Other placards followed; they ran as follows:—

GRAND SPECTACLE!

HIS MAJESTY . . . . MARIONETTES.

In the Chapel of Versailles.

GRATIS!

On a day to be hereafter announced.

Louis XIV. will fill the part of Gargantua; Madame de Maintenon, Madame Gigogne; the Abbé Gobélin, Pierrot; Père la Chaise, Satan (the lover of Madame Gigogne).

CHAPTER XXXI.

Queen Maintenon.

IT is the winter of 1685. The night is dark and starless. Fast falling snow makes the air thick and covers the ground as with a white mantle. An icy blast is blowing, chilling alike to man and beast. As eleven o'clock strikes, the Archbishop of Paris leaves his palace, spite of the inclement weather. He is alone in his coach. Midnight is past when he draws up outside the great gates of Versailles. These open silently. He drives onward, traversing the vast court-yard, passing the equestrian statue of Louis XIV., until he reaches the Cour de Marbre, between the two pavilions of the central portion of the château. Here the outer portal at the foot of the grand staircase is ajar. Bontemps, Governor of the Palace of Versailles, valet, confidant, and purveyor generally to the wants of his Majesty, stands behind it awaiting the Archbishop. He holds a light, which he carefully shades with his hand. Monseigneur de Harlay, Archbishop, descends from his coach shivering all over. His teeth chatter in his head, not only from the cold which is excessive, but from apprehension of what he is about to engage in. Bontemps precedes him up the stairs, holding the light in his hand. They traverse whole suites of rooms, a spacious hall, a long gallery, and many corridors. No word is spoken, every soul is asleep, and it is urgent they should remain so. Once within the King's apartments all is light, warmth, and luxury. The well-nigh frozen dignitary revives. Before him is the King, dignified, composed, and cheerful. With him are the Marquis de Montchevreuil and the Chevalier de Forbin, as witnesses; Père la Chaise is also there to assist the Archbishop. An altar is dressed in the centre of the room. As soon as his Majesty has saluted Monseigneur de Harlay, Bontemps is dispatched to fetch Madame de Maintenon. She loses no time in appearing. The marriage rites are performed by Père la Chaise, confessor to the King; the benediction is given by the Archbishop.

The marriage is to be secret; but Louis XIV. henceforth addresses her as "*Madame*." He receives his ministers in her saloon; the Marquise de Maintenon the while sitting upon a fauteuil in his presence. These are royal honours. Monseigneur le Dauphin

and the princes of the blood never forgive the marriage.
The contempt and hatred they feel towards Madame
de Maintenon cannot be concealed. As favourite they
had tolerated her; as wife they rebel against her. Yet
her will is law. The Duc de Maine and the Duc and
Duchesse de Bourgogne, son and daughter-in-law to
Monseigneur, are the only exceptions.

     *   *   *   *   *

We are again at Choisy. Every window is a blaze
of light, the terraced garden flashes with millions of
coloured lamps. The Dauphin and his consort, the
princes and princesses, courtiers, singers, actors, and
poets, fill the foreground. Brocade and satin sweep
the terraces; cocked hats and feathers, ribbons, lace,
plumes, jewels, orders, wave and glitter. There is the
sound of laughter and mad jest — joyous music and
voluptuous feasting, *petit soupers* and masked balls,
theatricals and concerts.

Long flights of marble stairs descend through
bosky groves, sweet with the scent of lilac and honeysuckles, to the Seine, on whose grassy banks, illuminated by torches and bonfires, a flotilla of boats are
moored under the overhanging woods. If the essence
of all the fêtes given in France was concentrated,
the result would be Choisy before the Revolution.
In the hands of Monseigneur it is a miniature
court, rivalling what Versailles was; a court where
youth, joy, and beauty reign supreme. Louis, now
old, desires that all the world should be old like-
wise — fast, pray, confess and hear sermons like
himself. Choisy is a scandal to him. The Dauphin
receives orders to quit, and take up his abode at
Meudon. Monseigneur, a short, stout, thick-set man,

with a fair complexion, and what would have been handsome features had his nose not been broken, appears before Madame de Maintenon, the real ruler of France. She is seated in her apartments, working as usual at her tapestry. She does not rise at his entrance, and her aspect is severe and repellant.

"Madame," says the Dauphin, seating himself at a gesture she makes, "can you explain to me what motive has induced his Majesty to banish me from my favourite residence of Choisy?"

Madame de Maintenon does not raise her eyes from her work. "Banishment you call it, Monseigneur; you mistake the term. Not banishment, simply a change of abode designed for your good, by his Majesty your august father."

"For my good? Surely I am of an age to judge for myself! If I cannot live where I please, I am under arrest. I am not aware in what I have merited the royal displeasure."

"Observe, Monseigneur le Dauphin," answers the Marquise, fixing her black eyes upon him, "the King feels no displeasure; on the contrary, he desires your more constant presence at his Court, near his person." The Marquise spoke these words with special emphasis.

"Madame, I am most grateful for the amiable manner in which you express his Majesty's flattering wish, but might not some plan be found to unite my presence at Court with my residence at Choisy?"

"Impossible, your highness. In a monarchy there can be but one sovereign. The Court must surround that sovereign. Now, permit me to observe, there are two Courts, and something like two sovereigns."

"I am not conscious, madame," replies the Dauphin, with dignity, "what action of my life, justifies such an accusation. If his Majesty desires to reprimand me, as a father, I ask the favour of hearing it from his own lips."

"Monseigneur," replies Madame de Maintenon, with affected humility, "it is his Majesty who speaks by my voice. I am less than nothing other than through him. If you desire to know what causes his displeasure, it is that in the magnificent fêtes you give at Choisy he observes that one most important element of society is omitted—an element his Majesty considers essential."

"What element, madame?"

"That of the Church, your Highness."

The Dauphin is suddenly convulsed with a fit of violent laughter. He takes a hasty leave.

"The Church at Choisy, *ma foi!*" he says aloud when he has safely passed the ante-room and is well beyond hearing. My old master Bossuet, and Bourdaloue, and the Versailles Jesuits assisting at midnight fêtes at Choisy—what a notion! I must tell this to Mademoiselle Choin. How she will laugh!"

Charlotte de Bavière, second wife of Philippe d'Orléans, brother of the King, hated the "old woman," as she called Madame de Maintenon. She saw through her and despised her. Madame de Maintenon returned her animosity with interest, but she dared not provoke her. There was something about this frank, downright German princess that was not to be trifled with. Whatever her eccentricities might be, they were respected; she was left in peace to drink as much beer and to eat as many *saucissons* as the peculiarity of her constitution required.

In person she was actually repulsive; her pride was a by-word and a jest; but she was a faithful friend and a true wife, and continued to live with her heartless and effeminate husband, Monsieur, in peace.

On her son, the Duc de Chartres, afterwards the Regent Orléans, she doted. In her eyes he was perfect. She was either blind or indifferent to his vices. But even he was not exempt from the violence of her temper. When she was told that he had consented to a marriage with Mademoiselle de Blois, daughter of Madame de Montespan, she struck him in the face. Then she flew to the King. The doors of the royal bedchamber are closed by the attendant Swiss, but the angry voices of Charlotte (Madame) and Louis in angry altercation, penetrate into the gallery of the Œil de Bœuf, where the Court awaits the moment of the royal lever.

"Sire," Madame is heard to say in her guttural German-French accent, "I am come to forbid the marriage of my son with Mademoiselle de Blois."

"How, my sister?" replies the full, deep voice of the King, that voice which usually created so profound an impression on the nerves of those whom he addressed.

"Yes, to forbid it. Had your Majesty desired an alliance between my son and a daughter of your consort, Maria Theresa, I should have considered it my duty to submit."

"Oh!" exclaims the King in a loud voice, and quick steps are heard pacing up and down the room, "you would have condescended to accept a princess-royal for your daughter-in-law!"   .

"Certainly, Sire; but because I committed a *mésalliance* myself in marrying your brother, Philippe d'Orléans——"

"*Pardieu!* madame," breaks in the King. "Do you talk of a *mésalliance* with a grandson of Henry the Great?"

"Certainly I do, your Majesty. What was Henry the Great, but an obscure Prince of Béarn, a beggarly little State among the valleys of the Pyrenees? Does your Majesty think that the hundred quarterings of my escutcheon will gain lustre by the arms of Bourbon?"

Louis is heard to stamp on the floor. "Madame," he cries, so loud that his words echo into every corner of the Œil de Bœuf, "Madame, you forget yourself. How dare you come here to insult me?"

"Sire, I come here to tell you the truth. My son, the Duc de Chartres, has forgotten himself by listening for one instant to your proposal. With my own hand I have chastised him as he deserves. I do not forget myself, whatever others may do. Philippe is too good for any princess in Europe. The blood in his veins is that of my ancestors—the Princes Palatine of the Rhine. We laugh at your modern houses—we laugh! Philippe is the best man in your Court. He knows everything—painting, music, poetry, science. None of you can understand him. You are too ignorant."

"Madame," the King is heard to say, "have a care—you are going too far!"

"No, my brother, I have not gone far enough," rejoins Madame. "You have forgotten the siege of Mons, where he fought under your own eyes—also

Steinkerque and Nerwinde. It is your fault that Philippe does not command **your** armies. He is equal to it. Who would not have such a husband? Sire, my son, the Duc **de** Chartres, shall never wed with your bastard!"

Again Louis is heard to stamp upon **the** floor. Then, in a voice hoarse with rage, he replies, "Madame, I shall hold **my** brother responsible for your insolence."

"Why have you provoked it, then?" is the reply **in** a calmer **tone**. Charlotte de Bavière has evidently re- lieved **her** own violence by exciting that of the King. "I have a right **to** resist such a disgraceful proposal. Withdraw your **marrige**, and I am again your good sister **and** friend as heretofore."

"We shall see, Madame, **we shall see!**" shouts the **King,** whose usual courtesy **towards women** is not proof against such an attack.

"Yes, Sire, we shall see. No person on earth shall make me sanction a blot **on my** name. My op- position shall not be only in words. The Duc de Chartres is my only son. I will stop the marriage in your presence. I will stop it at the altar of the chapel-royal."

"Madame, your pride has turned your head. **But** your husband, my brother, shall obey me."

"Your brother, Sire, will, I know, in this, as in all else, be advised by me. I can defend the honour of his house much better than he can himself, and he knows it. Your brother will do his duty, I shall do mine. I wish your Majesty good day."

The sound of the King's cane is audible, striking heavily on the floor as he strides up and down the room. The **door** of his bedchamber opens; Charlotte de Bavière, crimson in the face, appears. She calls her people together, and hastily departs, followed by the wondering glances of the courtiers, standing in groups about the Œil de Bœuf.

The King fearing that there was no chance of overcoming the opposition of Madame, either by persuasions or by threats, consulted Madame de Maintenon. With characteristic duplicity, she advised that what could not be done openly, must be brought about by stratagem. She sent for the Abbé Dubois, the *âme damnée* of the young Duke, his tutor and his companion, and by promises of money and speedy preferment she completely made him her own. Dubois promised to hurry on the marriage with or without the consent of Madame. The Duke, who loved his mother, and respected her scruples, only yielded when Dubois artfully represented to him the certain loss of all influence, as well as the personal animosity of the King, if he refused.

Philippe d'Orléans met Mademoiselle de Blois in the apartment of Madame de Maintenon. The marriage took place at Versailles.

Madame was furious at what she termed her "dishonour." She wept, abused, menaced, and scolded by turns. But finding that there was no redress, that the marriage was legal, and that further opposition might rouse the vengeance of the King, she gradually cooled down and received her new daughter-in-law with tolerable civility; particularly as the marriage with Mademoiselle de Blois continued the possession of the Palais Royal, with all its pictures, sculptures, and valuables, in the Orléans family, a gift which somewhat served to gild the bitter pill she was called on to swallow.

This marriage did not improve the Duke's conduct or character. He was galled by what he had been forced to do; his temper was soured; his excesses increased. Nor was the Duchess of a disposition to endear herself to any husband. Imperious, luxurious, and bitter-tongued, she always forgot that her mother, Madame de Montespan, was not the wife of her father, and treated the Duke as her inferior. He bore her extravagant pride, and listened to her harangues, reproaches, and taunts (expressed with real eloquence) in silence. Sometimes he called her *Madame Lucifer*.

With such parents their children grew up in habits of licentiousness, only equalled by the imperial ladies of Old Rome.

The Duchesse de Berry—the eldest of the Regent's daughters—kept her court at the Luxembourg with regal pomp. She received ambassadors seated on a throne, surmounted by a canopy sprinkled with the lilies of France. But she did not think it beneath her dignity to do the honours of certain *petits soupers* at the Palais Royal—too well known to need further mention here.

Her sister, Mademoiselle de Valois, was as remarkable for her beauty as for her lack of virtue.

Mademoiselle d'Orléans—third daughter of the Regent—was, if possible, more wanton than her sisters. To the eternal disgrace of the Church she was elected Abbess of Chelles. "*Tel père, tel fils*," says the proverb.

CHAPTER XXXII.

At Marly.

THERE is a lane on the heights over Paris, embowered by wooded hedge-rows, or skirted by open vineyards; this lane leads from Saint-Germain to Marly.

Below the village, deep in a narrow gorge, is the site of the once famous palace built by Louis XIV. Trees now wave and cattle browse on turf where once clustered twelve pavilions, linked together by arches and colonnades, in the Italian or villa style, to suit the royal fancy of a summer retreat.

Not a stone has been left by the Revolution; what were once gardens and a park, is now a secluded meadow. Blue-bells, thyme, and primroses carpet the mossy earth; and the thrush, the cuckoo, and the early swallow carol among pale sprays of beech and hazel. There are deep ditches and swampy pools, once carp-ponds and lakes, part of a plaisance, arranged in the solemn taste of that day, when nature itself was cut and trimmed *à la Louis Quatorze*.

When Louis fixed upon Marly as a residence he was tired of Versailles. He was old, he said, and needed relaxation. He wanted a *folie*, a hermitage— *un rien enfin*—where he could retire from the crowd and the restraints of his Court, sleep three nights in each week, and enjoy the society of his special favourites.

Either the King altered his plan, or his architect (Le Nôtre) disregarded the royal instructions. Millions were squandered on a residence, "which was to cost nothing." A forest of full-grown trees was brought from

Compiègne. The expense of draining the marshy soil, and elevating the waters of the Seine into the *Machine de Marly*, was never acknowledged.

What a stiff, solemn tyrant Louis is become! Selfish, exacting, pedantic, intolerant, dreaded by his children and grand-children, and exercising over them the most absolute control. Unhappy royal family, how one pities them! Marly was a dreadful infliction. Ill or well, they must go. The Duchess de Bourgogne might plead her interesting situation, and the positive prohibition of Fagon: no matter, her name is on the list—she must go. The Duchesse de Berry—that profligate daughter of the Duc d'Orléans—is in her bed seriously ill: her mother, the Duchesse d'Orléans, pleaded **for** her—in vain; if she could not walk she must be carried—to Marly she must go. She was dragged thither in a boat.

Madame de Maintenon herself **dared to** confess **to** no ache or pain that availed to rescue her from standing in the cold winds on frosty mornings—for the King loved the open air, and did **not** fear weather —beside him while he fed the fat carp in marble basins, decided upon a fresh alley to be cut through the woods, or upon a new cascade which was to pierce the hills, or a larger pavilion to be added to those already built.

Nothing could be a greater proof of favour than to be included in the "list" to Marly. It was an honour more craved for than a ribbon or a place at Court. The names of the distinguished few were written down in the King's **own** hand (a very bad specimen of caligraphy), after due consultation with Madame de Maintenon. She was fond of Marly, hence its favour as a residence. She had herself superintended the building, seated in her gilt sedan chair, the King, hat in hand, standing by her side. At Marly she could better isolate him than at Versailles. His loneliness threw him more under her influence and under that of the Duc de Maine. These two, pupil and governess, perfectly understand each other. There is to be a codicil to the royal will, virtually passing over the Duc d'Orléans, his nephew, to invest Maine with all the powers of a Regent. Madame de Maintenon represents this hypocritical son of De Montespan as a simple-hearted, unostentatious man, wholly occupied by his attendance on his Majesty and with his classical studies. The King, whose personal activity is diminished, and whose powers of mind are impaired, believes it. Louis, once renowned as the finest horseman, sportsman, runner, dancer, shot, and charioteer, driving four horses with ease and grace, in France, is now stiff and somewhat infirm. Too indolent to move about and inquire for himself, he sees and hears only through Madame de Maintenon. To others he is an unbending autocrat.

If Louis is feared as a parent he is hated as a Sovereign. The denunciations of his ci-devant Protestant wife in the interests of his salvation lash him into inexpressible terror of perdition. She suggests that he can best expiate the excesses of his youth by a holocaust to the Almighty of all the heretics within his realm. The Jesuits press him sorely. Terrified by threats of awful judgments upon impenitent sovereigns, Louis signs the Revocation of the Edict of Nantes. He expels the Jansenists, destroys their pleasant refuge on a wooded hill near Maintenon, accepts the Bull *Unigenitus*, exiles the Cardinal de Noailles, and fills the state prisons with recusant bishops.

The whole of France is in indescribable confusion. The south, where the reformed faith prevails, is deluged with blood. Many thousands of industrious and orderly citizens doom themselves to perpetual exile rather than abjure the Protestant faith.

Le Grand Monarque is now a lonely, melancholy old man. Defeat has dogged his armies; the elevation of his grandchild, Philip, to the throne of Spain has well-nigh brought France to destruction. Death has been busy with his family: the Dauphin is dead; his son, the Duc de Bourgogne, is dead; Adelaide de Savoie, his wife, most justly dear to Louis, is also dead; and now there only remains one little life, their son, the infant Duc d'Anjou, between himself and the extinction of his direct line. The Court at Marly is as lugubrious and austere as Madame de Maintenon and the Jesuits can make it.

Yet a shadow of the pomp and etiquette of Versailles is still kept up. On certain days after dinner, which takes place at noon, his Majesty receives the royal family. The folding doors of the royal suite are thrown open, and Louis appears. His hat with overtopping feathers is on his head, one hand is placed upon the breast of his coat, the other rests upon an ormolu table. He wears a diamond star; and a blue ribbon is passed across his breast. His coat is of black velvet, his waistcoat of red satin richly wrought with gold; he wears diamonds in his shoe-buckles and in his garters. On his head is a ponderous black wig, raised high on the forehead. This black wig gives his thin, hatchet-shaped face, seamed with wrinkles, a ghastly look. Louis changes his wigs many times each day to suit various occasions. He has wigs for all emergencies. In figure he is much shrunk, and is slightly bent. As he stands, his hand resting on the table for support, every movement is studied to impose silence and awe. To the day of his death he is majestic, and has the grandest, manners in the world.

The royal family, conducted through galleries and colonnades lined with exotics and orange-trees (for Louis loves orange-flowers, all other scents and essences, however, are forbidden), pass before him. They wear mantles or mantelets according to their rank. To the obeisances of those who enjoy the honour of the *fauteuil* his Majesty returns a decided bow. Others who occupy *tabourets* only, receive but a qualified acknowledgment. People who sit on *pliants* are not received at Marly at all.

After the reception come the visits. Those who by their rank are entitled to receive as well as to pay visits, flutter backwards and forwards, with painful activity. Madame la Duchesse or Madame la Princesse rushes out of one door and in at another, shouldering her train, to salute a royal personage and return before more company arrive to visit herself. Sometimes a call of ceremony is arranged to Saint-Germain, situated about two miles from Marly, where the unhappy James II. and his Queen, Mary of Modena, reside, as annuitants on the royal bounty. Here the question as to who should wear mantles and who mantelets, who should have *fauteuils* and who *tabourets*, complicates itself to such an extent (the etiquette of

the English Court having also to be duly considered)
that even his Majesty grows embarrassed. He cuts
the Gordian knot by not sitting down at all. He
exchanges a few casual phrases with the exiled Stuarts
standing, and forthwith returns to the *rural retreat* of
Marly.

* * * * * *

CHAPTER XXXIII.

"The End."

ON St. Louis day, 25th of August, 1715, the King,
then seventy-seven years old, felt seriously indisposed.
The disease from which he suffered was at first called
sciatica. On the 15th he dined in his bedroom at one
o'clock. Later he was able to rise and was carried
into the saloon of Madame de Maintenon, where he
met his ministers. Next day he presided at the
council of state held in a room adjoining his bed-
room. On the 25th he was sensibly **worse.** On the
28th, in consequence of fatal symptoms, his surgeon
Maréchal proposed to amputate his leg. The aged
King scanned the surgeon's face attentively.

"How long should I last then?" he asked.

Maréchal's hand was on Louis's wrist. His pulse
did not vary while he waited for an answer.

"In that case," returned Maréchal, "your Majesty
might hope to survive some days, perhaps some weeks
longer."

"Then it is not worth while," was the reply in a
steady voice. "How long can I live *now*, Maréchal?
Tell me the truth."

"Till Wednesday most probably, your Majesty."

"Ah! my death is to be on Wednesday. It is well. It is not so hard to die as I had thought."

He said no more at that time. Madame de Maintenon sat beside him. Père Letellier, his confessor, and a Jesuit, hovered about his bed. In his hand was a paper concerning the Bull *Unigenitus*, which he urged the King to sign. So merciless was his persistence, that the attendants drove him from the room. The Duc de Maine, and his brother, the Comte de Toulouse, watched. The royal will and codicil, sealed with seven seals, making Maine virtually Regent, was walled up until the King's death. The parliament was known to be in favour of the Duc d'Orléans. It was needful to be first in the field. Maine never took his eyes off his father. There lay that father, his prominent features sharpened by approaching death, upon his bed, such as we see it now, for no other monarch has lain in it since; the tester and framework of dark wood, from which gloomy satin curtains hang, carved and gilt, and guarded by a *ruelle* or balustrade of gilded pillars, which none dare pass. Upon his feet lay a counterpane, worked by the pupils of Saint-Cyr. On the walls, near enough for his eye to rest upon, hung the portrait of his mother, Anne of Austria, and two other pictures—St. John, by Raphael, and David, by Domenichino. These pictures never left him, even on his shortest journeys. On the mantlepiece, near the bed, was a bust of his dead favourite, Adelaide de Savoie.

At the King's desire, Madame de Ventadour brought in the five-year old Duc d'Anjou, son of the Duc de Bourgogne, his great-grandson and successor. "Allow me to kiss him, madame," said Louis, courteous to the last. The child was laid upon the bed, and burst out crying. Madame de Ventadour took him in her arms to comfort him. "My child," said Louis, bending his dim eyes upon the rosy-cheeked boy, "you will soon be King over a great people. Give thanks to God for all you possess. Keep peace with your neighbours. I have loved war too much. Do all that I have left undone." Again and again he kissed the frightened child, ere he would let him go.

Then he desired to speak with such nobles and courtiers as waited without. "I die," he said, "in the Catholic faith. I am myself ignorant of the merits of the various schisms which divide it. I have followed such advice as was given me. If I have erred, my advisers alone are responsible, not I. I call God to witness that what I say is true. Gentlemen, I bid you all good-bye. Forget my bad example. Pray for me."

Then the dying monarch turned his face towards Madame de Maintenon, who was seated within the *ruelle* of the bed. "Madame," he said in a low voice, "I regret no one but you. I have not made you happy." His voice hitherto firm, now faltered. "But I have one consolation in leaving you," he added, "we shall soon meet again." He tried to look at her, but Madame de Maintenon turned from him with disgust. She shuddered.

"What a rendezvous!" she muttered half aloud. "He cares for no one but himself." Bolduc, the King's apothecary, was near, and heard her say so. That very day she left him while he dozed, and drove away to Saint-Cyr.

On Sunday, the 1st of September, Louis died.

His confessor, the Jesuit Letellier, never returned.
Madame de Maintenon remained at Saint-Cyr. Save
the Cardinal de Rohan, and the parish priest of Versailles, all had forsaken him. No sooner had he
breathed his last, than precautions were necessary to
guard his body from insult.

While the first lord in waiting, standing at the
central window within the royal bedchamber which
overlooks the Cour de Marbre, the town of Versailles,
and the forest, broke his bâton of office, shouting in
a loud voice, "The King is dead! Long live the
King!" blasphemous songs and brutal jests passed
from group to group of low women gathered along the
streets.

When the funeral procession left Versailles, almost
secretly in the twilight, reaching the Bois de Boulogne
and the plain of Saint-Denis by tracks and country
roads, crowds followed it, bellowing horrible imprecations. Along the causeway, outside the barriers of
Versailles, temporary tents were pitched, where peasants
stood, glass in hand, to toast the corpse with curses.
These peasants and the townsmen of Versailles had
heard of millions squandered on royal mistresses, while
the people starved; of war abroad and persecutions at
home; of intolerance which spared no one; of ruin,
exile, imprisonment, and torture. The country people
and the populace did not acknowledge the dead as
Louis the Great. The citizens hated him. These men
neither knew nor cared that he had a sonorous voice,
a measured and solemn delivery that gave weight to
his smallest utterances, that leading a life of vice he
observed outward decorum, that he had a majestic
presence and a stately manner. These men weighed

him—manners against acts, life against words—and found him wanting. Posterity readjusted the scales and **pronounced** them just. The **great Revolution** declared the balance. Louis XVI. **expiated the** crimes **of** his ancestors on the scaffold.

THE END.